CANADA AT WAR

Conscription, Diplomacy, and Politics

CANADA AT WAR

*Conscription, Diplomacy,
and Politics*

J.L. GRANATSTEIN

UNIVERSITY OF TORONTO PRESS
Toronto Buffalo London

© University of Toronto Press 2020
Toronto Buffalo London
utorontopress.com

ISBN 978-1-4875-0705-3 (cloth)
ISBN 978-1-4875-2476-0 (paper)
ISBN 978-1-4875-3547-6 (EPUB)
ISBN 978-1-4875-3546-9 (PDF)

___

Library and Archives Canada Cataloguing in Publication

Title: Canada at war : conscription, diplomacy, and politics / J.L. Granatstein.
Names: Granatstein, J. L., author.
Description: Includes bibliographical references and index.
Identifiers: Canadiana (print) 20200278274 | Canadiana (ebook) 20200278339 | ISBN 9781487507053 (cloth) | ISBN 9781487524760 (paper) | ISBN 9781487535476 (EPUB) | ISBN 9781487535469 (PDF)
Subjects: LCSH: World War, 1914–1918 – Canada. | LCSH: World War, 1939–1945 – Canada. | LCSH: King, William Lyon Mackenzie, 1874–1950. | LCSH: Draft – United States – History – 20th century. | LCSH: Canada – Politics and government – 1914–1945. | LCSH: Canada – Foreign relations – 1914–1945.
Classification: LCC FC163 .G73 2020 | DDC 971.062/2 – dc23

___

Every effort has been made to obtain permissions for the reprinted material in this book. Any oversights brought to the attention of the publisher will be rectified in all future printings of the book.

University of Toronto Press acknowledges the financial assistance to its publishing program of the Canada Council for the Arts and the Ontario Arts Council, an Ontario government agency.

  Canada Council   Conseil des Arts
for the Arts   du Canada

Funded by the   Financé par le
Government   gouvernement
of Canada   du Canada

Contents

Preface   vii

Permissions   ix

Introduction   3

Section One: Conscription

1. "To win, at any cost": Politics and Manpower Policies, 1917   17
2. Conscription in the Great War   38
3. The Conservative Party and Conscription in the Second World War   50
4. The York South By-Election of February 9, 1942: A Turning Point in Canadian Politics   71
5. The "Hard" Obligations of Citizenship: The Second World War in Canada   89
6. Conscription and My Politics   102

Section Two: Diplomacy

7. "A Self-Evident National Duty": Canadian Foreign Policy, 1935–1939   111
   WITH ROBERT BOTHWELL
8. Mackenzie King and Canada at Ogdensburg, August 1940   137

9 The Hyde Park Declaration 1941:
   Origins and Significance   155
   WITH R.D. CUFF

10 The Man Who Wasn't There: Mackenzie King,
   Canada, and the Atlantic Charter   180

11 Happily on the Margins: Mackenzie King and
   Canada at the Quebec Conferences   194

Section Three: Politics

12 Financing the Liberal Party, 1935–1945   211

13 King and His Cabinet: The War Years   232

14 The Evacuation of the Japanese Canadians, 1942:
   A Realist Critique of the Received Version   249
   WITH GREGORY A. JOHNSON

15 Arming the Nation: Canada's Industrial
   War Effort 1939–1945   277

Section Four: Reflections

16 A Half-Century On: The Veterans' Experience   291

17 "What Is to Be Done?" The Future of Canadian
   Second World War History   299

18 Thirty Years in the Trenches: A Military Historian's
   Report on the War between Teaching and Research   308

Preface

The chapters in this volume present one historian's assessment of some key episodes in the first half of Canada's twentieth century, notably conscription in the two world wars, the shaping of foreign policy, and some domestic political issues. The central figure is unquestionably Mackenzie King, the nation's longest serving prime minister – and in my view one of Canada's greatest leaders – and the chapters, written over a long career of research and writing, cover some of the issues and policies that King and his government dealt with. The last section offers a few more personal reflections on the state of Canadian history.

As a researcher, I tried to find and use every archival collection on the subjects in which I was interested, and I was very fortunate that collections at the National Archives in Ottawa, in some departments of government, in other repositories in Canada, the United States, and Britain, and in private hands were beginning to be open to researchers as my career started in the mid-1960s, and as it continued. Much like everything I have written, the chapters here were based on the documents and the available published materials, and I believe they made and continue to make a good guide to the extant manuscript sources, books, and articles.

The essays were written over many years and presented in journals with many differing styles of documenting sources. I have not altered the endnotes as originally written.

A few of the chapters were written with colleagues, and I am grateful to them for permission to include them here and also grateful to the copyright holders for permission to reprint these papers. It gives me substantial pleasure to acknowledge that everything I write rests heavily on the work of distinguished scholars and friends, not least Charles Stacey, James Eayrs, John Holmes, Norman Hillmer, Robert Bothwell, John English, Desmond Morton, David Bercuson, and many more. I am indebted to them all, and I hope that I have added something to the rich mix of interpretations and ideas that shape the story of Canada.

JLG

Permissions

"'To win, at any cost': Politics and Manpower Policies, 1917," in Douglas Delaney and Serge Durflinger, eds., *Capturing Hill 70: Canada's Forgotten Battle of the First World War* (Vancouver: UBC Press, 2016), 205–25. With permission of the publisher from *Capturing Hill 70*, edited by Douglas Delaney and Serge Durflinger, UBC Press, 2016. All rights reserved by the publisher.

"Conscription in the Great War," in David Mackenzie, ed., *Canada and the Great War: Essays in Honour of Robert Craig Brown* (Toronto: University of Toronto Press, 2005), 62–75. Reprinted with permission.

"The Conservative Party and Conscription in the Second World War," *Canadian Historical Association Annual Report 1967*, 130–48. Reprinted with permission.

"The York South By-Election of 1942: A Turning Point in Canadian History," *Canadian Historical Review* 48 (June 1967), 142–58. Reprinted with permission.

"The 'Hard' Obligations of Citizenship: The Second World War in Canada," in William Kaplan, ed., *Belonging: The Meaning and Future of Canadian Citizenship* (Montreal: McGill-Queen's University Press, 1993), 36–49. Reprinted with permission.

"Conscription and My Politics," *Canadian Military History* 10 (Autumn 2001), 35–38. Reprinted with permission.

(and R. Bothwell) "'A self-evident national duty': Canadian Foreign Policy, 1935–1939," *The Journal of Imperial and Commonwealth History* 3 (1975), 212–33.

"Mackenzie King and Canada at Ogdensburg, August 1940," in J. Jockel and J. Sokolsky, eds., *The Road from Ogdensburg: Fifty Years of Canada-US Defence Cooperation* (Lewiston, N.Y.: Mellen Press, 1992), 9–29. Reprinted with permission.

(and R. Cuff) "The Hyde Park Declaration of 1941," *Canadian Historical Review* 55 (March 1974), 59–80. Reprinted with permission.

"The Man Who Wasn't There: Mackenzie King, Canada and the Atlantic Charter," in Douglas Brinkley and David Facey-Crowther, eds., *The Atlantic Charter* (New York: St Martin's, 1994), 115–28.

"Happily on the Margins: Mackenzie King and Canada at the Quebec Conferences," in D.B. Woolner, ed., *The Second Quebec Conference Revisited* (New York: Palgrave Macmillan, 1998), 49–64. Reprinted with permission.

"Financing the Liberal Party, 1935–45," in M. Cross and R. Bothwell, eds., *Policy by Other Means: Essays in Honour of C.P. Stacey* (Toronto: Clarke Irwin 1972), 179–99.

"King and His Cabinet, 1939–45," in J. English and J. Stubbs, eds., *Mackenzie King: Widening the Debate* (Toronto: Macmillan, 1978), 173–90.

(and Gregory A. Johnson), "The Evacuation of the Japanese Canadians, 1942: A Realist Critique of the Received Version," in G.N. Hillmer et al., eds., *On Guard for Thee: War. Ethnicity and the Canadian State 1939–45* (Ottawa: Supply and Services Canada, 1988), 101–30.

Arming the Nation: The Canadian Industrial War Effort, 1939–1945, Canadian Council of Chief Executives, 2005.

"A Half-Century On: The Veterans' Experience," in P. Neary and J.L. Granatstein, eds., *The Veterans Charter and Post–World War II Canada* (Montreal: McGill-Queen's University Press, 1998), 224–31. Reprinted with permission.

"'What Is to Be Done?' The Future of Canadian Second World War History," *Canadian Military Journal* 11, no. 2 (2011), 54–9. Initially published in *Canadian Military Journal*, vol. 11, no. 2, Spring 2011 at http://www.journal.forces.gc.ca/vol1/no2/09-granatstein-eng.asp

"Thirty Years in the Trenches: A Military Historian's Report on the War between Teaching and Research," *Canadian Military History* 19 (2010), 37–41. Reprinted with permission.

CANADA AT WAR

Conscription, Diplomacy, and Politics

Introduction

The two world wars have been the focus of my research for more than a half-century. I began writing on the Second World War with my PhD dissertation in the mid-1960s and more recently turned to the Great War. The effects of war on society fascinated me because conflict seems to act as a hothouse, speeding up the emergence of new ideas and crises and then sometimes forcing the quick adoption of these ideas and the resolution of crises – or not. There are victories and defeats in war, to be sure, but at the same time there is the certainty of rapid change. George Orwell defined the process: War, he wrote in 1941, "is the greatest of all agents of change. It speeds up all processes, wipes out minor distinctions, brings reality to the surface."[1] War subjects nations and their peoples to immense strains, and the dangers faced can sometimes tear societies completely apart or, at a minimum, transform attitudes at a much greater pace than in peacetime.

Canada was no exception. The First World War, the Great War to those who survived it, forced Canadian governments into decisions that initially must have seemed all but inconceivable to their leaders. Almost the first response to the conflict in August 1914 was the War Measures Act that put unprecedented and sweeping powers into the hands of the Cabinet. Soon after, more than 30,000 soldiers were dispatched overseas with the expectation that the war would result in a speedy British and French victory. Instead there were casualties beyond imagining – more than 5,000 Canadians killed, wounded, and taken prisoner in a few days of fighting at Ypres, Belgium, in April 1915. More troops went overseas in a steady stream, and more deaths followed month by month. By 1917, conscription had been put into law and in January 1918 into effect in an effort to keep the ranks up to strength. At the same time, radical change came quickly: taxes on income and excess profits, women's suffrage, the disenfranchisement of naturalized enemy aliens, the most blatantly gerrymandered election in Canada's history, prohibition, the repression of leftists, rudimentary rationing, and the greatest involvement of the state in the lives of the citizenry to that time. Canada's Second World War, much better run from Ottawa than the First, expanded the state's reach even further and to greater effect. Total war affected everyone.

My research began with the 1939–45 war. I had graduated from the Royal Military College in 1961 where I had studied history under scholars such as Richard Preston, Donald Schurman, and Ezio Cappadocia, and I had written a very lengthy undergraduate thesis on the history of Canadian peacekeeping to 1960, a subject that continues to interest me.² I had a commitment to serve three years in the army which in 1961–2 graciously allowed me to accept a Queen Elizabeth II Ontario fellowship and go to the University of Toronto to do a Master of Arts in History.

There I took John Saywell's superb seminar on post-Confederation Canadian politics. I didn't have a research topic in mind so he suggested the Communist Party in the Second World War. I started lining up access to Party records at the headquarters on Cecil Street in Toronto and then realized that, as a lieutenant in the army on leave to attend graduate school during the height of the Cold War, I might get into difficulty if every few days I was at the Party headquarters to read the files. I called the army's Central Command Headquarters in Oakville, Ontario, to explain the problem, was eventually passed on to the RCMP, and vetted. Much to my embarrassment, so too was Saywell (who the Mountie sergeant I dealt with said was not a "pinko" like so many University of Toronto faculty). And I was eventually advised that there was no objection to my researching my topic – providing I was debriefed after every visit to Cecil Street. This seemed ridiculous and too time-consuming, too onerous, so I apologized to Saywell for putting him under scrutiny, and took up his second and safer suggestion of researching the Conservative Party during the war. That saved me from a career rooting through Tim Buck's laundry lists and analysing the Communist Party's policy U-turns and failures and put me onto a more mainstream subject. There was more than enough in the Tory topic to make a good paper for Saywell.

Still in the army and after a year at Camp Borden training officer cadets and, somewhat bizarrely, running a motorcycle course for francophone padres (with then-Captain Desmond Morton as my immediate and benevolent superior), I managed to persuade the army to grant me leave without pay once more. In September 1963 I went to Duke University in Durham, NC, with a J.B. Duke Fellowship. There I made the wartime Conservatives my PhD dissertation subject, and I wrote under the supervision of the distinguished military historian Theodore Ropp, who, I discovered later, had written an unpublished manuscript on Canadian conscription which he had never mentioned. No one had yet systematically searched the available manuscript sources, and more politicians' papers were opening up at exactly the right time. (Indeed, I was repeatedly the beneficiary of asking for archival sources and getting them and securing special access by arrangement with individuals or government departments.) I did interviews with every participant I could find, beginning the intensive use of oral histories in much of my subsequent writing. I even went to Progressive Conservative Party headquarters where Flora MacDonald, later foreign minister in Joe Clark's government, directed me to the wartime files I wanted to see, which were literally in a heap on the floor of a basement storage room. In my thesis, I recorded the party's struggles to survive the war as it sought to find policies for a new era of social welfare that its members could support and wrestled in vain with Mackenzie King and the Liberal government.

The major domestic issue was, of course, compulsory overseas military service. While the party leadership was sometimes cautious, most Conservatives favoured it through almost all of the war, convinced – as they had been in the 1914 conflict – that francophones would not fight unless they were forced. So focused on conscription were the Tories that they actually called for it for the war in the Pacific and after V-E Day had ended the fighting in Europe. Not surprisingly, that stance did not help them in the election of 1945 in Quebec where the party won only 2 seats or elsewhere in Canada – except in parts of Ontario where they took 48 of their 67 seats in parliament. I completed my dissertation in 1966 and published it in 1967.[3]

The Conservatives at least had had the virtue of near consistency on their conscription policy. I did not. My research on the Tories in the 1939–45 war had persuaded me that conscription was the wrong way to raise an army, a view that I maintained in *Canada's War*,[4] a study of how the King government directed the war, and in *Broken Promises*,[5] my history of conscription written with J. Mackay Hitsman (who had died several years before publication). But as I continued to wrestle with this subject over the years, I began to realize – as I ought to have from the outset – that conscription was a life or death matter for the soldiers at the front. Understrength battalions suffered more casualties in action, the generals too often sending a battalion of 400 or 500 at defences that would have tested a full strength unit with twice the men. By the late autumn of 1944, as volunteers had dried up, the gaps in the ranks of the infantry in Italy and Northwest Europe had reached the crisis point. National Resources Mobilization Act home defence conscripts seemed to be the nation's only remaining source of trained infantry, and Mackenzie King, twisting and turning, finally ordered 16,000 conscripts overseas.[6] King struggled to survive in Parliament, and he fired one minister and had another resign. But despite the odds, and despite the anger in Quebec and English-speaking Canada about the way the manpower problems had been handled, the Prime Minister managed to eke out a narrow victory in the June 1945 election.

The needs of the front-line men had to matter most, I came to realize, and this forced me to soften my harsh view of compulsory service. A nation that had sent soldiers to fight had the obligation to support them to the fullest extent possible. The soldiers' lives and their military effectiveness had priority, and the real question for government was how to square the circle – how to balance the requirement for domestic peace with the manpower needs of the army. Sir Robert Borden, never my favourite prime minister, had decided in 1917 that the front line's demands took precedence over everything else, and he tore the country apart, pitting French Canadians, farmers, segments of organized labour, and ethnic communities against an aroused Anglo public that wanted to force men to fight. Canada was still a majority British nation, and Borden's ruthlessness won his Union Government a big majority in the election of December 1917.[7] That achievement hurt the Tories for decades.

These issues show up clearly in the chapters that make up the conscription section of this book. They are organized not in the order in which they were written but by chronology, two essays on the First World War and the next three on the Second World War. The final chapter explains how and why my views changed over the decades. The papers here trace events through the Great War where Arthur Meighen figured prominently, and in the Second World War where Meighen, briefly again the Conservative leader in 1941–2, tried to replicate the party's Great War conscription policy. Meighen failed, Mackenzie King prevailed, and conscription did not have quite the same devastating impact on French-English relations as in the earlier conflict.

The "hard obligations" of citizenship had to be met in some fashion in wartime, however, even though Mackenzie King kept those obligations in bounds. That King did prevail and that the nation did not fracture on linguistic lines in my view made him one of Canada's greatest leaders.[8] He might have been "Weird Willie," as a historian has recently characterized him, and he might have led a very double life, as one of Canada's greatest historians put it,[9] but King was a skilful, careful leader who understood that if the country ripped itself asunder at home, it could not fight effectively overseas. King's efforts produced a huge military, agricultural, and industrial war effort and made Canada into a prosperous middle power. Weird Willie indeed.

Mackenzie King was the dominant figure of the first section, and he is again in the second section which deals with his foreign policy at the end of the 1930s and through the war years. King was no adventurer. He had been a true believer in Britain's policy of appeasement – anything was better than another war with its huge costs in treasure and blood and its strains on the body politic. But King knew that the solidity of English-Canadian public opinion meant that Canada would have to fight if Britain went to war; indeed, while he disliked much of British interwar policy and distrusted many British leaders of the period including Neville Chamberlain and Winston Churchill, he wanted Canada to be at Britain's side.

Backing and forthing as he tried to hold his party and country together, King succeeded in bringing a more or less united country into war on September 10, 1939. Appealing to francophone Canada, he had promised no conscription for overseas service after Adolf Hitler broke his pledges made at Munich in September 1938 and swallowed all of Czechoslovakia in March 1939. The very next day, March 31, Ernest Lapointe, the justice minister and King's Quebec lieutenant, called on Canada to rule out neutrality in the coming war, implicitly pledging Quebec's support so long as its concerns were met by ruling out compulsory service. The English-speaking prime minister spoke to Quebec; the Quebec lieutenant offered reassurance to English Canada. The opening essay in this section, the first of many works I co-authored with Robert Bothwell,[10] laid out exactly how King had managed this.

The four remaining articles in the second section trace Mackenzie King's wartime relations with the United States and Britain. The chapter on the Ogdensburg Agreement examined the reasons why Canada in the summer of 1940 felt obliged to strike a defence alliance with the United States – and Winston Churchill's fiery, wrong-headed response to it. The chapter on the Hyde Park Agreement of 1941, written with Robert Cuff, was one of the first we did together.[11] A first-rate historian, Bob died much too young; our account of how and why the agreement mattered for the war years and affected Canada's future course stands up well. During the war, Canada clearly moved out of Britain's economic orbit and into that of the United States. Britain's military, economic, and political weakness had forced Mackenzie King's Canada to look south for protection and prosperity.[12] The last two chapters explore how Mackenzie King's Canada got on – or tried to get along – with the British and Americans as the Second World War progressed. King was cut out of the 1941 Atlantic Charter meeting between President Roosevelt and Prime Minister Winston Churchill in Newfoundland waters, but he did make it onto the sidelines of the two Quebec Conferences in 1943 and 1944. That held some value over and above the good media attention it secured for King, who took every advantage offered by photographs of him with the Allies' leaders.

The Diplomacy section demonstrates that King and Canada played its middling hand with some skill. For a start, King was no simpleton despite much of the historiography that focuses on his dog, his fixation with the hands of clocks, and his attending séances. He had been involved with foreign policy questions since the early years of the century, and he knew most of the key Anglo-American players. Moreover, his close Cabinet colleagues C.D. Howe and Louis St Laurent, and advisers Norman Robertson, Lester Pearson, and Hume Wrong were among the ablest ministers and civil servants Canada ever fielded. Still, to no one's surprise the Dominion did not get much of a share in running the Allied war effort. With a population of only 11 million people, Canada was never going to be able to butt into the Great Powers' game. Nonetheless, Canada greatly enhanced its reputation, protected its national interests, and generated an extraordinary war effort in the Second World War that gave Canada increased standing among the nations and made it the leader of the middle powers.

The third section deals with domestic political issues, and King again is the central character. Party finance interested me from the moment I came across the Norman Lambert Papers at the Queen's University Archives. Senator Lambert was the Liberal fundraiser and campaign manager and his notebooks detailed how much money he raised for the party and from whom. The papers made clear that the government party took its 5 per cent cut on government contracts. Lambert also offered one of the more compelling descriptions of Prime Minister King: "It is amusing," a journalist friend, Grant Dexter, wrote about Lambert in a memorandum about the conversation, "to hear him explain that he simply can't stand the worm at close quarters – bad breath, a fetid, unhealthy, sinister atmosphere, like being close to some filthy object. But get off a piece and he looks better and better."[13] King tried to stay above the mundane questions of party organization and finance though he perpetually complained that none of the Liberal party brass, not least Lambert, did anything to assist him. As his party organizer understood all too well, King's stature really did seem to improve with some distance.

More important was building and running a Cabinet, and here Mackenzie King was superb. He appointed strong ministers to whom he gave their head, and the wartime government had many such in St Laurent, Howe, J.L. Ilsley, Ernest Lapointe, and more. The duds were tolerated as long as necessary but then eased into the Senate, the bench, or sometimes a diplomatic post. Above all, regional balance had to be maintained, and French-speaking Quebec had to have its share of the posts. And if there were contentious issues – the creation of family allowances, for example – the prime minister was quite prepared to override opponents to get his way. Even with a strong group of ministers around the table, King was definitely the first among equals. On the other hand, when he had found himself the only one opposing the imposition of sweeping price controls in the autumn of 1941, King could yield to his colleagues. It was a good thing that the price control policy proved a great success.

The penultimate article in section 3 deals with the fate of the 22,000 Japanese Canadians during the 1939 war. Nothing I ever wrote, perhaps not even *Who Killed Canadian History?* published in 1998,[14] stirred up such an angry response as that. Greg Johnson, one of my PhD students at the time, assisted with research on this subject, initially for an article in *Saturday Night*, published in November 1986,[15] and he found the "Magic" transcripts, the results of the extraordinary decoding success of American navy codebreakers, in the US National Archives. Greg became the co-author of the subsequent academic piece. The declassified secret files, containing translations of the messages from the foreign office in Tokyo, made clear that the Japanese consul in Vancouver had been ordered to recruit spies from among the Japanese Canadians in BC and to seek out military information. How successful the consul was is unknown because the records seem to have been destroyed by the bombing of Tokyo during the war. Many people in the Japanese-Canadian community were very pro-Japan as Tokyo waged an aggressive war in China, and some Japanese-Canadian newspapers published large photo sections of propaganda supplied by the consulate. After Pearl Harbor on 7 December 1941, activities that had been permissible and even innocuous a few days before suddenly looked very different.

The result of Japan's stunning successes at the outset of the war in the Pacific was a palpable fear of invasion in British Columbia and a demand by the military, the media, the public, and provincial politicians there to eliminate any possible threat by removing the Japanese Canadians from the coast to the interior. Some 700 men deemed hard liners were interned in northern Ontario; the remainder of the Japanese-Canadian community was forcibly evacuated inland but not interned. They could not go westward toward their former homes and occupations, but they could and did go east to work and live. Most of what happened to this small visible minority was unquestionably based on racism and fear, but some of it did make sense. The government had almost no intelligence officers who could speak or read Japanese, and the absence of hard, verifiable intelligence meant that worst case scenarios became top of mind.

What was certain was that Greg's and my article made use of a substantial range of hitherto untapped archival sources and presented and interpreted much information that was new. This didn't appear to matter to our critics. David Suzuki, I was told, had threatened to punch me in the nose, and a meeting with Japanese Canadians pressing for redress included someone who asked me if what had happened to the Japanese Canadians was not the equivalent of the Holocaust. No, it wasn't.

What happened to the Japanese Canadians in 1942 and after, the vast majority of whom showed no ill intent to their country, nonetheless was unquestionably unjust. There were reasons for Ottawa to act as it had in a war that seemed about to involve the West Coast directly, a war that the Allies were thus far losing in the Pacific. But in a late 1980s Canada that had become aware of multiculturalism and had come to believe in the Charter of Rights and Freedoms as sacred writ that could and should be applied retroactively, there seemed no necessity to try to understand why the government had taken the actions it did. Anyone who called for a more nuanced approach to understanding the events of 1941–2 was shouted down and accused of racism. Readers can judge for themselves here and in the subsequent book I did with Patricia Roy, the leading historian of British Columbia, and two able Japanese scholars of Canada[16] if the shouting had any merit.

Finally in this section is a paper on Canadian wartime production that the Canadian Council of Chief Executives asked me to prepare in 2005. Wages rose, the Gross National Product doubled between 1939 and 1945, and raw materials, foods, munitions, supplies, and an endless stream of trucks, guns, ships, and aircraft poured out of the fields, mines, factories, and dockyards to arm the Canadian forces and those of Canada's allies. Driven by the "Minister of Everything," the remarkable C.D. Howe, Canada's productivity helped win the war and laid the groundwork for the country to mature into a prosperous nation in the postwar years. Canada had always been God's country, but after the Second World War it became God's *prosperous* country.

The last section of this book has three reflective essays and Prime Minister King is at last not the central character. The first chapter looks at the veterans' experience after the Second World War, a piece in a volume my friend Peter Neary and I published in 1998.[17] The second article, published in 2011, examined what had already been written on Canada's experience in that war and what gaps remained to be filled. The military history and the social, political, and industrial history of Canada during the war are areas now being explored at last – see the extraordinary list of titles in any of the recent publications in the Canadian War Museum's *Studies in Canadian Military History* series published with the University of British Columbia Press. I had begun this series to explore all aspects of the nation's military history when I was Director and CEO of the War Museum from 1998 to 2000, and I am delighted that it is without question the best continuing series publishing on Canadian history.

The final chapter, prepared for a festschrift in honour of Ezio Cappodocia that unfortunately did not proceed to publication, looked back at my career as a political-military historian. Canadian historians had moved away from the traditional approaches to their discipline in the 1970s and 1980s, and by the time I took early retirement from York University in 1995 the kind of history I researched and wrote did not seem to be highly valued by most my colleagues in the Canadian historical profession. I continued writing despite this – publishers and readers fortunately seemed to take a different view than academic historians.

Political, military, and diplomatic history still matter. It seems very odd to me that Canadian historians now pay so little attention to such subjects. Could it be that some believe that the political events of the Great War in Canada and the battles overseas are of no consequence? That Canada's shift from the British to the American sphere of influence is unimportant? That an issue like conscription that imperilled unity in two great wars should not be studied and taught? To me and to the literate Canadian public (including many students), such issues matter. The past is a foreign country, to be sure, but if we do not examine and understand the issues that once tormented Canadians we will never understand how we reached our present condition and status.

NOTES

1 George Orwell, "The Lion and the Unicorn," in *The Collected Essays, Journalism and Letters*, Vol. II (London: Penguin, 1970), 117.
2 Much of this BA thesis was published as "Canada: Peacekeeper: A Survey on Canada's Participation in Peacekeeping Operations," in Alastair Taylor et. al., *Peacekeeping: International Challenge and Canadian Response* (Toronto: Canadian Institute of International Affairs, 1968), pp. 93–187.

3 *The Politics of Survival: The Conservative Party of Canada, 1939–45* (Toronto: University of Toronto Press, 1967).
4 *Canada's War: The Politics of the Mackenzie King Government, 1939–1945* (Toronto: Oxford University Press, 1975; republished 1990, 2016).
5 *Broken Promises: A History of Conscription in Canada* (Toronto: Oxford University Press, 1977; republished 1985, 2015).
6 Michael Stevenson, *Canada's Greatest Wartime Muddle: National Selective Service and the Mobilization of Human Resources during World War II* (Montreal: McGill-Queen's University Press, 2001), and Daniel Byers, *Zombie Army: The Canadian Army and Conscription in the Second World War* (Vancouver: University of British Columbia Press, 2016), add much to the manpower story.
7 Two recent works that contribute greatly to the conscription story during the Great War are the late Richard Holt's *Filling the Ranks: Manpower in the Canadian Expeditionary Force, 1914–1918* (Montreal: McGill-Queen's University Press, 2017), and Patrick Dennis, *Reluctant Warriors: Canadian Conscripts and the Great War* (Vancouver: University of British Columbia Press, 2017).
8 Norman Hillmer and I surveyed historians in 1997 and ranked Mackenzie King Number 1 among prime ministers. "Historians Rank the Best and Worst Canadian Prime Ministers," *Maclean's* (21 April 1997), 34–39.
9 Christopher Dummit, *Unbuttoned: A History of Mackenzie King's Secret Life* (Montreal: McGill-Queen's University Press, 2017). C.P. Stacey's *A Very Double Life: The Private World of Mackenzie King* (Toronto: Macmillan, 1976) was an early attempt to probe King's psyche.
10 Other works Bothwell and I wrote together included *The Great Brain Robbery* (Toronto: McClelland & Stewart, 1984); *Pirouette: Pierre Trudeau and Canadian Foreign Policy* (Toronto: University of Toronto Press, 1990); *Petrified Campus* (Toronto: Random House, 1997); *Our Century* (Toronto: McArthur and Co., 2000); and *Trudeau's World* (Vancouver: UBC Press, 2017). David Bercuson, also a frequent co-author of mine on other books, was the third of the triumvirate that wrote the academic books. A scathing and much too critical interpretation of King and his pre-war policy is Roy MacLaren, *Mackenzie King in the Age of the Dictators: Canada's Imperial and Foreign Policies* (Montreal: McGill-Queen's University Press, 2019). See also Robert Teigrob, *Four Days in Hitler's Germany: Mackenzie King's Mission to Avert a Second World War* (Toronto: University of Toronto Press, 2019).
11 Cuff and I did two books together: *Canadian-American Relations in Wartime* (Toronto: Hakkert, 1975; second ed. published as *Ties that Bind*, 1977) and *American Dollars/Canadian Prosperity: Canadian-American Economic Relations, 1945–50* (Toronto: Samuel Stevens, 1978),

12 This topic was explored in the Goodman Lectures I gave at the University of Western Ontario in 1988, published as *How Britain's Weakness Forced Canada into the Arms of the United States* (Toronto: University of Toronto Press, 1989). My original title, inexplicably vetoed by the publisher (!), was *How Britain's Economic, Military, and Political Weakness Forced Canada into the Arms of the United States: A Melodrama in Three Acts*.
13 Grant Dexter memorandum, 22 April 1941, in F.W. Gibson and Barbara Robertson, eds., *Ottawa at War: The Grant Dexter Memoranda 1939–1945* (Winnipeg: Manitoba Records Society, 1994), p. 158.
14 (Toronto: Harper Collins, 1998).
15 "The Enemy Within," *Saturday Night* (November, 1986).
16 P. Roy, J.L. Granatstein, M. Iino and H. Takamura, *Mutual Hostages: Canadians and Japanese during the Second World War* (Toronto: University of Toronto Press, 1990).
17 P. Neary and J.L. Granatstein, eds., *The Veterans Charter and Post-World War II Canada* (Montreal: McGill-Queen's University Press, 1998)

SECTION ONE

Conscription

Chapter One

"To win, at any cost": Politics and Manpower Policies, 1917

After almost three years of fighting in France and Flanders, the Great War of words in Canada reached its peak. From the time that Prime Minister Sir Robert Borden arrived home in Canada from Britain and the battlefront in May 1917, the political conflict became intense. The issues were compulsory military service, the need to create a coalition government that could enforce it, and the steps to be taken to guarantee a coalition election victory. Borden was no great orator or intellect, but he was a focused, determined man willing to do whatever he must to ensure that Canada continued to do its utmost to help win the war. Although he had several times promised that conscription would not be implemented in Canada, he was willing to change course when that became necessary. If that meant dividing the nation and ruining his Conservative Party's prospects in French Canada and on the farms for a generation, that was a price he was willing to accept. What mattered to Borden was victory and the requirements of the immediate moment, not the future. Equally important to the prime minister, he personally and the nation he led had promised to support the men they put in the field. The heavy losses in the four divisions of the Canadian Corps at Vimy Ridge in April and Hill 70 in August had shaken Borden and his ministers. As he wrote almost two decades later, an army officer had told him "We had gone forth on the pledge of Canada's honour that we would be supported to the end. If reinforcements had failed, we might have failed."[1] To Sir Robert Borden, both his and the nation's honour mattered.

The prime minister had been in England when the Canadian Corps took Vimy Ridge at Easter, 1917. The victory and the plaudits he received for the Corps' achievements moved him; as much and even more, the 10,000 casualties that the victory had cost troubled him greatly. Recruiting for the front had slowed to a trickle in late 1916 and early 1917, casualties greatly exceeding the new volunteers at home.

In April and May 1917, casualties numbered 24,000; in the same two months, only 11,290 men enlisted.[2]

The government sought to release the approximately 50,000 volunteers in Canada for the Canadian Expeditionary Force (CEF) from defending the country against the possibility of German-American or Fenian raids from south of the border by creating the volunteer Canada Defence Force (CDF) with an intended strength of 50,000 home defence volunteers. "Release a Man to Fight in France by Enlisting in the Canada Defence Force," newspaper advertisements urged.[3] But men did not flock to the CDF, any more than they now did to the CEF. Why would a man put on a uniform that proclaimed his fitness to fight but his unwillingness to serve overseas? And if the CDF fell flat, would its enrollees not be put into the CEF, no matter what the army promised? By 25 April 1917, after a month of effort, fewer than 200 had enrolled in the CDF.

In any case, the United States had entered the war on 6 April, promising to bring millions of new men to the front as soon as they could be made ready. The side benefit for Canada was that the possibility of raids on Canada, never very great, disappeared completely. But the Americans' arrival, with an effectively trained and well-equipped force could not occur before at least a year. People understood that with the US now in the war, victory for the Allies seemed much more likely. But no one in England or Ottawa wanted to allow the preachy, moralistic President Woodrow Wilson the opportunity to proclaim that he and his nation had won the war. We need more men to bolster the Empire's position and win the war – that was the message that British Prime Minister David Lloyd George had given Borden.[4]

The problem facing the government in the spring of 1917 was that the Canadian Corps needed more infantrymen in the coming months to maintain its 48 battalions up to strength. Canada's fighting men had been overwhelmingly drawn from recent British-born immigrants, and the Canadian-born had been relatively slow to enlist, despite recruiting campaigns and "shaming" by patriotic women and men. French-speaking Canadians, in particular, were loath to enlist, seeing the war as none of their business because, in their view, it did not threaten Canada. Very simply, the majority of French-Canadians were more concerned with the preservation of their cultural, linguistic, and religious rights within Canada than with fighting a war in Europe. In Quebec, as a result, the public pressure was to stay out of khaki; in the rest of Canada, the pressure, hitherto not very successful with many of the Canadian-born, was for fit men to join up.

Sir Robert Borden in his 1916 New Year's Day message had committed Canada to fielding an army of a half-million men.[5] He had done this without consulting more than a handful of his cabinet ministers or the army's General Staff, but he must have known of the results of the 1911 Census. There were 3.859 million males in Canada, but of British subjects between 18 and 45 years of age, the only ones officially eligible for military service, there were only 1.029 million. Some 200,000 were medically unfit, leaving a manpower pool of 820,637 with some 146,000 fit enough to serve, but unfit for combat. The number of potential soldiers was not huge, especially given the almost insatiable demand for reinforcements for the front, but undoubtedly men were still available.[6]

A British Army Council study of late-1916 prepared for the War Cabinet in London noted that Canada had enlisted 9.6 per cent of its male population. While 37.5 per cent of British-born Canadians had joined, only 6.1 per cent of Canadian-born men of British origin had done so. The enlistment of foreign-born Canadians (6.5 per cent) and French Canadians (1.4 per cent) were also well below the national average. The French-Canadian enlistment rate, the Army Council study declared, was the lowest in "the white Empire."[7] A Sessional Paper laid before Parliament on 14 June 1917 stated that as of 30 April 1917, there were 125,245 Canadian-born English-speaking men overseas in the Canadian Expeditionary Force, 14,100 French-speaking men born in all parts of Canada (but only 6,979 serving in units organized in Quebec and presumably resident there), and 155,095 British subjects born outside of Canada.[8]

The numbers were probably far less firm than they appeared, but they were generally correct, and they pointed to the problem that faced the government and the military in the spring of 1917. The Canadian-born, and especially the French-speaking among them, had not come forward in sufficient numbers. The long casualty lists regularly printed in the newspapers had had their predictable effects. What Tim Cook has called "the war as an absent event" kept men at home. "These Canadians," he wrote, "were simply unwilling to leave their communities, jobs, and families, or were critically needed to grow food, manufacture munitions, work the mines, and operate the railway system. Did these men, all potential recruits, see themselves as soldiers of the soil and factory floor, or was the war simply an overseas event, to be followed in the daily papers with little inconvenience to oneself?"[9] Whatever their rationales, nothing any longer seemed to inspire enough of such men to volunteer to keep Canada's four divisions at the front up to strength, and the failure of the CDF was merely another indication of the voluntary system's failure. As a result, in the government's now firmly-held view, conscription had to be put in place to get the reinforcements that the Canadian Corps needed to keep fighting. The heavy casualties suffered in the battle for Hill 70 in August would increase the pressure for reinforcements even more, and this chapter demonstrates how effectively, indeed ruthlessly, the Borden government manoeuvred to pass conscription and ensure the subsequent election victory.

There were four pieces of legislation that the government rammed through Parliament in the summer of 1917 as it moved to deal with its manpower problems, to form a coalition with pro-conscription Liberals, and to ensure that it won the federal election that would allow it to implement and enforce conscription. The Military Service Act (MSA) was the key part of the package. Much less well known, but very important, was the Income War Tax Act (WTA) which brought some Liberal Members of Parliament closer to the government. The Military Voters Act (MVA) and the Wartime Elections Act (WTEA), two of the most extraordinary pieces of legislation in Canada's history, were designed to give Prime Minister Borden what he needed to persuade Liberals that they had no chance to win an election and to push the pro-conscription Grits to abandon Sir Wilfrid Laurier for a Union Government.

The prime minister presented his intention to introduce conscription to the House of Commons on 18 May. The Canadian Corps, Borden said, "cannot be maintained without thorough provision for future requirements. Hitherto we have depended on voluntary enlistment...," he went on, but "it is apparent to me that the voluntary system will not yield further substantial results.... All citizens are liable to military service for the defence of their country.... Therefore," the Prime Minister stated, "it is my duty to announce to the House that early proposals will be made to provide by compulsory military enlistment on a selective basis, such reinforcements as may be necessary to maintain the Canadian army in the field." The number of men required, Borden stated, "will not be less than 50,000 and will probably be 100,000...."[10]

The conscription measure, the Military Service Bill, did not come to the House of Commons until 11 June. In the interim, Borden met twice with Liberal leader Laurier on 25 and 29 May and asked him to join a coalition government, offering his party an equal number of positions in the Cabinet and, at the second meeting, to hold off the enforcement of conscription until after an election. A Union Government could ease the difficulties that Borden knew would arise with conscription; Laurier understood this as well, but he feared that with conscription and coalition Henri Bourassa and the *nationalistes* would become the unchallenged leaders of anti-government and anti-war opinion in Quebec.[11] The Liberal leader said he favoured a referendum or an election to decide on conscription, but Borden initially was not enthusiastic. As he noted in his diary the first evening he had met Laurier, "Our Ministers afraid of a general election. Think we would be beaten by French, foreigners, slackers."[12] Laurier consulted his followers, and Newton Rowell, the Liberal leader in the Ontario legislature and one of the Grits in favour of conscription, wrote him on 29 May that "Surely the time has come when we can all recognize that Canada is being defended in Flanders and in France just as truly and much more effectively that she could be defended on the banks of the St. Lawrence."[13] Knowing full well that his French-speaking compatriots did not share that sentiment, Laurier did not agree, and on 6 June, he told the prime minister that "he could not join coalition government as he is opposed to conscription. Fears Bourassa's influence...."[14] With great patience and a substantial measure of the utmost political ruthlessness, Borden would nonetheless continue his efforts to entice Liberals into the government.

The drafting of the conscription legislation, underway immediately on Borden's return, meanwhile fell to Arthur Meighen, the solicitor-general, relatively young, ruthless, and a great orator, and certainly the ablest member of the cabinet. Meighen received a draft bill prepared by staff that was modelled on American legislation and that called for a national registration followed by selection by lot from various classes by age and marital status. The dominion had adopted a voluntary national registration at the beginning of 1917 that had taken time and produced less-than-complete results.[15] Another registration, Meighen believed, would merely take up scarce weeks. Instead, he insisted that what should be done was to provide that when a certain class – it would be single men from ages 20 to 34 in the first instance – was called up, *all* members of the class were for the army unless they were exempted from service. Everyone and no one was to be conscripted, and Meighen's bill allowed exemptions, among others, for those engaged in war industry, those whose special qualifications meant that they could not be spared from their work, and conscientious objectors.[16] Exemption tribunals, to be set up across the country, would decide who was to be in uniform or not[17] and, as it turned out, virtually every man called up – more than 90 per cent in every province or 94 per cent overall-sought exemption.

The cabinet reviewed and revised Meighen's draft on 24 May, and the Military Service Bill came to the House of Commons on 11 June. The debate in Parliament was intense, lasting well into July with 99 MPs speaking, many of them Liberals expressing support for the measure. Ernest Lapointe, the Liberal MP for Kamouraska, however, called the bill "the most important since Confederation," and pronounced it unacceptable to Quebec because it was "a direct violation of all the pledges given by this Government, this Parliament, and all the public men of this country to the Canadian people."[18] Lapointe was correct, for as early as December 1914, Borden had promised there would be no conscription. Other French-speaking Liberals spoke in much the same vein as Lapointe, some in stronger terms. Laurier's final words in the debate were moving ones: "I oppose this Bill because it has in it the seeds of discord and disunion; because it is an obstacle and a bar to that union of heart and soul without which it is impossible to hope that Confederation will attain the aims and ends that were had in view when Confederation was effected." He went on: "All my life I have fought coercion; all my life I have promoted union; and the inspiration that led me to that course shall be my guide at all times so long as there is a breath left in my body."[19] It was magnificent, but Canada was at war, and Laurier failed to move the House. The bill passed on second reading on a vote of 119 to 55. Just five French Canadian MPs voted for the bill, only three of them from Quebec, two of them ministers. Twenty-six Liberals voted for compulsory service, and Laurier's following in English Canada was badly split.

In Quebec, meanwhile, the situation was volatile with anti-conscription meetings gathering steam since May and with several attacks on returned soldiers, the dynamiting on 9 August of the home of Lord Atholston, the owner of the pro-conscription *Montreal Star*, a plot to assassinate Borden, and street orators repeatedly urging armed resistance to the federal government and its Military Service Act.[20] Widespread violence seemed only days away. The Prime Minister noted in a mid-August letter to the anti-conscriptionist Archbishop Bruchesi in Montreal that in the still ongoing fighting at Hill 70 and Lens, fighting in which Quebec's 22nd Battalion was heavily engaged, 5,500 Canadians had fallen. "I should feel that their blood and that of all others who have fought would be on my head if the provisions of this law should remain unexecuted," he wrote.[21] Borden's task now was to use the Military Service Act, not signed into law until 29 August (after the fighting at Hill 70 and Lens had ceased), to help secure the coalition that he wanted.

When it finally concluded, the fighting around Hill 70 had cost the Canadian Corps 8,777 officers and men killed, wounded, and taken prisoner. In that same month of August 1917, there had been only 2,996 enlistments for the Canadian Expeditionary Force.[22] The *Calgary Herald*, as Serge Durflinger noted, was quick to point out on 31 August that the "Canadian losses at Lens require reinforcements," additional men who could only be found by enforcing the provisions of the Military

Service Act, passed two days earlier. Sir George Perley, Borden's minister in London, similarly told a journalist that, while the Corps' losses at Hill 70 could be made good from trained men in England, future losses could only be replaced with conscripts.[23] No one in the government in Ottawa or with the Canadians in England any longer doubted this.

The government's next step towards its goal was a financial measure. An income tax had never been the Borden government's preferred way to help finance the war effort. The war was to be paid for primarily by borrowing money, in effect fighting for the freedom of the future citizens of Canada who would carry the costs on their shoulders. At the beginning of the war in August 1914, Canada's small national government had financed itself through customs duties and excise and indirect taxes. By the end of the conflict, even after the introduction of a Business Profits Tax and the Income War Tax, the tariff and indirect taxes still generated some 90 per cent of tax revenue. Income tax itself generated less than 1 per cent of total tax revenue. In other words, the income tax was intended to serve a purpose other than generating revenue.[24]

So what was the intent of the Income War Tax Act of 1917? The war had undoubtedly created substantial pools of wealth in Canada. The manufacturers of munitions and vehicles, uniforms and weapons, had profited enormously from government contracts. So too had meat packers and the large producers of foodstuffs. In April 1917, Finance Minister Sir Thomas White told the House of Commons that the Business Profits Tax — which he had put in place in early 1916 and which he had originally estimated could produce $25 million in its first three years — would likely bring in $15 million in its first year of operation. But critics on the Opposition benches, in labour, and on the farms across the country claimed that the Business Profits Tax did little to make the rich pay, not least, as one Liberal MP put it snidely, "the multi-millionaires sitting on the treasury benches."[25]

White had consistently refused to consider an income tax, arguing that Canada was in competition for investment, and income taxes would be a disincentive for investors at home and abroad. In his 1917 budget, he instead proposed an increase in the Business Profits Tax. But the Opposition hammered at the government, demanding that the wealthy who paid little or no taxes should be forced to give their fair share.[26] Once Sir Robert Borden returned to Canada in May, and once he told Parliament that the government was to bring in a conscription of manpower measure, the debate in and out of Parliament shifted in tone. If men were to be forced to fight, surely now simple justice demanded the conscription of wealth. Farmers' organizations and newspapers indicated their support for such a measure, and even the plutocrats of the Montreal Board of Trade suggested that income taxation might be appropriate.

In the meantime, the prime minister continued his efforts to form a coalition that would implement conscription. During the debate on the Military Service Bill, many Liberals in Parliament had begun to call for a coalition without yet being prepared to cross the floor, Laurier's pleas for his party to stand together still having some force. The government's attempt to secure an extension of the life of Parliament had been debated in the Commons in mid-July, and Borden had already made amply clear that, without unanimity or near unanimity, he would not again ask Westminster to amend the British North America Act to make an extension legal as he had done a year earlier. What was significant was that the Liberals tried to amend the government motion by suggesting that a tax on wealth – the conscription of wealth – had to come before any extension.[27] On 18 July Borden withdrew his motion for an extension, making an election before the end of 1917 certain.

The government majority already had the votes to pass its conscription legislation, but its new need was to get Liberals into a coalition that could win the coming election. The introduction of an income tax measure could assist in achieving this. On 25 July, the day after the Military Service Bill had passed on second reading, White announced the introduction of such a bill – to meet the need, he said, for the greater expenditures that conscription would bring. He initially proposed eliminating the Business Profits Tax when the income tax came into effect, and at a time when the average yearly wage for men in manufacturing industries was some $762 a year, he called for only those earning more than $2,000 a year to be taxed. The Liberals objected strenuously to the details, not the principle, of the new measure. For example, F.F. Pardee, the Liberal Whip and a supporter of conscription, called the proposed tax "a flea-bite, a mere cheese-paring.... The rich man and the rich corporation who are protected by the men who are fighting our battles at the front should give to such an extent that it will hurt."[28] Newton Rowell, the Ontario Liberal leader and one of the Grits Prime Minister Borden wanted in his coalition government, called for a tougher measure in a speech on 26 July: "Men who are profiting by the war must make a full contribution to the cost of the war, and in addition, a radical, progressive income tax measure is urgently required."[29] White eventually agreed to keep the Business Profits Tax and to exempt the single earning less than $1500 and the married earning less than $3000. The basic tax was 4 per cent of income with surcharges on higher incomes, for example 25 per cent on incomes above $100,000. White estimated that the Income War Tax would generate $15 to 20 million a year.[30] As the one detailed study of the Income War Tax Act properly notes, it was "introduced as an inducement to Liberals to support a coalition government dedicated to enforcing conscription" and "it represented one of the largest concessions the government could make"[31]

But the Liberals in Parliament and in the provincial parties had not yet broken away from Laurier, and further measures, blatantly political measures, were needed to ensure electoral success. The first of these measures, the Military Voters Bill, made eminent sense in part. Everyone agreed that men in uniform, and soldiers who had finished their service honourably should be able to vote in a general election, including even those who had resided in Canada for only a short time before enlistment. After all, they had volunteered to defend Canada and the Empire. Men under 21 and Indians serving in the CEF were also eligible to vote, both for the first time. Women in uniform, Nursing Sisters, also received the right to vote; they too had assumed risks (and suffered casualties) and served the cause. The bill was introduced on 15 August 1917, coincidentally the day the Canadian Corps' battle for Hill 70 began in France.

Introduced by Minister of Justice Charles Doherty, the Military Voters Bill let a soldier cast his vote not for a specific candidate in a designated constituency, as had always been the case, but for either the Government or the Opposition. If the soldier could name the constituency in which he had lived on enlistment, or any constituency in which he had ever lived, his ballot would be counted there. If the military voter could not name a constituency, his vote would be assigned by the government-appointed electoral officer. This, as the Liberals in the House of Commons and across the country could see at once, was a clear path to electoral manipulation. That military voters might be expected to be for conscription, the quickest way to secure the reinforcements the Canadian Corps needed, was one thing. Soldier Harold Simpson from Prince Edward Island said it simply: "we want conscription and we want to see it without delay...." [32] Another member of the CEF, Ludlow Weeks, said "the fellows here have no use for the slackers."[33] But for the Grits, the possibility that votes might be directed where they were needed most by the Government candidates was chilling. The bill contained a clause directing that the overseas vote not be counted for 31 days after the election,[34] and this would let votes be applied where they could determine the outcome in close contests. [35] Using closure, the Conservative majority passed the Military Voters Bill in the House of Commons on 29 August 1917, and it became law at the end of September. The MVA was the first step in the Borden government's radical gerrymandering of the franchise.

The second hob-nailed boot crashed down on 6 September when Arthur Meighen, by this time, the minister of mines and secretary of state, introduced the Wartime Elections Bill. The Conservatives had been worried by their inability to break the Liberal hold on recently naturalized immigrants who had come to Canada between 1896 and 1911, the Laurier boom years. In October 1916, Meighen had privately told the prime minister that "Were it possible ... to meet the foreign population difficulty by well based legislation ... then it would undoubtedly be a splendid stroke of policy for us to extend the franchise to women wherever it is extended to them provincially. To shift the franchise from the doubtful British or anti-British of the male sex," Meighen argued, "and to extend it at the same time to our patriotic women, would be in my judgment a splendid stroke."[36] Splendid indeed. The results in provincial elections in Alberta and Saskatchewan in June 1917, where the Liberals swept back into power with a solid "foreign" vote reinforced these concerns. The task of drafting the new franchise bill was Meighen's.

His handiwork gave widows, mothers, wives, sisters, and daughters of soldiers the vote, the first women to be enfranchised in a Canadian federal election. At the same time, naturalized immigrants from enemy countries who had come to Canada after 1902 lost their right to cast a ballot; so too did conscientious objectors. Finally, the bill directed the federal government, not the provincial governments as had hitherto been the case, to appoint the enumerators to compile the electoral rolls. The Liberals denounced the bill in Parliament, but the Conservative majority again used closure to force it through the Commons on 14 September. The WTEA was law by the end of September, and estimates were that this extraordinary gerrymander potentially gave the vote to some 450,000 women while removing it from 50,000 to 70,000 of the foreign-born.[37]

Criticism of the WTEA in English Canada was muted, and Oscar Skelton, a leading professor at Queen's University (and a friend and future biographer of Laurier) was one of the few to express outrage. "The excuse given that the end justified the means, that any measure was warranted which would prevent the victory of a leader whose policy was traitorous and disastrous," he protested "added insolence to highway robbery."[38]

With the passage of the MVA and WTEA, the prime minister had now created the conditions he needed to win the coming election. Borden understood that the measures he had put in place were distasteful, but he was unmoved. As he wrote in his diary on 25 September and as he genuinely believed, "Our first duty is to win, at any cost, the coming elections in order that we may continue to do our part in winning this war and that Canada be not disgraced."[39] Borden's task now was to put together his conscriptionist coalition government.

This was to be no easy matter. The prime minister first had to stand by while the Liberals determined their course. He wanted to bring Newton Rowell, the Ontario Liberal leader, into his government, but Rowell was torn between his belief in conscription and his loyalty to Sir Wilfrid Laurier. At a meeting on 20 July in Toronto, Liberal MPs and candidates, called together to support conscription and coalition, instead supported Laurier, leaving Rowell confused and Laurier more hopeful. Conscription was only "a passing event," he said. "The important thing to remember is to keep the unity of the party on broad principles."[40] A month later, a conference of Western Liberals in Winnipeg once more voted against conscription and coalition and stayed loyal to the old chief. But Laurier's position was far from secure. A gathering of Ontario Liberal newspaper editors came out strongly for conscription and Union Government.[41] That was a clear sign that Borden had the province's wealthy media owners in his pocket.

Once the MVA and WTEA had passed through Parliament, however, the Laurier Liberals knew that the game was up. The Prairie Liberals had talked to the prime minister before the changes in the franchise, calling on Borden to step down as their condition to support coalition. Now, their electoral fortunes altered and their opposition to the prime minister gone, they stampeded toward a coalition under Borden. That solved one problem, but it created others. The prime minister's intent was to bring Liberals into his cabinet and caucus, and this meant that he had to drop some Conservative ministers.

Inevitably, that created hard feelings, not least from Manitoba's Bob Rogers, a fierce partisan dumped hard by Borden in mid-August because he was stirring up Conservatives to oppose coalition. Then Arthur Meighen, fearing that his rising status in the West might be weakened, fought strenuously to keep J.A. Calder, the Saskatchewan Deputy Premier and Liberal organization boss, out of the government, but he lost that struggle. Still, Meighen became Minister of the Interior, the key Western post that Calder had wanted.[42]

That was one portion only of the negotiations over inclusion and place that Borden had to manage. And then he and the party managers had to determine which candidate – a Conservative or a Liberal Unionist, many of them already nominated – would be the government candidate in dozens of ridings across the land. That too generated fury from Members of Parliament who might face their own political extinction for the sake of the coalition.

Nonetheless, two Grits joined the government in the first week of October, and by 12 October, six days after Parliament had been dissolved, Canada had a Union Government cabinet of 13 Conservatives (one nominally a "labour" representative) and nine Liberals, the Tories keeping most of the senior posts. Only three Liberals came from Laurier's caucus, the remainder from provincial parties in the West and Ontario. The creation of the Union Government was an extraordinary feat, one that demonstrated Borden's great patience and determination.

Borden's difficulties were not yet resolved. The new government faced serious problems as it contemplated the general election to be held on 17 December. The cabinet had only two French-speaking ministers from Quebec (neither of whom would survive the election though one would join the cabinet after being appointed a senator), and French Canada was solidly against conscription and for Laurier. The ethnic vote, or at least those who still had the franchise, was believed to be against the Union; so too was the Roman Catholic Church, its French-Canadian, Irish, and ethnic congregants much aggrieved by conscription and the manipulation of the franchise.[43] Labour, too, was opposed. One labour member of the Manitoba legislature, F.J. Dixon, stated baldly about conscription that "If I have to shed my blood, I would prefer to do it here, where I know it would be for freedom."[44] The government campaigners also feared opposition – and Liberal votes – from the men who were likely to be called up for military service.[45]

But in a Canada that was still heavily rural, the greatest concern was for the farm vote. Farmers had generally prospered during the war, but rural labour was scarce because men had enlisted and large numbers of women had moved to the cities to get work in munitions factories at a far better wage than they could earn, if they were paid anything at all, on the farm. If conscription were to take away what was left of young and fit farmworkers, production might drop, and food production was very important for the Allies (and Canada's exports).[46] The government was rightly very worried about the farm vote, and its concerns were not eased until the new Minister of Militia and Defence, General S.C. Mewburn, pledged on 24 November that "any farmers' sons who are honestly engaged in farm work and in the production of food stuffs – if they are not exempted by the Tribunals and are called up for military service – I will have them honourably discharged...."[47] Mewburn's promise was quickly confirmed by an Order-in-Council, and the farmers came to believe that conscription would take only some other man's son. As the election campaign coincided in part with the Canadian Corps' heavy losses in attacking Passchendaele in the Ypres Salient, to be guaranteed exemption from conscription meant something.

The men overseas naturally enough had their strong views on exemptions and conscription. One convalescent soldier, Private William Lowry, wrote home to say that "Conscription is now in force but this will not much effect the country, except in the big towns. This is on account of the number of exemptions...."[48] On the other hand, another, Robert Brown in the Royal Flying Corps, was pleased that his brother was "not old enough to be touched by conscription. I wouldn't want to see a brother of mine out here." But he expressed little surprise that men at home were seeking exemption: "Natural, I suppose, that they should object to being forced into a thing when they have had over three years to go in voluntarily.... Such men will not be of much use...." [49] And Private Harold Simpson, the farmer from Prince Edward Island, told his mother that "We do not want conscription of the men growing food for us... but we do want to see them get after some of single men holding down easy jobs and having a good time, in our cities and also such rural families as those in which there are several sons of military age and physically fit, still at home."[50] What the soldiers most seemed to want was to see French Canadians made to fight. "I guess Canada is having some time about conscription now," Frank Skeet, a 19-year-old from Swan River, Manitoba, with the 16th Battalion, wrote on 28 September. "I'd like to see them shove some of them Quebec French Canadians over."[51] The soldiers did their best to achieve this goal, voting massively for the Union Government – 215,849 to 18,522 for the Liberals.[52]

The Unionists were also concerned about the women's vote created by the WTEA. Most women suffragists across the country had cheered the measure, subduing their concerns about sending other mother's sons to fight and die and the manipulation of the franchise. Indeed, in their pleasure at the achievement of the vote for (some of) their gender, several leaders of women's organizations had urged Borden not to enfranchise all women for fear that foreign and French-speaking female voters might be opposed to conscription.[53] Once the election was called, the government was quick to mobilize the new voters: "To Women Voters. If your husband or father is on the fighting line, he will have less chance of being killed or injured if we send more men to help them ... Vote to save your kin."[54] In Montreal, however, the President of the Montreal Council of Women, Dr Grace Ritchie-England, called the WTEA unjust and endorsed Sir Wilfrid Laurier. For her pains, she was impeached and almost driven from office.[55]

The evident lack of French-Canadian support for the Union Government let Borden's campaign pull out all the stops in the Khaki Election. The overall theme was "they breed and we bleed," and Unionist campaign literature baldly stated that if Laurier won the election, "the French-Canadians who have shirked their duty in this war will be the dominating force in the government of this country. Are the English-speaking people prepared to stand for that?" "A vote for Laurier," John W. Dafoe's generally Liberal *Manitoba Free Press* said, "is a vote for the Kaiser."[56] Another piece of election propaganda charged that "Laurier means to quit the war," and Archdeacon H.J. Cody of St Paul's Church, a leading Toronto Protestant clergyman and later the President of the University of Toronto, told his parishioners that the election had only one issue: was it to be "Quebec uber alles" or not?

The anti-Quebec propaganda greatly affected soldiers overseas. Fred Milthorp, convalescing in England, wrote to his girlfriend that "if Laurier gets in, it looks as though Canada would drop out of the war.... it would be a shame if the French-Canadians won out against conscription."[57] The idealistic Private Simpson put it differently: "The soldiers in France forgot partyism and narrow political issues and voted for what they felt was the more speedy winning of the war, voted for reinforcements, for themselves, for the conscription of those who were not men enough to enlist, of their own free will," he went on, "and he voted without being influenced by political propaganda of any kind, voted as his conscience told him and I think voted right."[58]

In French-speaking Quebec, the public's attitude, or so Quebec City Liberal candidate and wounded junior officer Charles G. Power recalled, was "We don't care who wins the war at this stage but damn *les Anglais.*" The Liberal argument to the electorate was simple, Power said: "No conscription, and we will resist to the bitter end."[59] Union Government candidates in the province were threatened with bodily harm if they spoke in public,[60] and some historians later spoke of the situation French Canadians faced – a minority forced to fight against its will by an overweening majority – in revolutionary terms.[61] Campaigning for Laurier and against conscription, Henri Bourassa called the Union Government "the synthesis of all we detest, of all we despise." The Unionists, he charged, were mad for blood.[62] In effect, to French-speaking Quebec, conscription meant that French Canada's young men would be taken at gun point from the farms and villages, swallowed up by an anglophone army, and then slaughtered in the trenches."[63] The electorate's duty was clear.

The 1917 election, won on the enforcement of the conscription legislation, was the most openly racist and hateful in Canadian history. But Roger Graham, Arthur Meighen's biographer, is likely correct when he writes that the French-English divisions "were exacerbated as much by Henri Bourassa and the other Anglophobes of Quebec on the one hand, and the Francophobes in Ontario on the other, as they were by the [Military Service] Act itself. On both sides," Graham stated, "there were fanatics who deliberately sowed the seeds of national and religious discord and to blame the breakdown of national unity,' if, indeed, the term had any meaning before 1917, on the Military Service Act is to oversimplify grossly an exceedingly complicated and many-sided situation."[64]

Many-sided it may have been, but the vicious election campaign, in effect a plebiscite on conscription,[65] worked superbly for Borden. His Union Government captured 74 of 82 seats in Ontario (including one Ottawa riding won by a francophone doctor), taking 153 in all across the country after the military vote was counted and switched 14 seats to the government. Laurier's Liberals won all of the seats in Quebec except three strongly English-speaking ridings, taking 82 in all, but only 20 outside Quebec.[66] But on the civilian popular vote, matters were much closer – 841,944 to 744,849, though the soldiers' vote added more than two hundred thousand to the Unionist total. Borden had required the women's vote and the disfranchisement of "enemy aliens," as well as the soldiers' votes to hold power. Moreover, 117 of the Unionist seats were rurally based.

Borden had also needed the pledge to exempt farmers' sons from conscription.[67] (When Borden cancelled the farmers' exemptions in the spring of 1918 in response to the great German offensive, the outraged farmers turned to the formation of a new political party, and the West, in particular, would not be sympathetic to the Conservatives for a generation and more.)

Thus conscription had been "approved" by the electorate. But it was in truth a near run thing, with Quebec violently opposed, labouring men unhappy, many ethnics deprived of the vote, the undrafted fearful, the farmers bought off with pledges of exemption, and the enfranchised women and all the media and many of the good people of English Canada whooping and cheering that the French Canadians and slackers had been put in their place. Although thousands took to the hills to avoid military service, the first conscripts reported for training in January 1918.

Overseas, the men of the Canadian Corps, bloodied by the fighting at Hill 70 and Passchendaele, waited for what one soldier called "the mama's boys and the college fry" to arrive, the first few reaching front-line units in May 1918. Others derisively sang "Onward Conscript Soldiers / Marching as to war, / You would not be Conscripts / Had you come before."[68] The corps commander, Lieutenant-General Sir Arthur Currie, had been pressed by Ottawa to publish a message to his men that if the Union Government won the election, "survivors of the First Division still at Front will be brought [to] Canada on furlough." Currie refused, seeing this as blatant political interference, though he did write a note for publication in Canada that conscription was needed to support the soldiers at the front.[69] Far more important to him than forcing reluctant conscripts to fight, however, was the 5th Division, 21,000 strong in England, unable to be used for reinforcements because its General Officer Commanding was Major-General Garnet Hughes, the son of the former Minister of Militia and Defence, Sir Sam Hughes. Hughes was gone from the cabinet but still politically powerful, and his son, deemed unfit to command at the front by Currie, was nevertheless untouchable for a few weeks more. Beginning in February 1918, the 5th's infantry units were broken up and fed to the corps' front-line battalions.

A few days after the election, in the face of the campaign in English Canada to denounce French Canadians and their rejection of compulsory military service, Liberal Member of the Legislative Assembly of Quebec Joseph-Napoléon Francoeur presented a notice of motion stating that the province of Quebec would be prepared to accept the breaking up of the Confederation pact if the other provinces considered it an obstacle to the development of Canada. There was much discussion in the Legislature for two days in January 1918, and Quebec's Liberal Premier Sir Lomer Gouin, himself an anti-conscriptionist, made a vigorous defence of Confederation. He reminded Quebec that the federal system was the only suitable one for Canada, that separatism was impossible, and that Confederation had brought notable benefits to the province. The storm would pass, Gouin said. He was proud to be called a Canadian, and proud of his country, Canada. But at the same time, the premier made a point of recalling the sufferings of "our fathers" in the wake of insults and appeals to prejudices, and he declared that the slanders of the present moment were the work of a "small number" and not the majority of English Canadians. At the end of the speech, Francoeur withdrew his motion, declaring that it had had "the desired effect."[70]

It had, letting public opinion in the province vent. But there would be major riots in Quebec City in the next few months and continuing resistance to the Military Service Act's enforcement. More importantly, the memory of conscription in the Great War played a substantial part in shaping Quebec's attitude to military service in the Second World War, much more so than did the gallant service of the 22nd Battalion at Courcelette and at Hill 70. Although the Mackenzie King government handled compulsory military service much better than Borden's government had done and although a far higher number of francophones volunteered to serve, there were nonetheless fresh grievances to add to the historic ones. Quebec nationalism was strengthened by the two wars, and the issue of separatism or Quebec independence, raised in the wake of the Military Service Act and the 1917 election, would return. The events of the Great War of words at home, the events set in train by the fighting and heavy losses overseas at Vimy, Hill 70, and Passchendaele in 1917 and by Sir Robert Borden's determination that Canada do its full part, would reverberate through the rest of the 20th Century and into the 21st.

NOTES

1. Henry Borden, ed., *Letters to Limbo* (Toronto: University of Toronto Press, 1971), 276.
2. R.C. Brown, *Robert Laird Borden: A Biography, Vol. II* ([Toronto: Macmillan, 1980), 83.
3. *The Globe* (Toronto), April 10, 1917.
4. One Canadian junior officer, serving with the South Persian Rifles (!), noted in early June that he thought conscription unnecessary. "I would feel very, very sorry to see anybody have to go. Surely with the United States in the war, it should not be necessary." Canadian Letters and Images Project (CLIP), Daniel Lane to friend, June 6, 1917. CLIP is available online at www.canadianletters.ca
5. Henry Borden, ed., *Robert Laird Borden: His Memoirs*, Vol. I (Toronto: Macmillan, 1938), 528.
6. The best study of manpower is Richard Holt, *Filling the Ranks: Manpower in the Canadian Expeditionary Force 1914–1918* (Montreal: McGill-Queen's University Press, 2017). For a brief account, see J.L. Granatstein, *The*

Greatest Victory: Canada's Hundred Days, 1918 (Toronto: Oxford University Press, 2014), 60–1.
7 The National Archives (U.K.), Cabinet Records, CAB 32/1, Meeting 41, War Cabinet, January 23, 1917, Appendix 1.
8 This Sessional Paper, Number 143B, was not printed, but was secured from the House of Commons. Other figures suggest that Canada had 284,000 men in England and France in mid-1917. See J.L. Granatstein and J.M. Hitsman, *Broken Promises: A History of Conscription in Canada* (Toronto: Oxford University Press, 1977), 66.
9 Tim Cook, "Battles of the Imagined Past: Canada's Great War and Memory," *Canadian Historical Review*, XCV (September, 2014), 419–20.
10 Quoted in *Borden Memoirs*, II, 698–9.
11 Serge Durflinger credibly downplays Bourassa's role in the Quebec debate over conscription. See his "Vimy's Consequence: The Montreal Anti-Conscription Disturbances, May–September 1917," in Douglas E. Delaney and Nikolas Gardner, eds., *Turning Point 1917: The British Empire at War* (Vancouver and Toronto: University of British Columbia Press, 2016), l66ff.
12 Library and Archives of Canada (LAC), MG26H, Robert Borden Papers (Borden Papers), Diary, May 25, 1917.
13 LAC, MG26G, Wilfrid Laurier Papers (Laurier Papers), Rowell to Laurier, May 29, 1917. Quoted in A.M. Willms, "Conscription, 1917: A Brief for the Defence," *Canadian Historical Review*, XXXVII (December, 1956), 342.
14 *Borden Memoirs*, II, pp. 720ff. R.C. Brown and R. Cook, *Canada 1896–1921: A Nation Transformed* (Toronto: McClelland and Stewart, 1974), 268ff offers a good account.
15 The results of the voluntary registration can be found in Granatstein and Hitsman, 44ff.
16 On conscientious objectors, see Amy J. Shaw, *Crisis of Conscience: Conscientious Objection in Canada during the First World War* (Vancouver and Toronto: University of British Columbia Press, 2009).
17 Granatstein and Hitsman, 65–6.
18 House of Commons, *Debates*, June 20, 1917, 2584ff.
19 Ibid., July 24, 1917, 3723–7.
20 Martin Auger, "On the Brink of Civil War: The Canadian Government and the Suppression of the 1918 Quebec Easter Riots," *Canadian Historical Review*, LXXXIX (December, 2008), 507. See also Durflinger's account of the situation in Montreal, "Vimy's Consequence," 166ff.
21 LAC, Borden Papers, Borden to Archbishop Bruchesi, August 22(?), 1917.
22 G.W.L. Nicholson, *Canadian Expeditionary Force 1914–1919* (Ottawa: Queen's Printer, 1962), 297, and Appendix C, 546; Tim Cook, *Shock Troops: Canadians Fighting the Great War, 1917–18, Volume Two* (Toronto: Viking Canada, 2008), 306.

23 *The Ottawa Evening Citizen*, 30 August 1917.
24 Richard Krever, "The Origin of Federal Income Taxation in Canada," *Canadian Taxation*, III (Winter, 1981), 172–3.
25 House of Commons, *Debates*, April 24, 1917, 718.
26 See, for example, J.G. Turriff in ibid., January 26, 1917, 177.
27 For a post-modernist analysis see David Tough, "'The rich ... should give to such an extent that it will hurt': 'Conscription of Wealth' and Political Modernism in the Parliamentary Debate on the 1917 Income War Tax," *Canadian Historical Review*, XCIII (September, 2012), 382ff.
28 House of Commons, *Debates*, August 17, 1917, 4639.
29 Quoted in Tough, 394.
30 Krever, 187.
31 Ibid., 188.
32 Canadian Letters and Images Project [CLIP], Harold Simpson Collection, Simpson to mother, November 28, 1917.
33 CLIP, Ludlow Weeks Collection, Weeks to sister, December 6, 1917.
34 N.a., "A History of the Vote in Canada," Chapter II, www.elections.ca
35 The best account of the MVA in operation is Desmond Morton, "Polling the Soldier Vote," *Journal of Canadian Studies*, X (November, 1975), 39ff. Morton minimizes the fraud. Artillery Battery Sergeant Major Brooke Claxton likely voted for conscription overseas, but he nonetheless thought the Government tactics "rotten" for the electioneering and intimidation employed. D.J. Bercuson, *True Patriot: The Life of Brooke Claxton* (Toronto: University of Toronto Press, 1993), 28. Another soldier, Norman Nayler, wrote home that "I guess there are some funny votes for half of them don't know what they are doing it for." CLIP, Norman Nayler Collection, Nayler to brother, December 9, 1917. A pilot in the RFC said that he "Couldn't find out who were the candidates for our constituency so just voted for conscription." CLIP, Gordon Irving Collection, Irving to Fern, December 4, 1917.
36 LAC, Borden Papers, Meighen to Borden, October 17, 1916.
37 Tarah Brookfield, "Divided by the Ballot Box: The Montreal Council of Women and the 1917 Election," *Canadian Historical Review*, LXXXIX (December, 2008), 488; "A History of the Vote in Canada," www.elections.ca. The WTEA's impact on the franchise was substantial: in Quebec, low in enlistments and hence with small numbers of women voters, only 20.6% of the total population could vote; in Ontario, with many enlistments and many enfranchised women, 39.4% were eligible; in Saskatchewan, with many disfranchised "ethnic" voters, only 22.9% of the total population could vote. See John English, *The Decline of Politics: The Conservatives and the Party System 1901–20* (Toronto: University of Toronto Press, 1977, 196n.
38 Oscar Skelton, *Life and Letters of Sir Wilfrid Laurier*, Vol. II (New York: Century, 1922), 529–30; Skelton, "Current Events," *Queen's Quarterly*, XXV,

(October–December 1917), 230–2. See Norman Hillmer, *O.D. Skelton: A Portrait of Canadian Ambition* (Toronto: University of Toronto Press 2015), Chap. 3.
39 LAC, Borden Diary, September 25, 1917.
40 LAC, Laurier Papers, Laurier to W.C. Brewster, July 12, 1917, f. 196210.
41 Granatstein and Hitsman, 70–1.
42 See the account in Brown, 102ff.
43 On the Protestant-Catholic divide, see Robert Rutherdale, *Hometown Horizons: Local Responses to Canada's Great War* (Vancouver and Toronto: University of British Columbia Press, 2004), 178ff.
44 Quoted in John H. Thompson, *The Harvests of War: The Prairie West, 1914–1918* (Toronto: McClelland and Stewart, 1978), 119.
45 Granatstein and Hitsman, *Broken Promises*, 74ff.
46 W.R. Young, "Conscription, Rural Depopulation and the Farmers of Ontario, 1917- 1919," *Canadian Historical Review*, LIII (September, 1972), passim.
47 Quoted in a pamphlet in LAC, MG26J, W.L.M. King Papers, f. C3622.
48 CLIP, William Lowry Collection, Lowry to mother, October 4, 1917.
49 CLIP, Robert Brown Collection, Brown to mother, November 17 and 27, 1917.
50 CLIP, Harold Simpson Collection, Simpson to mother, January 8, 1918. Estimates were that only 100,000 farmers in all served, including those conscripted. See Mourad Djebabla, "Fight or farm: Canadian farmers and the dilemma of the war effort in World War I (1914–1918)," *Canadian Military Journal*, XIII (Summer, 2013).
51 Robert Sibley, "'Still the war rages on': Christmas war letters 1917," *Edmonton Journal*, December 27, 2014.
52 John English, *The Decline of Politics: The Conservatives and the Party System 1901–20* (Toronto: University of Toronto Press, 1977), 205.
53 Gloria Geller, "The Wartimes Elections Act of 1917 and The Canadian Women's Movement," Atlantis, II, (1976), 101–2.
54 *The Gazette* (Montreal), December 1, 1917.
55 Brookfield, *passim*.
56 Quoted in Granatstein and Hillmer, *Prime Ministers*, 70.
57 CLIP, Frederick Milthorp Collection, Milthorp to "dearest," December 4, 1917.
58 CLIP, Simpson Collection, Simpson to mother, February 25, 1918.
59 Norman Ward, ed., *A Party Politician: The Memoirs of Chubby Power* (Toronto: Macmillan, 1966), 102–3.
60 Lita-Rose Betcherman, *Ernest Lapointe: Mackenzie King's Great Quebec Lieutenant* (Toronto: University of Toronto Press, 2002), 15.
61 Béatrice Richard describes the situation after conscription as "un climat de guerilla." See Béatrice Richard, "Le ler avril 1918 – Emeute à Québec contre la conscription: resistance politique ou culturelle?" Conférence de Béatrice Richard, Montréal, 13 janvier 2013, La Fondation Lionel-Groulx;

Marc-André Cyr, "De l'engagement à la révolte, les Canadien français et les guerres mondiales," *Argument*, X (Printemps–été, 2008).

Durflinger's account of the Montreal agitation from May to September 1917, "Vimy's Consequence," passim. lends strong support to the claim of militant sentiment. See the discussion in Andrew Theobald, "Divided Once More: Social Memory and the Canadian Conscription Crisis of the First World War," *Past Imperfect*, XII (2006), pp. 3–4.

62 Robert Bothwell, et al., *Canada 1900–1945* (Toronto: University of Toronto Press, 1987), 131.

63 Richard Jensen, "Nationalism and civic duty: comparing world wars in Canada and America," *Canadian Issues* (Winter, 2004), 6ff. English Canadians were not alone in condemning French Canadians' lack of enthusiasm for the war; so too did France: "Selon les contemporains français, il semble que le Québec n'a pas fourni une contribution militaire à l'égal de sa population." Carl Pepin, "Du Military Service Act aux émeutes de Québec : l'effort de guerre canadien-français vu de France (1914–1918), » *Guerres mondiales et conflits contemporains*, 7 janvier 2011. On Quebec attitudes to France, see Brown and Cook, 263–4

64 Roger Graham, *Arthur Meighen: A Biography*, Vol. I (Toronto: Clarke Irwin, 1960), l94–5.

65 This is English's phrase in his *The Decline of Politics*, Chap. X.

66 English, 195, points out that in the 1917 election, 73 percent of Quebeckers voted Liberal and against conscription; in the 1942 conscription plebiscite, 74 percent in Quebec voted not to free the Mackenzie King government from its pledges against conscription.

67 Ibid., 196–7; Granatstein and Hitsman, *Broken Promises*, 81–2.

68 Quoted in Kenneth Radley, *Get Tough Stay Tough: Shaping the Canadian Corps 1914–1918* (Solihull, UK: Helion, 2014), 286–7.

69 LAC, MG30E100, Arthur Currie Papers, vol. 2, Telegram, December 3, 1917

70 Garth Stevenson, *Parallel Paths: The Development of Nationalism in Ireland and Quebec* (Montreal: McGill-Queen's University Press, 2006), 213–4. For a discussion of Quebec attitudes, see Stephane Roussel and J.-C. Boucher. "The Myth of the Pacific Society: Quebec's Contemporary Strategic Culture," *The American Review of Canadian Studies*. XXXVIII (Summer, 2008), 165ff.; Marian Scott, "Quebec's battle against conscription was a defining moment...." *The Gazette* (Montreal). July 25, 2014.

Chapter Two

Conscription in the Great War

I have been writing about conscription for more than forty years. I first touched the subject when I did my master's degree at the University of Toronto in 1961–2 and looked at the Conservative Party's misfortunes in the Second World War, misfortunes that arose out of its Great War policies and were compounded thanks to its views on manpower and Quebec in the 1939–45 war. That subject became my doctoral dissertation in 1966 and my first book, *The Politics of Survival: The Conservative Party of Canada, 1939–1945* (1967). From there I went on to write *Canada's War: The Politics of the Mackenzie King Government, 1939–1945* (1975), a study of the King government in the war and one in which I looked closely and very favourably at the way King had finessed the conscription issue so much better than Sir Robert Borden. My next book, with J. Mackay Hitsman, was *Broken Promises: A History of Conscription in Canada* (1977), and here for the first time I went through the manuscript sources on the Great War and, not surprisingly, concluded that I had been right: King had done much better than Borden, conscription was a disastrous issue for national cohesion and, moreover, it had little military impact in either war. I was positively derisory in my comments on the 24,132 conscripts under the Military Service Act (MSA) who had arrived in France by 11 November 1918 and no less so about the 16,000 home defence conscripts sent overseas after the conscription crisis of November 1944. Since more than 600,000 men had enlisted in the army in the Great War and 750,000 in the Second World War, the relatively tiny numbers of conscripts scarcely mattered, or so I believed. "Conscription has simply not worked in Canada," I said in the last lines in *Broken Promises*, "and there seems no reason to believe that it ever will."[1]

I held this position firmly until, in 1984, I read Denis and Shelagh Whitaker's book *Tug of War*, a study of the First Canadian Army's struggle to clear the Scheidt and open the great port of Antwerp for the Allies' use in the autumn of 1944. A Second World War Royal Hamilton Light Infantry officer and battalion commander of exemplary courage, Denis Whitaker understood, as I had not, that under-strength infantry units were at much greater risk in action. An infantry battalion with a nominal strength of 950 men could lose a third, a half, or even three-quarters of its strength in an afternoon, and every loss of a trained soldier left the unit weakened and its firepower reduced. Casualties fell most heavily on the brave, the section commander who led his men forward, the platoon sergeant who rallied the defence, the company commander who, in desperation, called down artillery fire on his own position. A section of ten could be reduced to five in a moment, but in the next attack a day later that same section ordinarily was expected to cover the same ground as if it were at full strength. Generals almost invariably assigned a battalion of 400 men the same kind of objectives to attack or the same portion of front to defend as they did when it was at or near full strength. With fewer men, the casualties increased as the firepower available in the offence or defence decreased. Unit cohesion, the intangible bonds that make men willing to fight and die for their comrades, also suffered from heavy casualties. Shattered survivors needed time to recover and to mourn.

To keep units up to strength, trained infantry reinforcements were essential. If replacements knew how to operate their weapons effectively and understood the basic principles of section and platoon tactics, they could add to the battalion's power. If they did not, if new men had to be shepherded by soldiers acting as nursemaids and shown what to do, they detracted from that strength and were a danger to themselves and their comrades. Moreover, arriving without the personal ties and loyalties that bound the regiment together, the new men were also friendless, completely lacking the personal support systems that were so essential if soldiers were to fight well. Such networks took time to develop, and if the replacements went into action at once, as they did too often, they did so all but alone. Especially after the losses in Normandy and in the Gothic Line battles in Italy, in the Second World War the army received too many ill-trained or untrained reinforcements and put them into the line at once. More Canadian soldiers died as a result.

The Whitakers' book forced me to rethink my treatment of conscription in the Second World War, obliging me to give the military necessities equal weight in the balance with the political requirements. In *The Generals: The Canadian Army's Senior Commanders in the Second World War* (1993), particularly in the chapter on Generals Maurice Pope and Ken Stuart, I tried to do so.

This brief essay is my attempt to be more even-handed in assessing conscription in the Great War. I admit that the military side of the equation receives its due weight forty years later than it should have. *Mea culpa.*

※

Recruiting in Canada had slowed after mid-1916 and by the spring of 1917 was running at only 4,000 men per month, far below replacement needs. Many of the volunteers opted for any corps but the infantry, making even those low numbers deceptive. This decline undoubtedly was a reaction to the high rate of casualties and to the gradual drying up of the pool of potential volunteers in English Canada. The British born, the portion of the population that provided a wholly disproportionate percentage of enlistments in the first two years of war, were now all but depleted. A British War Office study had calculated at the beginning of 1917 that 37.5 per cent of British-born Canadians had enlisted. Enlistment of the native born of British extraction was 6.1 per cent, and foreign-born Canadians had sent 6.5 per cent into the military.[2] "Those men who remained out of the army, their lapels regularly pierced with white feathers by women "recruiters," were under strong pressure to enlist. But the high number of casualties, the long lists of the killed, wounded, and missing that regularly appeared in the newspapers, were positive disincentives to joining the army.

At the same time, part of the difficulty was that the government could not decide if it was better to take a farmer or a tool and die maker and turn him into a soldier. Where could such a man provide the greatest service? Even after the National Registration taken at the end of 1916, even after the passage of the Military Service Act in the next year, and even after the destructive German offensives of March 1918 led the Borden government in a panic to cancel all the exemptions from conscription it had issued before and after the December 1917 election, this same problem existed.[3] The mismanagement of manpower that had begun with Sam Hughes's first call for men in August 1914 had never been properly corrected.

In French Canada, where enlistments were low and slow, there was no shortage of men, only of a willingness to serve overseas. The War Office study of Canadian manpower calculated that only 1.4 per cent of French Canadians had joined up, the lowest rate in the white empire.[4] Whether the secret British calculations were correct is almost immaterial. The numbers were known in the broad outline to Canadians, and the Quebec enlistment failure infuriated many English Canadians, who could neither appreciate nor understand the numerous and varied rationalizations produced in Quebec to explain this situation. The truth of the matter was that just as in English Canada the public pressure on men was to enlist, in Quebec the pressure was not to enlist. Hume Wrong, scion of a distinguished Toronto family, who had served overseas in a British regiment until being badly wounded and invalided home, wrote privately and only half-jokingly in May 1917, "I would welcome a little military activity in Quebec. My C.O. and I have arranged a little punitive expedition ... And I should delight in catching Bourassa and Lavergne [the anti-conscriptionist leaders]."[5] Many in English Canada shared that view – and they were not joking at all.

While it was primarily the refusal of the vast majority of Quebecois to enlist that drove the politics of the conscription issue at home, it was also the unwillingness of fit men in English Canada to serve. The government had tried every expedient to avoid an issue that even the dullest politician could see was bound to be terribly divisive, and not only in Quebec. Farmers, labour, ethnics, and parents of young, fit men – none of them wanted conscription that would take away men who did not want to fight from their jobs and families. On the other hand, those with sons, brothers, and fathers at the front wanted them to receive the fullest support. The manpower issue was a terrible one for politicians and the country.

Because many in the government had believed there was a threat from the 393,000 German-born Canadians and the 130,000 immigrants from the Austro-Hungarian Empire, substantial numbers of troops had been kept at home. The 1916 Prairie Census showed that 7.8 per cent of the west's population were born in enemy territory.[6] Just as worrisome, in the United States, German Americans, Irish Americans, or German sympathizers constituted a potential threat of invasion. The Fenian raids were within the living memory of men and women, and some soldiers, like the septuagenarian General W.D. Otter, had had their first taste of war against the Irish Americans fifty years before. The prime minister also worried about "thugs, gunmen, or other lawless individuals, instigated by German emissaries," who might carry out sabotage attacks, and he certainly feared raids across the border.[7] These fears kept 16,000 soldiers on guard duty against a threat that had scarcely ever existed, though the government could not ignore it. From October 1915 to September 1916 the government had also directed that a minimum of 50,000 Canadian Expeditionary Force (CEF) volunteers be retained at home on training or other duties to protect against all eventualities.[8]

As casualties mounted overseas, the chief of the General Staff, General Willoughby Gwatkin, looked for ways to replace the volunteers on home defence duties and get them into action. In January 1917, Gwatkin told the militia minister, Sir A.E. Kemp, that there were 62,000 men under arms in Canada, 50,000 of them CEF and 12,000 militia on active service. The response, approved by the cabinet in January and February 1917, was to recruit 50,000 men into a Canadian Defence Force (CDF) for home defence. The CDF began recruiting in March, seeking "men to volunteer for home defence by joining the active militia. An opportunity is now afforded to those who have been prevented from undertaking Overseas service to join this movement." The Militia Department proposed that CDF volunteers train with CEF volunteers, and serve at a slightly lower rate of pay and allowances on the same terms – to six months after the end of the war – as CEF recruits. The plan called for all 50,000 to be enrolled in April and to go off to summer camp in May.[9]

With the United States in the war after 6 April, there was no longer even the most remote possibility of a military threat from the south, though the prospect of sabotage (of which there had been almost none in Canada) did remain. Potential CDF recruits could figure this out, and they could also see that there was no need for 50,000 men to be retained in Canada. Most, no doubt, feared that if they joined the Canadian Defence Force they would be converted to the CEF and despatched overseas. As a result, volunteers who might have been eager to do their military service only in Canada stayed away from the CDF in droves. By 25 April fewer than 200 men had signed up. Preordained as it may have been, conscriptionists in the government, the military, the media, and the public viewed the CDF failure as proving that only compulsion could produce men now.[10] In the first month of recruiting for the CDF, coincidentally the month of the great Canadian victory at Vimy, casualties overseas were 23,939; volunteers for the Canadian Expeditionary Force numbered 4,761.[11] Conscription's hour had arrived.

To the surprise of the army leadership, Sir Robert Borden decided to impose conscription on his return from a visit to Britain and France in May. The prime minister had been persuaded by the Allies' grave situation and by the needs of the men at the front, and he was bound and determined to achieve his goal. For the next seven months, during and after the progress of the Military Service Bill through Parliament and through the formation of an almost wholly English-speaking coalition government and a bitter, divisive election in December 1917, conscription dominated the public debate.

Overseas, the soldiers watched and waited, most hoping that conscripts would provide the reinforcements the Corps needed. Lieutenant General Sir Arthur Currie had responded to Borden's congratulatory message on his appointment as Corps commander in June 1917 by saying, "It is an imperative and urgent necessity that steps be immediately taken to ensure that sufficient drafts of officers and men are sent from Canada to keep the Corps at its full strength."[12] This message, something that Currie believed to be true, had been read in Parliament during the debate on the Military Service Bill, where it annoyed anti-conscriptionists. But during the 1917 election campaign, when the government asked Currie (who many Conservatives knew to have been a Liberal) to issue a message to the troops endorsing the Union Government and conscription, he refused, seeing this request as blatant political interference with his command.

By this point, Currie thought it more important to break up the 21,000-strong 5th Canadian Division, sitting in England under Sam Hughes's son, Major General Garnet Hughes, than to impose conscription, which would take months to produce results. Hughes's division was untouchable so long as his father was minister; after Sam's ouster on 11 November 1916, the government, still fearing his wrath, refused to act to use its men for reinforcements for the four divisions fighting in France. To Currie, it was all politics, damn politics. There were enough men in England to replace the Corps's losses at Passchendaele, add to the strength of infantry battalions, and help to create new machine-gun battalions if only the government had the courage to confront Sam Hughes's malign influence. It did not, so Currie refused the government's request.[13] Arthur Currie was a tough, principled man, and he eventually secured the break-up of Hughes's division and its use as reinforcements for his hard-pressed infantry in February 1918.

Whatever Currie thought of the government and however he himself voted, like English-speaking Canadians at home, his men overwhelmingly cast their ballots for the Union Government and conscription. There was pressure applied to soldiers to vote the right way by some conscriptionist commanding officers, and there were stories of political skullduggery galore. It was nonetheless inescapable that 92 per cent of the military vote went to the victorious Borden, enough to switch fourteen seats from the Liberals to the Union Government.[14]

Conscription duly came into force, and the first 20,000 conscripts began to report for training on 3 January 1918, after the election. Only 1,500 francophones would form part of the first batch of reportees, the government was told, "owing to the fact that there were very few reports for service there; that the claims for exemption have been generally allowed. And that very few of the appeals, which are very numerous, have been disposed of."[15] More than nine out of every ten men called for service across the country had sought exemption, and many of those who were refused took to the hills. Many of the exemptions that were granted, not least to farmers who had been guaranteed exemptions just prior to the December 1917 election, were cancelled on 19 April 1918 as the great German offensive terrified the Allies. Borden told a delegation of protesting farmers that the war situation was critical and that the Canadian Corps needed reinforcements. He rejected the argument that he had broken a solemn covenant made during the election: 'Do you imagine for one moment we have not a solemn covenant and a pledge to those men?'[16] In Quebec, where evasion of the Military Service Act (MSA) was greatest, with 18,827 defaulters as against only 27,557 French-speaking men who were taken on strength of the Canadian Expeditionary Force,[17] there were contrary (and foredoomed to failure) pressures to create a francophone brigade out of conscripts and volunteers. Asked his views, Currie duly consulted his commanding officers and then vetoed the idea. None of his battalions would accept so much as a company of French Canadians. "My own opinion is that they should not be kept separate," Currie said privately; "they are Canadians the same as everybody else, and the sooner it is so regarded the better it will be."[18] The minister of militia and defence, now General S.C. Mewbum, urged the overseas minister to encourage good treatment of francophones in the army. "I honestly think it would be a good policy to have your officers go out of their way to treat them decently," he wrote to Sir Edward Kemp in London. "It will make all the difference in the world."[19] The 22e Battalion would remain the only French-speaking unit at the front.[20]

At the end of the day, Borden had hoped to generate 100,000 recruits by his conscription legislation, and he achieved this result. Of the 401,000 men called up for service, 99,651 were on strength of the CEF on 11 November 1918, the date of the armistice. Of that number, 47,500 had already proceeded overseas and 24,132 had been taken on strength of units in France.[21]

After almost three years in the trenches, the Canadian Corps was a veteran formation that had benefited greatly from its status as a national contingent, a position helped by the independence Currie had carved out for himself and his men. He saw to it that the Corps stayed together, fought together, and worked together, divisions and brigades learning from each other's successes and the failures of the other formations. Ordinarily, British corps were administrative groupings from which divisions could be plucked at will and assigned to another corps or army. The esprit and nationalism of the Canadians came in substantial part from being together. Very simply, the men of Currie's Corps had come to believe themselves unbeatable. Vimy, Hill 70, and the hell of Passchendaele, terrible in cost though they were, had persuaded the

Canadian soldiers that they were special. Most of the men at the front might have been British born, but the war turned them into Canadians, and they genuinely believed they could do what other armies could not, and they were right. That they had more resources was a critical bonus, an extra boost that reinforced the Corps's elan.

The Canadian Corps operated its own training schools and found and organized its own reinforcements by geographical area. British formations, by comparison, had no such independence, their schools being run in common and their casualty replacements drawn from a nation-wide and ever diminishing pool. Faced with a serious manpower shortage after the disastrous Passchendaele battles in the autumn of 1916, the War Office ordered a major reorganization: British divisions were to lose three battalions each, their men being parcelled out to bring the remaining battalions up to strength. British divisional organization by the beginning of 1918, therefore, consisted of three brigades, each with three infantry battalions, a 25 per cent reduction in fighting strength.

In early 1918 the British suggested that the Canadian Corps follow suit. The War Office wanted the Canadian Expeditionary Force to be reshaped into a two-corps army of six divisions. The men could be found, the brass hats suggested, by using the units of the 5th Canadian Division and the three battalions from each of the Corps's four divisions. This reorganization would have given Currie a promotion from lieutenant general to general and many of his officers a jump in rank.

With some difficulty, Currie persuaded the new minister of overseas military forces, Sir A.E. Kemp, to decline the suggestion of a Canadian army. There would be scant gain in fighting effectiveness, he argued, and the "overhead" – the extra brigade and division staffs plus the additional rear area units an army required to operate in the field – would be high. Moreover, there was the practical problem of a shortage of trained staff officers, a category of officer that took time and experience to produce.[22] The brigadier general, General Staff, at Corps headquarters, Currie's senior operational planner, was British, as were the two next senior staff officers, and the first Canadian GSO I, a divisional senior operational planner, did not take up position until November 1917.[23] "Unbusinesslike," Currie called it, cleverly finding precisely the right word to squelch the idea with Kemp, an industrialist at home.

Currie's refusal to countenance an expansion of his force – and his own promotion – led Stephen Harris lo write, quite properly, that "there was no finer demonstration of the professional ethos that requires loyalty to service before self."[24] Under Currie, in fact, the Canadian Corps had become a thoroughly professional army, a fighting force with expertise, a culture of its own, and a sense of responsibility to the nation.

As its leader, Currie exemplified the professional nature of his Corps. This professionalism shaped all his actions.

At the same time as Currie flatly refused to conform to the War Office's request that he adopt the British Expeditionary Force's weakening of its own divisions, he insisted on maintaining his four divisions at their strength of almost 22,000 men each. Currie wanted to retain three brigades, each of four battalions, in each of his divisions because he realized that stronger divisions were more effective. In addition, this organization offered a substantial benefit in a brigade attack. The usual two battalions up/two in reserve system meant that the follow-on or counter-attack force in the Canadian Corps was always strong. The reorganized British now had to employ two battalions up/one in reserve, which would weaken every brigade's second effort on the offensive and almost invariably produce higher casualties.

Added to the extra battalion in each Canadian brigade was the simple, but critical, fact that Canadian battalions in early 1918 also had, and continued to have, more men than British battalions, thanks to the reinforcements from the breakup of the 5th Canadian Division in England on 9 February 1918. On that date, Headquarters of the Overseas Military Forces of Canada ordered that eleven battalions of the division provide 100 men each to the Corps's reinforcement pool. The divisional artillery had already been sent to France, two field brigades and four mortar batteries arriving in August 1917. Currie used this extra increment of guns as a floater, serving wherever the situation required. Similarly, the three machine-gun companies and the three companies of divisional engineers went to the front before the breakup of the division. But the 5th Canadian Division's twelve battalions and almost 12,000 infantry were the key. The infantrymen reinforced the units in France; indeed, they permitted an extra 100 men to be added surplus to establishment for each battalion. This increased the fighting strength of the Corps's infantry units by 10 per cent, and it provided enough men to keep most battalions at or near full strength until the heavy casualties of the opening battles of the "Hundred Days," which began on 8 August 1918.

Thereafter, a ruthless scouring of men in Britain, rear area units, and hospitals for infantry reinforcements had to suffice until sufficient conscripts from Canada – "drafted men," the army preferred to call them – began to arrive in quantity. By the beginning of August and certainly by the Drocourt-Quéant battles at the beginning of September, MSA conscripts provided the great bulk of reinforcements for the Corps at the time it suffered its highest casualties of the war. The 24,132 conscripts who reached the front by 11 November amounted to more men than the 5th Canadian Division had provided – and fortunately they arrived just in time to let the Corps fight its most extraordinary actions and garner its greatest successes of the war. The four divisions in France had averaged just under 22,000 men each at the start of the Hundred Days. By its end, thanks to the Military Service Act conscripts and despite terrifyingly heavy casualties, they still averaged almost 21,000 all ranks, a diminution, but a relatively slight one.

The Canadians' comparatively satisfactory reinforcement situation also meant that the other arms and services of the Corps could have more men, more punch than British formations. British divisions had three engineer field companies and a battalion of pioneers; Canadian divisions had nine field companies and additional pontoon bridging specialists. British divisions had a machine-gun battalion of three companies; Canadian divisions could draw on a machinegun battalion three times the size, thus providing one automatic weapon for every thirteen men compared with one for every sixty-one men in British divisions. What this meant was that a Canadian division was vastly more potent than a British division and had 50 per cent more infantry.[25] A Canadian division was almost the equivalent in fighting power of a two-division British corps; the Canadian Corps was likely the equivalent of a middle-sized British army in power.

The Canadian Corps headquarters similarly controlled more resources that any British corps: 100 more trucks and a more efficient supply and transport organization, more and better signallers, a better maintenance organization to keep heavy equipment functioning, and, because Currie had kept the 5th Division's field artillery brigades intact, the Corps had an extra artillery increment. Moreover, the general officer commanding the Royal Artillery in the Canadian Corps could control all his artillery, unlike his British counterpart, who was more of an adviser. As a result, Canadian guns could be concentrated more easily, faster, and more effectively. The Canadians also had one heavy trench mortar battery per division; British corps had one battery under command.[26] In effect, the Canadian Corps, with its four large divisions and its extra punch, was easily the most powerful self-contained formation in France. The 5th Canadian Division's men and the MSA conscripts had provided the extra manpower that allowed the Corps this strength, and the luxury of additional firepower and units that were up to establishment allowed the Corps to score the victories that made its role so critical in the last three months of the war.

However, it was a very near thing. The Corps' Hundred Days from 8 August to the Armistice cost 45,835 casualties, almost 20 per cent of the casualties sustained by the Canadian Expeditionary Force over the entire war and, extraordinarily, more than 50 per cent of the strength of the Corps's four divisions and 45 per cent of the Corps's total strength on the opening day of battle. To put these totals in perspective, the casualties of the last hundred days were more than First Canadian Army suffered in the entire campaign in northwest Europe from 6 June 1944 to VE Day eleven months later.[27] Open warfare had proved even more costly than the bloody trench warfare that had preceded it, and by 11 November the Corps's units were almost literally on their last legs.

The MSA conscripts played their part in the final battles. Precisely how many conscripted men saw action remains unclear, and we have no firm sense of whether these unwilling soldiers performed well in action. What we do know is that if the war had continued into 1919, as most Allied government and military leaders expected, the 100,000 conscripts Borden's Military Service Act had raised would certainly have been sufficient to keep the Canadian Corps's divisions up to strength for that year. Politically divisive it most certainly was for a generation and more afterwards, but compulsory service had generated reinforcements when the voluntary system had broken down. Those reinforcements kept units up to strength, allowed the Canadian Corps to function with great effectiveness and efficiency in the final, decisive battles of the Great War, and helped to minimize casualties.

NOTES

1. J.L. Granatstein and J.M. Hitsman, *Broken Promises: A History of Conscription in Canada* (Toronto, 1977), 269.
2. Public Record Office (London) (PRO), Cabinet Records, Cab 32/1, War Cabinet, 23 January 1917, appendix 1.
3. At least this was Newton Rowell's view as late as June 1918. See National Archives of Canada (NAC), Robert Borden Papers, Rowell to Borden, 8 June 1918, ff. 53626ff.
4. PRO, Cabinet Records, Cab 32/1, War Cabinet, 23 January 1917, appendix 1.
5. J.L. Granatstein, *The Ottawa Men: The Civil Service Mandarins, 1935–1957* (Toronto, 1998), 113.
6. J.A. Boudreau, "Western Canada's 'Enemy Aliens' in World War I," *Alberta History* 12 (Winter 1964), 1.
7. Cited in Michael Boyko, "The First World War and the Threat of Invasion," York University, undergraduate paper, 1969, 17.
8. NAC, A.E. Kemp Papers, vol. 71, "Statement Showing Greatest Number of Guards Employed," 10 February 1917; vol. 115, 'CEF Strength in Canada.'
9. *The Canadian Annual Review 1917* (Toronto, 1918), 309.
10. Granatstein and Hitsman, *Broken Promises*, 49ff.

11 G.W.L. Nicholson, *Canadian Expeditionary Force, 1914–1919* (Ottawa, 1962), 546.
12 Daniel Dancocks, *Sir Arthur Currie: A Biography* (Toronto, 1985), 122.
13 NAC, Arthur Currie Papers, vol. 2, telegram, 3 December 1917; A.M.J. Hyatt, "Sir Arthur Currie and Conscription," *Canadian Historical Review* 50 (September 1969), 292–3.
14 See Granatstein and Hitsman, *Broken Promises*, 80–1; Desmond Morton, "Polling the Soldier Vote: The Overseas Campaign in the Canadian General Election of 1917," *Journal of Canadian Studies* 10 (November 1975), 39ff.
15 NAC, Borden Papers, Newcombe to Borden, 19 December 1917, f.53483.
16 Barbara Wilson, ed., *Ontario and the First World War, 1914–1918* (Toronto, 1977), lxiv.
17 NAC, Militia and Defence Records, file GAQ 10–473, Assistant Director of Records to District Officer Commanding, Military District No. 12, 9 March 1928.
18 D.P. Morton, "The Limits of Loyalty: French Canadian Officers and the First World War," in E. Denton, ed., *Limits of Loyalty* (Waterloo, 1980), 95–6.
19 NAC, Gen. R.E.W. Turner Papers, Kemp to Turner, 17 June 1918, f. 7051.
20 The 60th Battalion, raised in Quebec and with a substantial proportion of francophones, was in the 9th Brigade until early 1917. Then, because it was having difficulty maintaining its strength, the 60th was dropped from the order of battle and replaced by the 116th, whose commanding officer was a Conservative member of Parliament. See the official explanation in Nicholson, *Canadian Expeditionary Force*, 225.
21 In all, 470,224 soldiers served overseas of which 47 percent were Canadian born; 194,869 never left Canada of which 61.1 percent were Canadian-born, a figure that reflects the impact of conscription. See Desmond Morton, *When Your Number's Up: The Canadian Soldier in the First World War* (Toronto, 1993), 276–9.
22 Report of the Ministry: Overseas Military Forces of Canada 1918 (London, n.d.), 333–4.
23 John A. English, *The Canadian Army and the Normandy Campaign: A Study of Failure in High Command* (New York, 1991), 15.
24 Stephen Harris, *Canadian Brass: The Making of a Professional Army 1860–1939* (Toronto, 1988), 138; Desmond Morton, *A Peculiar Kind of Politics: Canada's Overseas Ministry in the First World War* (Toronto, 1982), 152ff.
25 Nicholson, *Canadian Expeditionary Force*, 382ff.
26 This description is based on the able account in Shane Schreiber, *Shock Army of the British Empire: The Canadian Corps in the Last 100 Days of the Great War* (Westport, Conn., 1997), 19ff.
27 John A. English, *Marching through Chaos: The Descent of Armies in Theory and Practice* (Westport, Conn., 1998), 62–3.

Chapter Three

The Conservative Party and Conscription in the Second World War

Conscription was the most contentious political issue of the Second World War. As in 1917, the question of compulsory military service divided the nation, setting *Canadien* against Canadian, Liberal against Conservative. As in 1917, the Liberal Party was torn with dissension over conscription. But as had not happened in 1917, conscription also became a divisive issue for English-speaking members of the Conservative Party.

If the unhappy Conservatives of the war years are remembered at all today, it is as conscriptionists. Arthur Meighen's return to the leadership in November 1941, on a platform of conscription and National Government comes readily to mind, while Dr. Robert Manion's repeated declarations of 1939 and 1940 that he opposed conscription are forgotten. Except for two relatively brief periods of the war, in fact, the leadership of the Conservative Party either took a position in opposition to conscription or remained mute on the issue. This is not to say that most Conservatives did not believe that ideally conscription was the fairest and best way to fight the war. They did. But if this is so, how can the wavering course of the party leaders be explained? Why did conscription divide the Conservative Party during the Second World War?

Dr. Robert J. Manion had become leader of the party in July 1938. A 56-year-old physician from Fort William, Ontario, he had first been elected to Parliament in 1917 as a Liberal Unionist. Unlike many others, Manion did not return to the Liberal fold after the war but became a minister in both of Meighen's short-lived administrations and in the Bennett government. He was an Irish Catholic and, although he was not fluent in French, Manion's wife was French-Canadian and his children were bilingual. At the leadership convention, Manion had received strong support from Quebec delegates who had apparently forgotten his wartime advocacy of conscription, and the new leader had confidence in his ability to break the Liberal stranglehold on the province. Manion also believed that he could bring the government down at the next election, for Mackenzie King had not succeeded any better than Bennett in coping with the depression.

Only the threat of war and the possibility of Canadian involvement, Manion believed, could put his plans for election victory in jeopardy. With few exceptions, English-speaking Conservatives believed that when England was at war, Canada was at war, and the most vocal among them favoured conscription from the outset. On the other hand, Manion's *Canadien* followers generally would have preferred to see Canada remain neutral in any new conflict, but recognizing the impossibility of this in the light of the three-to-one English majority, most accepted the necessity for a "limited liability" war. Canada could send economic aid and volunteers, they maintained, but under no circumstances would conscription for overseas service be accepted.

Manion's dilemma was all too obvious. If he attempted to woo Quebec by pledging the party against conscription and an all-out war effort, he would be attacked by anglophilic Tories and the metropolitan press; but if he refused to make the concessions demanded by Quebec, he stood no chance of gaining strength there, so strong were the memories of 1917. It might be possible to play a cautious game for a time, but Manion soon would have to make his move. His ultimate choice was scarcely in doubt. Manion had been chosen leader because it was believed that he would appeal to Quebec, and the French-Canadian delegates had been his strongest supporters at the convention. In addition, Manion had come to the belief that Canadian unity would not survive a second conscription crisis. "Apparently you do not see the need of trying to keep Canada from splitting down the middle," he wrote to one vociferous Vancouver conscriptionist. "I do. I cannot see for the life of me what good it would do to the Empire for Canada to get into a sort of semi-Civil War of its own."[1] Clearly Manion had chosen Quebec.

Manion made his play in March 1939, shortly after the Nazi rape of Czechoslovakia. Then he acted only after he had been "tipped off on Sunday night [March 26] that King was coming out anti-conscription and Lapointe was coming out in support of the idea that there could be no neutrality" in a war in which Britain was involved. "It was my idea of a proper compromise policy," he wrote to his son, "and I gave an interview to the press on Monday which covered the points ... as I felt if they beat me with this proposal I would be just trailing along behind."[2] "I do not believe Canadian youth should be conscripted to fight outside the borders of Canada," Manion told the press in Ottawa. "Canada can play her part in the Empire and in support of our democratic institutions by full co-operation with Great Britain through supplying munitions, foods, and other necessities to our allies, and by fully protecting Canada's own territory."[3] Manion's advice about King's plans proved correct, and on March 30 the Prime Minister came out against conscription for overseas service.[4] Both great parties were now on record against conscription and in favour of voluntary service – the policy that in essence Canada was to follow for the first five years of the war. Considering the past history of his party, and considering that Conservatism's strength was concentrated in English-speaking Canada, it is remarkable that the Conservative leader was the first to take a stand on this issue. Many in his party were most dissatisfied, however.

"I may say personally that I am very disappointed in Manion's leadership," wrote Dr. Herbert Bruce, a Toronto surgeon recently retired as Lieutenant-Governor of Ontario, even before his leader's declaration against conscription, "because he will not take a stand without first considering what the attitude of Quebec will be, so that in essence he allows Quebec to determine his policy and in this respect is following the lead of King ...."[5] At the same time, Manion's Quebec supporters were urging him to go further than King, demanding in fact that he declare against any automatic commitment by Canada in the event of England's becoming involved in war.

The attitude of Quebec Conservatives baffled Manion. "I do not see any reason," he wrote to Georges Héon, the lone French-speaking Conservative M.P. and a key worker in Manion's leadership campaign, "why I must, every time I open my mouth, talk of this damned issue, which stirs up trouble in both [Ontario and Quebec]; and, quite frankly, I don't see why so many of you chaps down there find it necessary to talk all the time on questions of this kind ... Why," he asked with understandable exasperation, "must it always be the subject in Quebec?"[6] Manion's vehemence did little to satisfy Héon and French-speaking Conservatives. It seems clear that neither really understood the problems of the other. Manion's attitude was already an extraordinary one for the leader of the Conservative Party to take and one which threatened the foundations of his support. On the other hand, Héon faced the herculean task of persuading French Canada that the Conservatives had changed, that Manion was not Meighen. The only way to overcome the legacy of 1917, Héon maintained, would be to state that Canada's "obligations to the Commonwealth should be limited to securing the inviolability of our territory."[7] This might have been stern medicine for Manion to swallow, but as he was on the verge of a clear breakthrough in the province of Quebec, it is not inconceivable that he would have gone along.

Manion and Premier Duplessis had arrived at an agreement early in August 1939 that guaranteed the Conservatives the full support of the Union Nationale organization. "You will be getting the entire support of the Duplessis government," the jubilant Manion was told, "without even having to spend one cent for travelling expenses."[8] With the assurance of support in Quebec, Manion was certain he could win the election, carrying the English-speaking Conservatives who were hungry for victory along with him. Perhaps he was correct, perhaps not. The question became academic on the morning of September 1, 1939, when the first reports of the Nazi invasion of Poland reached Canada.

The war disrupted everything. Within two weeks of the Canadian declaration of war, Duplessis had called an election, challenged Ottawa, and accused Mackenzie King of using the war as an excuse to destroy provincial autonomy. Duplessis' interjection of war issues revived the memories of 1917 with a vengeance, but the intervention of the Liberal Cabinet turned the mighty force of the conscription issue against the Union Nationale. There was nothing that Duplessis could do to counter the Liberals' clear and explicit promises against conscription, and his party was destroyed at the polls. The result was the death blow to Conservative chances in Quebec. The *coup de grace* to Manion and the party came a few months later when Mackenzie King staged his one-day session in January 1940, and dissolved Parliament. The Conservatives were caught without money, without organization, and without hard evidence of shortcomings in the war effort.

The party caucus met to discuss election strategy on January 26, the day following the abbreviated session. With the exception of one M.P. who had already indicated his intention of leaving public life, the Members unanimously endorsed Manion's policy against conscription for overseas service. This could hardly be interpreted as an appeal to Quebec, for after the Duplessis defeat few Conservatives could have held illusions about party strength there; it can only be interpreted, therefore, as reflecting a Conservative desire to maintain national unity and as a reaction to what was believed to be the mood of the electorate. At the same caucus, as Dr. Manion later recalled it, Earl Rowe, the M.P. for Dufferin-Simcoe, "without previous consultation with me – arose and proposed that in the ensuing election we stand on a national government platform. There was wild and enthusiastic acclaim and not one word of opposition."[9] Accordingly, after the caucus, Manion released a statement advocating "a truly national government in the sense that the very best brains among our people are drafted to serve in the Cabinet." If elected, he stated, "I shall form such a government."[10]

For any number of reasons, however, the National Government issue never got off the ground. Too few people had any faith in Manion as a war leader. The announcements by Mackenzie King and CCF leader J.S. Woodsworth that no members of their parties would join in a Manion government made the exercise appear as a cloak for the Conservative Party.[11] Die-hard Tories were offended by Manion's dropping the name "Conservative" and designating the party as "National Government."[12] Still others disliked what they regarded as Manion's "policy of catering to French and Catholic sentiment in Canada, instead of following the traditional Conservative course of militant imperialism."[13] Most important, perhaps, was that the issue of national government was too suggestive of the political strife of 1917. Certainly there was no enthusiasm for the war in Canada in the winter of 1940. The phoney war was not arousing the people. "It is a fantastic situation," wrote W.D. Herridge of his attempts to shape a war party out of Social Credit and other motley groups. "We try to form a war party in a country which scarcely realizes it is at war."[14] There was no popular support for conscription anywhere in Canada, Manion noted, and "before every meeting ... the first demand by our candidates was that I make it very clear that I was opposed to conscription for overseas service."[15]

But, despite Manion's repeated pledges against conscription, the Conservatives suffered once more from the memories of 1917. The mood of the country was such that the most effective weapon against Manion was the belief that his party, if elected, was more likely to implement conscription than the Liberals.[16] Any Conservative remarks on the war, therefore, only reinforced the fear that the Conservatives were too aggressive, too imperialistic, too likely to press for conscription as in 1917. Paradoxically, few Canadians believed that Mackenzie King favoured a massive war effort, and as a result the Liberals were able to stress the war more – and more effectively – than their opponents.[17] When Manion turned his attention to other areas of public concern, however, he was instantly attacked for neglecting the war, the central issue. Promises to increase the price of wheat were met by sardonic calls in the Maritimes to increase the price of fish at the same time.[18] The Conservative Montreal *Gazette*, for example, criticized Manion for not sticking to war issues, then proceeded to blast the unfortunate Conservative for his opposition to railway unification, the central issue to St. James Street and its mouthpiece.[19] In national broadcasts, Mackenzie King accused Manion of leaving a path strewn with "promissory notes.... At no place has he enunciated a war policy," King proclaimed. "At every place he has left behind a peace promise...."[20]

Feared as too aggressive by some sections of the electorate, attacked for neglecting the war by others, Manion's National Government Party sustained a crushing defeat. Only forty Conservatives were elected, twenty-five from Ontario and only one French-speaking Quebecker, as against 184 Liberals, the largest majority to that time. Manion, who had lost his own seat, believed his party had been beaten because "anti-war sentiment across Canada thinks King less aggressive ..."[21] People were afraid of conscription, and they were certain King would never implement it. "Undoubtedly," he added, "the big item was the fact that I had with me most of those who are sometimes called the ultra-Imperialists and the people largely felt that King is doing enough."[22] There were other reasons for the defeat, of course, but fear of conscription was high on everyone's list.[23] Whatever the reasons, however, Manion's brief tenure of the Conservative leadership came to an abrupt end at the party's first caucus a few days before the opening of the new Parliament. Manion had seen his policies and plans destroyed more by bad luck than by bad management. His attempt to seek an accommodation with Quebec had been destroyed by the war and by Duplessis' machinations. The chance of defeating King in the election was wiped out by the snap dissolution, by the electorate's disinclination to swap horses in midstream, and by folk memories of conscription. Manion had never had a chance.

His successor was Hon. R.B. Hanson of Fredericton, a stolid, heavy lawyer and Minister of Trade and Commerce for the last year of the Bennett government. The new Leader of the Opposition took over as the Allied front in France began to crumble. Almost immediately the whole tenor of the war changed for Canada, and public opinion began to demand action. The limited liability policies were scrapped, and as the Army's new Chief of the General Staff, General H.D.G. Crerar, wrote to a friend, "the pressure on the Government developed by recent events has completely blown off the restrictive lid of the Canadian military effort...."[24] The Conservative leader played an important part in the events of that terrible summer.

The fall of France spurred Hanson to action. "I thought the matter over ...," he wrote to R.B. Bennett in London,

> feeling that something drastic had to be done to stir [the government] out of their inertness and complacency. I finally decided on three things: (1) that [King] should declare a state of national emergency; (2) that he should pass legislation putting at the disposal of the state all the manpower and

material resources of the nation; and (3) that in order to effectively carry out (1) and (2), especially (2), he would have to have a National Government ...

Accordingly, I sought an interview ...

I prefaced my remarks by stating that I believed the position demanded immediate action, that I was not actuated in any degree by political or partisan motives, but that I felt I had to insist that steps be taken at once to meet the situation. I was laying down principles to him rather than details of any measures, and I placed before him proposals.[25]

"[Hanson] asked me," King recorded in his diary on June 17, "for the sake of the country, would I not feel that I could change my view on conscription." There was absolutely no chance of this. "In the first place," King said, "I believed it would create a worse situation in Canada than it would remedy." If it ever became necessary to introduce conscription for overseas service, "I would be ready to step out."[26] To his surprise, however, Hanson found Mackenzie King willing to accept conscription for home defence, and within a few days the National Resources Mobilization Act, which authorized such steps, was law.[27]

The Conservative leader was pleased with his success. "I have found that I can get action by going to King personally," he wrote, "and telling him that if he doesn't do this and so I will get the big newspapers after him and also get after him in the House. Then I can get some halfway measures." Conscription for home defence was only half a loaf, Hanson said, but it was better than no conscription at all.[28] But for the next six months and more, while Britain fought for her life, Hanson was preoccupied with the task of keeping the Conservative Party alive. The party was bankrupt, there was no organization, and if the Conservatives succumbed, the only alternative to the government would be the socialist C.C.F.[29] This, Hanson believed, was a terrible fate for the country.

Other Conservatives were not so concerned with the fate of the party, and they were beginning to demand an end to the restrictions in the N.R.M.A. that limited the service of conscripts to Canada. In the House, Hanson was confronted with a difficult problem. "From the very beginning," he wrote to a Calgarian who was urging him to action,

we have endeavoured to manoeuvre the position so that the Liberals will have to adopt conscription. Our view is that those who are anxious for conscription underestimate the sentiment in the country against it and that it is not opportune for us to come out at this time flatfooted for conscription. The time will arrive and that time will be when the voluntary system has demonstrated its failure. Meanwhile our rural Members are absolutely opposed to it, and without unanimity in the Party here I could not take this step. My own view is in favour of conscription but I cannot carry the rank and file of the Party with me and it is useless to take this step without that unanimity, which is so essential. You just have to balance things one against the other.[30]

As Hanson frankly admitted, he hoped to attach the blame for conscription in this war to the Liberals.

As he also had indicated, the caucus was not unanimous in its view of the manpower problem. The rural M.P.s, almost certainly reflecting the views of their constituents, opposed conscription, but some Members from urban areas did not share their fears. One of the most vigorous conscriptionists in caucus was Herbert Bruce, elected in 1940 as M.P. for Toronto Parkdale. In a speech on May 12, 1941, Bruce explained his position:

I am not a politician and I am speaking only for myself when I call upon the government to take immediate steps to meet the present urgent situation and make available by a national selective process the men necessary to bring our armed forces up to the strength that represents the fighting might of Canada.[31]

Bruce's speech went as far as any Conservative Member was prepared to go in the first six months of 1941, and despite his careful avoidance of the shibboleth "conscription," his speech was not well received by caucus. But, as Bruce wrote a friend, he "didn't care a d— about the fortunes of the Conservative Party," nor did he care what the other Members thought "because they are only thinking of the political effect."[32]

Impatient spirits outside the House agreed with Bruce. The Conservative press was becoming increasingly virulent in its attacks on the government's manpower policy,[33] and prominent Conservatives were coming out in favour of conscription. Murdoch MacPherson, a leadership candidate in 1938 and a former Attorney General of Saskatchewan, was the first to speak out bluntly, in a Regina speech on May 9, 1941. Warned of his intentions by John Diefenbaker, the M.P. for Lake Centre, Hanson telegraphed MacPherson that "there is no objection but you must make it plain that you are speaking for yourself and not officially. Our rural members emphatically object to coming out foursquare at this time desiring to fasten the odium on the government if possible." MacPherson agreed to speak on his own responsibility, but his pique was evident in his reply that "to avoid any complication am today resigning from provincial executive."[34] His speech received good coverage in the press, but its timing raised some doubts. "To many people," said Rod

Finlayson, one-time private secretary to R.B. Bennett, "it doesn't seem to be playing the game to make a demand for conscription just as the government is launching its recruiting drive...." The first major recruiting campaign had opened on May 11, just two days after the Regina speech. "I meet men here," Finlayson continued from Winnipeg, "who say they will not help in the drive. Briefly put, they want the drive to fail so that conscription will then become absolutely necessary."[35]

But the drive did not fail. Indeed, there was as yet no difficulty of serious nature in recruiting. In mid-1941, the Army had 218,000 volunteers, the R.C.A.F. was approaching a strength of 90,000, and the Navy numbered some 20,000 all ranks. For a country of only 11,500,000, simultaneously devoting every effort to increasing its agricultural and industrial production, 330,000 volunteers in two years was a highly creditable achievement. The position of the conscriptionists was a curious one, and it was made even more so by the simple fact that the Army overseas had not been committed to action as yet and so had incurred few casualties.

In these circumstances, why would anyone favour conscription? The reasons, based on an amalgam of emotion, prejudice, wisdom, and experience, are complex and difficult to unravel. Conscription had had to be imposed in the Great War, and those like Arthur Meighen who had been instrumental in securing it, believed that only similar legislation could produce results in this war. "How many Germans," Meighen asked in July 1941, "have been killed by Canadian Forces?"[36] Meighen's query, coming from one of the most lucid, if blinkered, men in Canadian politics, illustrates the emotional nature of the issue. Conscription was necessary to fight the war – regardless of the large air force and navy that had scarcely existed in the Great War; regardless of the tactical differences between the two wars; regardless of the greatly increased war production of 1941 compared with 1916; and regardless of the steady flow of volunteers. Conscription was necessary, and there could be no argument about this.

Certainly conscription was probably a fair method of raising men, and if its implementation would not have produced drastic effects on national unity, few would have opposed it. Most Conservatives tended to discount Liberal claims of preserving the unity of the two Canadian races, but many were not averse to calculating just how far Quebec lagged behind the loyal provinces. One memorandum in Arthur Meighen's papers estimates that, compared to Ontario, Quebec had contributed only 49 per cent of its share of Army volunteers.[37] The "disloyal bloody French," as one Toronto Conservative M.P. viewed them, simply would not fight.[38] In fact, as a perceptive Army report on "The

Recruiting Problem in the Province of Quebec" noted in June 1941, such an attitude could be held only by those "who fail to appreciate either the tactless blunders of a past generation, or the difficult and complex technical obstacles to proportional mobilization of French speaking Army units."[39] There were two fundamental problems. The civil education system in Quebec, one officer observed, was based on metaphysics, not physics, and did not produce men fitted for the technical services.[40] The second problem, of course, was language. Instruction in the technical corps and in most officer training units was entirely in English. Almost all training pamphlets were unilingual, and the *Canadien* could be pardoned for thinking that only the "poor bloody infantry" wanted him.[41] But despite these drawbacks, total Army enlistments in Quebec were 15,000 men higher – fifty-eight per cent – in 1941 than in 1916.

Meighen and his conscriptionist friends also neglected the consideration that popular opinion in Quebec, like it or not, viewed the proper aim of the war to be the defence of Canada, not overseas adventures. All these factors notwithstanding, conscription was still necessary, so thought the conscriptionists, if one was to be considered a true Conservative. There was no truer Conservative than Senator Arthur Meighen. He had favoured conscription from the opening shot of the war, but he had said nothing fearing that an immediate campaign would do more harm than good.[42] In the general election of 1940, he had remained silent although he had disagreed with Manion's position.[43] Even after the fall of France his voice had remained muted. By mid-1941, however, his indignation had reached a peak and he was ready at last. "I have not taken the field as an aggressive conscriptionist," he said, "being somewhat reluctant to appear as usurping the leadership. That the time has come I have no question," he continued, "and the Party cannot too soon take up its true position to suit me."[44]

Meighen's disgust mounted through the summer and fall of 1941 as Hanson continued to equivocate. As a result, Meighen and some supporters began to mull over the question of the leadership. In May the caucus had agreed that a conference would be held in November to select the date and site for a full leadership convention in 1942. But, as Meighen wrote to MacPherson, "I am steadily moving to the conviction that we ought to move faster than that and that the Conservative Party has to take this thing in hand as its own mission, that it must choose its leader and choose him soon and get into action on strong British total war lines without delay.... I believe that whatever is done should be done this Fall."[45]

Much to Meighen's dismay, the decision of the party conference in November was that he should abandon the Senate and once again become the leader. The conference reached this decision only after long, heated debate and amidst charges that the meeting had been packed. Disturbed by the opposition to him within the party and fearing for his health, Meighen hesitated. But only for a while. "I became convinced," he said, "and certainly my wife became convinced that I would lose what respect and regard the people felt for me if in the full light of day and with an appeal which had by that time reached Coast-to-Coast dimensions, I refused to try to do the one thing I can do, if, indeed, there is anything I can do, entirely well...."[46] There was no doubt about the new leader's policy. The battle would be for conscription and National Government. Mackenzie King would have to be excluded from any coalition, and this could only be accomplished if an alliance, strong enough to form a government, could be forged from Conservatives and conscriptionist Liberals. The policy was to be 1917 all over again.[47]

But the campaign for conscription was dead within three months when Mackenzie King's astuteness and Meighen's political ineptitude produced the predictable result. Choosing to run for the House in the Toronto riding of York South, Meighen fought his campaign entirely on war issues. York South, however, while traditionally Conservative, was heavily working class in composition, and Meighen fell easy victim to a two-pronged CCF campaign that stressed the Conservative leader's reactionary views on labour and welfare measures and called for a programme of advanced social reforms. Fearing the effects of Meighen's conscriptionist efforts, the Prime Minister assisted by announcing his decision to hold a plebiscite. The plebiscite would free King from his potentially embarrassing pledges against conscription for overseas service. Equally important in the short term, the plebiscite would cut the ground out from under Meighen and his supporters by offering a way around the Conservative leader's attempt to win his by-election simply on a show of hands between those for and against conscription. With the prospect of a vote on conscription before them, only those who wanted conscription immediately, regardless of the situation in the country, would be compelled to vote for Meighen.[48] King's reasoning was correct. Meighen's defeat in York South ended the external threat to the Liberal government.

The plebiscite also posed delicate problems for the Conservatives in the House. The Opposition M.P.s could denounce the government for its cowardice, but the dilemma confronting them was all too clear. "I have been giving some thought as to how I should vote ...," a perplexed Hanson wrote:

> If I vote "No," I am in effect telling King that he has been right all along and that he should adhere to his policy of "no conscription for overseas

service" ... if I vote "Yes" and to relieve him of all his obligations, I have not the slightest assurance in the world that he will do anything.[49]

Nonetheless, as all Conservatives were aware, they could not allow conscription to be defeated, and even Arthur Meighen had to indicate his support for the Government's campaign to be freed of its pledges.[50] Mackenzie King had manoeuvred his enemies into the unenviable position of having no choice other than to work for his policy.

The results of the plebiscite, however, compounded King's difficulties. Nationally, a majority favoured releasing the government from its pledges, and under pressure in the Cabinet, the Prime Minister had no option but to take action. As a result, on May 11, 1942, he introduced House of Commons Bill No. 80 to amend the National Resources Mobilization Act and repeal its limiting clause prohibiting the employment of conscripts overseas. But, as Mackenzie King told the House, the amendment did "not denote any change in government policy," and was intended only "to obtain for the government the freedom of decision and action approved by the plebiscite.[51]

Initially the Conservatives had been divided in their attitude to King's tortured contortions. From Toronto, Meighen pressed the harassed Hanson to pound away at King,[52] but the House leader felt bound by the wishes of caucus. "My position is extremely difficult," he wrote to Meighen on May 9, 1942:

> Our people here are absolutely averse to demanding conscription, on the theory that now the limitation is removed the responsibility is [King's], and [the government] have the information and the knowledge of the whole position, and that they should go forward. If we come out and declare now further for immediate conscription, it will give him the opportunity of saying when the time comes that the Opposition demanded it and that he was being driven into it. I am not merely reflecting my own view at the moment but the view of Caucus.[53]

But at a long caucus on May 12, the day after King introduced Bill 80 with the advice that it did not mean a change in government policy, the angry Members overwhelmingly rejected Hanson's advice and decided to press for conscription. Apparently only three M.P.s – John Diefenbaker (Lake Centre), Russell Boucher (Carleton), and Karl Homuth (Waterloo) – supported Hanson.[54] The Leader of the Opposition loyally accepted the situation, and said that "I intend, with all the force at my command, to demand the immediate and full institution of compulsory selective service over the whole field of the war."[55]

He was as good as his word. "To everyone's surprise," the American Minister in Ottawa noted of Hanson's assault on King on June 10, "Mr. Hanson instead of mumbling his reply let go with both fists and poured vitriol on Mr. King. It is the first and only time in the two years I have been here that he made an effective speech."[56] The criticism was unfair, hut the praise was deserved. Hanson summed up the nation's frustration at the Prime Minister's tactics with a few lines from Gilbert and Sullivan:

> A complicated gentleman allow me to present,
> Of all the arts and faculties the terse embodiment,
> He's a great arithmetician who can demonstrate with ease
> That two and two are three, or five, or anything you please;
> An eminent Logician who can make it clear to you
> That black is white – when looked at from the proper point of view;
> A marvellous philologist who'll undertake to show
> That "yes" is but another and a neater form of "no."[57]

"That 'yes' is but another and a neater form of 'no.'" That line captured Mackenzie King's plebiscite performance to perfection. But, boxed in by King's tactics, the Conservatives had no alternative other than to vote for the government's amendment of the N. R. M.A. "If we were to vote against the Government," Hanson had written earlier, "the thing would be very close – I have an idea that the government might possibly be defeated.... If I wanted to play politics and were disregardful of results afterwards, we might defeat him...." But he would not do this, Hanson concluded, as this "would bring down upon my head the execration of this generation and all future generations."[58]

Conscription ceased to be a major issue during the next two years. The war was seemingly off-stage, and the Conservative caucus was content to let Mackenzie King worry about the responsibilities that Bill 80 had given him. Arthur Meighen alone of the Conservatives continued to talk of the need for compulsory service, and Meighen soon was gone. Balking at his ineffectual and stubborn leadership and fearing that Meighen's tiresome insistence on conscription and national government would doom Conservatism to post-war defeat by the CCF,[59] the party began to veer to the left. The Port Hope Conference of September 1942, a meeting of lay Conservatives arranged by J.M. Macdonnell, H.R. Milner, and Rod Finlayson, took the first step toward a progressive Conservatism. Three months later the party chose John Bracken, the Liberal-Progressive Premier of Manitoba, as leader. Curiously, Bracken was the choice of both Meighen and the progressives. To Meighen, the

Manitoban was a convinced conscriptionist who could lead a reinvigorated drive for compulsory service and national government and at the same time beat the CCF in rural Canada.[60] The party progressives, however, rejected conscription and national government as useful issues. The duty of the Conservative Party, they believed, was to be in a position to defeat the CCF and form the government after the war when, they were convinced, the Liberals would be driven from office.[61] To do this, the party needed progressive welfare policies. Bracken was the man who could change the old Tory image and give reality to the party's new label, Progressive Conservative.

Through 1943 and early 1944, Bracken toured the country making speeches. The conscription cry was deliberately played down. The leader believed that King should pull his own chestnuts from the fire. And in addition the party was confident of its strength in conscriptionist Ontario, recently captured by George Drew's Tories. Now Conservatism was searching for support in the rural West and in Quebec, areas in which conscription was not a saleable commodity.[62] But soon Bracken began to lose control of his party.

The cause of the difficulties was the continued growth of the CCF. Bracken had been brought in as leader to counter the social-democrats, and the Conservatives had abandoned many of their cherished traditions at Port Hope and Winnipeg with this in mind. What had been the results? The CCF had taken 34 seats in the Ontario elections of 1943, won several federal by-elections, and captured the government of Saskatchewan in June 1944. Worse yet, every Conservative candidate in the Saskatchewan election had lost his deposit. Apparently, neither the name Progressive Conservative nor John Bracken's reputation were of much value on the prairies.

The failure in Saskatchewan, Bracken's backyard, ended the party's silence on conscription. Bracken had had his chance to offer the Progressive Conservative brand of social welfare, and he had gone nowhere. Now if the CCF were to be stopped, different issues would have to be found. What better issue could there be than conscription?

The pace was forced by Hon. C.P. McTague, a former Ontario justice and a member of the National War Labour Board until his resignation to become the party's National Chairman in early 1944. Addressing his own nomination meeting at Guelph, Ontario, just four days after the Saskatchewan election, the Toronto Tory dealt bluntly with the manpower question:

> Now as to where *this party stands on this matter,* let me state in simple unequivocal terms. To our army overseas and their relatives here we say you

should have reinforcements now, and they are all available now from the trained troops not now and never required for home defence.... National honour demands that without an hour's delay the necessary order in council should be passed making these reinforcements available....

The government's persistence in leaving these trained soldiers of the home army in Canada can only be construed as deference to the will of the minority in the Province of Quebec as voiced in the plebiscite.[63]

Seated behind McTague on the platform, Bracken apparently was unaware that his lieutenant was going to deal with manpower in these terms.[64] He could not let the matter pass without comment, however, and Bracken endorsed the policy.[65]

The caucus' response to these events was unfavourable. Only Dr. Bruce was pleased. "I was delighted with the nomination speech of Charlie McTague which came as a complete surprise to our members here," he wrote to his friend and fellow zealot, George McCullagh of the *Globe and Mail*. "In fact some of our friends were foolish enough to express criticism because this had been done without consulting caucus."[66] Attempts to push the balky caucus along McTague's path, however, were unsuccessful. Rodney Adamson, the M.P. for York West, noted the events of July 24, 1944, in his diary:

> Arrive Ottawa. [Met] at station.... Caucus at 10. Important. It is the Globe [and Mail] group. Have asked Bracken to have us divide the House on conscription, Caucus is 100% against taking this suicidal step. Really a great show and a sock in the eye for the Toronto crowd.[67]

Within three months, however, a genuine shortage of infantry reinforcements had developed overseas, and conscription once again dominated discussion.

The Progressive Conservative Party had no difficulty in determining its course of action in the conscription crisis of October and November 1944. For the first time in the war, public opinion was fully aroused against the government, and the Conservatives did not miss their cue. The party press accused King of risking military disaster in his attempts to win political advantage.[68] Conservative speakers charged the Prime Minister with "deliberately ruling according to the will of a minority.... Why did he not tell us at the time of the plebiscite in 1942," one Toronto Conservative demanded, "that he would not use the conscript army for fighting overseas if the Province of Quebec opposed it?"[69] In Parliament, House leader Gordon Graydon moved the party amendment to the government's motion of confidence: "This house is of the opinion that the government has not made certain of adequate and continuous trained reinforcements by requiring all N.R.M.A. personnel whether now or hereafter enrolled to serve in any theatre of war and has failed to assure equality of service and sacrifice."[70]

The Conservatives maintained the pressure of their criticism into February 1945, throwing the full weight of the party into a by-election in Grey North, Ontario, where the Minister of National Defence, General A.G.L. McNaughton, was seeking election. Bracken, still out of Parliament more than two years after his selection as leader, did not choose to run, but he campaigned in the constituency in support of the Conservative candidate. The leader's style was unusually hard-hitting and he lambasted the Liberals ferociously.[71] The result was an impressive victory for the party. Bracken had succeeded in making reinforcements the sole issue, and the by-election had been won with this tactic. It seemed significant, too, that the CCF candidate who had stressed reconstruction and social welfare had lost his deposit. Grey North raised Conservative hopes for the coming general election, but R.B. Hanson assessed the issue correctly: "If the Election is held before the Germans collapse, Bracken might win. But if peace comes soon and you lose the issue of reinforcements it might be otherwise."[72]

Peace in Europe came on May 8, 1945, but the Conservative leadership continued to ride the conscription horse. In his first major speech of the 1945 election campaign on May 16, Bracken promulgated his "Charter for a Better Canada". The portion of his speech that attracted the most attention, however, was his pledge to use conscripts in the war against Japan.[73] With fatal timing, the Conservatives had again nailed conscription to the party's masthead. Nowhere in Canada was there any enthusiasm for a major effort in the Pacific, and to make this party policy was madness. Bracken's speech was probably prompted by two reasons: first, conscription was still being demanded by influential figures in Toronto, led by McCullagh and the *Globe and Mail*; and second, an anti-Quebec line was believed to have strong appeal in English Canada and particularly in Ontario.[74]

The call for conscription for the Pacific served notice that the Tories had written off Quebec. Indeed, there was little left to write off. Bracken's scrupulous tiptoeing around the conscription issue in 1943 and early 1944 had been appreciated in the province, but attempts to cement an alliance with Duplessis had collapsed after the McTague speech.[75] The Conservatives had then tried to unite the anti-King forces and carried on talks with P.J.A. Cardin, the one-time Minister of Public Works who had left the Cabinet in 1942; with Camillien Houde, the Montreal mayor who had been interned from 1940 to 1944; and with

Frédéric Dorion, a nationalist M.P. since 1942.[76] These attempts finally collapsed in May 1945.[77] As a result, there were few Conservatives in Quebec left to object when Bracken flogged the race issue for all it was worth. "They have drained your firesides of your sons and they have deceived Quebec in this war," Bracken told an Ontario audience.

> The Government has now announced that it will expect the war in the Pacific to be fought by those who volunteer. The Government's policy in this respect is but another bid for Quebec's support....
>
> ... They are asking your sons to die in double the number of others and they are asking Quebec to continue to be misrepresented before the world. The patriotic among Canada's sons will again be asked to die for Canada, while others will stay at home to populate the land their brothers saved.[78]

Despite these efforts, Bracken's party lost the election of 1945. R.B. Hanson, who had not run for re-election, saw the causes of the defeat as being family allowances, Liberal campaign funds, and conscription. Family allowances were popular in poor districts and conscription for the Pacific was not. "The war," he said, "ended too soon."[79]

Why, then, did conscription divide the Conservative Party? Because of the legacy of 1917. Some in the party had learned the lesson of the Great War. National unity had to be maintained, and conscription would split the country. But many Tories had learned nothing. Conscription to them was not just a means but an end in itself. To rely on volunteers was to relieve the disloyal French Canadian of his share of sacrifice. To rely on volunteers was to betray the men overseas. To rely on volunteers was to admit that 1917 had been a mistake, that the party had been wrong.

But this is too bald a picture of the divisions of party opinion. Manion and Meighen were not the only Conservatives. The typical Conservative of the Second World War was undoubtedly R.B. Hanson. Hanson favoured conscription but feared its effects on his party. Conservatism could not afford to lead the nation on this issue, he believed, or the party would be doomed to spend still another generation in the political wilderness. It was far better to let the Liberals emerge from this war with the conscriptionist reputation.

All things considered, Hanson's course was undoubtedly the wisest one for the party to follow. The only way to counter Mackenzie King was to play his own game. But the gift of properly appraising political realities has never been a Conservative strongpoint. The Hanson course was rejected, and the result, carried to the extremes of political absurdity, was John Bracken's campaign to send conscripts to the Pacific. If there is any lesson to be drawn from the experience of the Conservative Party with conscription in the Second World War, it is this: expediency may be a four-letter word to editorial writers, but sometimes it is better for politicians to practise expediency than to stand on the wrong principles.

NOTES

1. Public Archives of Canada, R.J. Manion Papers, Vol. 13, Manion to J.A. Clark, September 13, 1939. As recently as 1936, however, Manion had written in his autobiography, *Life Is an Adventure*, p. 224, that "the only fair and just method of raising men for the army during war is by conscription...."
2. Manion Papers, Vol. 16, Manion to his son James, March 31, 1939.
3. *Toronto Daily Star*, March 28, 1939, p. 1.
4. House of Commons *Debates*, March 30, 1939, p. 2426.
5. Herbert Bruce Papers (Toronto), Bruce to Lord Beaverbrook, February 27, 1939. (The Bruce Papers are now at Queen's University.)
6. Manion Papers, Vol. 6, Manion to Georges Héon, August 1, 1939.
7. *Ibid.*, Héon to Manion, August 21, 1939.
8. *Ibid.*, Vol. 15, T.H. Onslow to Manion, August 5, 1939, enclosing Onslow to Dr. Robb, August 4, 1939.
9. *Ottawa Journal*, March 20, 1942, p. 10. This is a statement released by Manion in explanation of his reasons for advocating National Government.
10. Clipping from Saint John *Telegraph-Journal*, January 27, 1940, in Manion Papers, Vol. 61.
11. W.L.M. King, *Mackenzie King to the People of Canada* (Ottawa, 1940), pp. 36–53; Manion Papers, Vol. 14, J, Earl Lawson to Manion, February 13, 1940.
12. E.g., P.A.C., Hanson Papers, Hanson to T. Cantley, April 1, 1940.
13. University of New Brunswick, R.B. Bennett Papers, Notable Persons File, Norman Macleod to Bennett, January 30, 1940.
14. Saskatchewan Provincial Archives, G.H. Barr Papers, W.D. Herridge to Barr, February 5, 1940.
15. *Ottawa Journal*, March 20, 1942, p. 10. Cf. W.D. Herridge Papers (Toronto), Herridge to R.B. Bennett, May 24, 1941.
16. E.g., Manion Papers, Vol. 16, Manion to his son James, March 4, 1940; *ibid.*, Vol. 66, Diary entry, March 26, 1940; Hanson Papers, Hanson to A. Davidson, March 25, 1940.
17. E.g., *Halifax Chronicle*, March 25, 1940, advertisements; Queen's University, Norman Rogers Papers, 1940 Election Speeches. Address, February 19, 1940.
18. *Halifax Chronicle*, February 20, 1940, p. 8. Cf. Saskatchewan Public Archives, J.G. Gardiner Papers, Election Material, Address, "Manion at Brandon," n.d.
19. Montreal *Gazette*, February 20, 1940, p. 8.

20 *Mackenzie King to the People of Canada*, pp. 77–78.
21 Manion Papers, Vol. 66, Diary entry, March 26, 1940.
22 *Ibid.*, Vol. 17, Manion to his son James, April 18, 1940.
23 E.g., A.R. Adamson Papers (Toronto), Election Correspondence 1940, Memorandum, n.d.; Progressive Conservative Party Files (Ottawa), file PEI-Qla, Robb to P.W. Turner, April 4, 1940; Hanson Papers, Hanson to C.D. Gordon, April 5, 1940; P.A.C., Arthur Meighen Papers, E.N. McGirr to Meighen, June 22,1940; Manion Papers, Vol. 14, L.H. Snider to Manion, May 3, 1940
24 Directorate of History, Canadian Forces Headquarters, H.D.G. Crerar Papers, Crerar to L.B. Pearson, July 27, 1940.
25 Bennett Papers, Hanson to Bennett, July 4, 1940; Bruce Papers, Mrs. Bruce's Diary, June 17, 1940; J.W. Pickersgill, *The Mackenzie King Record*, Vol. I: *1939–1944* (Toronto. 1960), pp. 94–95.
26 *Ibid.*, p. 95.
27 The N.R.M.A. gave "special emergency powers to permit of the mobilization of all the effective resources of the nation, both human and material, for the purpose of the defence and security of Canada.... "*Statutes*, 4 Geo. VI, C. 13.
28 Hanson Papers, Hanson to T.G. Norris, June 20, 1940.
29 *Ibid.*, Hanson to J.M. Macdonnell, December 9, 1940; *ibid.*, Hanson to H.A. Newman, October 8, 1940.
30 *Ibid.*, Hanson to H.C. Farthing, May 27, 1941. Cf. Herridge Papers, Hanson to Herridge, May 25, 1941.
31 House of Commons *Debates*, May 12, 1941, p. 2729.
32 Bruce Papers, Bruce to George McCullagh, May 15, 1941.
33 E.g., Toronto *Evening Telegram*, April 22, 1941, p. 6. Cf. P.A.C., J.W. Dafoe Papers, Microfilm M-79, T. A. Crerar to Dafoe, April 25, 30, 1941.
34 Hanson Papers, Hanson to MacPherson, May 9, 1941, and reply, May 9, 1941.
35 *Ibid.*, Finlayson to Hanson, May 14, 1941. For detail on the recruiting campaign, see C.P. Stacey, *Official History of the Canadian Army in the Second World War*, Vol. I: *Six Years of War* (Ottawa. 1955), 121.
36 Meighen Papers, Meighen to Bennett, July 24, 1941.
37 *Ibid.*, Memorandum, n.d.
38 Adamson Papers, Diary entry, February 12, 1942.
39 Directorate of History file 112.3S2009 (D36), June 9, 1941. An earlier draft of this paper is in P.A.C., Ernest Lapointe Papers, Vol. 45.
40 Directorate of History file 112.3S2009 (D36), Memorandum, Director of Military Training to Chief of General Staff, June 25, 1941.
41 E.g., Edmond Turcotte, "What Canada's War Effort Might Be," in A.R.M. Lower and J.F. Parkinson, eds., *War and Reconstruction* (Toronto, 1942), p. 35.
42 Roger Graham, *Arthur Meighen*, Vol. III: *No Surrender* (Toronto, 1965), 89.
43 *Toronto Daily Star*, February 4, 1942, p, 9.

The Conservative Party and Conscription

44 Meighen Papers, Meighen to H.R. Milner, May 14, 1941.
45 *Ibid.*, Meighen to MacPherson, August 7, 1941.
46 *Ibid.*, Meighen to Hugh Clark, November 14, 1941.
47 Graham, III, 106.
48 Pickersgill, I, 313.
49 Hanson Papers, Hanson to H.A. Hanson, February 2, 1942.
50 Meighen Papers, Statement by Mr. Meighen, March 31, 1942.
51 House of Commons *Debates*, May 11, 1942, pp. 2280–81.
52 E.g., Hanson Papers, Meighen to Hanson, May 8, 1942.
53 *Ibid.*, Hanson to Meighen, May 9, 1942.
54 *Ibid.*, Memo for Caucus and attached notes, May 12, 1942. Cf. Bruce Papers, Bruce to Meighen, May 12, 1942; Adamson Papers, Diary entry, May 12, 1942.
55 Herridge Papers, Hanson to Herridge, May 25, 1942.
56 Harvard University, J. Pierrepont Moffat Papers, Vol. 47, Memorandum of Conversations..., 1 June 10, 1942.
57 House of Commons *Debates*, June 10, 1942. p. 3244.
58 Hanson Papers, Hanson to G.B. Jones, July 16, 1942.
59 E.g., P.A.C., R.A. Bell Papers, Vol. l, Bell to Hanson, September 11, 1942; Hanson Papers, D.K. Hazen to Hanson, September 12, 1941; *ibid.*, Grote Stirling to Hanson, October 5, 1942.
60 Meighen Papers, Meighen to L.G. Gravel, April 6, 1944; Pickersgill I 313-14; *Winnipeg Free Press*, January 20, 1942, p. 1.
61 *Ibid.*, October 19, 1942, p. 11. Cf. Queen's University, J.M. Macdonnell Papers, Vol. 52, Address to Toronto Conservative Businessmen's Club, June 12, 1942.
62 Hon. J.M. Macdonnell Interview, July 10, 1963; Rod Finlayson Interview, July 6, 1963.
63 Quoted in Progressive Conservative Party, *Progressive Conservative Speaker's Handbook, 1945* (Ottawa, 1945), War Policy, Section I.
64 Hon. R.A. Bell Interview, July 15, 1964.
65 Cited in "War Policy, John Bracken on Record," mimeo, n.d.
66 Bruce Papers, Bruce to George McCullagh, June 21, 1944.
67 Adamson Papers, Diary entry, July 24, 1944.
68 E.g., Montreal *Gazette*, November 13, 1944, p. 8.
69 Donald Fleming quoted in Toronto *Globe and Mail*, November 8, 1944, p. 4.
70 House of Commons *Debates*, November 27, 1944, p. 6622.
71 E.g., Bracken's speech at Meaford, Ontario, February 1, 1945, quoted in Progressive Conservative press release, March 1, 1945, copy in Directorate of History, A.G.L. McNaughton Papers.
72 Hanson Papers, Hanson to Bell, February 17, 1945.
73 *Ottawa Journal*, May 16, 1945, p. 13.

74 Adamson Papers, Diary entries, March 20, 21, 1945; Adamson Papers, Study of Public Opinion and Political Preference of Voters, West York," February, 1945.
75 Bell Papers, Vol. 1, Memorandum, "Problems of Organization" n.d.
76 *Ibid.*, Bona Arsenault to Bell, October 6, 8, 1944.
77 "Backstage at Ottawa," *Maclean's,* LVIII (July 15, 1945), 15.
78 Montreal *Gazette,* May 17, 1945, p. 1.
79 Hanson Papers, Hanson to G. Black, June 29, 1945.

Chapter Four

The York South By-Election of February 9, 1942: A Turning Point in Canadian Politics

Senator Arthur Meighen was selected as leader of the Conservative party in November 1941 by a party conference that originally had been called only to fix the date and site of a leadership convention. Meighen had been drafted for the leadership for a number of reasons: to industrialists he was the man alleged to be opposed to the increasing demands of organized labour; to businessmen and merchants he was the foremost critic of the Liberal government's price-freezing policy; and to members of parliament he was the strong, vigorous leader who would revive the faltering opposition in the House of Commons. But above all, to these groups in the Conservative party, Meighen was the leader of the forces in wartime Canada pressing for conscription of manpower for overseas service. If the new leader could direct an attack on the government, using the emotionally charged issue of conscription as his weapon, perhaps Mackenzie King's huge Liberal majority could be turned to the support of a national government, a national government that Meighen through the force of his still powerful personality might be expected to dominate.

The formation of a conscriptionist national government could only be disastrous for King and the Liberal party. Not only would King's personal power be destroyed, but the effects on Canadian unity would be shattering. In 1917 French Canada had reacted to conscription for a "British," "imperialist" war with riots and mass evasion. Knowing this, King had brought Quebec into the Second World War – equally a British war to many in the province – only by pledging himself, his government, and his party to a policy of no conscription for overseas service. For more than two years King had been able to honour his pledges, although conscription for home defence had been deemed necessary after the fall of France. Now with Meighen's return, the question of military service was to become the dominant issue once more.

Meighen needed a seat in the House of Commons in order to press effectively his case for conscription. This necessitated resignation from the Senate, finding a vacancy, and winning the subsequent by-election. But when Meighen finally secured a nomination for a "safe" seat, he found he was opposed by a candidate representing the Co-operative Commonwealth Federation. In the normal course of events the election of the leader of the Conservative party in a by-election would have been a mere formality. Complex forces were to meet head on in the York South campaign, however, and a war-weary electorate was to be offered social welfare as a cure for its ills. The decisive and unexpected result of the by-election was a watershed in Canadian politics.

Barring the possibility of a member's death or an unexpected general election, Meighen could only secure a seat in the House of Commons if one of the sitting Conservatives resigned, forcing a by-election. The problem, of course, was to pick a safe seat certain to return the leader. At the same time, with the party holding only thirty-nine seats in Parliament and being as well desperately short of legislative talent, no one wanted to deprive one of the more capable members of his place. Not surprisingly, perhaps, it proved rather difficult to induce a suitable M.P. to offer his seat.[1] Immediately Meighen had been selected as leader, two members had offered to resign in his favour. They were the Hon. Earl Rowe, member for the rural Ontario constituency of Dufferin-Simcoe, and Major Alan Cockeram from the Toronto riding of York South.[2] Apparently Meighen did not want either of these seats: rural ridings might not be safe ground for a conscriptionist; and Cockeram was on active service with his regiment, a valuable asset to a party claiming to represent the serviceman's interest. The most obvious choice after these two was the Toronto constituency of High Park, held since 1925 by the lacklustre A.J. Anderson, a 78-year-old lawyer. In precarious health, Anderson at one point agreed to give up his seat for his leader, but he soon reneged.[3] The sticking point apparently was the compensation required by Anderson for his sacrifice. Estimates of the amount demanded ranged from twelve to twenty thousand dollars, a sum that Meighen and his party presumably were not prepared to pay.[4] Finally, on November 26, Major Cockeram was allowed to resign, thus opening the way for Meighen's entry into the House of Commons.

York South seemed to be a safe seat for the Conservative leader. Since its formation in 1904, the constituency had never failed to vote

Conservative, often with large majorities. In recent elections, however, the Conservative plurality had been decreasing, and the victory of 1940 was probably attributable to the popularity of Cockeram, a decorated veteran of the Great War, a militia officer, and an outgoing individual. The electorate of approximately 33,500 had given Cockeram a comfortable 2,500-vote plurality over his Liberal opponent, and a 10,000-vote lead over the C.C.F. candidate, Joseph W. Noseworthy. Within the boundaries of York South lay the wealthy and exclusive suburb of Forest Hill Village, the middle class area of Weston, and the heavily populated working-class districts of York Township. The population was largely of British stock, although there were substantial numbers of Jews in the Village.[5] Some in the party would have preferred Meighen to choose another constituency, but it is hard to see how he could have done better at that time than to contest York South.[6]

With a seat now opened for him, the next problem for Meighen was whether or not he would face opposition. This question did not remain unanswered for long: on December 1 the C.C.F. again nominated Noseworthy to contest the vacancy. The nomination of a candidate was no mere whim of the local party organization but the result of a deliberate policy decision taken by the C.C.F. National Executive on November 15–16, shortly after Meighen's designation as Conservative leader.[7] As the archetypal representative of the "Old Gang" and of the "profit-seeking wolves of Big Business,"[8] Meighen was to be opposed by the C.C.F. wherever he chose to run.

With the exception of one Cape Breton seat won in the 1940 election, the C.C.F. had never returned a member of parliament east of the prairie provinces. On the outbreak of war in 1939 the movement, internally divided, had taken a somewhat equivocal stand on the question of Canadian participation, and this had seemingly destroyed it. The party's war policy, however, had undergone a slow metamorphosis from pacifism to conscription of wealth rather than men, to no conscription of men without conscription of wealth, and finally, by late 1941, to conscription of both men and wealth.[9] Coincident with this shift in policy, the C.C.F. found its programme of social welfare becoming more attractive to the public. The gloom of the war years seemed to be encouraging people to look ahead to a brighter postwar prospect, to a world free of depression and strife. When this feeling was coupled with full employment, stronger trade unions, and an admiration for the effective resistance of the "socialist" Soviet Union, the C.C.F. was the beneficiary. The party was ready to move into Ontario.[10] Joseph Noseworthy, the nominee in York South, was a good choice to lead the C.C.F. attack. He was the head of the English department at Vaughan Road

Collegiate, the neighbourhood high school, and as such he had a ready-made group of youthful supporters, a large number of former students, and many parents ready to work for him. Despite his crushing defeat at the hands of Major Cockeram in 1940, Noseworthy had a bare chance to win in the changed circumstances of 1942, but only if the vote was not split by the entry of a Liberal candidate.

What would the Liberals do? Meighen would be very dangerous to the government in the House of Commons, and his slashing attacks might destroy Mackenzie King's control of his increasingly restive English-speaking supporters. The York South Liberal Association (or rather one of the two feuding groups in the riding claiming that title) provided the answer on December 5 when it declined to contest the seat, declaring that as Cockeram had resigned only to facilitate Meighen's entry into the House, his wishes should be respected.[11] These were praiseworthy sentiments, but they concealed definite attempts to stop any Liberal from running against Meighen.[12] The Conservative leader, certainly, had no doubts as to the reason for this courtesy. Mackenzie King, he wrote long after the event, "would not put a candidate in the field knowing if he did so the vote opposing me would be divided, and he wanted it entirely concentrated, and did not care much under what auspices it was concentrated."[13]

Meighen's jaundiced view of Liberal motives was probably correct, although there were some extenuating factors. A "tradition" that the leader of a party seeking to enter the House in a by-election should not be opposed did exist, and the Liberals could claim that they were honouring this custom.[14] Furthermore it has been alleged that there was an agreement between the Liberals and the Conservatives that Meighen would be unopposed in York South if the Conservatives did not oppose Humphrey Mitchell, the newly appointed Minister of Labour, who was seeking election to the House in a by-election in Welland, Ontario, also scheduled for February 9, 1942. There is no doubt that Meighen made at least one attempt to get a candidate to run in Welland, but there is also no doubt that after his first choice refused to consider seeking the nomination, he dissuaded the Welland Conservatives from entering the contest.[15] Although Meighen later denied that there was any pact with the Liberals, many contemporary politicians believed that some agreement had been reached.[16]

In the weeks after his selection as leader, Meighen was busy with the difficult tasks of arranging his personal affairs and with party organization. He was painfully aware of the inadequacy of the party's representation in the House of Commons, but he was unable to induce the men he wanted to stand for election when vacancies could be found for them.[17] There was more success with finances. A new organization under Senator A.D. McRae, the architect of the Conservative victory of 1930, was formed.[18] "The arrangement with Meighen," R.B. Hanson, the Conservative leader in parliament since the resignation of Dr. R.J. Manion in May 1940, wrote some months later, "was that an entirely new financial set-up was made and he was guaranteed relief from any worry over finance."[19] Professor Graham has indicated obliquely that some $200,000 was to be provided for the party's needs,[20] and that this money was intended to finance a national movement for conscription. "We all realize that organization in the old Party line is not either wise or in our minds at all," Meighen wrote to one of his friends. "It is a national new movement we want to generate to get national results."[21]

Without its leader in the House of Commons, the national movement for a total war effort would be stillborn, and the first task was to get Meighen elected. The job of running the by-election campaign was turned over to J. Earl Lawson, a former M.P. for York South and Minister of National Revenue in the last days of the Bennett government. Lawson's chief aide was Leopold Macaulay, York South's Conservative representative in the Ontario legislature since 1926. Under the direction of these two experienced local politicians, a full campaign organization detailing responsibility for everything from publicity to "citizens' committees" was created and functioning before Christmas 1941.[22] Ample funds were available for the campaign, although all but a small portion of the $7,500 expended apparently came from Meighen's own pocket.[23]

While the campaign organization was wisely left in the hands of local politicians, Meighen himself determined the issue upon which he would base his fight for election. This issue – the only issue as far as Meighen was concerned – was the winning of the war, and this meant conscription and National Government. His decision to stand on this platform was probably intuitive and was grounded upon his belief that conscription was the foundation without which an effective war effort was an impossibility. It was obvious to Meighen that "no nation has any right to go into a war on any other basis than a compulsory selective service system."[24] None the less, to get the statistics necessary to bolster his beliefs, Meighen commissioned research into the war efforts of the other British dominions (none of which had imposed conscription for overseas service), into the war policy of the C.C.F., and into Canada's military condition. To get this information, Meighen corresponded with his friends across the country, asking for reports on the situation in their areas.[25]

Meighen's campaign advisers were not entirely pleased with the choice of campaign issues. As early as December 9, before Meighen's first meeting with the executive of the York South Conservative Association, Earl Lawson urged his leader not to oppose an excess profits tax and to support the conscription of wealth and industry as well as the conscription of manpower.[26] Remembering the unemployment and distress of the 1930s when parts of the constituency had been among the hardest hit in the nation, Lawson based his advice on a realistic assessment of political conditions in the riding. His warnings, and those of other Toronto Conservatives, fell on deaf ears, however, for Meighen was concerned solely with the war.[27]

Meighen's obsession was readily apparent in his first major address of the campaign, a local radio speech on January 9. After a brief attack on the C.C.F. for blocking his election by acclamation, the candidate turned directly to his joint themes of National Government and conscription. His thesis was simply put: "we are not organized politically as we should be ..." and "as a consequence of an unsuitable political set-up we are not organized militarily as we should be." In proof of this contention the Conservative leader cited the example of New Zealand, claiming that the small Pacific dominion had contributed a proportionately greater share to the empire's war effort than had Canada.[28] How could this alleged disparity be made up? "We need more men for overseas service," Meighen claimed. "We cannot organize this nation without ample power to direct the energies of every man and woman to the place where those energies are needed. That power this government refuses to exercise. The cold hand of political expediency has held it in its grip. A trembling servitude to a sinister tradition has gone far to benumb the striking power of Canada." In Meighen's opinion there could be no excuse for refusing to conscript men in any war. Certainly Mackenzie King's reason – "that if we compel Canadians to serve where Canadians have to fight to save Canada, we will destroy the unity of the Nation," as Meighen put it – was foolish. "Can any normal mind accept such a preposterous contention?" he asked. Despite his belief that the government's course thus far had been a cowardly one, the Conservative leader offered to share the burdens with the Liberals: "If wanted, we of the Conservative party will ... help within [the government]; if not wanted, we will help from without; but we insist on action. We shall not be satisfied with substitutes or subterfuge. To the utmost of our strength we shall urge abandonment of things secondary and things that make for division and delay...."[29]

Arthur Meighen's speech was forcefully, even brilliantly, delivered, but in the context of wartime Canada its content left much to be desired. The Hon. T.A. Crerar, King's Minister of Mines and Resources and a colleague of Meighen in the Union government of the Great War, wrote to a friend about the opening salvo of the Conservative Leader's campaign: "Meighen's speech the other night was a characteristic one. He offers to place himself on the altar of his country in a National Government-and then proceeds to make it impossible. I doubt if I have known anyone during my political life with less political instinct or sense than Meighen has. In this he is the victim of his limitations."[30] Who could doubt Crerar's judgment? Meighen showed no glimmer of understanding for the objections of French Canada to overseas conscription. For attempting to abide by his pledge to Quebec, Mackenzie King was guilty of "trembling servitude to a sinister tradition." Anyone who agreed with King and his manpower policy lacked a "normal mind." Meighen's views with their emphasis on victory and sacrifice were truly patriotic, but they were hardly open to compromise. In Canada as elsewhere, compromise was the stuff of politics – even in wartime – and without it eventual defeat was inescapable. Meighen, however, had made one further error of more immediate import.

The opening speech of the campaign was notable for Meighen's almost total neglect of his actual opponent. Other than to level a perfunctory blast at the C.C.F. for daring to force a test at the polls, Meighen had scarcely glanced in Noseworthy's direction. All his heavy fire was directed at the King government. There was no appeal to the voters of York South, no recognition of the C.C.F. campaign for social welfare measures, and no sign of an understanding of local issues. Meighen's faith in the broad interests of his electorate was evidently real – but was it realistic? Might not the electors feel that Meighen was using them only as a springboard to a better platform? Might not the Liberals of the constituency resent Meighen's attacks on their party's policy and translate this resentment into votes – if not for Noseworthy, then against Meighen? More directly, might not Meighen's total reliance on war issues alienate an electorate that was being promised social reform by his opponent?

A new factor was interjected into the campaign on the day after Meighen's opening address. By a "spontaneous and enthusiastic expression of the people's will,"[31] a Committee for Total War was organized at a meeting held in Toronto's Royal York Hotel. The Committee's avowed purpose was to mobilize public opinion behind a policy of conscription and to exert pressure on Ontario's members of parliament, in the hope of forcing this predominantly Liberal group to desert Mackenzie King and demand conscription.[32] The Committee for Total War, more popularly known as the "Toronto 200," had met at the call of three prominent businessmen, J.Y. Murdoch of Noranda Mines, C.L. Burton of the Robert Simpson Co., and F.K. Morrow, a Toronto financier and corporation director. In the background was C. George McCullagh, publisher of the Toronto *Globe and Mail*, Toronto's zealously conscriptionist morning newspaper. McCullagh had been one of the organizers of the scheme to bring Meighen back from retirement in November 1941. Now he was hoping to organize all Ontario into a grass roots movement that could propel Meighen into power.[33]

The formation of the Toronto 200 marked the shift of the conscription campaign into high gear. Meighen's election campaign was merged into a province-wide effort, featuring a lavish use of the mass media, all paid for "by a small group of patriotic citizens."[34] In Toronto, of course, the *Globe and Mail* spearheaded the campaign, turning over its news columns to the Committee's activities.[35] In other communities, similar drives were underway. As the *Globe and Mail* put it on January 13, "The heather is on fire in Ontario."[36] Indeed it was, and if the fire was not as spontaneous as the Toronto newspaper claimed, it was none the less dangerous. The threat of a revolt of Ontario back-benchers, coupled with the imminent return of Meighen to the opposition ranks, posed one of the gravest threats of the war years for the Liberal government.

The demand for conscription in January 1942 was entirely "political and psychological," Mackenzie King believed, for no practical difficulty had yet been experienced in finding volunteers for Canada's overseas armies. The government's opponents were trying to make conscription for overseas service "the symbol, in English-speaking Canada, of a total war effort,"[37] and although he believed this view to be wrong, King could see that his pledge not to conscript men for overseas service would be a potentially embarrassing commitment when casualties began to mount. As early as mid-December 1941, therefore, he had begun to feel that the government would have to be released from its pledges by a plebiscite.[38] "We might get into Parliament," King told his cabinet, itself restive on the issue of conscription, "and find the party divided; already, there were some for and some against.... The situation might become such that to settle the matter there might have to be a change of Government. One thing I did not want was to see any Government managing Canada's affairs of which Arthur Meighen would be the head, or a member...."[39] Characteristically, King saw that the idea of a plebiscite would also serve to cut the ground out from under the Conservatives.[40] With Meighen, McCullagh, and the Toronto 200 all demanding conscription, the plebiscite concept offered a way around the Conservative leader's attempt to win his by-election simply on a show of hands between those for and against conscription. With the prospect of a plebiscite before them, only those who wanted conscription immediately, regardless of the situation in the country, would be compelled to vote for Meighen.[41] Accordingly, the Speech from the Throne that opened the 1942 session of parliament on January 22 included the following statement of policy: "My ministers ... will seek, from the people, by means of a plebiscite, release from any obligation arising out of any past commitments restricting the methods of raising men for military service."'[42]

The announcement of the plebiscite produced the predictable charges of political cowardice from the opposition. Meighen was "shamed and humiliated by our Government's despicable evasion.... It is a base and cowardly insult."[43] Major Cockeram, on leave from his regiment to participate in Meighen's attempt to win his old constituency, called the plebiscite the "rankest insult to men on active service."[44] Mitchell Hepburn, the Liberal premier of Ontario, announced that because of the plebiscite he would support Meighen's bid for election. As George Drew, the Ontario Conservative leader, was already in the fight, Hepburn's entry seemingly united all right-of-centre shades of the Ontario political spectrum behind the Conservative chieftain.[45]

Mesmerized by the conscription issue, Meighen believed that the announcement of the plebiscite would increase his chances for success in his attempts to destroy the King government. Who would not be outraged by this shameful attempt to evade the responsibility for settling the conscription question? "A fair, decent breakaway from King in the House on this plebiscite would be a magnificent achievement," he wrote. "It would probably lead to the only move that would save the situation...." This move, he continued, "is for the Government members assisted by us if they want us, to unitedly tell the country what has to be done...." What had to be done, it was evident, was the inauguration of total war – conscription and National Government.[46]

Other observers were not misled by the effect of King's call for the plebiscite, for the new dilemma facing the Conservatives was becoming clear. The announcement of the forthcoming vote on conscription seemingly had solidified the Liberal party behind the Prime Minister,[47] and the chances for the breakaway foreseen by the Conservatives were now decreasing despite the best efforts of Meighen and the Toronto 200. In the light of this changed situation, attacks on the plebiscite inevitably became attacks on the question posed by King – conscription or not? Whatever their contempt for King's political expediency, the Conservatives could hardly afford to see the idea of conscription defeated. As Senator McRae wrote to Meighen, "like it or not,' the party had to work to bring out the largest possible affirmative vote in the plebiscite. The Prime Minister, he added, "has once more proven himself the most astute politician Canada has ever had."[48] So he had. King's plebiscite had destroyed Meighen's main issue; more important yet was the Conservative leader's failure to realize this. The Co-operative Commonwealth Federation organization in York South, however, was not about to make this same mistake.

The strategy and organization of the C.C.F. in the Toronto constituency were superb. By deliberate plan the policy of Noseworthy's headquarters was to stir up interest in the campaign and to force Meighen to defend his past record. This strategy was working better than expected, E.B. Jolliffe, a vice-president of the Ontario C.C.F., wrote to national party headquarters on January 18. The *Globe and Mall*, he reported, was beginning to attack the C.C.F. each day, and Meighen was being forced to devote more and more of his time to defending himself and to setting out his "real" views on social security.[49] At the same time the C.C.F. message of social reform and total war was being delivered to every home in the riding by an army of dedicated volunteers, gathered together from the entire metropolitan area.[50] In sharp contrast to the usual C.C.F. penury, money was available for the by-election fight. A national appeal for funds and extensive canvassing in Toronto produced more than $5,000,[51] and as the party relied on volunteer workers, this money could be used for radio and press publicity.

The plebiscite, which had effectively forced Meighen into an untenable position, hardly bothered Noseworthy's campaign. The C.C.F. candidate readily fell back on his already well-worn themes of social security and "conscription of wealth" and redoubled his attacks on Meighen's record. "Tories of his type," Noseworthy said of his opponent's attempts to defend himself, "always become interested in the poor at election time." "The Tory clique who drafted Mr. Meighen," he charged on another occasion, "want to give us the old 1914–18 leadership for the war, and they want the same type of leadership for the reconstruction period that follows the war." This clique, Noseworthy claimed, was using conscription to divert attention from other phases of the war effort, "such as the mobilization of all our material resources. They hope, moreover, to give to the Conservative party ... a momentary flicker of life. They hope to get through the election of my opponent some control of our war policy."[52]

Faced with this barrage of C.C.F. charges, Meighen began to water down his stand on social welfare as the campaign drew to its close. First, however, he found himself embroiled in a dispute with the *Toronto Daily Star*, the one local newspaper unfriendly to him. The *Star* had reported Meighen as saying in a speech on January 29 that "if we have to conscript wealth to win the war, we will, but people of common sense don't advocate that until the last gasp." Six days later, Meighen belatedly claimed that he had been misquoted and announced that he now favoured the conscription of wealth.[53] This last-minute conversion was scarcely believable.

After the entry of Mitchell Hepburn into the campaign at Meighen's side, Noseworthy's efforts received an evidently unsolicited boost when

Arthur Roebuck, the Liberal member for Toronto Trinity and Hepburn's Attorney General from 1934 to 1937, attacked both his old leader and Arthur Meighen in two hard-hitting radio speeches. Roebuck claimed that he was acting on his own responsibility, but it would appear that he asked for and received Mackenzie King's permission to join in the fray.[54] His entry roused other Liberals. Brooke Claxton, the M.P. for Montreal St. Lawrence-St. George, approached Senator Norman Lambert, former President of the National Liberal Federation and the controller of party finances, for $1,000 for the C.C.F. in York South. Apparently acting on his own responsibility, Lambert made arrangements with David Lewis, national secretary of the C.C.F., for the transfer of the money.[55] It would seem that this $1,000 was the extent of direct financial assistance.[56] In Toronto, the C.C.F. received other forms of assistance. T. Wilbur Best, a prominent businessman in York South who had earlier supported Meighen's campaign, withdrew his endorsement of the Conservative leader. Because Meighen was unfairly attacking the government, he wrote in an open letter to the *Toronto Daily Star*, "I am ... withdrawing my support from Mr. Meighen like most other Liberals in the riding."[57]

Whether "most other Liberals" shared Best's opinion was questionable, but the election results of February 9 were not. Noseworthy, who had won exactly one poll in his first try for office in 1940, carried 159 of 212 in the by-election and won easily with a 4,456-vote majority. What had happened? Meighen had run well in Forest Hill Village, winning 23 of 30 polls and a majority of 1,537 votes. In middle-class Weston, the Conservative leader held his own, even picking up the only three polls that had voted Liberal in the general election two years earlier. Only in York Township had he done poorly, so poorly in fact that it was there that the election was lost. The working-class districts of York South had cast 11,720 votes for the Conservative candidate in 1940, but only 7,683 for Meighen, a loss of 4,037 votes. In the 1940 election, Noseworthy had won only one poll in the township; two years later he captured 141, most of which had been Conservative in 1940. Only in the areas of the township bordering on Forest Hill Village and in the "better" districts had the electorate chosen Meighen. What had happened, it is clear, is that Meighen had done well in the wealthier sections of the constituency but had lost in the working-class districts.[58]

Other factors than the defection of the working-class vote had undoubtedly contributed to the C.C.F. victory. The weather, first, had been uncommonly bad, Toronto having been struck by "the worst blizzard ... in recent years" barely 48 hours before the polls opened,[59] and this may have been responsible for keeping the turnout of voters below that in the 1940 election. If the C.C.F. organization was as efficient in getting out the vote as in canvassing, this could have been an important factor in determining the outcome. And what of conscription? In the plebiscite held ten weeks after the by-election, York South voted 93.7 per cent in favour of releasing the government from its pledges.[60] Presumably, then, the announcement of the plebiscite had some effect in destroying part of the Conservative leader's support. The one certainty in all this however, is that almost 4,100 Conservative voters in York Township had either stayed home on election day or else had switched their allegiance to the C.C.F. candidate. As a result, Meighen was defeated decisively "and defeated in the strongest riding in Toronto, which means the strongest Tory riding in all of Canada." "Defeated," exulted the jubilant Mackenzie King, "while supported by financial interests and the press – everything in the way of organization and campaign power that could be assembled for any man...."[61]

The loss was a bitter blow to Meighen. "While I was the most doubtful of any of our organization as to the outcome in South York," he wrote indignantly, "the result, I must admit, was much worse than I thought possible. Truly it is discouraging that the foul and despicable methods which were initiated right at the beginning there and carried on without the slightest regard for truth, and on a wholesale scale, could be successful in a constituency almost wholly of Anglo-Saxons. Undoubtedly the average level is not what it was, and just as undoubtedly we are in for real trouble as a result." Politics in Canada, the defeated Meighen concluded bitterly, were even more rotten than in the France of 1940.[62] Later, Meighen would attribute his defeat to the "common resolve of not one, not two, but three party leaders – the Liberal, the CCF, and the Communist ..." and to the absence from the riding of 4,000 men on active service.[63]

Meighen's reaction to his defeat was understandable, but his analysis of the causes of the *débâcle* was as wrong as his choice of issues. Certainly the C.C.F. campaign with its focus on Meighen's personality and past was not a gentle one, and it seems likely that some Liberal aid was given directly to the C.C.F. But it is none the less difficult to escape the conclusion that the cause of the defeat was Meighen's inept campaign. His political myopia, aggravated by unreasoning patriotism, had led Meighen to fight his battle solely on the issues of the war and to neglect all positive mention of social welfare until the closing days of the campaign. This obsession with conscription and National Government had left him in an exceedingly vulnerable position when the government announced the plebiscite. By his attacks on the King government and by his reliance on the support of the Toronto 200 and of renegade Liberals, Meighen undoubtedly weakened his position with the Liberals of York South. At the same time, and most decisively, the Conservative leader had alienated the working-class voters of the constituency by his attitude to social reform. The C.C.F. strategy of painting Meighen as a profiteer, a strike-breaker, and a tool of the "interests" undoubtedly assisted in this process. As one of Meighen's key lieutenants noted mournfully, "I think the C.C.F. are starting to make inroads in the working vote of both parties."[64] With its well-organized, well-run campaign, the C.C.F. had capitalized on Meighen's errors and scored a stunning upset. In the process, the attractiveness of social welfare as an election issue had been effectively demonstrated. The primary result of Meighen's defeat was to destroy the hopes and plans of those who had arranged his selection as leader in November 1941. With the rebuff in York South, the drive for conscription and National Government fizzled out. In the end, even Meighen was forced to say that he would vote "yes" on the plebiscite.[65] At the same time the C.C.F. victory gave tremendous impetus to the fledgling social democratic movement. "From that moment," wrote C.C.F. leader M.J. Coldwell, "the C.C.F. ceased to be an interesting minority movement"[66] and rapidly expanded to the point where it threatened the major parties. Buoyed by the unexpected victory over Meighen, the C.C.F. increased its strength rapidly and in September 1943 the polls showed the socialists leading the old parties in national support.[67] This was to be a temporary condition, but the effects of the new C.C.F. strength were none the less striking.

The threat of a left-wing government was terrifying to the old-line parties. As a first stage in their attempts to counter the C.C.F., both parties were virtually forced to liberalize their platforms and to adopt extensive social welfare schemes. For the Conservatives, weak even before York South, this urgent movement to progressive Conservatism led eventually to a new party name and a new leader without prior ties to the Conservative party – Premier John Bracken of Manitoba. Meighen's defeat, then, had truly far-reaching effects, both in shaping the course of the war effort in Canada and in moulding the form of society that was to follow the peace.

NOTES

1 Public Archives of Canada (P.A.C.), Arthur Meighen Papers, Meighen to M.A. MacPherson, Nov. 27, 1941.
2 The Hon. W. Earl Rowe Interview, Sept. 9, 1964; House of Commons, Debates, Jan. 30, 1942, p. 177 (J.F. Pouliot, M.P., citing Judith Robinson, "Tory Patriot Offers Costly Seat." [Toronto] News, date unknown).
3 Meighen Papers, J.R. MacNicol, M.P., to Meighen, Dec. 5, 1941.
4 A. Rodney Adamson Papers (Port Credit, Ontario), Diary, entry for Dec. 4, 1941: "... Anderson asked $12,000 for his seat. Shocking this just the curse of the Tory party again [sic]"; House of Commons, Debates, Jan. 30, 1942, p. 177.

5 The population of the constituency of York South, as reported by the 1941 census, was 78,167. Of this number 5,740 lived in Weston, 11,757 in Forest Hill Village, and 60,670 in York Township. Dominion Bureau of Statistics, *Eighth Census of Canada, 1941* (Ottawa, 1944), II, 35. Well over three-quarters of the population was of British stock (ibid., II, 442–3). Income distribution was sharply varied in the three districts forming the riding. The head of a household in Forest Hill earned an average of $3,504 yearly and lived in a house valued at $12,611. In Weston the salary was $1,715 and the house value $4,583, and in York Township the figures were $1,622 and $3,783 respectively, (ibid., IX, 162–7). The York Township averages above are boosted by the "better" districts bordering on Forest Hill Village. Without these areas, the figures would doubtless have been lower.

6 The Hon. R. A. Bell Interview, July 15, 1964. Bell stated that he had tried to stop Meighen from running in York South, feeling that he could not win there, but that he could win High Park. On the other hand, J.R. MacNicol, M.P. for Toronto Davenport, wrote Meighen that he was relieved he was not to run in High Park because "there are many foreigners and railroad men [in High Park]" (Meighen Papers, MacNicol to Meighen, Dec. 5, 1941). Election results in High Park show a progressive decline in Conservative strength. In 1925, the plurality was 10,344; in 1930, 6,042; in 1935, 2,592; and in 1940, only 205 votes.

7 P.A.C., C.C.F. Records, National Executive Minutes, Nov. 15–16, 1941; Toronto *Globe and Mail*, Dec. 2, 1941, p. 2.

8 Phrases from a York South campaign pamphlet in author's possession.

9 Leo Zakuta, *A Protest Movement Becalmed: A Study of Change in the CCF* (Toronto, 1964), p. 60.

10 G.L. Caplan, "The Failure of Canadian Socialism: The Ontario Experience, 1932–1945," *Canadian Historical Review*, XLIV (June, 1963), 99; David Lewis and Frank Scott, *Make This Your Canada* (Toronto, 1943), pp. 3, 14, 25; M.J. Coldwell, *Left Turn, Canada* (New York, 1945), pp. 26–30.

11 Toronto *Globe and Mail*, Dec. 6, 1941, p. 4. Details on the split between the two riding associations may be found in *Toronto Daily Star*, Dec. 3, 1941, p. 8, and Dec. 5, 1941, p. 8

12 F.J. MacRae, the Liberal candidate in 1940, was visited by the Postmaster General, the Hon. W.P. Mulock, and was politely advised not to seek the nomination (MacRae Interview, June 2, 1965).

13 Meighen Papers, Meighen to Theodore Ropp, July 9, 1957; *ibid.*, Meighen to H.E. Wilmot, Jan. 17, 1942.

14 For example, when Dr. R.J. Manion entered the House in a by-election in November 1938 the *Canadian Annual Review of Public Affairs, 1937 and 1938*, p. 58, noted that "the Liberal Party extend[ed] the usual courtesy to a newly-elected Party Leader" by not opposing him.

15 Meighen tried to persuade M.A. MacPherson to run (Meighen Papers, Meighen to MacPherson, Dec. 13, and reply, Dec. 16, 1941). For Meighen's efforts at dissuading the Welland Conservatives, see *ibid.*, Meighen to T. F. Forestell, Dec. 16, 1941.
16 P.A.C., John W. Dafoe Papers, Microfilm roll M-80, the Hon. T.A. Crerar to Dafoe, Jan. 31, 1942: "We did not nominate a Liberal against Meighen and there was some understanding – how complete it was I do not know – that the Conservatives would not nominate against Mitchell." Meighen's denial of an arrangement is in Meighen Papers, Meighen to John Bird, Feb. 17, 1942.
17 Meighen tried to persuade MacPherson and George Drew to enter the Commons (Meighen Papers, Meighen to H.R. Milner, Nov. 28, 1941, and Meighen to MacPherson, Nov. 27, 1941). Apparently, he also attempted to persuade W.D. Herridge to follow a similar course (W.D. Herridge Papers (Toronto, Herridge to A.P. Waldron, Nov. 24, 1941).
18 R. B. Hanson Papers (Fredericton), File 0–160-F, Hanson to Meighen, March 23, 1942. (The Hanson Papers have since been deposited in the P.A.C.)
19 Ibid., File 0–167, Hanson to D.C. Coleman, May 30, 1942.
20 Roger Graham, *Arthur Meighen*. III. *No Surrender* (Toronto, 1965), 162-3.
21 Meighen Papers, Meighen to Milner, Nov. 28, 1941.
22 *Ibid*. J. Earl Lawson to Meighen, Dec. 22, 1941
23 Meighen put up $7,300 himself, while $159.85 was received in contributions (*ibid.*, C.F. Moore to Meighen, March 10, 1942). Cf., Graham, *Meighen,* Ill, 161.
24 Toronto *Globe and Mail*, Jan. 30, 1942, p. l.
25 Bell Interview, Aug. 24, 1964. Bell prepared an elaborate memorandum on recruiting in the dominions which proved inconclusive, hut upon which Meighen proceeded to base his attacks. Meighen's researchers also looked into the C.C.F. press, but found nothing useful (Meighen Papers, Milner to Meighen, Jan. 12, 1942, and "CCF Attitudes Toward War," n.d.). Meighen's principal correspondents on the military situation were Senator McRae and MacPherson {e.g., Meighen Papers, MacPherson to Meighen, Dec. 31, 1941, containing a report prepared by A.H. Bence, Saskatoon Conservative M.P., which is revealing as to the tenor of the reports; "I am afraid that there is nothing that I can point out of a critical nature as far as the local situation is concerned").
26 Meighen Papers, Lawson to Meighen, Dec. 9, 1941.
27 F. G. Gardiner, Esq., Interview, Sept. 8, 1964. Gardiner was Reeve of Forest Hill at this time and a key figure on the campaign staff. He recalled that his urging of social welfare on Meighen became so tiresome to the Conservative chief that he took to calling him "Social Security" Gardiner each time they met. Leopold Macaulay confirmed this interpretation (interview, Sept. 17, 1965).
28 The example of New Zealand was not entirely suitable. Not only did that country lack the manufacturing and mineral resources that absorbed much of Canada's manpower, but its government was formed by Labour.

29 Meighen's speech is printed in full in *Toronto Daily Star,* Jan. 10, 1942, p. 31. This theme was repeated again and again {Toronto *Globe and Mail,* Jan. 17, 1942, p. l; Jan. 21, 1942, p. 4; Jan. 30, 1942, p. l).
30 Dafoe Papers, Microfilm roll M-80, Crerar to Dafoe, Jan. 13, 1942.
31 Toronto *Globe and Mail,* Jan. 12, 1942, p. I.
32 *Ibid.,* p. 8, address by the Committee chairman, J.Y. Murdoch.
33 Adamson Papers, Diary, entry for Jan. 10, 1942: "Today is the day of the 'All Out War' meeting at the Royal York. Murdoch and Burton and George McCullagh. Will it prove another Globe stunt [sic]"; Dafoe Papers, Microfilm roll M-80, Crerar to Dafoe, Jan. 13, 1942; Meighen Papers, C.O. Knowles to Meighen, Feb. 18, 1942. Meighen denied knowledge of the Toronto 200 "until the call for the meeting was being complied with" (Hanson Papers, File S-175-M, Meighen to Hanson, Feb. 13, 1942).
34 Toronto *Globe and Mall,* Jan. 12, 1942, p. 8. Full-page advertisements were placed in every daily and weekly newspaper in Ontario. The *Toronto Dally Star* printed a memorandum distributed at the meeting detailing the plans for publicity (Jan. 12, 1942, p. 10).
35 On one typical day (Jan. 13, 1942) at the beginning of the drive, the *Globe and Mail* had five stories about conscription on page 1, two on page 2, one on page 6, two on page 8, all of page 9, and one on page 10.
36 *Ibid.,* p, 1. The fire spread to the prairies, and a Total War advertisement was placed in a Regina newspaper (Saskatchewan Provincial Archives, J.G. Gardiner Papers, T.H. Wood to Gardiner, Jan. 20, 23, 1942).
37 J. W. Pickersgill, *The Mackenzie King Record.* I. *1939–1944* (Toronto, 1960), 333.
38 *Ibid.,* I, 314; Dafoe Papers, Microfilm roll M-79, Grant Dexter to Dafoe, Nov. 18 and Dec. 22, 1941
39 Pickersgill, *Mackenzie King Record,* I, 314.
40 *Ibid.,* I, 313
41 Ralph Allen, *Ordeal by Fire* (New York, 1961), p. 416; Graham, *Meighen,* Ill, 108
42 House of Commons, *Debates,* Jan. 22, 1942, p. 2.
43 Meighen Papers, tel., Meighen to John Bracken, Jan. 23, 1942.
44 Toronto *Globe and Mail,* Jan. 30, 1942, p. 1.
45 *Ibid.,* Jan. 29, 1942, p. 1. Hepburn's letter and Meighen's reply to this offer of support are printed here.
46 Meighen Papers, Meighen to A.B. Watt, Feb. 2, 1942.
47 Houghton Library, Harvard University, J. Pierrepont Moffat Papers, memorandum of conversation with Mr. J.W. McConnell, Jan. 24, 1942, and "Notes on Political Situation," Feb. 7, 1942.
48 Meighen Papers, McRae to Meighen, n.d. Cf. *Winnipeg Free Press,* Feb. 3, 1942, p. 1
49 C.C.F. Records, E. J[olliffe] to David Lewis, Jan. 18, 1942. For examples of Meighen's defence: Toronto *Globe and Mail,* Jan. 17, 1942, p. 1; Jan. 21, p. 4; Feb. 4, p. 4.

50 Noseworthy reported that "several hundred" canvassers were organized (C.C.F. Records, Noseworthy to Lewis, 9, 1942). For the reactions of a typical canvasser, see Hester James, "I Canvassed for Noseworthy," *Canadian Forum*, XXII (April, 1942), 16–18.
51 The budget was expected to range between $3,600 and $5,000 (C.C.F. Records, F.A. Brewin to Lewis, Jan. 9, 1942). E.B. Jolliffe states that the maximum figure was exceeded (Interview, June 2, 1965).
52 *Toronto Daily Star*, Jan. 22, 1942, p. 9; Feb. 3, p. 5; Feb. 4, p. 8. Meighen's biographer devotes fifteen pages to the C.C.F. campaign (Graham, *Meighen*, III, 109–24).
53 In an extraordinary front-page statement on Feb. 5, 1942, the *Star* denied having misquoted Meighen. The reporter who had covered the meeting in question, the *Star* stated flatly, had specifically asked Meighen if his words were intended and had been informed that they were, Meighen's charges against the *Star* are in the issue of Feb. 4, 1942, p. 9.
54 At a party caucus on Jan. 29, King asked his M.P.s to support government candidates in the by-elections set for Feb. 9 (Pickersgill, *Mackenzie King Record*, I, 343–44; Roebuck interview, July 15, 1964). After this caucus Roebuck apparently persuaded the dubious King that there was a chance to beat Meighen and convinced him that he should be allowed to enter the campaign on his own responsibility. Roebuck was likely motivated by his extreme dislike for both Hepburn and Meighen; his feeling was strong enough that he was willing to pay for his own radio time – or so it appears (Roebuck Interview; Jolliffe Interview). Roebuck's speeches are in the *Toronto Daily Star*, Feb. 2, 1942, p. 3, and Feb. 4, p. 9
55 Douglas Library, Queen's University, Norman Lambert Diaries, Jan. 29, 30, 1942. According to the diary, the money was picked up in Toronto by Andrew Brewin of Noseworthy's campaign staff. In a letter to the author, dated Nov. 23, 1966, Mr. Brewin stated that his recollection was that there was no direct contribution from the Liberals. (I am indebted to the Rev. Neil McKenty, author of a forthcoming profile of Mitchell Hepburn, for drawing the Lambert Diaries to my attention.)
56 The possibility exists, however, that additional funds could have been transferred by the Liberal "bag man" in Toronto. See *ibid.*, Jan. 31, 1942.
57 *Toronto Daily Star*, Feb. 7, 1942, p. 21. Meighen alleged that the King government had forced those Liberals who had endorsed him to withdraw their support on pain of losing their war contracts (Meighen Papers, Meighen to Bird, Feb. 17, 1942, and Meighen to T. Ropp, July 9, 1957). Best, the only Liberal to publicly withdraw his support, vigorously denies that any pressure was put upon him (letter to author, Oct. 19, 1964).

No evidence at all has been discovered, other than Meighen's letters, that Liberal "wardheelers" campaigned for Noseworthy (Graham, *Meighen*, III, 126–7). Jolliffe stated that some Liberals appeared with cars

88 Section One: Conscription

on election day to drive voters to the polls, but he emphatically denied that there was additional assistance (Jolliffe Interview).

58 The following table, derived from Chief Electoral Officer, *Report on the General Election of 1940* (Ottawa, 1941) and *Report on By-Elections Held* in 1942 (Ottawa, 1943), shows the distribution of the vote in 1940 and 1942:

		Forest Hill	York Twp.	Weston	Total
	Lib.	2,138	9,586	1,140	12,864
1940	Con.	2,454	11,720	1,172	15,346
	C.C.F.	350	4,742	280	5,372
	Lib.				
1942	Con.	3,218	7,683	1,051	11,952
	C.C.F.	1,681	13,565	1,162	16,408

Details of polls won and lost are derived from the *Reports* and from the *Toronto Daily Star*, Feb. 10, 1942, p 8.

Professor Grahams assessment – "the bulk of the normally Liberal vote had gone to Noseworthy" – seems questionable in the light of the above examination *(Meighen, III, 130)*

59 *Toronto Daily Star*, Feb. 9, 1942, p. 10
60 *Canada Gazette*, LXXV (June 23, 1942), "Statement of the Result of the Plebiscite... ." The results in York South were 29,860 in favour of releasing the government from its pledges and 1,178 against.
61 Pickersgill, *Mackenzie King Record*, I, 348. King was so pleased by the defeat of his hated antagonist that he told C.C.F. leader M.J. Coldwell that "if titles were in order, I'd make you a K.C.B." (The Hon. M. J. Coldwell Interview, July 6, 1963).
62 Meighen Papers, Meighen to M.G. O'Leary, Feb. 12, 1942. This paragraph is repeated in at least two other letters by Meighen (Hanson Papers, File P-450-M, Meighen to Hanson, Feb. 11, 1942; Bonar Law-Bennett Library, University of New Brunswick, R.B. Bennett Papers, Meighen to Bennett, Feb. 12, 1942). Cf. Adamson Papers, Diary, entries for Feb. 6, 7, 9, 1942
63 Arthur Meighen, *Unrevised and Unrepented: Debating Speeches and Others* (Toronto, 1949), p. 420 (speech of Dec. 9, 1942); Toronto *Globe and Mail* Feb. 10, 1942, p. 1. No voting arrangements were made then (or now) for military voters outside their home constituencies in by-elections. Chief Electoral Officer, *The Canadian Forces Voting Rules* (Ottawa, 1960), p. 7.
64 *Toronto Daily Star*, Feb. 10, 1942, p. 5.
65 Meighen Papers, Statement, March 31, 1942: "True the device of a plebiscite is evasive, dilatory and un-British... . But this disgraceful thing is upon us... .'
66 Coldwell, *Left Turn, Canada*, p. 26
67 The C.C.F. had 29 per cent, the Liberals and Conservatives each 28 per cent. Letter to author from Mrs. B.H. Sanders, director of the Canadian Institute of Public Opinion, Feb. 7, 1962.

Chapter Five

The "Hard" Obligations of Citizenship: The Second World War in Canada

In the spring of 1944, the leadership of the Canadian army in Canada was exerting itself to persuade approximately 60,000 home-defence conscripts enrolled under the National Resources Mobilization Act (NRMA) to volunteer for active service overseas. Some of the conscripts, derisively labelled "Zombies" by a harshly critical public in English Canada, had been in the army since 1941, and after years of similar efforts to persuade them, they were by now well-hardened to resist appeals to their patriotism.

The main effort to "convert" Zombies into general service volunteers was taking place at Vernon, B.C. 13 Canadian Infantry Brigade had some 5,000 men, almost all of whom, except for the officers and some of the non-commissioned officers, were conscripts, many of them French-speaking. The brigade's commander was Brigadier W.H.S. Macklin, a permanent force officer of intelligence and ability. In May, Brig. Macklin sent a long report on his efforts at conversion. He and his officers had spoken to the men of all the infantry battalions in groups, and battalion officers had interviewed their men individually. The Protestant and Roman Catholic padres had added their support, the senior Catholic padre telling Macklin that "he had reduced more than one man to tears without succeeding in persuading the man to enlist." Distinguished veterans of the fighting in Italy also spoke to the troops, including Major Paul Triquet, a Victoria Cross winner with the famous "Van Doos."

The results were better than some might have expected, with 769 men "going active," but there remained a large group of NRMA soldiers who simply could not be persuaded to volunteer for active duty, who "resisted successfully every appeal to their manhood and citizenship." Macklin tried to explain why by noting the differences between general service soldiers and conscripts:

> The volunteer feels himself a man quite apart from the N.R.M.A. man. He regards himself as a free man who had the courage to make a decision. He

seldom takes the trouble to analyze the manifold reasons put forward by those who won't enlist. He lumps them all together as no more than feeble excuses masking cowardice, selfishness and bad citizenship. In many cases no doubt he is right ... The rift is there all the time ... It can be detected with ease in the attitude of the men. The volunteer is conscious of his position. He is proud of it. He is anxious to work. He salutes his officers and speaks to them with self-confidence. The N.R.M.A. soldier slouches at his work. He tends to become sullen. He nurses his fancied grudge against "the Army" ... He has little self-respect and therefore little respect for his officers.

Many of the French-Canadian conscripts – or so the commanding officer of le Regiment de Hull, Lt.-Col. L.J. St Laurent, said in an appendix to Macklin's report – were willing to serve overseas, but only if the government ordered them to do so: "These men have never been trained from childhood to make important decisions or to think for themselves. They have always been led or advised. They are not yet fully educated for democracy." Others were "passionately and strongly attached to women's apron strings with a childish simplicity. Their mothers, wives or sweethearts have warned them that to sign active ... would break their hearts." Still others did not want to fight for "the English" or "les Anglais," for so they saw the Second World War. History and prejudice, in other words, also played their part.

And what of the English-speaking NRMA soldiers? Macklin was blunt in his assessment of their reasons for refusing to volunteer:

> they vary all the way from a large number who have no patriotism at all or national feeling whatever, to a few intelligent men who, I believe, honestly think that by holding out they will force the Government to adopt Conscription [for overseas service] which they feel is the only fair system.
>
> The great majority are of non-British origin – German, Italian, and Slavic nationalities of origin probably predominating.[1] Moreover most of them come from farms. They are of deplorably low education, know almost nothing of Canadian or British history and in fact are typical European peasants, with a passionate attachment for the land. A good many of them speak their native tongues much more fluently than they speak English and amongst them the ancient racial grudges and prejudices of Europe still persist. Here again the process of converting these men into free citizens of a free country willing to volunteer and die for their country will be a matter of education, and I think it will be slow. At present there is negligible national pride or patriotism among them. They are not like Cromwell's "Good Soldier" who "knows what he fights for and loves what he knows." They do not know what they are fighting for and they love nothing but themselves and their land.[2]

Macklin's long assessment had much that was wrong with it. His contrast of the Zombies, slouching and lacking confidence, with the general service soldiers, proud and saluting with zeal, is almost glibly ludicrous, especially when it must have taken some substantial courage and confidence in their position for the conscript soldiers to resist the combined pro-volunteer forces of public, press, army brass, and the GS soldiers around them. Even so, there was much that was correct about the report, most notably its comments that might be lumped together under the heading of "building citizenship." If Macklin could be believed, Canada in the Second World War was paying a price for its troubled history, which had pitted French against English for three centuries, and for its failure to integrate effectively its relatively recent immigrants and to teach them to accept the traditions and values of Canada. The "hard" obligation of citizenship, the willingness to volunteer and die for their country, however crudely that thought was phrased in the brigadier's memorandum, was something that many Canadians of all origins had accepted during the war. That the obligation was far from universally accepted, however, was all too clear, as the experience of 13 Brigade made clear.

Why? Why were so many Canadians apparently unaware of the importance of the issues at stake in the Second World War, as just a war as the world has ever seen and one that brought U-boat sinkings into the Gulf of St Lawrence and an attack by a Japanese submarine on the west coast?

The reasons are complex, too much so to be easily simplified. For French Canadians, they relate back to the Conquest of 1760, to the sense of having been conquered by an alien race, culture, and religion. How then could Quebec join willingly in defending the British crown when it was that crown – and its English-Canadian adherents – who ruled over them, scorned their language and faith, and discriminated against them in manifold ways? Even after Confederation, the military forces of the new dominion were British in composition, outlook, appearance, and training; efforts to create Quebec regiments that, for example, might wear the Algerian-style uniform of Papal Zouaves foundered on Ottawa's insistence that such garb was un-British – and its unstated concerns that overt military Catholicism was equally so.*

---

* Such attitudes persisted into the Second World War, and Quebecois reacted sharply against them. A French-speaking member of the Canadian Women's Army Corps, undergoing language training in Kitchener, Ontario, recalled a skit at course's end where *Québécoises* sang: "Vous n'aurez pas les petites Canadiennes / Et malgré vous, nous resterons françaises / Vous avez pu angliciser la plaine / Mais notre coeur, vous ne l'aurez jamais." Quoted in Carolyn Gossage. *Greatcoats and Glamour Boots. Canadian Women at War (1939–1995) (Toronto 1991)*, 45–6

Imperial wars such as the South African War, where the Boers, a small people much like French Canada, were crushed by the full weight of the empire, and the Great War, where English-speaking Canadians demanded that everyone rush to defend Britain's interests, only reinforced the reluctance of *Québécois* to participate in the military affairs of Canada.[3] Moreover, the shock to the country produced by the conscription crisis of 1917 meant that in the postwar years politicians pledged repeatedly that war would never come again and, even if it did, conscription would never be employed. Quebec's resistance to compulsory military service in 1917 had effectively altered the political debate in Canada.

For those of non-British origin in the rest of Canada, the reaction to war was not dissimilar. For a Ukrainian, a Pole, a German, or an Italian, Britain's wars were not necessarily just, and rhetoric about the need to serve king and country in a scarlet tunic on a parade square in peacetime inevitably rang as hollow as the demand to serve in muddy khaki in a trench in Flanders. The almost automatic firings of foreign-born workers at the outbreak of war in 1914, the internment of citizens of Germany and Austria-Hungary, and the wholesale gerrymander of 1917, when the Wartime Elections Act stripped recently naturalized Canadians of the franchise, all reinforced a natural tendency to keep to one's own kind.[4]

Worse still, the lesson that ought to have emerged from the wartime experience simply failed to do so. Instead of making every effort to integrate the French-speaking, politicians in both major national parties devoted themselves to winning Quebec's support by seeking more independence for Canada, a worthwhile and long overdue aim but one that implied that the country's national interests would be the major determinant in deciding which, if any, wars to fight. Such interests, of course, were never defined. Conscription became *the* shibboleth phrase, never to be uttered except to frighten voters at election time. And the armed forces were reduced to such a level of inconsequence that scarcely anyone could conceive of Canada being able to fight successfully any state more powerful than Liechtenstein.[5]

For those of non-British stock, the nation did almost nothing to bind up the wounds of the Great War. There were no attempts worth recounting to integrate those of other than British or French stock into Canada's life and values. The comments of one Ukrainian Canadian growing up in post-war rural Saskatchewan may be taken as typical: "There was no outside world for us. Our own world was very closed – it was the only one we knew. We were so removed! This was the early twenties – our world was Ukrainian. We did what we did in our own way, in the way we felt like doing it. We were all the same, basically one single Ukrainian community, joined together by bonds of national identity and especially by a shared language. We lived Ukrainian ... Everything we did in daily life was permeated with this sense of being Ukrainian, even though we were living in Canada."[6]

Public school education, while compulsory, did little to crack such ethnic exclusiveness. The singing of "God Save the King," "Rule Britannia," and "The Maple Leaf For Ever," and the reciting of patriotic poetry, could do little in and of themselves to teach the values of the wider Canadian community. What was peculiarly and distinctively Canadian about such values as were taught was similarly unclear. British imperial patriotism – the legacy of Nelson, Wellington, and Haig and a map that was heavily painted with red – did little to commend itself automatically to non-British immigrants. And Canada, a country whose nationalism and sense of itself then and later were still largely unformed, had almost nothing else to put in its place other than the much-expressed conviction that the dominion was different from – and better than – the United States. Of course, this situation was less true in Quebec, insulated by language and where the church controlled education and where "la race" was popularly seen to be in danger. If French Canada had its own concept of self, the Canadian tragedy was that there was little sense of shared values as they were understood in the rest of the country; moreover, the anti-immigrant attitudes in Quebec were quite possibly the sharpest in Canada.

The result of these failures was clear. By the 1930s, as fascist leaders in Europe and Asia began their march toward another war, domestic fascism made substantial inroads in Quebec primarily and to a slightly lesser extent in other parts of the country. Anti-Semitism and anti-immigration feelings were widespread.[7] At the same time, Nazi and Fascist elements, actively sponsored by the German and Italian consulates, were at work. The consuls distributed propaganda, shaped the educational curricula in schools they sponsored, raised money and volunteers for "patriotic" causes such as the Italian war against Ethiopia, and set up Fasci or Deutscher Bund societies, most especially in Toronto, Montreal, and on some parts of the prairies.[8] The Canadian government did nothing to check such activities which were, after all, largely legal. The Royal Canadian Mounted Police, obsessed with the hunting down of Communists and so understrength that it could provide almost no Italian or German translators to read the foreign-language newspapers, could be of only limited assistance. And until the Germans' seizure of the rump state of Czechoslovakia in March 1939, the Canadian government continued to advertise in Nazi and Fascist newspapers published in Canada.

The chief bureaucrat in Ottawa in charge of formulating a response to what, by spring 1939, was at last recognized as a problem was Norman Robertson of the Department of External Affairs. Shrewd, intelligent, and sympathetic to the difficulties that immigrants to Canada had to face, he made suggestions that were both hard and soft in character. He urged the government to cease its "administrative encouragement" of Nazi and Fascist groups by stopping its advertising and by blocking government employment for "notorious fascists." "The lower middle class attitudes and origins of Fascist and Nazi groups make them particularly susceptible to this sort of social ostracism," he said, adding that Fascists should be "sent to Coventry with the Communists." The government could also employ tax audits as a weapon, refuse immigrant entry to propagandists, and ensure that a close check was made of the records of applicants for naturalization from Germany and Italy, "in the same way that the Police now check the records of persons believed to be of radical or communist sympathies." The government could also consider revoking the naturalization of those whose membership in Nazi or Fascist organizations such as the Bund or the Fasci was "incompatible with the loyal fulfillment of the oath of allegiance they have taken on naturalization."[9]

Robertson was a genuine "small-l" liberal, and, while such suggestions troubled him, he believed that the state had the right and duty to defend itself against those who would destroy it. But he recognized that many of the German and Italian Canadians caught up in the Bundist and Fasci activities were almost literally blameless, so little had Canada done to suggest what was or was not expected of them. In a memorandum written about the same time as his hard-line one, Robertson had pointed to the steps that might yet be taken to correct the situation. These included English classes "under Canadian auspices – night schools and adult education associations" and the possibility of giving "preferred employment to refugees," something that no government would have lightly contemplated in the Depression. He also wanted social work among immigrant groups, and he lamented that "we've lacked a Jane Addams – no Hull House or Henry Street Settlement – nor any University Settlement work worth mentioning." Other things could be done, too, such as provision of legal aid and medicine for the poor, use of the CBC and National Film Board to instil citizenship, outreach by the political parties, and enlistment of the churches and such organizations as the YMCA into the process of Canadianization. The goal was "a positive affirmation of [the] concept of Canadian Citizenship based on loyalty & domicile [and the] repudiation of 'blood & soil.'"[10]

Even if the government had had the will to act along those lines – and there was no indication that it did – the outbreak of war came too soon, and suspect Germans, German Canadians, Communists, Italians and Italian Canadians, and Japanese and Japanese Canadians were eventually rounded up and interned. The RCMP, often lacking hard information about such elements in the population, proposed broad-brush action, but Robertson largely short-circuited that. Instead, only the leaders and those suspected of treasonous activities were arrested and interned, though not without complaint, then and subsequently, from civil libertarians.[11] In all, 2,423 people were arrested during the course of the war, including 847 Germans, 632 Italians, and 782 Japanese, although only 263 remained in internment at war's end.[12]

How much of a threat those interned amounted to is unclear. Certainly there were no cases of sabotage attributed to German, Italian, or Japanese sympathizers. Robert Keyserlingk's assessment seems largely justified: "The main purpose of moves against German Canadians was less to turn up dangerous agents than to calm the public and make it appear that the government was in control of the Nazi threat at home." His conclusion would fit the Italians and Japanese as well.[13]

What impact the government's actions had on the public – and on ethnic Canadians – is less clear than the intent. Barry Broadfoot recounts the story of an Alberta family of German descent that had all four of its sons in the armed forces. "My father, he didn't say much," Broadfoot's interviewee put it, "but my mother said that all the boys, every one, had to go into the war so that this would prove that we were good Canadians."[14] When the government asked Canadians to release it from its pledges against conscription for overseas service in April 1942, those areas in the west with heavy concentrations of German- or Ukrainian-Canadian voters said "no" by large majorities.'[15] That support at home, much as Brigadier Macklin and his officers would lament years later, must have reinforced the reluctance of home-defence conscripts from those communities to volunteer for overseas service.

So too did the discrimination that ethnic Canadians faced all across Canada. A 1943 report by the Wartime Information Board, the government's propaganda agency, suggested that many immigrant groups were isolated and suffered from low morale: "Letters still appear in the press complaining that 'foreigners' are staying home and taking the jobs of 'real' Canadians who enlist. If this is so, it is not surprising, for numbers of these people, naturalized or not, have suffered years of humiliating discrimination because of their names, accents, or appearance ... [This] cuts its victims off from the only experience which can make them feel like Canadians. And until they feel like Canadians they can have little urge to fight for Canada."[16]

That was self-evidently the case, although the government's propaganda agencies and the Nationalities Branch of the Department of National War Services had been trying for some time, in a clumsy fashion and often with hidden cash subsidies, to reach out to and influence ethnic groups. Prof. Watson Kirkconnell of McMaster University was one of those employed in this campaign. One of his efforts, a pamphlet published in 1940, argued that no European national group could be considered "alien" from the Canadian "way of life," a phrasing that left out entirely the non-white, and he urged his compatriots to "never assume that our fellow Canadians of any origin are *by nature* unworthy of our sympathy, respect and goodwill."

The extent to which such bad sociology succeeded is unclear, and W.R.Young, the leading student of Canadian wartime propaganda, concluded regretfully that "propaganda directed at the ethnic community had a divisive rather than a unifying effect."[17] Certainly that was true in the large Ukrainian community, where Communist and anti-Communist divisions remained sharp even after Ottawa brokered the formation of an umbrella Ukrainian Canadian Committee in 1940, not least because of resentment at the government's refusal to anger the Soviet Union – the ally bearing the brunt of the war against Germany – by endorsing independence for Ukraine.[18]

The dominion government had little more success in Quebec. The propaganda campaign directed at the province from Ottawa simply failed to blunt the widespread sentiment there that Canada ought not exert itself in the war. The fall of France did almost nothing to alter that view, and the new collaborationist government of Marshal Pétain, with its emphasis on "Travail, famille, patrie," was initially much admired.[19] Worse, the political promises that there would be no conscription had been repeated so often between 1919 and the national election of 1940 that they had become an article of faith.

When in April 1942, W.L. Mackenzie King's government asked the entire country to release it from the promises that it had directed at Quebec, the sense of outrage and anger from Montreal to the Gaspé was as sharp as or sharper than it had been in 1917. A massive grass-roots campaign was mounted by *la Ligue pour la défense du Canada*, a group that included Henri Bourassa, André Laurendeau, and such young leaders as Pierre-Elliott Trudeau and Jean Drapeau. The conscription plebiscite produced a huge "non" vote in Quebec – 72.9 per cent, or appreciably close to 90 per cent among French-speaking voters – and from French Canadians elsewhere in Canada.[20] King's government as a consequence was virtually forced to delay implementation of compulsory service until battle losses in Northwest Europe and Italy in late 1944 forced its hand.[21] Of course, those delays – and the undoubted additional casualties they produced when infantry battalions went into action short of their needed reinforcements[22] – produced marked outrage in English Canada and worsened relations between French Canadians and their compatriots. That King and the Liberals won re-election in the teeth of the bitterness in the country in June 1945 must be counted a near miracle – and a testament to the weakness of the opposition Tories and CCFers.

The moral of this tragic story seems clear: the dominion government could not undo its peacetime failure to integrate Quebecois and ethnic Canadians into the larger community with clumsy propagandizing crafted under the stress of war. Canadians in the Second World War were fighting for democracy and freedom, and the nation's cause ought to have commended itself to all who were fortunate enough to live here. It did not, because many Canadians, French-speaking and others, believed incorrectly that their interests, Canadian interests, were not directly threatened by Hitler, Mussolini, and Tojo. Others, victims of prejudice and discrimination or economic victimization, believed that they owed scant loyalty to a nation that had failed them. Those who had suffered from the economic collapse of the Depression could not readily have been reached by educational campaigns. But the others might have been. Had Canadian citizenship and distinctively Canadian values been inculcated in the inter-war years, the wartime selling of the "hard" obligations of citizenship might well have been easier.

Has Canada made progress in integrating all its peoples into a common idea of citizenship since the Second World War? To ask the question unfortunately is to answer it. Separatism in Quebec is at historic highs in the opinion polls, and Canada, as it has existed since 1867, may not continue for many more years. In English Canada, moreover, there is increasingly serious opposition to the policy of multiculturalism, enshrined in law for two decades, on the grounds that it has divided Canadians rather than unifying them and alienated minorities from rather than integrating them into the mainstream. Still, the inescapable facts are that there are now almost two million members of "visible minorities" among the 26 million Canadians, and the Canadians whose origins are neither British nor French now number some 38 per cent of the total. That proportion is still rising, and it may well reach 50 per cent within the next decade or so.

What are the implications of this for the "hard" obligations of citizenship? During the Gulf War of early 1991, to cite the most recent example, Canadians of Arab origin were undoubtedly treated badly and identified with the enemy government of Iraq, most often incorrectly.

The Canadian Security Intelligence Service and the RCMP mounted a heavy-handed effort to watch, interrogate, and in some cases intimidate the Arab and Muslim communities, and the media focused on those Iraqis and others who expressed support for Saddam Hussein's invasion of Kuwait. This unhappy state of affairs led a Toronto journalist, Zuhair Kashmeri, to write a book, *The Gulf Within: Canadian Arabs, Racism and the Gulf War*, and to advance a startling new direction for the foreign policy of an increasingly multicultural Canada.

Canada, Kashmeri said, "did not consider the views of its large Arab and Muslim communities before it decided to join the U.S.-sponsored coalition in the Gulf." He was certainly correct that there was no consultative mechanism in place at the beginning of the Iraqi crisis and correct, too, that the needs of Canadian Arabs and Muslims were simply overridden. For Kashmeri, this was simply unacceptable, and he quotes favourably the views of Rev. Tad Mitsui, a Japanese-born United Church of Canada minister who sees "race involved in judging who is an enemy and who is a friend. For example, Canadians will never think of America as an enemy, and neither can they think of the British or the French as enemies ... But it is so easy for Canadians to think of Arabs as the enemy." Mitsui says, "I think this is not fair. Why can't Pakistan be our friend no matter what? Why can't Iraq, to take the case to its extreme, be our friend? ... And if you expand that logic, if Canada should exist as a multicultural, multiracial country, you cannot take sides with anybody."

For Kashmeri, Mitsui's logic is clear and compelling: "Since multiculturalism advocates celebrating the differences, allowing the traditions and cultures to co-exist, the extension of that policy in foreign policy is a stance of neutrality." Neutrality in the Gulf War would have dampened the backlash suffered by Arabs and Muslims in Canada, and the fear felt by people like Mitsui and Kashmeri "is that today it is Iraqis, tomorrow it could be any of the other nationalities settled here, if Ottawa continues to fall behind Washington in the American quest for a post–Cold War 'New World Order.'"[23]

Whether Canada simply fell in behind Washington in the war with Iraq, as Kashmeri blithely concludes, is debatable. So is whether Canadian national interests can ever be separated on the major international issues from those held in the United States, the superpower with which this country uneasily shares the continent. But the Mitsui-Kashmeri views, which, if they could be extended back to 1939, would have obliged Canada to remain neutral in the war against Hitler lest German Canadians be offended, are simply not debatable in their larger thrust. Canada is not a neutral and pacifist nation, it never has been and, given its geographical location, it never can be. Canadian Arabs and Muslims unhappily felt discriminated against in early 1991 just as did Canadian

Germans in 1914 and 1939. But the significant point surely is that in 1991 there was no indication whatsoever that the German Canadians reacted any differently to the war with Iraq than did the majority of their fellow citizens. In other words, German Canadians over time became Canadians, shaping their political and international attitudes out of the same mix of ideas, received wisdom, and national interests as their compatriots. They had integrated into the mainstream intellectually and, in large measure, physically through intermarriage. Over time, presumably, so will the recently arrived Arabs and Muslims, despite the best efforts of Canada's Department of Multiculturalism.

But to suggest that only a policy of neutrality can preserve social peace in Canada and truly embody the national ideal of multiculturalism is utterly nonsensical. Most Canadians came to believe that Iraq was a dangerous, expansionist power in a vital region, and one that had not hesitated to invade its neighbour, to send missiles against other neighbouring states, and to use ecological terrorism as a war-fighting method. They might well have demanded that a neutral Canada drop its pacifists' cloak and stand up for the principles of collective security which it had pledged to support in the United Nations Charter and other international covenants. The prospects for an even more violent public debate if they had been denied would have been omnipresent.

The implications seem clear. If multiculturalism means toleration of ethnic and religious differences, the great majority of Canadians will support it. If, however, it means putting their political traditions aside and shaping their world-view to conform to a half-baked concept of multicultural neutrality, there is simply no doubt that the policy of multiculturalism will be tossed forcibly into the dustbin. At the end of the 1930s, Norman Robertson called for a positive affirmation of Canadian citizenship based on loyalty and domicile. During the Second World War, Brigadier Macklin sought free citizens of a free country, willing to volunteer and die for their country. Old-fashioned as they sound today in the post-Cold War era, those two approaches to the hard obligations of citizenship have much more to recommend them than a policy of multicultural neutrality devoid of substance.

NOTES

1 This was probably incorrect. A study of the 60,000 NRMA soldiers in late 1944 found roughly the national proportions of English-speaking, French-speaking, and non-British or French origin among the conscripts. See J.L. Granatstein and J.M. Hitsman, *Broken Promises: A History of Conscription in Canada* (Toronto, 1985), 207.

2 National Archives of Canada (NA), J.L. Ralston Papers, vol. 50, Mobilization of 13 Bde on an Active Basis, 2 May 1944. There is an abbreviated version of this memorandum printed in C.P. Stacey. *Arms, Men and Governments: The War Policies of Canada 1939-1945* (Ottawa, 1970), 591ff.
3 See, for example, Robert Rutherdale, "Préparons-nous à la guerre': Francophone Patriotism in Trois-Rivières at the Outbreak of the First World War," a paper presented at the Canadian Historical Association, 1989; D.P. Morton, "French Canada and War, 1868–1917: The Military Background to the Conscription Crisis of 1917," in J.L. Granatstein and R.D. Cuff, eds., *War and Society in North America* (Toronto, 1971), 84ff.
4 See Donald Avery, "Continental European Immigrant Workers in Canada 1896–1919: From Stalwart Peasants to Radical Proletariat," *Canadian Review of Sociology and Anthropology* I 2 (1975) 59ff.; and John English, *The Decline of Politics: The Conservatives and the Party System 1901–1920* (Toronto, 1977), 153ff. The response of native-born Canadians to the Great War was surprisingly cool. Of the more than 600,000 members of the Canadian Expeditionary Force who served during the war, almost exactly half were born in Britain, a figure that suggests strongly that the call of home loyalties was directly related to the country of birth.
5 Granatstein and Hitsman, *Broken Promises,* chap. 4.
6 L. Luciuk, ed., *Heroes of Their Day: The Reminiscences of Bohdan Panchuk* (Toronto, 1983), 26.
7 See, among others, Lita-Rose Betcherman, *The Swastika and the Maple Leaf Fascist Movements in Canada in the '30s* (Toronto, 1975); Michael Oliver, *The Passionate Debate: The Social and Political Ideas of Quebec Nationalism 1920–1945* (Montreal, 1991), chap. 7; and C.H. Levitt and W. Shaffir, *The Riot at Christie Pits* (Toronto, 1987).
8 See, for example, John Zucchi, *Italians in Toronto: Development of a National Identity 1875–1935* (Montreal, 1888), chap. 7; L.B. Liberati,"The Internment of Italo-Canadians during World War II, "a paper presented at the Canadian Ethnic Studies Conference 1989, 4ff; J.F. Wagner, *Brothers beyond the Sea: National Socialism in Canada* (Waterloo, 1981); and R.H. Keyserlingk, "Breaking the Nazi Plot: Canadian Government Attitudes towards German Canadians 1939–1945" in G.N. Hillmer et al., eds., *On Guard for Thee* (Ottawa, 1988), 55ff.
9 NA, Norman Robertson Papers, vol. 12, file 134, Memorandum, 24 May 1939; NA, Department of External Affairs Records, vol. 822, file 701, O.D. Skelton to Ernest Lapointe, 26 May 1939. See also J.L. Granatstein, *A Man of Influence: Norman A. Robertson and Canadian Statecraft, 1929–1968* (Ottawa, 1981), 82ff.
10 Robertson Papers, vol. 12, file 134, What can be done ..., n.d.; Granatstein, *Man of Influence,* 83.

11 Granatstein, *Man of Influence*, 83 ff.
12 Keyserlingk, "Breaking the Nazi Plot," 63–4.
13 *Ibid.*, 61. On the Japanese, see Patricia Roy et al., *Mutual Hostages: Canadians and Japanese during the Second World War* (Toronto, 1990), especially chaps. 2, 4, and 7.
14 Barry Broadfoot, *Six War Years 1939–1945: Memories of Canadians at Home and Abroad* (Toronto, 1974), 15.
15 Granatstein and Hitsman, *Broken Promises*, 171; R.J. MacDonald, "The Silent-Column: Civil Security in Saskatchewan during World War II," *Saskatchewan History* (Spring 1986) 56–7.
16 Quoted in W.R. Young, "Chauvinism and Canadianism: Canadian Ethnic Groups and the Failure of Wartime Information," in Hillmer et al., eds, *On Guard for Thee*, 43.
17 Cited in *ibid.*, 35. See also W.R. Young, "Building Citizenship: English Canada and Propaganda during the Second War," *Journal a/Canadian Studies* 16 (Autumn–Winter 1981) 123.
18 B.S. Kordan and L. Luciuk, "A Prescription for Nationbuilding: Ukrainian Canadians and the Canadian State, 1939–1945," in Hillmer et al., eds., *On Guard for Thee*, 80 ff.
19 W.R. Young, "Working for Unity: The Problems of Public Information in Quebec during the Second World War," Canadian Historical Association paper, 1979, passim.
20 Opinion polling before the plebiscite also found differences in support for conscription between those in upper-income brackets, who favoured it by 72 per cent, and those in lower brackets, whose support was only 54 per cent; urban dwellers (68 per cent) were also more supportive than rural voters (57 per cent). *Public Opinion Quarterly* 6 (Summer–Fall 1942) 312–3, 488–9.
21 Granatstein and Hitsman, *Broken Promises*, chaps. 5–6.
22 See W. Denis Whitaker and Shelagh Whitaker, *Tug of War* (Toronto, 1984), especially chap. 10.
23 Zuhair Kashmeri, *The Gulf Within* (Toronto, 1991), 126ff.

Chapter Six

Conscription and My Politics

When I graduated from the Royal Military College in 1961, I wanted to do American history in graduate school and to write about Franklin D. Roosevelt and the New Deal. But I was advised by my RMC professors that US history was too crowded a field and that Roosevelt had been overdone (amazing that they could have said that in 1961!). "There was more room in Canadian history," they said. So, ever obedient, I went off to the University of Toronto on leave without pay from the Army to do an MA and was fortunate enough to find myself in John Saywell's superb class in Canadian political history. I didn't have a topic in mind and asked Saywell to suggest something. "How about the Communist Party in World War II?" he said, adding that no one had yet done that. I duly began to read into the subject and went to Party headquarters on Cecil Street in Toronto and asked if could read their files. After some hesitation, the party officials agreed, and I began. It suddenly hit me that I was a young officer in the Canadian Army and it might not help my career to be spending afternoons on Cecil Street. So I telephoned the Intelligence officer at Central Command Headquarters in Oakville and asked him what to do. "Call Sergeant X at RCMP headquarters," he said, so I did. The Sergeant was not happy with me but promised to get back, and he soon did. I had been checked out and was OK; so had Saywell, and he wasn't a pinko, like so many professors at Toronto. And I could write on the Party providing that each time I came out of the Party headquarters, I was de-briefed.

This seemed a bit burdensome when all I wanted to do was to secure my MA, so I went to see Saywell, apologized for being the cause of his being investigated, and asked him to suggest a new subject. "How about the Conservative Party in the Second World War?" he shot back. "No one has done that either." So there I was, saved from being trapped in the sectarian ghetto of Marxism, and the subject of the Tories led inexorably to conscription.

To look at the Tories meant examining how a party self-destructed over conscription, over the legacy of the Great War, and over the insistence of former Prime Minister, Senator and once and future wartime party leader Arthur Meighen on repeating past history. To Meighen and those who thought like him, French Canadians were slackers, and the Liberals were soft on winning the war, on conscription, and on Quebec. And, of course, working on the Conservative Party in World War II led necessarily to seeing just how Mackenzie King beat the Tories, kept Quebec behind him, and the conscription issue under control. King had learned from the Great War experience, and the Conservatives and Arthur Meighen had not.

Now this was in the early 1960s just as the Quiet Revolution was getting underway. I had some understanding of Quebec, I thought, because I had gone to Collège Militaire Royal de St-Jean and lived in the province for three years. I was even – briefly – bilingual. I was predisposed to be sympathetic to the modernization of Quebec then underway, and the work I had done on the Conservative Party during the war showed me how necessary it was to study a Canadian party to understand Quebec and to come to terms with its reality.

Then from 1963 to 1966 I was in the United States at graduate school at Duke University. My PhD thesis topic was an expansion of the work I had done for Saywell – eventually published in 1967 as *The Politics of Survival: The Conservative Party 1939–1945*. I was hired at York in 1966, the same year I left the Army where I had worked at the Directorate of History at National Defence Headquarters. As the author of a book on the Conservatives – there were few others – I found myself participating in the party leadership convention of 1967, though I was never a party member. Nonetheless, I was against John Diefenbaker and against his idea of "One Canada" which I interpreted as a code word for putting Quebec in its place. And I supported the "deux nations" line that was espoused at the Tories' Montmorency policy convention and the Toronto leadership convention. I can remember trying to explain what this meant to skeptical Prairie delegates, and there is no doubt in my mind that it was my understanding of conscription and the Second World War that shaped my attitudes. And when Robert Stanfield, a moderate, intelligent man, was selected as leader and Diefenbaker was dumped, I rejoiced.

But Stanfield was not to become Prime Minister. The Liberals chose Pierre Trudeau in 1968, and he swept to power. I was not a supporter – I was resolutely NDP in my politics even though I had participated in the Tory convention of 1967 – but I was infuriated by the way some older Canadians complained about Trudeau's failure to serve in the military during the war, exactly the way Tories had complained about Mackenzie King's lack of military service during the Great War (but never Meighen's similar decision to stay in politics at home). This was anti-Trudeau, anti-Quebec racism, I was convinced. And even though I had gone to RMC and served in the peacetime Army, I was against the Vietnam War, then tearing the US apart. I have no doubt at all that this reinforced my anti-conscription attitudes. I had seen friends at Duke desperately seeking ways not to be drafted, and I had met many young US military officers there who were just as desperately eager for a chance to fight. I sided with those who did not want to go.

My attitudes were reinforced by my research on the King government during World War II, the research that eventually became *Canada's War: The Politics of the Mackenzie King Government, 1939-1945*, published in 1974. This research simply confirmed King's political genius for me because of the skilful way he had balanced the interests of English and French Canada during the hard days of war. Keeping the country together was his aim, and wartime pressures posed the worst threat to unity. He had succeeded, fending off the Opposition but also the unthinking – as I saw them – conscriptionists in his own party: Defence Minister J. Layton Ralston and Navy Minister Angus L. Macdonald and others. All the Liberals had been shaped by their Great War experience – Ralston had been a battalion commander in Flanders – and clearly all the attitudes of the Second World War had emerged from the Great War. History lived, history repeated.

After that book on the King government, I decided to write a history of conscription with J.M. Hitsman (who regrettably died while the book was in process). Now it will not surprise you that as I turned to look in depth at the Great War for the first time, I was already convinced that conscription was a bad thing. Nothing that I turned up in my research convinced me otherwise. There was the country's colonial relationship with Great Britain – and no good reason why Quebec should buy into that; there was the poorer health and earlier marriage age of Quebec men; there were the recruiting bungles of Militia minister Sam Hughes; and there was what I saw as the straight-out racism of English Canada. The election of 1917 was to me the nadir – with the charges in the press that if Laurier won, he'd win leading the cockroaches of the kitchen of Canada to victory; the claims that the Kaiser would cheer if the Liberals and anti-conscription forces won; and the charges from otherwise intelligent men that French Canadians were, because of their failure to enlist in the requisite numbers, innately cowards. I found this simply repellent, and what I wrote reflected my distaste. Indeed, I said in the preface of *Broken Promises: A History of Conscription in Canada*, published in 1976, that I fervently hoped that my children would never be conscripted for anyone's war. And I meant it.

Now my position was unquestionably based on my research – and also on the era in which I was living. I didn't support Trudeau politically, but I agreed with the Official Languages Act, and I looked with some pleasure at the rise of Quebec's self-confidence. I shared the view that Quebec had real grievances in Confederation. Conscription, after all, was one, the attempt of English Canada to make everyone fight Toronto's view of what the wars should be. I had been on the editorial board of *The Canadian Forum* which took a benign view of the possibility of Quebec independence, and I had vehemently opposed the imposition of the War Measures Act in the October Crisis of 1970. The Vietnam War was over by the time I wrote *Broken Promises,* but its effects were still being felt. There is no doubt that these things shaped my approach. Yes, I believe that the evidence also supported the view I took, but the times, I now think, were just as important.

What began to change my mind? The times, for one. I might be a bit slow, but I suddenly came to realize in 1980 that René Lévesque, a man I thought the most attractive politician in Canada, wanted to split the nation. I still remember going on a trip to do research at Bishop's University in Lennoxville, Quebec, in the spring of 1980 during the Referendum campaign and suddenly realizing that those bastards wanted to tear apart my country. The times they were a-changing for me – and for Canadians.

But what definitively swung me around was the publication of *Tug of War: The Canadian Victory that Opened Antwerp,* by Denis and Shelagh Whitaker in 1984. Whitaker had been a brave and much decorated officer in the Royal Hamilton Light Infantry in World War II, and his book on the Scheidt campaign of the fall of 1944 opened my eyes. As an infantry officer, Whitaker understood, as I had not, that men serving in understrength units were in serious danger. I had jeered at the 24,132 conscripts who had arrived in France by the Armistice in November 1918 as meaning nothing when we had enlisted 625,000 volunteers in all. I had dismissed the 16,000 NRMA men sent overseas as result of the conscription crisis of 1944 as meaningless when Canada had 750,000 men in khaki. I was wrong. The 24,000 Great War conscripts were enough to sustain the Canadian Corps for at least 6 months of heavy fighting; 16,000 home defence conscripts would have met First Canadian Army's reinforcement needs through the rest of the war.

The reason why this mattered only became clear to me after reading Whitaker's book. The casualties fell on the infantry in disproportionate numbers. An infantry battalion of 950 men could lose one-third of its men in a day, and every loss of trained soldiers, of brave soldiers – it was the bravest who suffered the most casualties – left the sections and platoons and companies understrength. A section often could be reduced to five in a second; a platoon of 30 could be at 15 in a day; a company of 120 could be reduced to 60. That understrength section, platoon, and company, that weakened battalion, had to cover the same ground and mount the same attacks. And with fewer men, the casualties increased. In other words, trained infantry reinforcements were essential to keep units up to strength and to minimize casualties. And as the army struggled in October 1944 to keep its units up to strength, it re-mustered men from other corps to the infantry. Whitaker was scathing as he explained that such men had forgotten or never knew much about infantry fighting – they simply didn't know how to arm a grenade or fire a Bren gun. They were a danger to the experienced infantry, and they were quick to become casualties. (Trained men, General Chris Vokes once said, had a 75 per cent chance of survival; untrained had none.) This was especially hard on French Canadian units, which had to scrape even harder for men because of relatively lower enlistments – and had to take on English-speaking officers because there were so few French-speaking.

The Whitaker book changed my mind about conscription and removed the blinkers from my eyes. I was a (peacetime) soldier, but I had simply not factored in the risks to the men in the field. I had not made the connection between conscription and the front, between a hundred trained reinforcements and the success of a battalion in operations. It is also true that I was predisposed to have my mind changed. The Vietnam War was long over, and I had become interested again in current defence policy and appalled by the state of the Canadian Forces. I was remembering my RMC and army roots. Moreover, I was unhappy with the Quebec bargaining position on the constitution and increasingly unsympathetic – indeed, straight out opposed – to Quebec independentist ideas and arguments which I viewed as based on lies and misrepresentations. In other words, the new information – new to me – in Whitaker fed into my growing dislike for Quebec's aspirations. And that led me to re-appraise my position on conscription.

Now was this bad? I think not. It is a good thing for historians to constantly re-assess their interpretations, and I make no apology for that. But I do wish I had been as aware as I am now of the extent to which contemporary politics had shaped my attitudes and approaches.

I think my awareness of this is most evident in *The Generals: The Canadian Army's Senior Commanders in the Second World War*, which I published in 1993. This is, I think, just about the best thing I have written, and certainly it was the easiest – the book just about wrote itself. In it, I came to terms with the impact RMC had on my personality and life, and I wrote my most balanced interpretation of conscription. In one chapter, I looked at two generals who had served with distinction in the Great War – Maurice Pope and Ken Stuart. Pope was half-French Canadian and the military adviser to Mackenzie King, with two sons overseas; Stuart was the former Chief of the General Staff and senior officer at Canadian Military Headquarters in Britain who many deem responsible for the conscription crisis of 1944. Pope saw that conscription could split the country, and he overcame his worries for his sons to argue strongly against it in November 1944. Stuart innately favoured conscription but had said it would not be necessary; then when casualties mounted and reinforcements dried up, he changed his mind and argued its necessity. Both men tried to act in good conscience; both put their definition of country and nation first; and both were correct. If I had fallen prey to the temptation to let contemporary events shape my history in the past, in *The Generals,* I think, I overcame it.

But the lesson you should draw from this is that the present shapes our understanding of the past. I am resolutely anti-ideological, and I dismiss Marxism and Marxist approaches to history as nothing but Groucho Marxism. I believe now as I have always done that the sole task of a historian is to try to understand what happened and why. But I know now that my politics, shifting and changing as I applied my analyses to events as I lived them, shaped what I wrote as a historian. I am not sure if I could have avoided this or even if this should be avoided. I only know what I did not in 1967, 1974, and 1976 – that events in which I was a participant or observer determined to some substantial extent what I wrote. I doubt we can protect against this; we can, however, be aware of it, and that at least should play a part in how we read what historians have written.

SECTION TWO

Diplomacy

Chapter Seven

"A Self-Evident National Duty": Canadian Foreign Policy, 1935–1939

J. L. GRANATSTEIN AND ROBERT BOTHWELL

"If you were to ask any Canadian," Stephen Leacock wrote in 1939, "'Do you *have* to go to war if England does,' he'd answer at once, 'Oh, no.' If you then said, 'Would you go to war if England does,' he'd answer, 'Oh, yes.' And if you asked, 'Why,' he would say, reflectively, 'Well, you see, we'd *have* to.'"[1]

Leacock's typical Canadian of 1939 had solved the conundrum that confronts the historian of Canadian foreign policy between the wars: support for Britain was first a moral duty, and a political duty, if it was one at all, a long way after. The subject of long and complicated constitutional struggles, Canadian autonomy once achieved turned out to be like free will: it existed to enhance the righteous choice. Neutrality, like the devil, was there to provide a colourful background and to ensnare unsophisticated French Canadians, occasionally fractious academics and some unwary Englishmen.

What did puzzle Canadians in the last prewar years and long after was where Prime Minister W. L. Mackenzie King stood on the question of Canada's "duty to Great Britain." Critics at the time dealt only in terms of probabilities, for until the sticking point of September 1939, neither King nor fate presented them with a clear, irretrievable decision. The fluidity of Mackenzie King's policy in external relations has continued to bedevil historians looking for clarity and consistency, if not on the public level then at least in the confidential memoranda that underlay and presumably expressed the thought of the Canadian government.

The result, however, is a more private and confidential expression of the same vagueness and imprecision that blurred King's public persona. It is, however, possible to discern certain self-contradictory rather than complementary themes in King's conduct of foreign policy. Pre-eminent was his distaste for war and fear of Canadian involvement in any future world conflict. Accompanying this wholly reasonable position was the realisation that neither Canada's international nor her internal situation would permit isolation from a major European war. Responding to these two imperatives, King's policy between 1935 and 1939 veered and wobbled according to the interpretation that he put on the international situation of the day. But as a contemporary observer recognised, King had always believed 'that *if* Britain became engaged in a serious struggle Canada would again bleed and impoverish herself on Britain's behalf'.[2] The profundity of this conviction and King's knowledge of the damage that another war could do to Canadian national unity defined his efforts-not to keep Canada out of any war, which he knew to be virtually impossible, but to encourage the possibilities of peace.

The prime minister's chosen policy for peace was appeasement. The abandonment of the restraints imposed upon Germany by the Treaty of Versailles, the reunification of the German *Volk,* the end of the pompous legalities of the League of Nations, all these commended themselves to Mackenzie King. They were objectives that could be achieved without violence, through deliberate negotiation. King had made his career out of industrial and political negotiation, and he was, as the British high commissioner in Ottawa correctly observed, "temperamentally as well as politically attracted by a policy of settlement by negotiations."[3]

King's predilections were powerfully reinforced by his domestic circumstances. The Liberal Party, which he again led to victory in 1935, had traditionally based its appeal in Quebec on its opposition to imperial adventures and, more recently, to conscription for overseas service. The leader of the federal Liberals in the province, Ernest Lapointe, was King's right-hand man and indispensable in the cabinet. At one point, King had promised Lapointe the post of secretary of state for external affairs, and the latter was disappointed when King relegated him to the Ministry of Justice in 1935 and kept External Affairs for himself. Even so, Lapointe retained his interest in foreign policy and acted as a restraint on King's initiatives in the field.[4] None of King's other ministers, however, showed more than sporadic interest in questions of foreign policy.

As secretary of state for external affairs, King headed a department of exceptional intellectual distinction. The under secretary, Dr. O.D. Skelton, had been his hand-picked choice in 1923 to direct Canada toward autonomy. Skelton could be relied upon to suspect and resist British schemes to involve Canada in imperial adventures.[5] Like Skelton, the department's counsellor, Loring Christie, was a confirmed isolationist who believed that Canada's sovereign interests could only be damaged by irresponsible foreign adventuring when the vital task was to build up Canadian strength at home. Christie even went so far in his resistance to foreign entanglements as to suggest autarky as a desirable end of Canadian policy.[6] Both of these men worked to keep Canada neutral and, in particular, neutral in British war. Under Skelton and Christie, some members of the department, such as Norman Robertson and Scott Macdonald, could nevertheless argue for Canadian support for the failing democracies of Western Europe. Skelton encouraged their criticism but ignored it. Other officers such as J.W. Pickersgill and Hugh Keenleyside, were close to the Skelton line and still others, including L.B. Pearson, then serving in London, defy categorization.[7]

Information flowing to and about Canada derived from Canadian missions abroad and foreign missions in Ottawa. Canada's two principal external posts, London and Washington, were both headed by political appointees, Vincent Massey in London and Sir Herbert Marler in Washington. While Massey was prominent and sometimes influential, he was not trusted by his prime minister who viewed him, correctly, as Anglophilic in the extreme. Massey was strictly ordered to abstain from any gesture that might give credence to Canadian participation in a common imperial foreign policy.[8] Marler, ageing and ill, was no heavyweight in diplomacy, but his inclinations reflected and even exaggerated Mackenzie King's public attitudes.[9] Both Marler and Massey soon learned that King looked on their offices as decorative post-boxes, and at no time between 1935 and 1939 was either man given significant authority to represent or interpret the views of the Canadian government Indeed, neither was even informed of crucial changes in Canadian policy. In Marler's case this did not prove particularly significant, but in Massey's there were important consequences.

Marler's weakness was partially compensated for by the ability of the American minister in Ottawa, Norman Armour. Armour's dispatches reflect his considerable ability and effectiveness. He was on good terms with Mackenzie King and regularly furnished President Franklin D. Roosevelt with information and analyses of the Canadian scene.[10] When he left Ottawa in January 1938, he was replaced by a series of short-term political appointees, none of whom had any particular impact on the Canadian scene.

The British were represented by two high commissioners during this period, Sir Francis Floud and Sir Gerald Campbell. Both were conscientious, but neither was an intimate of Mackenzie King and neither was particularly well-informed on Canadian matters. Their isolation was reflected in their despatches home, full of their dislike for Mackenzie King and their mistrust of his intentions and bona fides. In the case of

Campbell, his prior knowledge of Canada can best he epitomised by his self-description at the time of his arrival in Ottawa: "I had mighty little idea ... of what it means to a Dominion to be independent of all control from the country it once called Mother."[11]

The prime minister worked in a situation where all effective decision-making power was concentrated in his own hands and where, with the possible exception of Armour, no foreign diplomat had real influence. The government's willingness and ability to convey its thoughts on external policy to other governments was dependent entirely on the prime minister who alone could express the views of the administration. If he didn't, no one else could.

Mackenzie King's involvement with the darkening European crisis began as soon as he took office in October 1935. Italy had just invaded Ethiopia, and the Canadian government with the rest of the League had appeared to take a strong stand against aggression through the imposition of sanctions. But sanctions, as King well knew, could lead to war. His unease was reinforced by warnings of a hostile reaction from Quebec, conveyed by Ernest Lapointe. Dr. Skelton, who regarded the League as a creature of Britain and France, vigorously opposed Canadian participation in irrelevant European entanglements. Mackenzie King's subsequent exit from the sanctions dilemma was hasty and undignified: Canada would follow where others led, knowing they would not lead. The brief "Canadian initiative" of oil sanctions was disavowed.[12]

The oil sanctions were the first victim of King's preoccupation with internal tranquillity. He believed that the League and its supporters could easily lead the world to war while judicious negotiations could preserve peace. An insistence on the international status quo, symbolised for him by the League's commitment to defend its members against aggression, could jeopardize attempts to reach a more equitable, if less legalistic, settlement of grievances. The prime minister was prepared to see the League linger on, if its fangs were pulled, as a forum for international negotiation and conciliation. Such an approach, he argued, might even lure more members to Geneva, and thus create for the first time a truly universal organization.[13] But sanctions were anathema and the thought of them could provoke King into extreme statements. In 1937, for example, he treated Sir Ronald Lindsay, the British ambassador in Washington, to "a diatribe ... against sanctions.... He said that Canada was resolved to maintain neutrality in any war at any price, and that on no account would she be dragged into any hostilities."[14] As far as Lindsay was concerned, King's "attitude corresponded very closely to that generally adopted in America."[15] For certain aspects of Canadian policy, especially where O.D. Skelton was concerned, this observation was just. As a summation of Mackenzie King, it leaves something to be desired.

King was fully aware that his background and conduct left him open to the charge of being a pro-American isolationist and, as he told the American minister in Ottawa, some called him "the American."[16] But given Canadian political and racial difficulties, what could be more natural than for King to emulate the policies of his American neighbour and remain aloof from European conflict? This interpretation gains plausibility because of King's close relationship with Roosevelt. The two met once or twice a year after 1935 for friendly consultation on Canadian-American and international problems. Moreover, when King returned to office, he told Armour "that he wanted to choose 'the American road' if we made it possible for him to do so." At the same time, Dr. Skelton emphasised that Canada had come to "a very important crossroads," not only economically but politically.as well.[17]

For his part, Armour pointed out to his superiors "the wisdom of the development of an increasingly close economic and political relationship with Canada which will protect it from the vicissitudes which might flow from the adventure of all-British economic imperialism." The dangers of standing off from Canada were "not only of an economic but also of a political nature."[18] King also told Armour that "we must stand together on all these questions" that might affect North American "mutual interest and wellbeing,"[19] and the prime minister still cherished what assistant secretary of state William Phillips called his "pet idea that Canada can play a useful role as an intermediary between the United States and Great Britain."[20]

King's policy of close relations with the United States had a British dimension, of course. He wanted to bring the two countries together as a force for peace, for if the British and the Americans could achieve economic and then political cooperation, his hopes for world stability would be greatly enhanced. King told Armour in 1936 that he was trying to impress on the British "the importance of trying to meet our [American] views ... It was up to them," he said, "to join with Canada and the United States in presenting a united front, etc., politically and economically."[21]

King's emphasis on economic agreements reflected the pre-occupation of the 1930s with economic recovery as a priority of foreign as well as domestic policy. World recovery through freer trade was a staple belief of some members of the Roosevelt administration, one that King apparently shared. This economic peace would have to apply outside the Anglo-American-Canadian triangle, too, and just before the 1937 imperial conference, Roosevelt and King concocted a plan for universal economic appeasement through a world conference to be held in Geneva. Its aim would be to dispose of the *"evils* (economic and social) ... which are the *fundamental cause of war."*[22] In brief, King hoped to involve the United States in a programme of economic appeasement.

At the same time, he believed that international conditions were steadily deteriorating. Affairs in Europe, King told secretary of state Cordell Hull, "were continuing very confused and improving but little, if any in numerous ways while they were becoming worse in other ways." He was "very discouraged."[23] The Americans had nothing to offer except preachings of economic appeasement and words of good will. In these circumstances King found "the American road" increasingly difficult to reconcile with the possibility of war, war in which Canada might be involved.

The imperial conference did nothing to reassure him. Although King had presented himself to Roosevelt and Hull as the interpreter of their views to the British, and although Armour had reported that the Canadian delegation would press for economic appeasement,[24] the conference did not turn out this way. Britain's new prime minister, Neville Chamberlain, was impatient of what he saw as the American penchant for words without deeds[25] and King does not seem to have struggled to alter his mind. The Canadian accepted an agenda that placed economic questions on the sidelines and, in addressing the assembled prime ministers of the empire, he confined himself to mentioning that, "Both the President and the Secretary of State are firmly convinced of the value and possibility of a policy of economic appeasement as a constructive means of lessening political tension. Their reciprocal tariff policy," he lamely concluded, "is a step in this direction ..."[26] The "Permanent Conference on Economic and Social Problems" over which King and Roosevelt had enthused in March was buried. That line of Anglo-American cooperation was dead and, as far as King's policy was concerned, so was economic appeasement. In the future, political appeasement would be King's principal hobbyhorse.

In the depressing state of the world in 1937, political appeasement seemed a necessity if war was to be averted. Certainly King's advisers were uniformly bleak in their world view. From London, Lester Pearson had written that "if I were responsible for Canadian policy, I would assume that war in Europe is certain within five years ..." In his view, Canada's "chief interest now is to avoid being involved in any circumstances," although, he added, "I admit we may not be able to avoid it."[27] Loring Christie had also reached that conclusion. Writing to Lord Lothian in 1936, he predicted an inevitable war into which Canada

"A Self-Evident National Duty" 117

would be dragged. Worse, the decision for war lay with England alone, not Canada.[28] But despite his assumption of futility, Christie continued to struggle against Canadian involvement right up to September 1939. His chief, Dr. Skelton, was less definite on the inevitability of war but even more convinced about the necessity of Canadian neutrality.

The problem for Mackenzie King was that despite his best efforts defence was becoming an important issue in Canadian politics. The American minister reported in May 1937 that "defence has been the dominant political question in Canada, no other subject even approaching it in sustained interest or importance."[29] The same thing was true at the imperial conference, of course.

There the British wanted to discover how far Canada would go toward setting up common defence facilities and planning for a joint economic war effort. The answer was not different than it had been at earlier imperial conferences: not very far at all. The minister of national defence, Ian Mackenzie, explained the Canadian position to the conference:

... Canadian public opinion would not, under present conditions, support any larger appropriations than those voted this year by Parliament... . Canadian public opinion was definitely opposed to extraneous commitments... . The most important contribution they could render at this time, when dark shadows seem to be hovering over the world, was, as far as possible, to preserve *unity* in their councils... .

The minister concluded by urging the conference not to weaken the links of empire "by placing too much strain on them...."[30]

The effect of Canada's determination to resist "strains" was to weaken Britain's rather fragile enthusiasm for any kind of forward policy in defence. In fact, Britain's attitudes to Canada during these years were an odd mélange of skepticism and hope. In December 1934, as the British slowly began to rearm, Sir Maurice Hankey reported that he had found only "calculating aloofness" on a visit to Ottawa. The secretary of the Committee of Imperial Defence felt compelled to raise "the brutal question of whether Canada would come to our assistance in another war," a question that Hankey resolved satisfactorily by discounting the influence of the "'highbrows,' isolationists, French Canadians, Irish disloyalists ... [and] intellectuals" and by asserting that "the men of action," whether or not they were a majority, "would be sufficiently numerous to stampede the country."[31] Two years later, with Mackenzie King in power, Hankey was less confident: "We realise that in the present state of Canadian opinion no Canadian Government could commit itself to active participation in a war...." The Dominions secretary, Malcolm MacDonald, added a minute to suggest that "We do not want Mackenzie King to think that we really contemplate Canada not being in a war with us."[32]

From the British point of view, King was being extremely difficult. Repeated attempts to secure Canadian cooperation in munitions production came to naught,[33] and when Ian Mackenzie and his prime minister held to this position at the conference, Hankey was seriously disturbed: "all our efforts at the conference failed to obtain from Canada any really satisfactory assurance that we should be able to count with certainty on obtaining supplies from her in time of war." This was vital, for "It would be clearly disastrous if we laid our plans on the assumption that we could count on Canada, and then when the day came we found that we had been building upon false premises."[34]

The major effect of the conference was to drive home to the British the need to handle Canada with care. First, since some of the information supplied by the imperial government seemed to excite opposition among the dominions, certain confidential material was withheld from the visitors. Then, the British gave in to Canadian demands (backed by South Africa) and agreed to a communiqué that was virtually meaningless wherever it touched on defence and foreign policy. Chamberlain was directly responsible for these expedients. With them he bought a façade of empire unity without which, as he told a London audience, Great Britain would be merely "a fourth-rate Power."[35]

If the British were discouraged by the results of the imperial conference, King was not. Although he indefatigably resisted British schemes at every such meeting, he was nonetheless always deeply stirred by the trappings of Empire, particularly prominent in 1937 because of the coronation of George VI. Norman Armour, for one, had shrewdly allowed for an irrational factor in King's behaviour. As he wrote in May, the prime minister "is emotional and warm-hearted. He is, for his own peace of mind in political life, too easily hurt by criticism and apt to be influenced by his surroundings...." He did not, Armour said, "wish to give the impression that Mr. King will be swept off his feet during the forthcoming conference," but it was a possibility.[36]

Armour was right. King left the heady atmosphere of the conference for Berlin where he had an audience with Herr Hitler. Before leaving, he had told Malcolm MacDonald that he would inform the Nazi leader "that if Germany should ever turn her mind from constructive to destructive efforts against the United Kingdom all the Dominions would come to her aid and that there would be great numbers of Canadians anxious to swim the Atlantic!"[37] King was as good as his word in his interview with the Fuehrer,[38] and British newspapers reported that he had made a public commitment in a speech in Paris on 2 July:

> We have our own representation in other countries [and that] is evidence of that great liberty and freedom, which, above all, we prize, and were it imperilled from any source whatever [this] would bring *us* together again in preservation of it.[39]

King's staff were appalled at what their master had done. Christie told Lothian that he doubted King himself knew what he meant in Paris.[40] Skelton reminded his prime minister that "no government of a free country can determine what course its people will follow in years to come and under circumstances which no one can now envisage, and ... it would be futile to rely on such undertakings ..."[41]

The British, of course, were delighted by King's interview with Hitler (although the high commissioner in Onawa doubted King had been as forceful as he claimed)[42] and by his Paris remarks. Chamberlain referred to the latter as a "remarkable speech" meaning "that in case of any threat toward England, it would bring Canada at once to her side."[43] Still, the British were not entirely certain of Canada, however optimistic Chamberlain might sound in public statements. Late in 1937, the Dominions Office concluded glumly that the Canadian position was doubtful in the event of war. If "democracy" were threatened and if the Canadians could be sustained by a sympathetic American attitude, then Canada might come to the aid of the mother country.[44] But the doubts were real, and there were grounds for them.

Most Canadians, the American Legation reported in mid-1937, wanted "continued membership in the British Commonwealth, and in the League of Nations, with avoidance of entanglements that might lead Canada into another overseas war."[45] How entanglements could be avoided while membership was retained was unclear, but Skelton was certain in his own mind that "From the military standpoint there can be little question that today our connection with the United Kingdom ... is, on a balance of advantages, a net liability rather than asset."[46] The chief of the general staff, however, did not see things that way. He was pleased that his officers could plan to defend Canada "and, incidentally, to make some contribution toward the defence of all those countries that may some day necessarily associate themselves for the purpose of preserving their liberties...."[47] That prospect gave External Affairs nightmares. Skelton and Christie persistently assaulted the defence estimates between 1937 and 1939 on the grounds that the military were secretly preparing an expeditionary force. If the plans were prepared and the occasion offered, the Canadian reaction would be a foregone conclusion: an expeditionary force like that of 1914.[48] Ironically, at this juncture the British themselves were still hoping to avoid sending an army to the continent. The prevailing philosophy of "limited liability" prescribed a small army and a concentration on air defence and sea power.[49]

As for Mackenzie King, he had left London in 1937 with confidence in Neville Chamberlain's sincerity and ability. "Limited liability" was a concept that appealed to him, as did Chamberlain's determination to seek a peaceful accommodation with Hitler.[50] During the winter and spring of 1937–8, therefore, there was no change in King's attitude or in the policy of the government. The internal debate continued, but no external occasion arose to disturb the tranquil surface of events. As the British government acquiesced in the *Anschluss* and prepared to sacrifice Czechoslovakia to Hitler, Canada was peaceful.[51]

The Sudetenland crisis woke the dreamers on both sides of the Atlantic, and the British again began anxiously to watch developments in the dominions. The high commissioners were their ready source of information, and Sir Francis Floud summed up the position of King and Canada in a long letter to Sir E.J. Harding, the permanent undersecretary at the Dominions Office. Mackenzie King, the high commissioner said, wanted to keep his eye "on what he considers to be the main objective, viz. the preservation of Canada's unity" and thus he was content "again and again to insist on the supremacy of Parliament as the interpreter of the people's wishes if and when the time comes." The prime minister "resolutely refuses to take any other line," Floud continued, "and it is clear that however unsatisfactory this may be for those who are charged either here or at home with working out anything in the nature of Imperial defence plans, we cannot hope, under the present regime, to get any further." Moreover, in Floud's view, Canada seemed legally "well equipped at least to avoid getting herself entangled unofficially as it were in a war in which we were engaged." This was not a view that many Canadians shared.[52] Still, the high commissioner was guardedly hopeful as he wound up his letter:

> Since it is inconceivable to you and to me that we shall embark on an aggressive war, and that any war in which we do ever get engaged will be other than a war of direct self-defence after an unprovoked attack, or a war which we are bound to wage in fulfillment of express undertakings shared by Canada or a war in which our undertakings are not actually shared by Canada but which is manifestly equivalent to a war of self-defence, it is surely equally inconceivable that Canada will not be with us in the end.

> All I myself really fear is a period of hesitancy, and I am afraid that we
> cannot necessarily count on Canada being in with us from the very begin-
> ning. There might be a delay of days, and those days might lengthen into
> perhaps two or three weeks.... After all, what is the alternative? Person-
> ally I think that whatever Canada's own attitude might be, she would be
> brought in on our side in any case by the enemy's own action.[53]

To have Canada back into war in such a fashion was not particularly palatable to many Englishmen – or to many Canadians.

But as the Czech crisis developed British fears should have eased. At first Mackenzie King carefully refrained from public statements, but in private he had made up his mind even before the press reports of German threats and Sudeten riots alarmed the public. On 31 August, he confided to his diary:

> I made it clear to both Mackenzie and Power [the Minister of National
> Defence and the Postmaster General] that I would stand for Canada doing
> all she possibly could to destroy those Powers which are basing their ac-
> tion on *might* and not on *right*, and that I would not consider being neutral
> in this situation for a moment. They both agreed that this would be the
> Cabinet's view....

Dissension in Quebec was predictable, but King made *it* clear that this would not deter him. His Quebec ministers would simply have to lead the province in seeing its obligation to participate. In that other hive of isolationism, the Department of External Affairs, Dr. Skelton told the prime minister that he agreed "that the Government could not, without suffering immediate defeat," adopt non-intervention as its policy. As Skelton read the national mood, Canada "would be strong for interven-tion and even for participation by a possible expeditionary force...."[54]

This assessment did not deter Skelton from doing his best to hold King to the straight and narrow. He reminded the prime minister on 11.September that, "we are the safest country in the world-as long as we mind our own business." He recognized the internal factors that would make it difficult for Canada to resist "the call of the blood" particu-larly from "the older and middle aged generations which control public opinion in English Canada."[55] King's response, set out in his diary, was that Skelton's memorandum was

> Excellently done, but all the way through referring only to self-interest
> of each part as determining its action, and leading to a sort of isolationist
> attitude so far as Canada is concerned. I believe myself that whilst care

must be taken as to determine the part that Canada may be called upon to play, and the steps toward that end, that our real self-interest lies in the strength of the British Empire as a whole, not in our geographic position and resources. That not to recognize this would be to ultimately destroy the only great factor for world peace, to lose the association of the United States and the British Empire and all that it would mean for world peace. That it would place Canada in an ignominious position.

I am clear in my own mind that cooperation between all parts of the Empire and the democracies is in Canada's interests in the long run and in her own immediate self-respect. The only possible attitude to be assumed.[56]

The attitude King now criticised in Skelton was precisely that which he had recently allowed to be sent out over his name. Quite evidently, King too felt "the call of the blood."[57]

King reaffirmed his stand repeatedly in conversations and correspondence with his ministers. To Charles Dunning, the minister of finance, he wrote on 3 September that "My mind is wholly clear as to the course we should pursue."[58] He spoke to Norman Rogers, the minister of labour and, some said, King's favourite among his ministers, and recorded that

> We both agreed that it was a self-evident national duty, if Britain entered the war, that Canada should regard herself as part of the British Empire, one of the nations of the sisterhood of nations, which should cooperate lending every assistance possible, in no way asserting neutrality, but carefully defining in what ways and how far she would participate.[59]

The next day, 14 September, Chamberlain's decision to fly to Germany to see Hitler was announced. It is doubtful that King knew of this in advance, but it is abundantly evident that he approved of Chamberlain's dramatic gesture. "I am sure," his public statement proclaimed, "the whole Canadian people will warmly approve this striking and noble action on the pan of Mr. Chamberlain. Direct personal contact is the most effective means of clearing away the tensions and misunderstandings that have marked the course of events in Europe in recent months...."[60] King thus reinforced Chamberlain's peace policy, but he did not go so far as to indicate in public what Canada would do if Chamberlain's mission failed.

There was no one who could tell London of Canadian policy for the prime minister did not confide his thoughts on Canada's "self-evident national duty" to Vincent Massey. As the high commissioner later wrote, he received no messages of any kind from King in this period.[61] Massey had his own views, however, and he criticised the "timid and isolationist Canadian Government" and its "inert" prime minister, at the same time as he assured the editor of *The Times* that he personally was "all against a world war fought with the object of keeping large dissident minorities under Czechoslovak rule."[62] A few days earlier, however, he had told the dominions secretary that "he had no doubt that if Great Britain got involved in war, Canada also would be in the war."[63] As the crisis developed, Massey was sent a copy of King's statement of 17 September, in which the Canadian government expressed its appreciation for Chamberlain's "efforts to preserve the peace of Central Europe." Beyond that, the statement did not commit Canada to a predetermined course of action in "hypothetical contingencies."[64]

For a while it seemed that Chamberlain's first visit to Hitler had achieved the basis of a peaceful settlement. His second visit on 22 and 23 September was far less hopeful and war again seemed close. In Ottawa, the prime minister met with his cabinet to decide if the government should issue a statement of its intentions should Chamberlain's mission fail. Mackenzie King had envisaged "as expressive of our position" a statement that, "The world might as well know that should the occasion arise, Canada will not stand idly by and see modem civilisation ruthlessly destroyed." Skelton was predictably "greatly shocked at this," King recorded, "and felt it was going back on my whole position with respect to having Parliament decide, etc. I told him I thought we would have to indicate long before Parliament met what our policy would be, though Parliament itself would decide whether that policy should be carried out." In cabinet, King found that W.D. Euler from Ontario was flatly against any statement and against war, and at least one other minister insisted that parliament should really decide Canada's course.[65] From Geneva, Ernest Lapointe also discouraged a statement and deplored the turn of events.[66] Under the circumstances caution won out and King decided to withhold his statement although, as Christie later told a friend, "he felt like a cad" in so doing.[67]

The crisis grew worse over the next few days as the British government struggled to find a way out that would at once preserve peace and the appearance of peaceful concession while still satisfying Hitler. Massey reported on 26 September that he along with the other high commissioners had spent most of an hour with Chamberlain "and heard from him intimate accounts of his efforts.... My impression is that he and his Government feel that they have exhausted every means of avoiding catastrophe and that they are none too confident that it can be averted."[68]

The Canadian cabinet met again on 27 September. Mackenzie King presented another draft statement for approval, this one being less specific and noting only that Canada was in complete accord with

Chamberlain's policy. There was still dissension, however, and King tried to counter it by remarking that

> I doubted if the British would send an expeditionary force to Europe; did not think an expeditionary force would be expected from Canada. That our part would probably consist in supplying munitions, air pilots, etc., and looking after our own defences.

Reflecting on the meeting, King characteristically sounded a high note:

> Personally, I feel very strongly that the issue is one of the great moral issues of the world, and that one cannot afford to be neutral on an issue of the kind.[69]

The statement was approved and duly issued, simply urging the country to "keep united" and adding that the government "is in complete accord with the statement Mr. Chamberlain has made to the world today."[70]

King's public statements were all the British had to go on in their estimates of Canadian policy. From the uninformed Massey, they gathered that Canada would be a reluctant combatant at best. From Ottawa, Sir Francis Floud had predicted "hesitancy" but eventual participation. But descriptions of the climate of opinion were far different from official promises. Lacking reliable reports on Canada, the British seem to have lumped it with the other dominions into something called "Dominion opinion." The result has been that from 1938 on historians have regularly invoked the dominions as "obscure but important factors."[71] There was more obscurity than importance from the Canadian side. At no point did King threaten Chamberlain by withdrawing his support; at no time did he encourage him by openly promising it. The influence of such a non-policy lies entirely in the eye of the beholder.

American observers in Ottawa had no doubt which course Canada would follow. The legation reported that "as the crisis became more acute, Canadian opinion fell strongly behind the line of action taken by Mr. Chamberlain. This was demonstrated not only in the press but also by the expression of officials in Onawa."[72] Certainly this was an accurate reflection of the prime minister's attitude. But there were others including some who shared the prime minister's readiness to back Britain, who were sceptical of the vocal interventionist support. Dr. R.J. Manion, the Conservative Party chief and the leader of the opposition, characterized the pro-British enthusiasts to his son as "the usual crowd of old bachelors and childless parents."[73] Dr. Skelton, too, was convinced that opinion in Canada was shaped by middle-aged

Anglo-Saxon enthusiasts. Youth, he hoped, would be on the side of peace.[74]

Almost everyone was relieved by the dénouement at Munich. The American legation reported "great relief,"[75] while Mackenzie King publicly rejoiced and privately buried the potential divisions in his cabinet. Almost a year later he admitted to the governor-general that he had had serious doubts about his ability to bring a united cabinet and country into a war in September, 1938.[76] Some Canadians, however, saw the Munich settlement with a jaundiced eye. Four days after the agreement, Skelton pointed out that, "The settlement is not one to be proud of in itself."[77] Christie was pleased that peace was preserved but he saw danger from the east. Russia, he argued, would try to provoke a war between Germany and the Western powers.[78] From London, Lester Pearson predicted another crisis:

> I am pessimistic enough to think that an armaments race is not necessary to cause trouble: the nature of the German state, the aggressive spirit of Nazi-ism, the feeling of triumph through power from recent successes, and the equally strong feeling of British and French impotence, should be enough to cause another crisis before long.[79]

But for the time being there was peace, and King and Skelton took the opportunity for a vacation cruise in the Caribbean. Naturally, they refought the events of the past few months, and Skelton used the opportunity once again to press his autonomist theories on his chief. His arguments were familiar enough, but King's reactions were not. In Kingston, Jamaica, the prime minister summed up his undersecretary as "a Canadian, pure and simple, [who] did not feel British connection meant anything except the possibility of being drawn into European wars; thought the younger generation were all against it."[80] And when Skelton stated that Canada relied for its security on the United States, King was perturbed:

> I do not like to be dependent on the U.S.; change of leaders there might lead to a vassalage so far as our Dominion was concerned. There was more real freedom in the British Commonwealth of Nations, and a richer inheritance. This I truly believe.[81]

In fact, King found himself fundamentally in disagreement with Skelton:

> ... I felt more and more-the materialistic "scientific" point of view which Skelton had in all things – a critical frame of mind, also a "republican" attitude. I felt his negative viewpoint and inferiority complex in so many

things – a real antagonism towards monarchical institutions and Britain, a sort of communist sympathy – lack of larger view in reference to world affairs – an isolated Canada – which I cannot accept. It told on me and him, and raised a sort of wall of separation between us. He seeks to dominate one's thought, is intellectually arrogant in some respects.... I can see I must control policy and be the judge of my own conduct and other affairs – to lead and not be controlled, while in many ways he is the best of Counsellors and guides....[82]

Yet for months after Munich, King's public policy was scarcely distinguishable from Skelton's private opinions. In cabinet, however, he seldom deviated from his decision at the time of Munich to come to Britain's aid if need be. He told the defence committee of the cabinet that the "gangster nations" were a threat and that Canada had to be prepared against them.[83] (Not so prepared, however, as to indulge in reckless spending after the "emergency" had passed. Defence estimates were still watched closely and pared to the bone.[84]) In December, King emphasised the dangers of the situation to cabinet "to show [them] the necessity of Canada joining with other nations in impressing Dictators with the determination of the Democracies to make themselves more powerful to resist aggression."[85] On 16 January he quoted Sir Wilfrid Laurier's 1910 dictum to the House of Commons:

If England is at war we are at war and liable to attack. I do not say we will always be attacked; neither do I say that we would take part in all the wars of England. That is a matter that must be guided by circumstances, upon which the Canadian parliament will have to pronounce and will have to decide in its own best judgment.

Later that day King wrote that, "... I simply developed what had been most in my mind and particularly in regard to Canada's relations to Britain in time of war, made up my mind that I would not allow myself to take the one-sided view that I was crowded into, speaking on External Affairs, last session which ignored the possibility of Canada being at war when Britain was at war." Finally, with a new scare filling the telegrams from London, King told his ministers at the end of January that Canada would be attacked if Britain was at war. Lapointe conceded that Canada would indeed be involved in such a war, but the minister of justice urged delay in making any pronouncement until public opinion matured further. King agreed.[86]

Political realism might dictate delay but it also prescribed the policy that eventually emerged. Christie remarked cynically that, "A

Government does not determine its own activities – its activities are determined for it by the course of events."[87] The Canadians now had only to wait for the course of events to manifest itself. In the meantime, King sternly rejected all attempts by Skelton to lead him back to belief in the old policy of "no commitments." His "only mistake" so far, he wrote in his diary, had been in not saying "what was the real position about the reality side of things, thereby letting it be assumed that I was indifferent to this aspect, and was holding solely to the academic position – crisis or no crisis."[88]

A crisis there soon was. On 15 March 1939 Hitler seized what remained of Czechoslovakia. Two days later, Chamberlain was forced to denounce the German action and mentioned in his remarks that the dominions supported Britain. He was, his biographer noted, "informed by strong representations as to opinion in the House, the public, and the Dominions ..."[89] Mackenzie King was annoyed by the implication that he had been consulted on the shift in British policy to a harder line. "I wish very much that he had made no mention of other parts of the British Empire," he wrote, "as it immediately raises the most difficult question with which we are faced in Parliament. It gives the jingos a chance to press for a clear cut statement on standing by Britain, and [it is] more difficult to make clear the wisdom of giving no blank cheque with respect to wars."[90]

Skelton seized the opportunity to warn King once more of the folly of relying on Chamberlain. The British leader's qualities, whatever else they were, were not those of a diplomat: "He is a self-confident to the point of arrogance, intolerant of criticism, and at the moment sore because he thinks in the eyes of the world Hitler has made a fool of him." Worse, he was descended from the hereditary enemy of all Liberals:

> He is also a Chamberlain, born and bred in a Tory imperialist school, and cannot imagine that any part of the British Empire has any choice but to halt when he says halt and march when he says march. Hence his references, unconscious or deliberate, to turning to our partners in the British Commonwealth, to having the approval of the whole British Commonwealth for declarations of which they knew nothing in advance ... Hence also other British Ministers calmly announcing what "our Dominions" will do. They are not men to whom blank cheques may safely be given.[91]

King's mood was cautious, therefore, in the last week of March. When Sir Gerald Campbell, Floud's successor at the High Commission in Ottawa, came to call on 24 March, King read him a lecture. The prime minister was worried, Campbell reported, that Canada might be invited to join an alliance between England and eastern European countries. "This he said would cause grave embarrassment and in particular he expressed regret that it should apparently have been necessary for the United Kingdom to associate herself with the U.S.S.R." A "Balkan dispute" would not be a sufficient *casus belli* for Canada, King warned. The high commissioner concluded that King was "if anything less disposed to cooperate with other countries in the defence of democracy than is the Government of the United States."[92]

Campbell's harsh words were understandable, but he seemed to be neglecting King's long-contemplated public statement of Canada's position in the event of war on 20 March. In it, the prime minister went further than ever before, telling parliament that if there was any danger of bombs raining on London, Canada would step forward to Britain's aid.[93] But after marching two steps to the front, King characteristically took one pace back when on 30 March he spoke again to the House of Commons. He worried beforehand that his remarks would not be "as immediately helpful to Britain as I should like ... but, in the long run, [it is] the kind of thing that will keep this country together, and enable us to do most effectively in the end whatever may be decided upon."[94] The speech was Skeltonian both in conception and in phraseology:

> The idea that every twenty years this country should automatically and as a matter of course take part in a war overseas for democracy or self-determination of other small nations, that a country which has all it can do to run itself should feel called upon to save, periodically, a continent that cannot run itself, and to these ends to risk the lives of its people, risk bankruptcy and political disunion, seems to many a nightmare and sheer madness.[95]

The prime minister's policy clearly was to balance bellicosity with caution; the requirements of the domestic scene demanded this.

King's careful speech of 30 March was balanced the next day by a vigorous attack on the idea of Canadian neutrality from Ernest Lapointe. Taken together, the two helped lay the ghost of conscription at the same time as they reassured those unduly concerned over King's firmness ten days before. The prime minister accurately gauged the effect of the speeches. He would "suffer ... from an impression of aloofness so far as relations between Canada and Britain are concerned," but with Lapointe's, the two speeches amounted to "a sort of trestle sustaining the structure which would serve to unite divergent parts of Canada, thereby making for a united country."[96]

The long-run significance of King's position in March 1939 lies more in the hidden diary than in the public utterances. King wanted to support Britain, and his statement on March 20 was an accurate reflection of everything he had been saying since the Imperial Conference of 1937, if not before. His concern on March 30 was to bind up national unity, then as always *his* fundamental preoccupation. It was a classic case of *reculer pour mieux sauter.*

Still, British policy could infuriate him, and Skelton's analysis of Chamberlain's underlying attitude to the dominions was proving more and more perceptive. On 31 March Chamberlain extended an unconditional British guarantee to Poland and Rumania. In effect, Canada was now committed to support Poland in precisely those hypothetical circumstances against which Skelton and Christie had always warned. And if Chamberlain's record of perspicacity in foreign affairs was uninspiring, it positively shone when compared with the Poles'. King was properly provoked at not having been consulted. "This, a conditional declaration of war was made certainly without anything in the nature of consultation or the possibility of consultation with Canada or any of the Dominions."[97] In London, the new dominions secretary, Sir Thomas Inskip, helpfully explained to the high commissioner that he had thought their governments "would not have wished that the United Kingdom should invite them to share responsibility for the decision."[98]

A month later when Sir Gerald Campbell called on King to propose a blanket statement of support for British policy, King's resentment boiled over. According to the high commissioner's account of the interview, the prime minster had said that there was

> considerable opposition in Canada to the manner in which the United Kingdom appears to be becoming entangled with Balkan and East European countries and above all with Russia. There were many people in Canada including some Ministers, and I gathered this included him, who disliked entanglements of this kind.... He could not forecast in advance of Parliament what line Canada would take if the United Kingdom went to the help of one of these countries and as a result were herself attacked.[99]

To make matters worse for the confused Campbell, King and Skelton agreed the same day that "Germany knew quite well that Canada would go into the fight if Germany were in any way an aggressor."[100]

In a curious way, King's relationship with the high commissioner was almost symbolic in nature. It was as if Campbell was there to expiate in person all the crimes and follies of Great Britain's foreign policy. The abuse and hectoring under which he suffered, however, did not mean very much, for once Campbell was disposed of King went on to indulge in an orgy of royalist and Anglophile feeling during the spring tour of George VI and Queen Elizabeth.

The royal tour evoked a fervent display of loyalty from Canadians. As L.B. Pearson wrote from London at the time, the visit "does make even more complicated certain complicating features of Canada's imperial relationship." The British public now had the "conviction that all this talk of Canadian isolation and neutrality is academic eye-wash, and that the reception given by Canada to the King has proved, if it needed proving, 'the great heart of Canada is sound.'" Pearson seemed concerned with the problem of "eradicating this impression,"[101] but time had run out.

Word arrived on 21 August that the Soviet Union would sign a non-aggression pact with Germany. Mackenzie King, who had been thinking of a fall election, abandoned his contemplations for the time being and prepared for war.[102] Dr. Skelton, who a month before had judged Lord Halifax to be "the best British Foreign Minister in years," now deplored "the greatest fiasco in British history."[103] And in his diary, King criticised the "blundering there has been in England's foreign policy all along the way."[104] None the less, democracy was at stake and the prime minister was prepared to meet the challenge.

It remained only for Dr. Skelton to write the epitaph for Canada's foreign policy as he had conceived and sporadically implemented it. On 25 August, he minuted that

> The first casualty of this war has been Canada's claim to control over her own destinies. If war comes to Poland and we take part, that war came as a consequence of commitments made by the Government of Great Britain, about which we were not in one iota consulted, and about which we were not given the slightest inkling of information in advance.[105]

Skelton was writing about his conception of foreign policy, and however closely it correlated with Mackenzie King's on certain points, it had never been the official, authorised foreign policy of the government. For both men, delay and obfuscation had been instrumental – but instrumental for different reasons. King believed that Canada would perish if it did not go to war, while Skelton believed the exact opposite. After reading Skelton's anguished memorandum, however, King felt the need to console his "best of Counsellors." He telephoned his under-secretary to say "how wholeheartedly he agreed with the memorandum of 25 August. If we get through this, Mr. King stated, there will be an Imperial Conference at which there will have to be some very plain speaking."[106]

"A Self-Evident National Duty" 131

This account of certain aspects of Canadian foreign policy between 1935 and 1939 has attempted to refute the legend of Mackenzie King the isolationist and neutralist. It has concentrated on the events of 1937 and 1938 because these were in a sense dress rehearsal for September 1939. The plot was the same, but refinements to the script were required, and some of the actors needed extra coaching. But when the prologue was ready for the audience in August 1939, it achieved its purpose.

At no point was King an isolationist in his basic conception of Canadian relations with the Empire. Between 1935 and 1939 he was convinced that events abroad would necessarily affect the peace and well-being of Canada. If collective security proved dangerous, then the world, not Canada alone, must abandon it. If economic appeasement proved ineffective, then King would support its political manifestation. The Prime Minister sought a close relationship with the United States at least partly because he thought he could influence British policy in that way, and bring Britain and the United States into a harmonious relationship – and one with stabilizing consequences for the world. When, in 1937, he decided that Canada would have to tread a road the United States could or would not, he effectively postponed his pre-occupation with bringing the United States into a "North Atlantic triangle." While relations with Roosevelt remained close, the influence of the United States on Canadian policy from 1937 to 1939 must be adjudged slight.

In many of his opinions on foreign policy, King revealed himself to be unreasonably optimistic, prejudiced and unrealistic. But in his basic perception that foreign policy can be no more effective than one's internal strength will support, he was profoundly right. King's backing and filling, his evasions and hesitations do not make inspiring reading. But his actions, particularly between 1937 and 1939, indicate his sure grasp of the public mood and his recognition that public opinion cannot be wished into existence simply because one course of action or another is "right." When King took a united Canada into the Second World War, he gave Canadians a policy that not only was right to him, but one that seemed right to them.[107]

NOTES

1 Stephen Leacock, "Canada and Monarchy," *Atlantic Monthly*, (June 1939), 735.
2 J. Pierrepont Moffat to Secretary of State, 21 Dec. 1940, in Nancy Harvison Hooker, *The Moffat Papers* (Cambridge, Mass., 1956), 342. An excellent assessment of King's concern with national unity in the late 1930s is H. Blair

132   Section Two: Diplomacy

Neatby, "Mackenzie King and National Unity," in H. L. Dyck and H.P. Krosby, *Empire and Nations* (Toronto, 1969), 54 ff. For a contrary view, see K.W. McNaught, "Canadian Foreign Policy and the Whig Interpretation," *Canadian Historical Association Report, 1957*, 43ff.

3 Prem. 1/242 (Public Record Office, London), High Commissioner, Ottawa, to Dominions Office, 27 Oct. 1938.
4 Sec F.W. Gibson, "The Cabinet of 1935," in F.W. Gibson (ed.), *Cabinet Formation and Bicultural Relations* (Ottawa, 1970), 115 ff.
5 Cf. Norman Hillmer, "The Anglo-Canadian Neurosis," a paper presented at "Britain and Canada: A Colloquy," Windsor Great Park, England, 3–5 Sept. 1971.
6 Christie wrote many lengthy memoranda on Canadian foreign policy. Those that best expresses his thought are "The Canadian Dilemma," Nov. 1938 and "Responsible Government: The Last Stage," 1926, both in the Loring Christie Papen (Public Archives of Canada), 23.
7 The best published account of the pre-1939 history of the Department is Gilles Lalande, *The Department of External Affairs and Biculturalism* (Ottawa, 1969), 3ff.
8 See Vincent Massey, *What's Past is Prologue* (Toronto, 1963), 231ff; Cab. 21/494 (P.R.O.), High Commissioner, Ottawa to Dominions Office, 24 March 1939.
9 For an assessment of Marler by the British Ambassador, see F.O. 371/22820/A4461/250/45 (P.R.0.). For an appraisal by a shrewd Canadian reporter, see Lothian Papers, 17/381/241–2 (Scottish Record Office), Grant Dexter to Lothian, 4 April 1939.
10 See, for example, the remarkable series of memoranda by Armour from October 1935 on the subject of King and trade negotiations in F.D. Roosevelt Papers, PSF, Box 33 (Roosevelt Library, Hyde Park, New York).
11 Sir Gerald Campbell, *Of True Experience* (New York, 1947), 97.
12 Cf. R. Bothwell and J. English, "Dirty Work at the Crossroads: New Perspectives on the Riddell Incident," *Canadian Historical Association Report, 1972*.
13 For King's 1936 speech at Geneva, ushering the League "out into the darkness", sec Nicholas Mansergh, *Survey of British Commonwealth Affairs: Problems of External Policy, 1931–1939* (London, 1952), 119–20.
14 F.O. 371/20670/A2182/2082/45, Lindsay to Vansittart, 8 March 1937.
15 *Ibid.*
16 Roosevelt Papen, PSF, Box 33, King to W.D. Robbins, 17 December 1934, encl. with Robbins to Roosevelt, 18 December 1934. Robbins added that King "is inclined ... to play the game with us".
17 *Ibid.*, Armour to Phillips, 22 and 24 Oct. 1935.
18 *Ibid.*

"A Self-Evident National Duty" 133

19 *Ibid.*, Memorandum by Armour, 25 Oct. 1935.
20 *Ibid.*, Phillips to Roosevelt, 7 Nov. 1935.
21 State Department Records (U.S. National Archives), 842.20/37$^{1/2}$, Armour to J. Hickerson, 13 Nov. 1936.
22 Roosevelt Papers, PSF, Box 33, King's "Permanent Conference on Economic and Social Problems – Notes," 6 March 1937. An almost identical version appears in James Eayrs, *In Defence of Canada* (3 vols. to date; Toronto, 1964–72), II, 223–5. See A.A. Offner, *American Appeasement* (Cambridge, Mass., 1969), chapter 7, for American preoccupations at this time.
23 State Department Records, 500.A19/61, Hull's Memorandum of conversation, 5 March 1937.
24 *Ibid.*, 841.01 Imperial Conference 1937/28, Armour to Secretary of State, 5 May 1937.
25 See esp. Keith Middlemas, *Diplomacy of Illusion* (London, 1972), 54–5.
26 John Munro, ed., *Documents on Canadian External Relations* (7 vols. to date; Ottawa, 1969–74), VI, Baldwin to King, 18 Nov. 1936, 121–2; Baldwin to King, 23 Jan. 1937, 124–5; King's speech to Imperial Conference, 21 May 1937, 161. (Cited hereafter as *DCER*, VI).
27 Department of External Affairs Records (Public Archives of Canada), file 4–1, Pearson to Skelton/?/, n.d. The letter bears the notation "late 1935 or early 1936".
28 Lothian Papen, 17/327/218–22, Christie to Lothian, 20 Oct. 1936.
29 State Department Records, 841.01 Imperial Conference 1937/28, Armour to Secretary of State, 5 May 1937. For examples of public discussion, see "The Folly of Canadian Rearmament," *Canadian Forum* (Feb. 1937), 6–7; "Armaments Expenditure," *Ibid.* (March, 1937), 3; G.M.A. Grube, "Pacifism: The Only Solution," *Ibid.* (June, 1936), 9–10; and *Canada: The Empire and the League* (Toronto, 1936) for discussion of Canadian policy by various politicians and intellectuals in the summer of 1936.
30 *DCER*, VI, 203.
31 Cab. 63/81, "Impressions of Canada," Dec. 1934.
32 Cab. 21/671, Hankey to Baldwin, 22 Oct. 1936 with minutes by MacDonald.
33 E.g., see *DCER*, VI, 175–6; External Affairs Records, vol. 42, file 241–1, "Procedure Respecting British Munitions Contracts in Canada," 26 June 1937; Eayrs, op. cit., II, 116.
34 Cab. 21/670, Hankey to Sir E.J. Harding, 9 May 1938.
35 Sec R. Tamchina, "In Search of Common Causes: The Imperial Conference of 1937," *Journal of Imperial and Commonwealth History*, I (Oct. 1972), 79–105.
36 State Department Records, 841.01 Imperial Conference 1937/28, Armour to Secretary of State, 5 May 1937.

37 Cab. 23/88, Cab. Conclusion 34(37) 5, 16 June 1937.
38 Eayrs, op. cit., II, 226ff.
39 Reported in *Montreal Gazette*, 3 July 1937.
40 Lothian Papen, 17/346/157–157a, Christie to Lothian, 10 July 1937.
41 External Affairs Records, vol. 9, file 59, Memorandum to Prime Minister, 17 July 1937.
42 Prem. 1/334, Floud to Sir H. Batterbee, 9 Aug. 1937.
43 Reported in *Montreal Gazette*, 9 July 1937.
44 D.O. 35/543/D28/5 (P.R.O.), "Probable Attitude and Preparedness of Dominions in Event of War," n.d.
45 State Department Records, 842.00/ 504, "Canada, Political Estimate," June 1937.
46 External Affairs Records, vol. 2, file 4–3, "Note re Canada's Foreign Policy, Particularly in Relation to the United Kingdom," n.d.
47 C.G. Power Papers (Queen's University, Kingston, Ontario), General Staff memorandum, "The Defence of Canada-A Survey of Militia Requirements," 7 Jan. 1938.
48 External Affairs Records, vol. 8, Christie's "Notes on General Staff Paper," 17 Jan. 1938. Cf. C.P. Stacey, *Arms, Men and Governments* (Ottawa, 1970), 71.
49 See Peter Dennis, *Decision by Default* (London, 1972), 81–140 and Michael Howard, *The Continental Commitment* (London, 1972), 96–120.
50 Eayrs, op. cit., II, 60–1.
51 See Middlemas, op. cit., chapter 7. For the quiescence of Canadian press opinion, see State Department Records, 842.00 P.R., periodical reports for the summer months of 1938.
52 See, e.g., the discussion in R.A. MacKay and E.B. Rogers, *Canada Looks Abroad* (Toronto, 1938), chapter 15.
53 D.O. 35/543, Floud to Harding, 21 June 1938.
54 Mackenzie King Diary, 31 Aug. 1938, quoted in Stacey, 7.
55 External Affairs Records, vol. II, file 66–2, "Central European Situation," 11 Sept. 1938. See also Christie's memo, *ibid.*, "Re Ideological Crusading," 4 April 1938 and Skelton's, *ibid.*, "Re Chamberlain's Policy," 14 April 1938.
56 W.L.M. King Papers, (P.A.C.), Diary, 12 Sept. 1938.
57 See *DCER*, VI, 1085–7.
58 Charles Dunning Papers (Queen's University, Kingston, Ontario), King to Dunning, 3 Sept. 1938.
59 King Papers, Diary, 13 Sept. 1938.
60 *DCER*, VI, 1090. The Canadian people did agree, for the American legation reported "strong support for the British stand" and no sentiment for neutrality. State Department Records, 842.00P.R./136, "Periodical Report on General Conditions in Canada," 17 Sept. 1938

61 Massey, op. cit., 262.
62 *The History of the Times*, (London, 1952), IV, part II, 938.
63 Prem. 1/242, memo by M. MacDonald, 13 Sept. 1938. "He also told Lord Halifax that 'the majority' in Canada would be against 'action' at this point in the hope of avoiding war." Middlemas, op. cit., 342
64 *DCER*, VI, 1093–4.
65 King Papers, Diary, 23 Sept. 1938.
66 Eayrs, op. cit., II, 68.
67 Norman Lambert Papers (Queen's University, Kingston, Ontario), Diary, 10 Oct. 1938.
68 *DCER*, VI, 1096–7.
69 King Papers, Diary, 24 Sept. 1938.
70 *DCER*, VI, 1097.
71 Middlemas, op. cit., 5, is the latest; see also Keith Feiling, *The Life of Neville Chamberlain* (London, 1946), 371–2.
72 State Department Records, 842.00 P.R./137, Periodical Report, 3 Oct. 1938.
73 R.J. Manion Papers (P.A.C.), vol. 16, Manion to James Manion, 7 Oct. 1938
74 See above n. 55. Cf. External Affairs Records, vol. 2, file 4–4, H. Keenleyside's memorandum "Western Canadian Opinion and the European Crisis," November [?], 1938; *ibid*., vol. II, file 66–2, for a collection of varying reactions to the crisis, and MacKay and Rogers, op. cit., 249–324
75 State Department Records, 842.00 P.R./137, Periodical Report, 3 Oct. 1938
76 Stacey, op. cit, 7.
77 External Affairs Records, vol. 54, file 319–2, "After the Munich Agreement," 3 Oct. 1938.
78 *Ibid*., file 254–36, "Re the Russian Game in the European Crisis," 10 Dec. 1938.
79 *Ibid*., file 319–1, Pearson to Skelton, 4 Nov. 1938.
80 King Papers, Diary, 24 Oct. 1938.
81 *Ibid*.
82 *Ibid*., 14 Nov. 1938.
83 *Ibid*., 13 Nov. 1938.
84 *Ibid*., 7 Oct. 1938
85 *Ibid*., 2 Dec. 1938.
86 Canada, House of Commons *Debates*, 16 Jan. 1939, 52; King Papers, Diary, 27 Jan. 1939. Cf. Massey, op. cit., 273–6.
87 External Affairs Records, vol. 721, file 47, "Re: Defence Estimates," n.d.
88 King Papers, Diary, 27 Jan. 1939.
89 Feiling, op. cit., 400.
90 King Papers, Diary, 17 March 1939. Arnold Heeney believed that 15 March ended King's last hopes for peace, Arnold Heeney, *The Things that Are Caesar's* (Toronto, 1972), 55.

91 External Affairs Records, vol. 2, file 4–5, "As to a Statement of the International Position," 20 March 1939.
92 D.O. 114/98, Campbell to Dominions Office, 24 March 1939.
93 Canada, House of Commons *Debates*, 20 March 1939, esp. 2043.
94 King Papers, Diary, 29 March 1939.
95 Canada, House of Commons *Debates*, 30 March 1939, 2605–13. Cf. Bruce Hutchison, *The Incredible Canadian* (Toronto, 1952), 242–6.
96 King Papers, Diary, 31 March 1939.
97 *Ibid*
98 F.O. 371/22969/C5265/15/18, Hankinson to Harvey, 30 March 1939 encl notes of the meeting. Massey was there but with no right to speak on behalf of the Canadian government. For Massey's reaction, and for reasons why King was right not to trust his judgment, see Massey, op. cit., 236ff. Cf. Lester B. Pearson, *Mike: The Memoirs of the Rt. Hon. L.B. Pearson*, I: 1897–1948 (3 vols.; Toronto, 1972, 1973, 1975), 105–6.
99 D.O. 114/98, Campbell to Dominions Office, 26 April 1939.
100 King Papers, Diary, 24 April 1939.
101 External Affairs Records, vol. 48, file 265, Pearson to Skelton, 9 June 1939.
102 Hon. J.W. Pickersgill interview, April, 1970; Hutchison, 248–9.
103 External Affairs Records, vol. 54, file 319–2, Memoranda 19 July 1939 and 22 Aug. 1939.
104 King Papers, Dairy, 22 Aug. 1939.
105 External Affairs Records, vol. 54, file 319–2, "Canada and the Polish War: A Personal Note," 25 Aug. 1939.
106 *Ibid*., memo, 28 Aug. 1939.
107 See Lester Pearson, "Forty Years On: Reflections on Our Foreign Policy," *International Journal*, 22 (Summer, 1967), 67 which offers Pearson's comment that after being a prime minister concerned with national unity he had more understanding of Mackenzie King's difficulties.

Chapter Eight

Mackenzie King and Canada at Ogdensburg, August 1940

In 1935 there took place the first conference on Canadian-American affairs held under the joint auspices of Queen's and St. Lawrence Universities and the Carnegie Endowment for International Peace. There were four of these biennial conferences, gatherings that brought together some of the better known Canadian and American scholars of North America with businessmen, bureaucrats, and public figures.

In June 1941, the last of these conferences was held at Queen's University with almost two hundred in attendance; among those present were distinguished scholars such as S.F. Bemis, A.L. Burt, A.B. Corey, Edward Meade Earle, Chester Martin and Frank Scott; Pierrepont Moffat, the American Minister in Ottawa and Malcolm MacDonald, the British High Commissioner, attended; so did Clifford Clark, the Deputy Minister of Finance in Ottawa, Hugh Keenleyside and Escott Reid of the Department of External Affairs, Adolf Berle of the State Department, and at least two Canadian Army generals. In other words, the foreign policy establishment (Canadian-American sub-section) turned out en masse.

Well they might have. The relations between Canada and the United States had been transformed by the war. From being a slightly independent, slightly reluctant tail on a British kite, to use an analogy employed by the British quarterly *The Round Table*, the events of 1940–41 had made a desperately eager Canada simultaneously into a tail on the kite of a still-neutral United States. In very real terms, with most of its military strength overseas in Britain, Canada had become a protectorate of the United States. Franklin Roosevelt had already given public indications of his willingness to protect Canada in prewar addresses at Chautauqua, NY, and Kingston, Ont., and he had pressed Canada to do more to defend itself in those speeches and in several private prewar conversations with Prime Minister Mackenzie King.[1] The President and Prime Minister had recognized the new military and political situation in Europe (and potentially in the Pacific) by their creation of the Permanent Joint Board on Defense. This first defense alliance between the Dominion and the Republic marked an undoubted turn in North America's history.[2] It was followed quickly by the Hyde Park Declaration of April 1941 which went a long way toward uniting the two North American economies for war purposes.

What did the conferees of June 1941 at Kingston think of these events? Ogdensburg had occurred ten months before they met, Hyde Park only eight weeks previously. The war was still proceeding very badly for Britain and the Commonwealth, and the debacle in Greece and Crete, following on what seemed an unending succession of defeats, was fresh in everyone's mind. The Nazi invasion of the Soviet Union, begun a few hours before the conference opened, was a new development of still-intangible weight, though few knowledgeable people believed that Stalin's Russia would hold out for long. The United States, though not yet a belligerent was helping Britain as much as it could through lend-lease aid and through naval patrols in the western Atlantic, but very few Canadians contemplated victory in the war so long as the United States stayed out. John W. Dafoe, the editor of the *Winnipeg Free Press* and the chair of one of the sessions, put this very clearly when he quoted Lester B. Pearson, then a little-known Canadian diplomat, as having said that, we might lose the war, and we had to face that fact."[3]

Facing facts is always difficult, and not just for Canadians. Few of those presenting papers or offering comments at Kingston seemed to grasp the new reality that now existed in North America. Grant Dexter, the Ottawa correspondent for Dafoe's paper, while implying that the Ogdensburg Agreement had permitted Canada to devote the maximum military force possible to the overseas struggle, used much of his paper on Canadian-American defense relations to juxtapose Mackenzie King's preference for listing the defense of Canada as the nation's first priority with that of his defence minister, Colonel J. Layton Ralston, who was "equally insistent in declaring our first obligation to be aid to Britain, that the English Channel is our front line." Dexter also did his part to reinforce the myth of Canada as the "linch-pin" between Britain and the United States with his references to Mackenzie King as "'the key man throughout" the negotiations that preceded the bases-for-destroyers deal of 3 September 1940.

The reporter, however, was on sounder ground when he suggested that the Ogdensburg Agreement "would have been impossible" had the Conservative party been in power in Canada instead of King's Liberals. Dexter reminded the conferees that the House Leader of the

Conservatives, Hon. RB. Hanson, a lacklustre New Brunswick politician, had attacked the agreement as "political window dressing" and darkly noted King's longstanding leanings toward the United States. The Tory leader in the Senate and former prime minister, Arthur Meighen, had denounced the Ogdensburg arrangement in November, as Dexter said pointedly, "after he had plenty of time to think it over."[4]

Dexter's comments provoked some heated and revealing discussion. J.M. Macdonnell, the President of the National Trust Co. and an important Conservative party supporter, excused the Hanson and Meighen remarks as being the result of "the exigencies of party politics" which force politicians "to take stands and to use words which, if they were in a different situation, they would not. It was naturally very painful to Mr Meighen and Mr Hanson to see Mr King do the thing which was so obviously useful to Canada." Macdonnell was an able and principled man, but those remarks were simply silly.

While holding no brief for Hanson, Professor R.G. Trotter of Queen's University's History Department argued that many Canadians believed that Ogdensburg might produce "a lessening of our contribution to the cause that was at issue, and perhaps in a holding back of the necessary United States aid." Remember, Trotter said, that Americans, unlike Canadians, believed that Britain had been beaten. Was Ogdensburg "going to mean for Canada retreat into defeatism"? If it had turned out to be so, he argued, "you would have found before very long a torrent of condemnation of Ogdensburg which no policy of guiding public utterances and newspaper utterances in discreet ways would have been able to keep suppressed."[5] Perhaps Trotter's comment was what led one American participant from the floor to raise the attacks on and near firing of the gadfly socialist and nationalist Professor Frank Underhill of the University of Toronto. Underhill's heinous crime was that he had said in an address in late August 1940 that the Ogdensburg Agreement would inaugurate a new era in Canadian relations with the United States and Britain.[6]

Obviously, the manner in which the conference participants perceived Britain and its chances of surviving the war against Nazism largely determined their view of the Ogdensburg Agreement and its significance. Was it, as Trotter seemingly suggested, King and Canada turning their back on a defeated Mother Country? Or was it a device to let Canada, its own security guaranteed by the United States, do its utmost for Britain?

The one participant at the conference who cut through these predictable and blinkered views was Frank Scott, who had spent 1940–41 at Harvard University and was then teaching law in the summer session there. The McGill University professor, poet, and backroom figure in the social-democratic Cooperative Commonwealth Federation had the wit and intelligence to understand what was happening. Although he had been deeply moved by the course of the war and had begun to question his prewar isolationism, those belated second thoughts did not alter Scott's perspicacity. First, he said, after the Ogdensburg Agreement and the one year of operation of the PJBD, Canada had been strategically incorporated into the United States' scheme of defense for this hemisphere in a way that we have never been before. Second, he went on,

> we see an equivalent economic integration (after the Hyde Park Declaration) between Canada and the United States. We are in the curious position that the more we do to assist Great Britain in the economic war effort, the more we are obliged to co-operate with the United States. So that we have a sort of double co-operation directly growing out of our present position. We help Great Britain, and therefore we must be more closely associated with the United States.

"Anyone," Scott maintained, "who has read either the Hyde Park Declaration or the Ogdensburg Agreement will see there principles of permanent relationship that will go far beyond the actual war period." What this meant was that the "British Empire is no longer able to maintain itself in the kind of world we are living in today, strategically, without allies." That being so,

> then it will follow that American policy will very directly control and limit the freedom of British Commonwealth policy in the coming world. Canada will be affected by this development; and our policy, like our military strategy and like our economic relationships, will be much more closely parallel to that of Washington.[7]

There it all was, clearly and succinctly laid out. Although there was substantial discussion after Scott's comments, incredibly no one picked up on them, although Scott, as was so often the case in his long career, had unquestionably grasped the salient issues of the hour. The world had changed since September 1939. Britain, once an unquestioned great power, was now fighting for its life and was enormously dependent on the support of the Commonwealth and not least Canada. To support Britain militarily and economically, Canada had to deepen its relations with the United States. The Hyde Park Declaration, effectively linking the wartime economies of North America, was one outward sign of this; the Ogdensburg Agreement, the first Canadian-American defensive alliance, was the other. And why had both the Agreement and the Declaration been essential for Canada? The answer was clear to Scott: because Britain's weakness had now put Canada's defense into jeopardy and, moreover, Britain was now too weak to finance the Canadian war effort or to pay for the goods it needed from Canada. In other words, Britain's economic and military weakness had forced Canada permanently, as it turned out, into the arms of the United States.[8]

Mackenzie King instinctively understood all this. The Prime Minister was, hoary legend notwithstanding, an imperialist, a monarchist, and a fervent believer in Britain. (He was also a nationalist and a continentalist, of course, thus combining within himself all of those Canadian traits that still bedevil outsiders trying to comprehend the country.) What King could not abide was being high-hatted by the British or the failure of some British politicians and officials to comprehend that he was the elected Prime Minister of Canada, responsible for the safety of His Majesty's realm in North America and all of its citizens. For example, had King known that Sir Gerald Campbell, the High Commissioner in Ottawa at the time of the Ogdensburg Agreement, had written scornfully of the Prime Minister's "general attitude of putting Canada first and Great Britain second"[9] he would have been apoplectic. Of course, he put Canada first; he was its leader.

That simple fact governed all of King's actions during the war and, most especially, during the terrible spring and summer of 1940. The British and French defeat of May and June, not made much more palatable by the Dunkirk evacuation; the surrender of France and the establishment of the puppet Pétain regime; the terrible pressures on the Royal Navy and Royal Air Force – all these posed political problems for King's government at the same time as they forced the revving up of the Canadian war effort, to this point barely idling.

Most important for King, and for President Roosevelt, was the prospect that Britain might not withstand the expected Nazi invasion. If that happened, Canada would lose its two divisions of troops in Britain, its trained aircrew there, and possibly the four destroyers of the Royal Canadian Navy, sent there on 23 May 1940; in other words, most of the country's trained military manpower would be consumed in the flames of defeat. That was bad enough; much worse, the Royal Navy might fall into Nazi hands and then North America itself could be subject to an invasion in the near future. King played his part, at Roosevelt's urgent request, in conveying American concerns about this possibility to Winston Churchill, the new British Prime Minister.[10]

Certainly, Canada's economy and its physical security were now threatened as never before, a subject of genuine concern for the government. The Cabinet War Committee, the small group of ministers who directed the war effort, had to face up to the realities. As King put it to his colleagues in late May, the defense of Canada under the new conditions demanded urgent consideration. The country, he said, was virtually undefended,[11] and the Prime Minister took good care lo ensure that the President knew this. As he wrote in his diary the day his ministers agreed to send every possible ship to British home waters, "Let them see how completely depleted we were of defence on both coasts. It was due to the U.S. who stood to suffer if our shores were wholly neglected. It was due to our own people to get from the U.S. all the help we possibly could."[12]

King wanted that help, and he took pains to have a long talk with the newly appointed American Minister to Canada, Pierrepont Moffat, who arrived in the capital on 11 June. A professional diplomat (unlike the spoiled sons of rich men or major campaign contributors Washington ordinarily sent and sometimes still sends to Ottawa), the very able Moffat was well connected at the State Department, and he and King, as well as the officials of the Department of External Affairs, soon were on good terms and working closely together. In a dispatch on 16 June, Moffat noted that King had asked:

> if the time has not come for conversations between our Navy Department and naval and air officers from Canada. He recalled that some informal conversations between staffs were held about three years ago concerning the Pacific. Of course at that time both countries were at peace. Now Canada is a belligerent. Possibly a request for such limited staff talks, if made, might be exceedingly embarrassing to the President; this is the last thing he would wish. On the other hand, given the fact that our own interests would be served by the preservation of the British Fleet, he thought that the President might feel that such talks were amply warranted.[13]

King's style and method showed clearly in that dispatch. First, he was very obviously the representative of the small country seeking help from the leader of the great power. Then, he was the fellow politician, acutely aware that Roosevelt was facing re-election in November and unwilling to cause him any additional difficulties with the isolationist elements in the United States. And finally, having carried Roosevelt's messages about the fate of the Royal Navy to Churchill, King was able to use "the preservation of the British Fleet" as a card to try to get the staff talks he wanted and needed. Astonishingly, given the Nazi triumph in Europe and Britain's perilous position, that feeler took almost a month to produce results, but the military talks, the first serious and

Mackenzie King and Canada at Ogdensburg 143

detailed military discussions ever to take place between the two countries, finally were held in complete secrecy in Washington on 11 July.[14] Though without commitment, the discussion, as the American minister later noted, "at least had the result that American aid would be effective" in the event of any attack on Canada.[15]

What was the country's military situation at this time? Almost certainly, the Cabinet War Committee took a bleak view of matters. On 9 July, for example, the ministers had decided that no further commitments to send troops or materiel out of Canada would be made without full consideration and specific authority in each particular case.[16] Apparently, there had been no consultation with the military authorities before that decision was taken.[17] The newly-appointed Chief of the General Staff, General H.D.G. Crerar, had returned to Canada from Britain late in July and, after assessing the reports that his vice-chief had brought from the meetings in Washington, met the Cabinet War Committee on 26 July. Professional soldier that he was, although one of the very few Canadian officers whose intelligence was held in high repute by the mandarins of the Ottawa bureaucracy, Crerar did not believe that a German invasion of Canada was likely, no matter the result of the struggle for Britain. Raids were a possibility, however. In consequence, the country's Atlantic coast was to be strongly defended and garrisoned, with three brigade groups (or something more than 15,000 men) kept available for counterattacks. In the event of raids, Crerar said, he expected military assistance to come from the United States. For this reason and others, "frank exchange" of information with the Americans was essential, and the Chief of the General Staff wanted a military attaché to be posted to Washington.[18]

No one in Ottawa any longer had doubts about the necessity for frank exchanges with the Americans. Hugh Keenleyside, a counsellor in the Department of External Affairs and King's envoy for the discussions on the Royal Navy with President Roosevelt, was the leader in urging accommodation to the new economic and military realities. In a paper on 17 June, he noted that the United States "will expect, and if necessary, demand, Canadian assistance in the defence of this continent and this Hemisphere. If the United States is forced to defend the Americas, Canada will be expected to participate; thus the negotiation of a specific offensive-defensive alliance is likely to become inevitable."[19] Two weeks later, on 30 June, Keenleyside prepared another memorandum of the points that might be discussed "if the Prime Minister should decide to meet President Roosevelt with a view to discussing closer co-operation." The most important paragraphs covered defense and included Canadian construction of the Alaska Highway, something long desired by the Roosevelt administration, coordination of war production and consultation on war finance, and further staff talks "including the gradual switching of the Canadian Forces to the use of United States mechanized equipment."[20] If Britain was conquered, the use of American-pattern equipment would be virtually essential. Closer cooperation seemed to be the order of the day, and not only in Ottawa. In the American capital, planners like Berle, the Assistant Secretary of State, were also beginning to consider what might happen if Britain fell,[21] and their minds obviously were turning toward a "new hemispheric concept," "the new American empire." "I can describe it as nothing else," wrote the Canadian journalist Bruce Hutchison in a private memorandum he sent to Mackenzie King. Berle's "whole assumption was that Canada's economy would be merged with that of the U.S., but he did not foresee political union.[22] Something of that sort probably would be necessary, or so the Bank of Canada concluded after a study of the economic implications if, as it was euphemistically phrased, "communications with the United Kingdom were cut." The economy faced virtual collapse in such an eventuality, with widespread unemployment a direct consequence of the disappearance of overseas trade. The Governor of the Bank in mid-August told the Prime Minister that Canada would have to appeal to Washington for assistance in such an event, and the only card we had to play was that the "United States will have to plan its defence on continental terms at least, and Canada will be an integral and necessary part of their plan."[23]

Essentially this same conclusion had already been reached by a group of influential academics, younger politicians, and bureaucrats (the group, many of whom had been neutralists before the war, in effect constituted Canada's foreign policy community) who met in Ottawa in mid-July to draw up a "Program of Immediate Canadian Action." Including in its number Robert Bryce of the Finance Department, Members of Parliament Brooke Claxton and Paul Martin, and Jack Pickersgill of the Prime Minister's Office staff, the Program group sounded the same note as Keenleyside and the Bank of Canada. Public opinion "is ready for a frank recognition by the government of the need for action." The government had to take the initiative. "If Canada allows this opportunity to go by default and the United States is subsequently obliged to require us to cooperate, we might as a result be unable to maintain our independent identity."[24]

But the taking of bold initiatives was not ordinarily Mackenzie King's way. He knew as well as anyone of Canada's new military and economic dependence on the United States, but the campaign for the presidency was in its initial stages, the Selective Service Bill was moving through Congress, and the numerous and apparently powerful isolationists were in full cry. If he moved too quickly, too publicly, Mackenzie King feared that he might find himself accused of trying to drag the United States into the war, something that might sorely embarrass the President – and Canada.[25] It was better to ensure, as he had already done, that Roosevelt had the fullest information about Canadian defenses; it was enough to have cooperated to the fullest in conveying Roosevelt's concerns about the fate of the Royal Navy to Churchill. King was a master of political timing, a shrewd judge of when not to act and when to do so. As far as the Prime Minister was concerned, any additional moves in the direction of North American defense cooperation had to be left to Roosevelt, no mean judge of timing himself.

There would not be too much longer to wait. In July, Pierrepont Moffat had noted that there was still little talk about North American defense, as that somehow seemed to imply continued "reverses" in Europe.[26] On 14 August, however, the diplomat reported to the State Department on the "growing public demand" for "some form of joint defense understanding with the United States." To Canadians, the Minister in Ottawa said, a treaty or even publicly announced staff talks seemed "a reasonable reinsurance policy. The old fear that cooperation with the United States would tend to weaken Canada's ties with Great Britain has almost entirely disappeared. Instead, Canada believes that such cooperation would tend to bring Britain and the United States closer together, rather than to force Britain and Canada apart."[27] Roosevelt saw this letter; whether or not he assessed the impact of a joint defense understanding in the way Moffat did remains unknown; the President may have had his own ideas on bringing Canada and the United States closer together.

Whatever the reason, Roosevelt was now moving toward formalizing the slowly-developing military relationship with Canada. The President had long been concerned about the weak Canadian defenses on the Atlantic and Pacific coasts, areas he had himself cruised on presidential trips. He had talked about such problems with Mackenzie King both before and after September 1939, and he had pressed the first staff talks on the two countries' military chiefs before the outbreak of war. Moreover, he had offered a blanket pledge of protection to Canada in his famous address at Kingston, Ontario in the summer of 1938. Now, exactly two years after his Kingston speech, Roosevelt knew that there was a major threat to North America.[28]

On 13 August, therefore. Roosevelt talked with Loring Christie, the Canadian Minister to the United States, and said that he was thinking of sending staff officers to Ottawa to discuss the defenses of the east coast. He "had in mind," Christie reported to Ottawa, "their surveying the situation from Bay of Fundy around to the Gulf of St Lawrence. They might explore the question of base facilities for United States use, including possible desire to make such facilities available at say Chester or Louisbourg [N.S.]. Roosevelt also said that he might telephone King soon."[29] The next day, however, the President met with some of his key advisers, including Henry Morgenthau, Jr., about the best way to handle the announcement that negotiations for a destroyers-for-bases deal with Britain were underway. "Everyone," Morgenthau wrote in his famous diary, "argued it should be done that day. It was finally Roosevelt's idea to do it at his press conference and only handle what we were to receive from the U.K. in the form of bases. He also got the idea on the spot that he would see Mackenzie King."[30] The President told the press, among other things, that he was carrying on conversations with Canada on the defense of the coasts and, after the fact, he called Mackenzie King to tell him what he had said and to invite him to meet at Ogdensburg, New York, the next evening, Saturday 17 August, close to where he was to inspect troops. As King recorded it in his own famous diary, the President had said that "We can talk over the defence matters between Canada and the United States together. I thanked him," King wrote, "and said I would be very pleased to accept the invitation."[31]

The next day, the Prime Minister briefly met with Colonel Ralston, his new Minister of National Defence, and received from him a list of equipment Canada sought from the United States. King duly handed the requests to Roosevelt. Apparently, that was his only briefing prior to the meeting with Roosevelt;[32] equally important, King took no advisers with him.[33] Accompanied only by Pierrepont Moffat, the Prime Minister drove to Ogdensburg, arriving at the President's railway car at 7 p.m.

Was King surprised or concerned by Roosevelt's suggestion of a Permanent Joint Board on Defense? There is no indication in his papers or diary then or subsequently that he was. The subject, as well as several others relating to the destroyers-for-bases deal and the provision of American equipment for the British and Canadian forces, was dealt with quickly. King did query Roosevelt's intention in wanting to make the Board permanent. "I said I was not questioning the wisdom of it," King wrote later in his diary, "but was anxious to get what he had in mind." What the President meant was not "to meet alone this particular situation but to help secure the continent for the future." King agreed readily, and as he telegraphed to Churchill on 18 August, "The wording of the jurisdiction of the board has purposely been so framed as to permit joint action of Canada and U.S.in defence of Pacific as well as Atlantic coasts."[34]

The Prime Minister was not so accommodating when the question of American bases in Newfoundland came up. King had explained that "as we had undertaken protection of Newfoundland and were spending money there, the British Government would probably want our Government to co-operate in that part" of the destroyers-for-bases arrangement. Canada, in the Prime Minister's view, had present and future rights in Newfoundland, then being governed as a virtual Crown colony by a Commission of Government appointed in London, and had no intention of seeing the United States take control of the island. In his telegram to Churchill, King made the same point: "You are aware, Canadian Government is already assisting in defence of Newfoundland and is, at the moment, contemplating additional large expenditure. There will probably be necessity for co-operation between the three governments in matters pertaining to that island."[35]

Perhaps King's protection of Canadian "rights" in Newfoundland got under Roosevelt's skin. When King explained further "that we would not wish to sell or lease any sites in Canada but would be ready to work out matters of facilities," Roosevelt first replied that "he had mostly in mind the need, if Canada were invaded, for getting troops quickly into Canada." Of course, that was "all right," as far as King was concerned; so too were annual manoeuvres on each other's soil. But then Roosevelt remarked, or so King recorded it, that he had told Lord Lothian, the British Ambassador to the United States, that he could not understand why Britain had hesitated about leasing West Indian bases to the United States: "That as a matter of fact, if war developed with Germany and he felt it necessary to seize them to protect the United States, he would do that in any event. That it was much better to have a friendly agreement in advance."[36]

There was an implicit threat and a warning there, a Rooseveltian iron fist draped in the velvet of warmest good fellowship, though one presented wholly in a British-American context. If King, ordinarily a man of great shrewdness and perception, recognized the meaning of FDR's words, however, he never gave any indication in his diary or papers then or later. The President had raised the question of bases in Canada with Loring Christie on 15 August, and he had done so a second time with the Prime Minister; King had rejected any such idea quite firmly. (A few days later, on 20 August, Chubby Power, King's Air minister, told representatives of the Newfoundland government that while Canada was willing to offer the United States forces facilities in Canada, under no circumstances would the country transfer sovereignty of Canadian soil to American hands. King's statement, in other words, was quickly translated into a fixed government policy.)[37] Roosevelt's response to King's rejection was to put the Prime Minister on notice: to ensure the safety of the United States in the Western Hemisphere, to be certain that Canada's lamentably weak defenses on the Atlantic and Pacific did not put his country in jeopardy, he would do whatever he judged necessary. To put it in its most extreme form, for example, if necessity required the seizure of facilities in Halifax or Saint John, so be it. A "friendly agreement in advance" was the President's aim, and with the PJBD he had achieved it just as he had with the destroyers-for-bases deal.

There was a clear sign of United States determination – even though it was, in this case, frustrated by stronger still Canadian resistance – in the autumn of 1940 when the PJBD produced the Joint Canadian-United States Basic Defense Plan, 1940. This plan aimed to meet the situation that would result if Britain was overrun and the Royal Navy lost, and it gave strategic control of the Canadian forces to the United States, subject only to consultation with the Canadian Chiefs of Staff. In such dire circumstances as the defeat of the United Kingdom, the Canadian government obviously considered that this provision made sense. The next spring, however, after Britain had continued to fight and after hope of ultimate victory had begun to revive in Canada, the Board produced its second plan, ABC-22, to take effect if and when the United States joined with the Allies against the Axis Powers. When the American members again tried to secure strategic control of the Canadian forces, something the Canadians now interpreted as including tactical command as well, and to integrate much of eastern Canada and all of Newfoundland into their Northeast Defense Command and all of British Columbia into the Northwest Defense Command, Ottawa resisted fiercely and won its point. Mackenzie King had a backbone when he needed one, and the United States backed off in the interests of amity. All that was conceded was the "co-ordination of the military effort" of the two countries "to be effected by mutual cooperation,"[38] which meant almost nothing. Even so, it was clear that living cheek-by-jowl with a great power under a "friendly agreement" was not going to be easy.

Living with Canada's other great power and Mother Country always proved difficult, especially for Mackenzie King. The Prime Minister, as we have seen, had promptly telegraphed Churchill about the Ogdensburg conversations and Agreement, offering the British leader a full and fair account. He had even added that "In conversations with the President and (secretary of War) Mr. Stimson, I stressed the fact that Canada viewed so strongly the significance of the conflict in the U.K. area as constituting the first line of defence of this continent that we had parted not only with our own destroyers and aircraft to the extent we had but were also allowing you to retain guns which some time ago we had ordered for Halifax."³⁹ Concerned though he was by the defense of Canada, there is no reason to doubt that King genuinely believed those words. Moreover, "this descendant of a rebel," as the High Commissioner in Canada put it in a letter to Lord Lothian, "was fully convinced that at last he had rendered both Great Britain and Canada a service, and he was inclined to put the former before the latter." But what was the response from London? A "'wettish blanket" and a "somewhat dampening" reply, or so Sir Gerald Campbell called it.⁴⁰

That was a fair enough assessment. Churchill had told his War Cabinet on 21 August that King "was putting himself into a difficult position from the point of view of Canadian politics, and that he would find it difficult to obtain approval for the arrangements by which the United States Army would be granted facilities for manoeuvres on Canadian soil." For this reason, as the minutes phrased his comments, Churchill had "introduced one or two cautionary phrases in his telegram."⁴¹ So he had:

> I am deeply interested in the arrangements you are making for Canada and America's mutual defence. Here again there may be two opinions on some of the points mentioned. Supposing Mr. Hitler cannot invade us and his Air Force begins to blench under the strain all these transactions will be judged in a mood different to that prevailing while the issue still hangs in the balance.⁴²

Churchill's reasoning was completely uninformed about the mood in Canada, and he simply failed to recognize the obvious fact that Mackenzie King had the same primary responsibility he did to ensure the ultimate security of his own country. The press and public response to the Ogdensburg Agreement demonstrated irrefutably that Canadians supported King's actions at Ogdensburg.⁴³ Nonetheless, Churchill's "cautionary phrases" hit King like a slap in the face, producing real resentment in the Prime Minister and in his War Cabinet.⁴⁴ As King told Sir Gerald Campbell, the British High Commissioner:

> I said it showed how much appreciation was given in British quarters to anything that did not suit their particular mood at the moment. That when matters were going bad, Churchill had been ready enough to appeal very urgently to the U.S. for help and to ask my co-operation in getting it. When, however, it looked as if the British might still win because of the immediate successes of their air force, they were ready to pull away from U.S. co- operation.

Campbell's only reply was that he was glad Churchill had not sent a telegram of that kind to the United States.[45]

What shook King, the British patriot and Canadian politician, was the British leader's criticism of the Agreement. Churchill's words seemed to lie behind – or at least to lend support to – the imperialist criticism of Ogdensburg that Conservative leader Hanson began to offer early in September.[46] However much the peril to Canada's coasts, the Prime Minister knew all too well that there still remained a constituency in the country, one that was powerful and rich, that invariably favoured a policy of the last man and the last dollar to help Britain. These were the people who failed to realize that the events of 1940 had changed the world, and Canada's place in it, forever. For most of its history, fear of U.S. power had driven Canada close to Britain; now, fear of the consequences of Britain's weakness obliged Canada to seek shelter in the American embrace. Moreover, these were the same people who had torn Canada apart in 1917 to enforce conscription, the same ones who had formed the Union Government that excluded Quebec, the men who had destroyed Sir Wilfrid Laurier and, not incidentally, cost Mackenzie King election to Parliament in 1917. For King, these imperialists were dangerous and unrealistic in their desire to help Britain to the very maximum. They failed to realize that by so doing Canada was left completely denuded of defense and completely dependent on American military protection and economic assistance.[47] King, at least, understood the realities of the day: if Canada was to help Britain, the United States had to defend Canada.

Conclusion

The paradoxical nature of Canada's position, in retrospect, is completely clear. Canada had been forced to turn to the United States for military assistance because of Britain's weakness after Dunkirk. Every military action, every ounce of economic assistance to help keep Britain in the war weakened the country further. A private soldier or a pilot or a dollar's worth of munitions sent to Britain was one that would certainly be lost if and when Britain was invaded; and if Britain fell, then North America was in peril. Aid to Britain, in other words, while absolutely necessary, nonetheless weakened Canada; and a militarily and economically weak Canada had only one place to look for protection and help: the United States. As Frank Scott put it at the Canadian-American conference at Queen's University in 1941, "We are in the curious position that the more we do to assist Great Britain the more we are obliged to co-operate with the United Sates. We help Great Britain, and therefore we must be more closely associated with the United States."[48] Mackenzie King wanted to help Great Britain as much as possible, and he understood and accepted that this obliged him to seek closer links with Roosevelt's America. There was no point in railing against fate, no point in complaining. The harsh realities of August 1940 offered no time for that.

NOTES

1 King likely realized that he was being told to do something about them. Of course, not *all* Canadians enjoyed being lectured by Roosevelt. See, for example, the mockingly critical comment in an unsigned Department of External affairs memorandum after Roosevelt's speech at Kingston in August 1938. Printed in Robert Bothwell and Norman Hillmer (eds.), *The In-Between Time* (Toronto, 1975), p. 168. On FDR's concern for hemispheric defense, see the able M.A. paper by Angelika Sauer, "The Mission of Goodwill, Mackenzie King, the United States and Appeasement, 1936–38," Carleton University, 1988, pp. 119ff.
2 This event is, of course, a staple of after-dinner speeches *on* this continent. See, e.g., Paul Martin's address at the twenty-fifth anniversary celebrations in Ogdensburg on 18 August 1965 in Department of External Affairs, *Statements and Speeches*, no. 65/20.
3 R.G. Trotter and A.B. Corey (eds.), *Proceedings of the Conference on Canadian-American Affairs, 1941.* (Toronto: Ginn Co., 1941), p. 227.
4 Ibid., pp. 39, 42, 47–8. Dexter could not know that Hanson's phrasing in his address of 2 September was taken from a letter Meighen had written him. National Archives of Canada [NAC], Arthur Meighen Papers, vol. 141, Hanson file, 27 August 1940.
5 *Proceedings*, pp. 62, 65–66.
6 Ibid., p. 175. To his credit J.W. Dafoe noted that, despite the "bloodthirsty remnants of past times" who had pursued the unnamed Underhill (in attendance at the conference), "he has been successfully defended so far, and I do not think he will lack defenders again," ibid., p. 176. On the Underhill affair, see Douglas Francis, *Frank H. Underhill: Intellectual Provocateur* (Toronto: University of Toronto Press, 1986), pp. 114ff. One sample of Underhill's views in print is "North American Front," *Canadian Forum* (September 1940), pp. 166–67
7 *Proceedings*, pp. 247–48. On Scott, see Sandra Djwa, *The Politics of the Imagination: The Life of F.R. Scott* (Toronto: University of Toronto Press, 1987), pp. 191ff
8 See J.L. Granatstein, *How Britain's Weakness Forced Canada into the Arms of the United States* (Toronto: University of Toronto Press, 1989).

Unfortunately, I was unaware of Scott's comments of June 1941 when I wrote this book.
9 Public Record Office, London, Foreign Office Records, FO 800/398, Campbell to Lord Lothian, 27 September 1940.
10 Roosevelt's use of King to convey his worries about the Royal Navy's possible disposition has been well-covered. See, e.g., J.W. Pickersgill, *The Mackenzie King Record Vol: 1 1939–1944* (Toronto: University of Toronto Press, 1960), pp. 115ff, and J.L. Granatstein, *Canada's War: The Politics of the Mackenzie. King Government 1939–1945* (Toronto: Oxford University Press, 1975; republished, 1990), pp. 120ff.
11 NAC, Privy Council Office Records, Cabinet War Committee Minutes, 29 May 1940.
12 NAC, W.L.M. King Papers, Diary, 23 May 1940.
13 United States National Archives, State Department Records, 711. 42/194, Moffat to Hull, 16 June 1940.
14 The Canadian account of the discussions can be found in David R. Murray (ed.), *Documents on Canadian External Relations, Vol. VIII:* 1939–41 (DCER1) Part II (Ottawa, 1976), pp. 156ff.
15 Foreign Relations of the United States (FRUS) 1940, vol. III (Washington, 1958), p.145.
16 Cabinet War Committee Minutes, 9 July 1940.
17 C. P. Stacey, *Arms, Men and Governments* (Ottawa: Queen's Printer, 1970), p. 131
18 Cabinet War Committee Minutes, 26 July 1940. Military attachés were opened soon after. The 3rd Canadian Infantry Division was soon in formation and based in the Maritimes for use as a mobile reserve and a Command Headquarters (Operational) was created. See C.P. Stacey, *Six Years of War* (Ottawa: Queen's Printer, 1955), pp. 80, 163.
19 NAC, Department of External Affairs Records, vol. 781, file 394, "An Outline Synopsis," 17 June 1940. See on this, H.L. Keenleyside, *Memoirs of Hugh L. Keenleyside, Vol II: On the Bridge of Time* (Toronto: McClelland and Stewart 1982), pp 47–48.
20 DCER VIII, p. 105. See another Keenleyside memo, of same date, pp. 103–4.
21 Department of State Records, 740.0011EW1939/4700. Memo by Berle, 12 July 1940. The Canadian Minister in Washington said "we ought to talk, hypothetically of course, about possible grave changes which might take place. I presumed he referred to the contingency of a British defeat."
22 King Papers, Black Binders, vol. 19, Memorandum, 12 June 1940.
23 Ibid., Graham Towers to King, 15 August 1940, ff. 252698ff.
24 Copy in University of British Columbia Archives, Alan Plaunt Papers, box 9, file 1. See also *Memoirs of Hugh L. Keenleyside*, pp. 49–51. On the dissemination of the "Program," see Plaunt Papers, box 8, file 20, Plaunt to

John Baldwin, 13 August 1940. Brooke Claxton sent King a copy on August 23, pointing out that "on this main point you had taken practically the same line." King Papers, ff 241683-4. In early 1939, a neutralist manifesto entitled "Canadian Unity in War and Peace. An Issue of Responsible Government" had been put out by many of the same individuals. See David Lenarcic, "Ready, Aye Ready? Neutralism on the March, Autumn 1938–Spring 1939." draft York University Ph.D. chapter.
25 See Pierrepont Moffat's opinion in FRUS 1940, III, p. 145.
26 Houghton Library, Harvard University, Pierrepont Moffat Papers, Personal Correspondence, vol. 17, Moffat to W. Emerson, 12 July 1940.
27 FRUS 1940, III, p. 145.
28 See Canadian Minister to Washington Loring Christie's account of a conversation with Roosevelt on this point in October 1940 in DCER VIII, pp. 150-1. See also James Eayrs, *In Defence of Canada*, Vol. II: *Appeasement and Rearmament* (Toronto: University of Toronto Press, 1965), pp. 176ff.
29 King Papers, Black Binders, vol. 19, Christie to King, 15 August 1940; Stacey, *Arms, Men and Governments*, p. 337; DCER, VIII, p. 127.
30 J.M. Blum, *From the Morgenthau Diaries* (Boston, 1959–67), II, P. 180.
31 Pickersgill, *The Mackenzie King Record*, p. 131.
32 King Papers, Black Binders, vol. 19, Ralston to King, 17 August 1940.
33 John Hilliker, *Canada's Department of External Affairs, Vol. I: The Early Years 1909–1946* (Montreal: McGill-Queen's University Press, 1990), p. 234-5.
34 Foreign Office Records, FO 800/398, King to Churchill, 18 August 1940. For the significance of "Permanent," see David Beatty, "The Franklin Roosevelt Corollary to the Monroe Doctrine and the Ogdensburg Agreement," for "Ogdensburg 40," a conference at the University of Toronto, June 1980, p.7.
35 FO 800/398, King to Churchill, 18 August 1940. For the Newfoundland view of the destroyers-for-bases deal, see the able account by Peter Neary, *Newfoundland in the North Atlantic World 1929–1949* (Montreal: McGill-Queen's University Press, 1989), pp. 136ff.
36 Pickersgill, *The Mackenzie King Record*, pp. 13lff. King had Keenleyside's memorandum, "The Provision of Bases," with him when he met Roosevelt. See DCER, VIII, pp. 132-3
37 See David MacKenzie, *Inside the Atlantic Triangle: Canada and the Entrance of Newfoundland into Confederation 1939–1949* (Toronto: University of Toronto Press, 1986), p. 44.
38 See Granatstein, *Canada's War*, pp. 131-2.
39 FO 800/398, King to Churchill, 18 August 1940.
40 Ibid., Gerald Campbell to Lord Lothian, 27 September 1940.
41 Ibid., F0371/24259, Extract from War Cabinet Committee Conclusions, 231 (40) 21 August 1940.

154 Section Two: Diplomacy

42 King Papers, Black Binders, vol. 20, Churchill message att. to Campbell to King, 22 August 1940. On the Roosevelt-Churchill minuet that may have lain behind the King-Churchill gavotte, see Fred E. Pollock, "Roosevelt, the Ogdensburg Agreement, and the British Fleet All Done With Mirrors," *Diplomatic History 5* (Summer 1981): 203ff.
43 For example, see Moffat Papers, Personal Correspondence 1940, Moffat to C.M. Gauss, 29 August 1940; King Papers, J4, vol. 139, "Press Comment on- the Ogdensburg Agreement," n.d.: 54 editorials in 37 Canadian papers revealed no opposition
44 Pickersgill, *The Mackenzie King Papers*, p. 140.
45 King Diary, 26 August 1940; King Papers, Secretary of State for External Affairs to High Commissioner in Britain, 16 September 1940, ff. 247320–2. On the 23 September, King received another telegram from Churchill, one drafted in response to pleas from the High Commissioner, that did much to mollify him. See Pickersgill, *The Mackenzie King Papers*, p. 143.
46 See King's telegram to Vincent Massey suggesting that former Prime Minister R.B. Bennett, now living in England, was the source of Churchill's criticism. King Papers, tel, 16 September 1940, ff. 247320–2.
47 Historians, however, have not been numerous in their denunciations of a "sell-out" at Ogdensburg. See Granatstein, *Britain's Weakness*, Chapter 11; cf. Donald Creighton, "Presidential Address," *Canadian Historical Association Annual Report*, 1957, p. 8.
48 *Proceedings*, pp. 247–8.

Chapter Nine

The Hyde Park Declaration 1941: Origins and Significance

J.L. GRANATSTEIN AND R.D. CUFF

"Done by Mackenzie and F.D.R. at Hyde Park on a grand Sunday, April 20, 1941." So Franklin Roosevelt inscribed the original typed copy of one of the most significant economic agreements reached between Canada and the United States during World War II. The simple six paragraph statement expressed the desire of President Roosevelt and Prime Minister Mackenzie King that "in mobilizing the resources of this continent each country should provide the other with the defense articles which it is best able to produce ..." The declaration anticipated that Canada "can supply the United States with between $200,000,000 and $300,000,000 worth of such defense articles" over the next year, purchases that would "materially assist Canada in meeting part of the cost of Canadian defense purchases in the United States." The agreement also specified that "In so far as Canadian defense purchases in the United States consist of component parts to be used in equipment and munitions which Canada is producing for Great Britain, it was also agreed that Great Britain will obtain these parts under the lease-lend act and forward them to Canada for inclusion in the finished articles."[1]

Mackenzie King regarded Hyde Park as a triumph of personal diplomacy. When he spoke to the House of Commons about the declaration on 28 April he emphasized how it would reduce Canada's exchange problem with the United States and how it would contribute to the rationalization of continental defence production and so aid both Britain and the war effort. "But beyond its immediate significance," he continued, "the Hyde Park declaration will have a permanent significance in the relations between Canada and the United States. It involves nothing less than a common plan for the economic defence of the western hemisphere." More, the declaration was "a further convincing demonstration that Canada and the United States are indeed laying the enduring foundations of a new world order, an order based on international understanding, on mutual aid, on friendship and good will."[2]

Even if it did not live up to King's exuberant claims for it, the Hyde Park declaration was generally hailed in Canada by Liberals and Conservatives, by businessmen and farmers. It seemed to resolve some of Canada's pressing short-term problems and apparently without cost to the dominion. But simple and straightforward as it was, the agreement still raises some important questions for the historian. Why was it necessary? What was the international context in which the agreement was signed? How did Ottawa officials decide on the necessity for such an agreement? And how did Mackenzie King secure Roosevelt's co-operation?

These questions should help us reflect upon three broad historical issues of general importance: first, Canada's place at this time in the so-called North Atlantic triangle; second, the general patterns of Canadian-American economic relations that began to emerge during the war years; and, finally, the context of Canada's role in the emerging "new world order" of the postwar years. These general themes should remind us of the obvious: Hyde Park did not occur in a vacuum. It was, rather, a consequence of Anglo-American financial diplomacy, and it followed in the wake of a series of prior agreements between the United States and the United Kingdom.

The Roosevelt administration had made a number of breaches in the neutrality walls before 1941. But such measures as repeal of the arms embargo in 1939 and the destroyers-for-bases deal in 1940, though of importance to the Allies, had not solved Britain's growing shortage of gold and US dollars. This was an issue that reached crisis proportions after the British assumed liability for French contracts in American with the fall of France in June 1940. British purchases in North America, the chancellor of the exchequer estimated on 21 August 1940, would run to $3.2 billion over the next year. But Britain's total resources in foreign exchange and American securities amounted at best to £490 million, and some of the securities virtually could not be sold.[3] The prospect was one of bankruptcy. "Boys," the British ambassador, Lord Lothian, told the press on his return to the United States in late 1940, "Britain's broke. It's your money we want."[4]

The British plight, however, was not immediately perceived as such in Washington. Some key administration officials, especially in the State Department, repeatedly demonstrated scepticism about the extent of British financial hardship and a parallel belief in the opulence of empire. They advised British representatives to sell such direct investments in the United States as Shell Oil, Lever Brothers, and Brown and

Williamson Tobacco in order to acquire both dollars and public good will.[5] They urged further that London seize gold supplies which Canada held in trust for the French, a proposal that would trouble Canada's relations with both Britain and the United States well into the next year.[6] President Roosevelt, who held an exaggerated view of British holdings, personally told Lothian in November 1940 that Britain would have to liquidate $9 billion worth of assets in the Western hemisphere before she could expect to make a convincing case for aid.[7]

At this point, the administration's request for liquidation owed less to a determination to break up the empire than to a concern to overcome isolationist opposition in Congress, to prove that the British were indeed in dire need. "Between 1939 and 1941," writes the latest student of Lend-Lease, "the formulation of American economic policy rested primarily with [Secretary of the Treasury Henry] Morgenthau and the Treasury Department, which thought essentially about restraining Nazism and pacifying public opinion."[8] The consequences for Britain and the empire were serious nonetheless.

The Anglo-American financial difficulties that would eventually produce Lend-Lease had their parallel on a somewhat smaller scale in Anglo-Canadian relations, although sometimes the frictions were as great. There had been much irritation in London about Canada's unwillingness to assume more of a financial burden in the first few months of the war, particularly in connection with the British Commonwealth Air Training Plan,[9] but there had been equally sharp comments in Ottawa in 1939 and early 1940 about the British government's reluctance to place munitions orders in Canada.[10] Both British orders and British pressures increased following the fall of France, and feeling mounted in Whitehall that Canada should begin to use her own gold reserves and direct investments in the United States. Furthermore, British representatives, partly in response to American demands, continued to press Ottawa for the French gold.[11]

Spurred by the desperate war situation, the Canadian government soon took a series of steps to provide Britain with additional Canadian dollar supplies, among which the repatriation of Canadian securities held by British citizens was the most important. On 31 March 1941 the British deficit with Canada was $795,000,000. Of this amount, 31.4 per cent was met by gold transfers, 42.4 per cent by debt repatriation, and 26.2 per cent by the accumulation of sterling balances in London.[12] The British wanted Ottawa to contribute more by way of sterling overdrafts, in effect a form of dollar loan, in part to reduce the pace of redemption of Canadian securities. Moreover, by late 1940 the flow of British gold to Canada had come to a halt.

Britain's deteriorating financial position had serious implications for Canada. The historian of British war finance has pointed out that "Whether the Dominion Government provided the United Kingdom with Canadian dollars in exchange for repatriated Canadian securities or for a sterling balance, the dollars had to be found by the Dominion Government either by taxation or by the sale of securities to the Canadian public."[13] The problem for Canada was that the strain on the economy was already very great indeed. Estimates by Finance Minister J.L. Ilsley in February 1941 were that war expenditures in fiscal 1941 would run to $1.4 billion while an additional $400 million would be needed for repatriation of securities from Britain and $433 million would be required for civil expenditures. In addition, Ilsley calculated, the municipal and provincial governments would spend $575 million. The total was $2.8 billion, well over half the national income.[14] If the British financial position deteriorated further, the demands on Canada would increase, and the result might be, as Mackenzie King gloomily ruminated, "a greater burden than the people of Canada can be led to bear."[15] A solution to British financial problems was an absolute necessity for Canada.

Even under peacetime conditions Canada's economy was based on a "bilateral unbalance within a balanced 'North Atlantic Triangle.'"[16] Canada had a chronic deficit with the United States, in other words, but it had been balanced – and generally more than balanced – by a surplus with Britain, Western Europe, and empire countries. Much of that market had disappeared as a result of the war, of course, and Britain was now financially strapped. In the meantime, trade had increased with the United States, most of it as a direct result of the war. In April 1941 the deputy minister of finance foresaw a deficit of $478 million in Canada's balance of payments with the US, and by June Canadian officials estimated that American imports had increased by $400 million per year over the 1938 figures while Canadian exports to the United States had risen by only half as much.[17] So long as 30 per cent of the components required for British munitions orders had to be secured by Canada from the United States, there was little prospect of a reduction in the deficit. The result, in sum, was that Canada faced the problem of having to finance Britain's deficit while itself facing an increasing deficit of American dollars. The double bind was tightening.

The King government took a series of actions in its efforts to right this adverse balance with the United States after Canada entered the war. A Foreign Exchange Control Order to prevent capital exports was issued in 1939, and it was accompanied by increased efforts to broaden exports, stimulate American tourism in Canada, and to increase gold production. Further measures followed in the spring and fall of 1940, including the stabilization of the exchange rate at 10 per cent below parity with the American dollar and a refusal of American dollar exchange for Canadian travellers to the United States. In December 1940 the government took its most serious step in a move that coincided with the end of British gold flows to Canada. The passage of the War Exchange Conservation Act prohibited importation of a long list of products (including cereals, processed and canned fruits and vegetables, spirits and wines, electric appliances and jewelry) from countries outside the sterling bloc.[18] Clearly the measure was aimed at reducing imports from the United States. Simultaneously the government lowered duties on a large number of imports from Britain and levied heavy excise taxes on automobiles and other articles which required large imports of American components.[19] These measures were expected to save $70 million in exchange.[20] But the adverse trade balance continued its inexorable increase.[21]

Equally as important as the devices the government used to cope with the exchange problem are the options it rejected. In late October 1940, for instance, the very able US minister in Ottawa, Pierrepont Moffat, had informed Washington that "Canada's biggest worry at the moment is financial – how to acquire more dollar exchange." "The need," he said,

> is not yet desperate but the problem is rapidly becoming acute. It could, of course, be staved off if our legislation were amended and loans or credits granted to Canada, but there is some slight opposition to this prospect in financial circles here which argue that the future headache of servicing a large increase in Canada's foreign debt would be worse than any possible current headache. If loans or credits are not soon forthcoming then we must face the fact that Canada will have to take one or more of the following three measures: (A) Seizure against compensation and sale in New York of large blocks of American securities now held by Canadians; (B) Blocking in whole or in part the transfer to American owners of dividends from American companies; and (c) Selective purchasing from the United States under license, with strict rationing of non-essentials, among which are included American fruits and vegetables. There is much popular pressure in favour of number three ...[22]

The reaction in financial circles in the United States to any move to block dividends flowing out of Canada would have been very sharp, of course. The War Exchange Conservation Act, then, was extremely significant for what it omitted.

At the same time, however, several points that would become issues in subsequent Canadian-American negotiations appeared in early strategy discussions. Clearly Ottawa officials wanted to avoid borrowing in the United States. Moffat had reported opposition to the idea in October, and O.D. Skelton, the undersecretary of state for external affairs, had observed that Ilsley believed "it would be disastrous to face a future of making heavy interest payments to the United States year after year in perpetuity, or, alternatively, having a war debt controversy ."[23] On this point, in fact, Canadian and American policy converged, for one of the central objects of Lend-Lease would be to avoid just this kind of postwar entanglement with the British.

A second point to emerge, and one which would remain central to Canadian policy in the subsequent months, was Canada's determination to hold on to her investments in the United States. Estimates of the amount in question varied from $275,000,000 to over $1 billion.[24] And while Finance Department officers were prepared to consider a sell-off *in extremis*, they clearly hoped to avoid such an unpalatable measure. The Canadian investments provided a cushion that protected Canada from some of the strains imposed by the nation's heavy foreign indebtedness and, among a host of additional economic reasons, there was the real difficulty involved in compelling Canadians to sell their holdings in American securities at what some investors would feel to be sacrifice prices.[25] Both the British and the Americans would challenge Ottawa's position, but without success.

Finally, King and his officials took a very cautious approach to putting controls on United States imports, and with good reason. Such controls flew in the face of the prewar trend toward liberalized trade between the two countries and would be certain to antagonize US Secretary of State Cordell Hull, one of Canada's champions in the American capital. They would also invite powerful opposition from American domestic interests, and this could block amicable agreements in other, more crucial policy areas. This kind of calculation almost certainly entered the decision to omit fresh fruits and vegetables from the December list of excluded imports. As Ilsley frankly told Parliament, "we had to weigh ... the inevitable public reaction there would be in many of the agricultural districts of the United States, the embarrassment this restriction would cause ... and the danger which would ensue not only to our own trade relations with the United States, not only to the market which our trade agreement with that country gives to so many of our primary producers, but to the whole trade agreement policy of the United States ..."[26]

As 1940 gave way to the new year both Canadian and British calculations centred increasingly upon the proposed Lend-Lease Act.

Introduced by Roosevelt into Congress on 10 January, the bill was designed to speed up munitions production, to eliminate the need for cash payments on Allied orders, and to increase Roosevelt's freedom in foreign affairs. It empowered the president to have manufactured "any defense article for the government of any country whose defense the President deems vital to the defense of the United States." These articles he could "sell, transfer title to, exchange, lend, lease or otherwise dispose of" to those governments.[27]

For the next three months officials in London and Ottawa waited upon Congress to accept this dramatic shift in the ground rules of US aid. But British and Canadian calculations diverged in at least two important respects. For London, the introduction of Lend-Lease would end the first stage of negotiation with the United States and open wider the doorway to America's productive and financial might. For Ottawa, however, the passage of the Lend-Lease Act would mean not only that the first stage of negotiations was about to begin but that Britain might close the door to future orders in Canada. Canadian enthusiasm for any Lend-Lease aid to the war effort, therefore, coexisted with anxiety over the future of Anglo-Canadian relations.

What would happen to British orders placed in Canada once Lend-Lease became law? This was a key question for Canadian officials. C.D. Howe, the minister of munitions and supply, told his Cabinet War Committee colleagues on 18 February that he was "gravely concerned" that the American legislation might lead the British to shift orders for raw materials, food, and munitions to the United States where the terms seemed easier.[28] Some ten days later Howe was pressing for the despatch of a strong negotiating team to Washington to talk with both American and British officials, and he was warning his colleagues that the diversion of orders could have "disastrous" results on the country's industrial programme.[29]

That the British fully appreciated the impact Lend-Lease would have on Anglo-Canadian relations seems certain. Some lesser ministers bemoaned what they saw as Canada's accelerating drift out of the empire and into the American orbit,[30] but the Treasury, however, clearly wanted Canada to use Lend-Lease to the fullest. This was crystal clear in a memorandum prepared at Treasury for the newly named high commissioner to Canada, Malcolm MacDonald. "What we want Canada to do," the Treasury brief bluntly said, "is (a) to reduce her purchases in the United States to an absolute minimum ... (b) To make use herself of the 'Lease and Lend' Bill if the United States Government will agree to his, in order to obtain the maximum she can from the United States without payment. (c) In so far as Canada still has an adverse balance with the

United States ... to cover this with saleable Canadian marketable assets (e.g. United States securities, etc.) held by Canada." This prescription was recognized as being difficult for the Canadians to swallow. They would need heavier taxation, the Treasury brief noted, and they would have to accept some inflation. "But clearly their objective should be to meet our needs so far as possible by saving and taxation and to reduce inflation to a minimum." The brief concluded by noting that the British held a good hand in negotiating with Canada: "These are points of domestic policy on which we have no right to dictate to Canada, but it is as much in their interests as in ours to act along these lines, seeing that our only alternative, if we are unable to pay for our orders in Canada, is to place them instead in the United States in cases in which we should be able to obtain the goods under the 'Lease and Lend' Act."[31]

This Treasury position was consistent with the British line throughout the war thus far: Canada could do more. But the British now possessed a powerful weapon in Lend-Lease, and access to the $7 billion Congressional appropriation which accompanied it greatly increased their manoeuvrability. Unless and until Canada could reach a settlement with the British on purchasing policy, Lend-Lease would increase the unpredictability of Anglo-Canadian financial relations.

And what of Canada's relationship with the United States under Lend- Lease? Opinion was developing among top officers in the Finance Department that Canada should have none of it. The British Treasury's representative in North America noted that Clifford Clark, the deputy minister of finance, was opposed, despite his country's adverse balance with the United States and steeply mounting loans to Britain. Clark believed that acceptance would place Canada in a weaker position vis-à-vis the United States than Britain, separated by an ocean from American power, and that the Americans later might drive a very hard bargain on tariffs.[32] The prime minister accepted this reasoning, too. As he wrote in his diary on 13 March, "We do not intend to avail ourselves of the Lend-Lease Bill but to allow its advances wholly to Britain. There is, of course, a bigger obligation because of it all than appears on the face of it. I have no doubt the US would undoubtedly keep the obligations arising under the Lend-Lease Bill hanging pretty much over her head to be used to compel open markets or return of materials, etc. It is a terrible position for Britain to be in ..."[33]

As we have seen, one of the assumptions of the Ottawa planners that led to their hesitancy about Lend-Lease was their fear that Washington would demand a liquidation of Canadian assets in the United States similar to that pressed upon Britain. They were also aware that some Americans believed that Canada had not done as much as she could to aid Britain. There was, for example, the matter of French gold that Canada was holding in trust for France and refusing to turn over to the British, and there were also complaints that Canada was charging the British for all her purchases while the United States was being expected to give Britain supplies for free under Lend-Lease.[34] Treasury Secretary Morgenthau personally told Clifford Clark at an early stage in the Canadian-American conversations that Canada would not be permitted to come under Lend-Lease unless "steps had been taken to realize at least a portion of Canadian securities in the United States." Nor was Morgenthau particularly worried that any rapid Canadian liquidation would further depress stock market prices, already reacting to the British sale of the Viscose Corporation.[35]

What Canada clearly was seeking was some way to have whatever benefits were available under Lend-Lease to solve her exchange problems, while avoiding the kinds of sacrifices demanded of the British both in the short run (liquidation of direct investments) and in the long run (weakened bargaining position in the postwar years). The problem was to hit on a formula that obviated direct Lend-Lease aid, that did not add to Morgenthau's problems with Congress, and yet still reduced Canada's call on US dollars. The ideal situation from Canada's point of view would be an arrangement whereby Washington agreed to buy some of its war needs in Canada and also to supply the components Canada required for manufacturing munitions for the British. And if, in addition, Washington could be persuaded to buy Canadian output for shipment to England under Lend-Lease, Ottawa would have access to British purchasing while avoiding the current requirement of financing it.

The War Cabinet heard one part of this formula on 12 March. The deputy minister of finance had seen Morgenthau and suggested that the raw materials and components Canada required to manufacture munitions for Britain should be eligible for Lend-Lease on the British account.[36] Grant Dexter, the ubiquitous *Winnipeg Free Press* reporter, met with T.A. Crerar, the minister of mines and resources, on the 25th, and similarly learned that the government was "trying to persuade the US to include in the Lease and Lend category, the raw materials shipped to Canada for manufacture and reshipment to [Britain]." That would give some relief on balance of payments. The problem was that "Washington, [Crerar] said, is pretty sticky with Canada so far as Lease and Lend goes."[37]

Washington indeed was being sticky. Morgenthau, feeling bound by his pledges to Congress, was not very helpful when Canadian and British financial officials saw him on 18 and 19 March. If there were exchange problems, Canada should begin to liquidate her securities, he said, and as for the question of bringing the British component of Canadian imports from the United States under Lend-Lease, that was for Harry Hopkins to decide.[38] Hopkins was Roosevelt's friend and confidant and the man charged by the president with the administration of Lend-Lease. As a result, Clifford Clark was convinced by the end of March that Morgenthau was the chief obstacle to a favourable settlement,[39] and he was increasingly of the view, as he told Grant Dexter on 9 April, that "a good deal of education was needed in the U.S. to prove to them that it was not in their own interest to put Canada through the wringer ..."[40] This task of education would ultimately fall to Mackenzie King.

In the meantime, the British had agreed to maintain their orders in Canada. Word had reached Ottawa in mid-March that the British would not divert orders from Canada if the Canadians would agree to assume financial responsibility for them.[41] This was something close to blackmail, even if the British no longer had any alternative to such a course, and the Canadian government had to go along. By 27 March Finance Minister Ilsley had drafted a telegram agreeing to finance British orders placed in Canada.[42] To this extent the British had used Lend-Lease to bargain very effectively and toughly with Ottawa. But this agreement with London may have served to strengthen Canada's hand with Washington. It further justified the Canadian request for an arrangement to ease the exchange problem, and it also visibly demonstrated an intensification of Canada's financial war effort.

Congress passed Lend-Lease on 11 March, and the time to settle with Washington had now arrived. At the Cabinet War Committee on 21 March, Ilsley said that his deputy minister, Clifford Clark, was convinced that only direct representations to President Roosevelt could produce immediate and sympathetic consideration of Canada's difficulties in retaining and financing British purchases in Canada. At this meeting the Prime Minister indicated that he was planning a trip to Washington in April.[43] It now would be up to King personally to secure a favourable agreement from the Roosevelt administration.

Negotiation was the kind of task at which Mackenzie King excelled. He was a shrewd judge of men, and he was as confident in his own prowess as a negotiator as was President Roosevelt. Both leaders believed that their charm, when applied full force, was an effective weapon. And both men, after a series of meetings since 1935, knew each other fairly well. To Roosevelt, King was "Mackenzie" and a skilful, long-lived politician. To King, Roosevelt was still "Mr President" but there was a good deal of genuine admiration in this relationship. Archibald MacLeish, the poet and head of the Library of Congress, saw King in February 1941 and wrote to the president of his host's parting words: "he asked me if I would remember him to you and then turned and came back and said, with a sudden and very real warmth: "Give him my love." I have never heard words spoken with more sincerity."⁴⁴ Though one can scarcely conceive of similar words being seriously spoken by Roosevelt, the president, as L.B. Pearson noted, "had a better understanding of the position and importance of Canada than most Americans in official places." ⁴⁵ That was probably more important than mere sentiment. Mackenzie King, too, had a genuine understanding of the United States and its political problems. He had, for example, deliberately refrained from saying anything whatsoever about Lend-Lease during the long debate about it in the Congress. More, he had taken no steps to explain the Canadian war effort to the United States during the last several months.⁴⁶ This was conscious and deliberate policy, for by keeping a low profile for Canada he kept the dominion from impinging on the American consciousness as yet another nation seeking a handout. He may even have hoped to ease Roosevelt's difficulties with Congress by his silence, for the isolationist America Firsters eagerly seized on bellicose foreign speeches and used them as evidence of interference.

King left for Washington on 15 April and saw the president the next day. Their first conversation was mainly about hemispheric military matters, the subject that clearly was uppermost in Roosevelt's mind. The United States was going to extend its patrols farther out into the Atlantic, he said, and the president demonstrated that he was well briefed about the defence of the Labrador coast. Mackenzie King "purposely refrained from discussing financial matters," he recorded in his diary, "as I saw how tired he was, and did not wish to introduce this subject until we got away when we could discuss it quietly."⁴⁷

The next day King saw Secretary of State Hull and Treasury Secretary Morgenthau in separate appointments. Hull was friendly and the two men chatted politely about a wide range of subjects. King soon got down to business, however, and told Hull that he hoped it would be possible to have "the components of materials we were producing for Britain secured from America on the Lend-Lease American basis and that America would place orders with us for things that we could produce."⁴⁸ The reciprocal nature of the proposed arrangement was clear, a shrewd tactic on King's part for reciprocity was a sacred totem of international relations to Hull. Ironically, however, Hull was extremely lukewarm about Lend-Lease, and the great aid bill had been pressed for mainly by Morgenthau.⁴⁹

The treasury secretary was in an expansive mood but he stressed his difficulties with Congress and told King that in order to get Lend-Lease passed he had had to make clear that Britain was bankrupt. As far as Morgenthau was concerned, Canada was not yet in that state. King recorded that the secretary "thought our situation was all right till the end of the year," and the prime minister had to stress to Morgenthau that Canada in fact was in great difficulties at that moment. King then raised his idea for a virtual system of barter in war materials between Canada and the United States and found Morgenthau interested and willing to do "anything possible ... on this scale to help to get us purchasing power." The secretary also said "they would pay in dollars for things manufactured by us. I said it would go to purchasing American war material." The two agreed that Clifford Clark would meet the secretary the next day to discuss matters further.[50]

Matters seemed to be in hand at last. And on Sunday, 20 April, just before he was to go to Hyde Park, Roosevelt's home on the Hudson River, King met with Clark and E.P. Taylor of munitions and supply. The deputy minister of finance gave King a draft statement that expressed the optimum state of affairs from the Canadian point of view. Mackenzie King, after making a few amendments, carried this draft with him when he went off to spend his "grand Sunday" with the president.[51]

It was indeed to be a grand Sunday, particularly for Canada and Mackenzie King. The visit was long and friendly, and Roosevelt again talked at length about hemisphere defence, aid to Britain, and American bases in Canada and Newfoundland. Later in the afternoon Roosevelt said that he had seen Morgenthau and had the Canadian situation explained to him. "He thought perhaps it might be going a little too far to have something manufactured in Canada for the U.S. to Lease-Lend to England,"[52] King recorded.

After a pleasant dinner the discussion turned in earnest to the subject King had come to discuss. The prime minister produced his draft agreement and showed it to the president who "Said he thought it was first rate." There were only two changes requested by the president. As he had indicated earlier in the afternoon to King, he deleted any reference to the United States purchasing goods in Canada for subsequent Lend-Lease to Britain. The president also added aluminum to a list of war materials Canada could supply to the United States. The amended Canadian draft was agreed to over the telephone by Morgenthau, and the Hyde Park agreement was fact. It had all been incredibly easy.[53]

King was justifiably proud of his success, and he was heaped with praise by his Cabinet colleagues. C.D. Howe, in particular, his munitions plants now virtually assured of continuous full production, was glowing. "Said something about being the greatest negotiator the country had or something about the world's best negotiator," King wrote

The Hyde Park Declaration of 1941   167

in his record. "Could hardly believe so much could have been accomplished in so short a time. Said it straightened out the most difficult problems they had had for months."⁵⁴ So it did. But what is most significant is that King secured his agreement without being forced to make any major concessions. After all the long and frustrating negotiations Clifford Clark and his colleagues had had with their American counterparts, nothing in the end was demanded of Canada.⁵⁵

Once the agreement was signed, the rest was housekeeping. As early as 24 April the United States army began to honour the agreement even before the modalities were clarified.⁵⁶ The details were not arranged until 14 May when Clifford Clark and Sir Frederick Phillips of the British Treasury signed a brief memorandum in Washington that put on record Britain's willingness to secure approximately $220 million worth of goods under Lend-Lease for despatch to Canada. This would represent "the actual value of the 'United States content' of Canadian war supplies to the United Kingdom."⁵⁷ Morgenthau accepted this arrangement, and the remaining details were worked out in a similar fashion.⁵⁸

The Hyde Park Declaration, of course, did not solve all of Canada's manufacturing and exchange problems. There were continuing difficulties in maintaining British purchases in Canada that lasted until Canada itself adopted its Mutual Aid programme in early 1943.⁵⁹ As the agreement worked out in practice, moreover, the positive effects for Canada owed less to the provision of components intended for Britain under Lend-Lease than to increased American purchases in Canada. These mounted very fast, reaching $200 million by mid-1941, and totalling $275 million in 1942, $301 million in 1943, and $314 million in 1944.⁶⁰ Additional U.S. dollars soon flowed into Canada when the United States began heavy defence expenditures in the Canadian Northwest after Pearl Harbor, and when American investors, speculating on a revaluation of the undervalued Canadian dollar, began sending large sums north of the border. The result was that Canada's shortage of US dollars was over by 1942 and the holdings, in fact, grew large enough the following year that controls had to be imposed to keep them within bounds.⁶¹

Ironically, therefore, many of the benefits for which King negotiated so successfully at Hyde Park would probably have accrued to Canada in any case after Pearl Harbor. The increased United States orders for defence materials, for example, would probably have been placed as soon as the Americans entered the war. The long-term economic significance of the agreement, then, was not great except insofar as it foretold the integration of the North American economies that we live with today. But Hyde Park was important, primarily for the way in which it was negotiated.

The origins of the declaration provide an insight into the broader historical patterns of these years. First of all, it is clear that Hyde Park emerged as a consequence of a bilateral arrangement between the United States and Britain. It is true that the Canadians were aware of the discussions that led up to the introduction of Lend-Lease into Congress in January 1941. But apparently at no time were they included in these negotiations. Nor did British and American officials have Canada very much in mind as they established the Lend-Lease framework, except to hope that Ottawa would release the French gold to ease Britain's US debt. The British, moreover, did not make any prior arrangements as to the source of their North American purchases, and this in turn caused grave apprehension among Canadian planners. For the most part, then, Canadian officials had to manoeuvre within economic boundaries staked out by the Americans and the British for their own purposes and goals. But this fact in itself was not necessarily detrimental to the Canadian position, nor did it make any subsequent action a foregone conclusion. On the contrary, Canada received several significant benefits from the prior Anglo-American negotiations, not the least of which was the opportunity for an agreement like Hyde Park.

Well before Mackenzie King set off for Washington in April, Canadian business circles, for example, realized the several opportunities which passage of Lend-Lease legislation would open up to Ottawa. Kenneth Wilson of *The Financial Post* had outlined them in a prescient article as early as 1 February 1941 in which he noted that Lend-Lease could lessen the need for import controls and exchange restrictions against the United States. The Act offered three alternatives in this respect: the United States could ease Canadian dollar commitments by providing certain defence items; the United States could agree to buy certain materials from Canada and thus provide a supply of dollar exchange; and, finally, the Americans might finance branch-plant expansion in Canada for munitions expansion, buy the output, and then send it to England through Lend-Lease.[62] This last, of course, was the most multipurpose proposal of all. In the end Mackenzie King pressed for a variation of all three alternatives and counted himself a lucky man to come away from Hyde Park with even the first two.

But why was King able to leave Hyde Park that Sunday in April with anything at all? And why without reciprocal concessions? Roosevelt did not demand that Canada turn over to the British (and hence ultimately to the United States) the French gold held in trust in Ottawa. He did not force the sale of Canada's American securities, nor did he demand withdrawal of the various Canadian measures designed to conserve exchange. The answers to these questions illustrate both general features of Canadian-American relations during the war years as well as the unique importance of the cordial relationship between the prime minister and the president.

In its broadest perspective, the agreement at Hyde Park did not matter much to the United States, even though there was an American preoccupation with hemispheric defence through 1940 and 1941. The very absence of any mention of the agreement in the memoirs of the major members of the Roosevelt administration instrumental in working out Lend-Lease and the details of Anglo-American finance attests to this fact. The financial costs of Hyde Park were very small to the United States as well, particularly when they were compared with the $7 billion appropriation devoted to Lend- Lease. Nor did the agreement require a separate appropriation which would have singled out Canada for Congressional scrutiny. At the same time, however, it should be noted that the United States would secure access to Canadian war material of kinds and types it required. So, obviously, there was some benefit for Washington in the agreement.

Still, it was the United States that was offering the favour and Canada that was gratefully accepting it. Part of the reason for the Americans' willingness to help Canada must simply have been the genuine goodwill that existed between the two leaders, governments, and peoples. Two Canadians who spent much of the war working in Washington for the Canadian government tried to explain this goodwill in an essay in 1945. They stressed that Canada's natural resources were vitally important to the United States, that the Canadian war effort was a highly creditable one, and that Ottawa was physically close to Washington. "We could always bring a man to Washington to talk to his opposite number and since they spoke the same language and had the same approach to problems the results were generally satisfactory." Moreover, Canada was a cash customer of the United States and was not seeking a handout. "In short," they said, "the United States trusted us, liked us, understood us, had no reason to fear us, and shared with us the common objective of defeating the enemy."[63] This is close to being a classic formulation of the "good neighbourhood" theory of continental relations, but some of it may be true for all that.

More realistically, another harder factor that must be mentioned is that by the beginning of the Second World War the United States had an investment in Canada of $4.15 billion, and this amounted to fully 60 per cent of the total foreign investment in Canada.[64] For the United States to squeeze Canada involved squeezing its subsidiaries as well, and too vigorous action might have forced Ottawa to take action against the branch-plants and their shareholders in the United States.

Above all, however, was the willingness of President Roosevelt to receive Mackenzie King and to listen to him. Had the issue not reached Roosevelt there is no certainty that the result would have been so favourable to Canadian interests. Of course, Roosevelt was committed heart and soul to the defeat of the Axis, and he was willing to go just as far as he could to aid Britain and the Allies. But his primary concern was with military and strategic questions, and he was far less interested in economic matters that he may not have entirely understood in any case.

Mackenzie King was clearly aware of this and he pitched his appeal to Roosevelt in terms that were precisely calculated. In an interview with Grant Dexter the day after the agreement was signed, King revealed the approach he had employed:

> ... Roosevelt had said to King that he didn't know much about the exchange situation: that he would like King to tell him about it and outline the policy which Roosevelt should follow. King hadn't bothered about the economics of it. He told Roosevelt that if he were in his place, he would have regarded [sic] only for the neighbourly phase of it. What the US and Britain had done was one thing. Canada as the neighbour on this continent, the only one that really mattered, was another proposition entirely. If the US insisted upon taking from Canada what few possessions she had in the U.S. it would only give voice to anti-U.S. sentiment in this country. Why not buy from Canada as much as Canada is buying from the U.S. – just balance the accounts. Roosevelt thought this was a swell idea ...[65]

Roosevelt was much better briefed than this account suggests, and certainly he was not the passive figure King paints him as here. But the Dexter memorandum catches perfectly the style and tone of an appeal that was calculated to work with Roosevelt far better than statistics, charts, and financial data. The prime minister knew how to court a king.

For Mackenzie King the lesson of Hyde Park was that Canada and the United States were "laying the enduring foundations of a new world order ..."[66] A new world order was being created and there can he no doubt of that. Britain was being reduced to the status of a lesser power and the United States was reaching the superpower status she still occupies. But for King to suggest as he did that Canada was shaping this new order with Washington was wishful thinking. It would have been more to the point for King to say that Canada was working to achieve such benefits as it could under the new American order. The Hyde Park agreement may indicate that Canada could do this much with some success in 1941.

APPENDIX: THE HYDE PARK DECLARATION[67]

Among other important matters, the President and the Prime Minister discussed measures by which the most prompt and effective utilization might be made of the productive facilities of North America for the purpose both of local and hemisphere defence and of the assistance which in addition to their own programme both Canada and the United States are rendering to Great Britain and the other democracies.

It was agreed as a general principle that in mobilizing the resources of this continent each country should provide the other with the defense articles which it is best able to produce, and, above all, produce quickly, and that production programmes should be coordinated to this end.

While Canada has expanded its productive capacity manyfold since the beginning of the war, there are still numerous defense articles which it must obtain in the United States, and purchases of this character by Canada will be even greater in the coming year than in the past. On the other hand, there is existing and potential capacity in Canada for the speedy production of certain kinds of munitions, strategic materials, aluminum and ships, which are urgently required by the United States for its own purposes.

While exact estimates cannot yet be made, it is hoped that during the next twelve months Canada can supply the United States with between $200,000,000 and $300,000,000 worth of such defense articles. This is a small fraction of the total defense programme of the United States, but many of the articles to be provided are of vital importance. In addition, it is of great importance to the economic and financial relations between the two countries that payment by the United States for these supplies will materially assist Canada in meeting part of the cost of Canadian defense purchases in the United States.

In so far as Canadian defense purchases in the United States consist of component parts to be used in equipment and munitions which Canada is producing for Great Britain, it was also agreed that Great Britain will obtain these parts under the lease-lend act and forward them to Canada for inclusion in the finished articles.

The technical and financial details will be worked out as soon as possible in accordance with the general principles which have been agreed upon between the President and the Prime Minister.

NOTES

1 The agreement is found in the Appendix to this paper.
2 Canada, House of Commons, *Debates,* 28 April 1941, 2289. See also Louis Rasminsky, "Foreign Exchange Control: Purposes and Methods," in J.F. Parkinson, ed., *Canadian War Economics* (Toronto 1941), 127. For press views on Hyde Park, see Public Archives of Canada [PAC], W.LM. King Papers, c275492ff
3 These figures are from Corelli Barnett, *The Collapse of British Power* (London 1972), 14. In 1943 the Treasury representative in Ottawa valued UK holdings of US securities at $950 million on 13 August 1939; at $616 million on 31 December 1940; and at $372 million on 3 August 1941. PAC, Department of Finance Records, vol. 3437, R.G. Munro to W.C. Clark, 5 Feb. 1943. In 1944 Lord Keynes estimated that total UK reserves were $4.2 billion in September 1938, $2.45 billion in September 1939, and precisely $12 million in April 1941. King Papers, Memo, "British Requirements for the first year of Stage II," nd [Oct. – Nov. 1944], c251055ff
4 Cited by David Dilks, "Appeasement Revisited," *University of Leeds Review,* xv, May 1972, 51
5 Warren F. Kimball, "Lend-Lease and the Open Door: The Temptation of British Opulence, 1937–1942," *Political Science Quarterly,* LXXXVI, June 1971, 240–1. See also Warren F. Kimball, *The Most Unsordid Act, Lend-Lease, 1939–1941* (Baltimore 1969), 64–5, 86–7
6 R.S. Sayers, *Financial Policy 1939–1945* (London 1956), 335–6
7 John M. Blum, *Roosevelt and Morgenthau: A Revision and Condensation of* From the Morgenthau Diaries (Boston 1970), 341
8 Kimball, "Lend-Lease and the Open Door," 258. In this article Kimball makes the distinction between the generally benign motive that guided Morgenthau and the origins and passage of Lend-Lease and the aggressively economic motives which dominated its subsequent use by Secretary of State Cordell Hull, who shaped the broader economic policies of the Roosevelt administration.
9 There is a large body of material on this subject. See, for example, Public Record Office [PRO] London, Cabinet Records, CAB 65/2, War Cabinet Minutes, 2 Dec. 1939. For a Canadian view, see King Papers, Notes and Memoranda, vol. 151, folio 1274
10 See for example, M.M. Postan, *British War Production* (London 1952), 229; Queen's University Norman Rogers Papers, "Record of Visit to the United Kingdom ... 18 April-9 May 1940," entry for 19 April 1940, 5; King Papers, vol. 295, tel. no. 97, King to Churchill, 8 June 1940, 250514
11 Sayers, *Financial Policy,* 328–32, 335
12 House of Commons *Debates,* 29 April 1941, 2338; King Papers, W.C. Clark to King, 9 April 1941, 288021 ff. Clark hoped to persuade the US to allow

Canada to get a share of the British gold. See Department of Finance, W.C. Clark Papers, file B2–8-9-1, memo by Clark, "Report on Visit to Washington, March 17–11, 1941."

13 Sayers, *Financial Policy* 338
14 H.D. Hall, *North American Supply* (London 1955), 230. A later and probably somewhat more accurate estimate for fiscal 1941–2 puts the national income at $5.95 billion. War spending was estimated at $1.45 billion, aid to Britain at $1.15 billion, and civil expenditures at $1 billion. The total of public expenditure amounted to $3.6 billion or 60.5 per cent of national income. King Papers, "Canada's War Effort," 4 April 1941, ff 288088fL See also Clark Papers, file B2-8-9-1, Canada's War Effort and Budgetary Position," 4 March 1941, and PAC, Ian Mackenzie Papers, file 2–29, Senior to Mackenzie, 28 April 1941. By comparison, in the Great War the percentage of national income devoted to war at no time rose above 15 per cent.
15 J.W. Pickersgill, ed., *The Mackenzie King Record*. I: *1939–1944* (Toronto 1960), 189; Queen's University, Grant Dexter Papers, Memoranda, 11, 25 March 1941
16 Sayers, *Financial Policy*, 322–3
17 King Papers, memo, W.C. Clark to King, 9 April 1941. 288014ff; Rasminsky, "Foreign Exchange Control." 120. In fact the actual figures were worse even than this estimate.

	Canadian exports to US	Canadian imports from US
1938	$270,461,000	$424,730,000
1939	380,392,000	496,898,000
1940	442,984,000	744,231,000
1941	599,713,000	1,004,498,000

M. Urquhart and K. Buckley, eds., *Historical Statistics of Canada* (Toronto 1961), 181–2

18 House of Commons. *Debates*, 2 Dec 1940, 610–12. See also Clark Papers, file 82-8-9-0 for detail on Canada's exchange situation in late 1940. On US representations over the War Exchange Tax of 1940, see King Papers, Robertson to Skelton, 14 June 1940, c230902.
19 Finance Minister Ilsley summarized these measures in House of Commons *Debates* 29 April 1941, 2338–9
20 J.S.B. Pemberton, ed., "Ogdensburg, Hyde Park and After," *Behind the Headlines*, 1, April 1941, 18
21 R.W. James, *Wartime Economic Cooperation* (Toronto 1949), 18. See the good summary, "Canadian Wartime Economic Control Measures," *Bulletin of the Institute of International Finance of New York University*, no 118, 30 Dec. 1941
22 United States National Archives, Washington, State Department Records, 842.00/601, tel. 322, Moffat to Secretary of State, 24 Oct. 1940

23 PAC, Department of External Affairs Records, vol. 35, memorandum, "United States Exchange Discussions," 20 Nov. 1940
24 Urquhart and Buckley, *Historical Statistics*, 168. *The Financial Post* on 1 March 1941 reported a US Commerce Department estimate of Canadian holdings as $1.18 billion. But W.C. Clark told King that figures reported to the government were only $275 million at 28 February 1941. King Papers, Clark to King, 9 April 1941, 288018. On the Canadian determination to hold on to these US assets, see ibid.; Dexter Papers, memo, 11 March 1941; Public Record Office, Foreign Office Records, F0371/28795, Phillips to Treasury, 4 March 1941
25 King Papers, Clark to King, 9 April 1941, 288023ff. On British pressure, see PRO, Treasury Records, T160/1054, "Canadian Financial Assistance to this Country," nd [14 March 1941] att. to MacDonald to Sir Horace Wilson, 17 March 1941. On US pressure, see Hall, *North American Supply*, 236
26 House of Commons *Debates*, 2 Dec. 1940, 556; King Papers, Robertson to King, 7 April 1941, 287996ff. *The Financial Post* later reported that Washington had protested the exclusion of fresh fruits and vegetables, hinting at reprisals against Canadian exports (5 April 1941, 1). These fruit and vegetables amounted to more than 20 per cent of total US exports to Canada. Urquhart and Buckley, *Historical Statistics*, 180, 182. For the Canadian-American trade agreements of 1935 and 1938, see R.N. Kottman, *Reciprocity and the North Atlantic Triangle, 1932–1938* (Ithaca 1968)
27 For the text of the Lend-Lease Act, see Edward R. Stettinius, Jr, *Lend-Lease Weapon for Victory* (New York 1944), 335–9
28 PAC, Privy Council Office, War Cabinet Committee Records, minutes, 18 Feb. 1941. Cf *Financial Post*, 18 Jan. 1941, 1
29 War Cabinet Committee Records, minutes, 26 Feb. 1941
30 The secretary of state for dominion affairs, Cranborne, sent a long memo to Churchill on this subject in which he criticized the US efforts at hemispheric consolidation which "must ultimately not only poison the relations [between the US and the UK] but also drive a wedge between US and Canada." PRO, Prime Minister's Office Records, Premier 4/43B/2, 5 March 1941. Cf UK Treasury Records, T16o/ 1340, L.S. Amery to Kingsley Wood, 10 May 1941 which indicates that such fears increased after Hyde Park.
31 Ibid., T160/ 1054, "Canadian Financial Assistance to this Country"; documents on UK Foreign Office Records, FO371/28791–8; Dexter Papers, memorandum, 9 April 1941. This kind of UK attitude particularly bothered O.D. Skelton, the undersecretary of state for external affairs. As he wrote in a memo of 20 December 1940, "We should cooperate with the United Kingdom fully and freely in discussions with the United States but we should carry on our own discussions with Washington on these subjects. We have our own angle on the Western Hemisphere and it is Canada that

should be laying down the policy in these matters." Memo, "Hemispheric Economic Preparations," in Department of External Affairs, Records, file 1497–40 (Part 1) (a file retained in the department).

32 Clark estimated that Canada's adverse balance with the US would be $400 million for the year from August 1940 and might be $600 million for the year after that. Canada's remaining capital assets were, in US dollars, $136 millions of gold, $115 millions of dollars, and $378 million in marketable securities. The British Treasury officer observed that if British estimates of their adverse balance with Canada of $1.2 billion were correct it was difficult to see how Canada could carry on. "The proportion of their national income which is required for supplying their war effort ... is on any showing astonishingly high ..." These factors notwithstanding, the Canadians were still opposed to taking Lend Lease. UK Foreign Office Records, FO371/28792, Phillips to Treasury, 4 Feb. 1941; FO371/28795, Phillips to Treasury, 4 March 1941: James, *Wartime Economic Cooperation,* 32; A.F.W. Plumptre, *Mobilizing Canada's Resources for War* (Toronto 1941), 71 ff; King Papers, C.D. Howe to King, 8 April 1941, 288010ff. But see ibid., Clark to King, 9 April 1941, 288032-3 which defines conditions in which Lend-Lease might be acceptable.

33 Pickersgill, ed., *Mackenzie King Record,* I, 189. King was quite right on this point, for the Roosevelt administration under Hull's influence did use Lend-Lease ultimately as a lever to try to break up the imperial preference system and to convert Britain to economic multilateralism in the postwar years. See Richard N. Gardner, *Sterling-Dollar Diplomacy* (New York 1956), 42–56. In analyzing the variety of motives among American postwar planners, E.F. Penrose observed that some Washington officials "were jealous on political grounds of any ties between Canada and Great Britain that were not shared by the United States." E.F. Penrose, *Economic Planning for the Peace* (Princeton 1953), 27. Norman Robertson, in King Papers, Robertson to King, 7 April 1941, 287996ff, seemed to feel that tariff adjustments might help Canada solve some of its exchange problems with the US.

34 For a report indicating critical US opinion, see War Cabinet Committee Records, Minutes, 11 Feb. 1941. For the question of French gold, see UK Treasury Records, docs on T160/ 1045; UK Prime Minister's Office Records, Premier 4/43A/ 16, J. Garner to J.M. Martin, 15 Aug. 1940; Pickersgill, ed., *Mackenzie King Record,* I, 180–7

35 King Papers, Robertson to King, 12 March 1941, C250323ff and Clark to King, 9 April 1941, 288026. The Viscose sale was the result of a personal request Roosevelt made to Churchill for a spectacular indication of British good faith to appease Congressional opponents of Lend-Lease. See Kimball, *Most Unsordid Act,* 224–5. *The Financial Post,* 29 March 1941, 12, noted the symbolic nature of the event. The briefing papers Clark took

176   Section Two: Diplomacy

to Washington are in Clark Papers, file B2-8-9-1. See particularly his "Report" on the visit for some British opinion on the forced sale of their holdings.
36 War Cabinet Committee Records, minutes, 12, 13 March 1941. See on this point two memos in the King Papers, Brockington to King, nd, C250301, and Robertson to King, 12 March 1941, C250324-5. The Canadian members of the Permanent Joint Board on Defence had suggested cooperation between Canada and the US in the field of war materials and the integration of production facilities as early as December 1940. These proposals had already been canvassed in the Washington bureaucracy. US State Department Records, 842.20 Defense/61, memo, Hickerson to Welles, 21 Dec. 1940; the memos by H.L Keenleyside in External Affairs Records, vol. 67, file 383; Skelton's memo to King in ibid., vol. 826, file 725, 23 Dec. 1940; and material on ibid., file 1497–40 (Part 1)
37 Dexter Papers, memo, 5 March 1941
38 Hall, *North American Supply*, 236–7; War Cabinet Committee Records, minutes, 21 March 1941
39 Ibid.
40 Dexter Papers, memos, 9, 18 April 1941
41 War Cabinet Committee Records, minutes, 12, 13 March 1941
42 Ibid., 27 March 1941; Sayers, *Financial Policy*, 339
43 War Cabinet Committee Records, minutes, 21 March 1941. Cf Clark Papers, file B2–8-9–1, Clark's "Report on Visit to Washington." There is no evidence to suggest that the Americans were interested in forcing the British to buy only in the United States as a condition of Lend-Lease aid. But clearly such a condition would not have been completely unreasonable, and this might have weighed on the minds of Canadian planners.
44 F.D. Roosevelt Library, Hyde Park, Roosevelt Papen, PSF–1, Diplomatic Correspondence–Canada, MacLeish to Roosevelt, 15 Feb. 1941
45 L.B. Pearson, *Mike: The Memoirs of the Right Honourable Lester B. Pearson*, I: *1897–1948* (Toronto 1972), 226
46 Pickersgill, ed., *Mackenzie King Record*, 1, 190–1
47 Ibid., 190. On the arrangements for the visit and for briefing papers, etc., see King Papers, Black Binders, vol. 409, file 107. The military, for example, were concerned with Newfoundland and Canada's place in the UK and US military talks. Ibid., 287973A-5, 287976. 287991–2
48 Pickersgill, ed., *Mackenzie King Record*, I, 190. King and Hull also discussed the proposed integration of Canadian and American defence production, formally suggested by Canada on 17 March. US State Department Records, 842.20 Defence 71, memo by A.A. Berle, 17 March 1941. For Hull's version of his talks with King, see Library of Congress, Washington, Cordell Hull Papers, box 57, folder 196, memos, 17 April 1941; for the Canadian

The Hyde Park Declaration of 1941 177

Legation's, see External Affairs Records, file 91-CY-4OC, H. Wrong to Robertson, 25 April 1941 (a file retained in the department).
49 Hull had wanted the British to put up collateral for Lend-Lease. Cordell Hull, *The Memoirs of Cordell Hull* (2 vols., London 1948), II, 923. But of his cordiality to Canada there could be no doubt. "Throughout my twelve years at the State Department," he wrote, "no sector of our foreign policy gave me more satisfaction or brought more fruitful results than our relations with Canada." Ibid., 1479
50 Pickersgill, ed., *Mackenzie King Record*, 1, 190–2; External Affairs Records, vol. 93, file 573 (vol. 3), N. Robertson to King, 18 April 1941; Ibid, file 91-CY-4OC, Wrong to Robertson, 25 April 1941. See Clark Papers, file s2-8·9·1, "Memorandum of Meeting with Morgenthau, April 18, 1941" for Clark's meeting with the secretary. The memo indicates that Morgenthau passed King's suggestion on to the president, who liked it.
51 Pickersgill, ed., *Mackenzie King Record*, 1, 193–4. According to Wrong, he, Clark, and J.C. Coyne of the Legation staff had drafted the statement. External Affairs Records, file 91-CY-4OC, Wrong to Robertson, 25 April 1941
52 Pickersgill, ed., *Mackenzie King Record*, 1, 197
53 Ibid., 198–202; War Cabinet Committee Records, minutes, 21 April 1941; Dexter Papers, memo, 21 April 1941. Some US officials were distinctly unhappy with the procedures used to negotiate the agreement. See Harvard University, J. Pierrepont Moffat Papers, vol. 19. Hickerson to Moffat, 30 April 1941
54 Pickersgill, ed., *Mackenzie King Record*, I, 202. Cf. King Papers, Howe to King, 25 April 1941, 288034Aff for Howe's detailed response to the terms of the declaration.
55 Press and public could scarcely believe this was so. There was much speculation that Canada had agreed to repeal its 10 percent special war tax on imports and the ban on pleasure travel to the US. *The Financial Post*, 26 April 1941, I. The *New York Times*, 21 April 1941, 1, groping for Canadian concession, speculated that the US had secured "a word to say about the form Canadian efforts to aid Britain would take." Rumours were squelched by Ilsley in Parliament. House of Commons, *Debates*, 29 April 1941, 2339–40. See also Roosevelt Papers, PSF, Canada 1–41, King to Roosevelt, 24 April 1941; US State Department Records, 842.20 Defense/71, Desp. 1380, Moffat to Secretary of State, 25 April 1941
56 C.P. Stacey. *Arms, Men and Government': The War Policies of Canada 1939–1945* (Ottawa, 1970), 490
57 Memo, 14 May 1941 on US State Department Records, 740.0011 European War 1939/11542
58 Ibid., Morgenthau to Hopkins, 15 May 1941; UK Treasury Records, T160/1335, tel. PURSA Savings no. 2, British Supply Council in North

America to Supply Committee, London, 26 July 1941 and atts. The difficulties should not be underestimated. See External Affairs Records, file 91-CY-4OC, Wrong to Robertson, 25 April 1941; Clark Papers, file B2-8-9-1, memoranda re conference in Washington, 11–16 May 1941
59 Sec PAC, C.D. Howe Papers, file S-5(91); Hall, *North American Supply*, 237ff; UK Treasury Records, T160/ 1340, tel. 1662, High Commissioner, Ottawa, to Dominions Office, 27 October 1941; UK Prime Minister's Office Records, Premier 4/44/9, WM (42), 3rd conclusion, item 4; 4th conclusion, item 8; ibid., WP (42) 14, 7 June 1942; UK Cabinet Records, CAB 65/25, WC 3(42), 11–12
60 J. de N. Kennedy, *History of the Department of Munitions and Supply* (2 vols.; Ottawa 1950), 1,475; James, *Wartime Economic Cooperation* 34–5. James seems to doubt the $200 million figure for orders by mid-1941. Ibid., 35, 193–4. See also Clark Papers, file B2-8-9-1, memoranda re conference in Washington, 25–31 December, 1941 which downplays the results of Hyde Park in 1941. The effect of the declaration on 1942 exchange problems. however, was seen to be great although other difficulties remained. For further detail see External Affairs Records, vol. 1009, file 35, 'Forecasts of Canada's US Dollar Position,' 9 March 1942 and February 1943
61 James, *Wartime Economic Cooperation*, 35–6. Fully $689 million in Canadian securities were purchased by US investors between 1942 and 1945. See W.T.G. Hackett, "The 'Bank,' The 'Fund,' and the Canadian Dollar," in J. D. Gibson, ed., *Canada's Economy in the Changing World* (Toronto 1948), 119–20; C.D. Blyth, "Some Aspects of Canada's International Financial Relations," *Canadian Journal of Economics and Political Science* {CJEPS], XII, 1946, 303–4
62 *The Financial Post*, 1 Feb. 1941, 1
63 S.D. Pierce and A.F.W. Plumptre, "Canada's Relations with Wartime Agencies in Washington," CJEPS, XI, 1945, 411. "The agreement," commented W.C. Clark, "... represents the fruition of long years of the application of friendliness, goodwill, and common sense to the international relations of the two countries." W.C. Clark, "From the Canadian Point of View," in Reginald C. Trotter and Albert R. Corey, eds., *Conference on Canadian American Affairs* (Toronto 1941), 86. Cf the comment by A.A. Berle in a memorandum to Secretary of State Hull: "My own view is that we have a special relation to Canada; and that Canadian defense comes so close to our own that we have to consider Canadian needs as though they were to a considerable extent the needs of the American armed forces." US State Department Records, 842.20 Defense/71, 28 Feb. 1941. For a very much more qualified view of the continental relationship, see King Papers, N.A. Robertson to King, 22 Dec. 1941, C161568ff
64 Urquhart and Buckley, *Historical Statistics*, 169

65 Dexter Papers, memo, 21 April 1941. King was following Clark's advice in taking this tack. See Clark Papers, file B2–8–9-1, Clark's "Report on Visit to Washington, March 17–21, 1941": King should base "his arguments upon the larger considerations and the more intangible factors in the long term relations between our two countries." Roosevelt also knew how to please his courtiers: "Sometimes I indulge myself in the thoroughly sanctimonious and pharisaical thought, which I hope you are also occasionally guilty of, that it is a grand and glorious thing for Canada and the United States to have the team of Mackenzie and Roosevelt at the helm in days like these. Probably both nations could get along without us, but I think we may be pardoned for our thoughts, especially in view of the fact that our association has brought some proven benefits to both nations." Roosevelt Papers, PSF I, Diplomatic Correspondence – Canada, Roosevelt to King, 5 Nov. 1941
66 House of Commons *Debates*, 28 April 1941, 2289
67 External Affairs Records, File 1497–40, tel. 62, Secretary of State for External Affairs to Secretary of State for Dominion Affairs, London, 22 April 1941 (a file retained in the department)

Chapter Ten

The Man Who Wasn't There: Mackenzie King, Canada, and the Atlantic Charter

Fifty years ago this week [August 1941], an antisubmarine aircraft of the Royal Canadian Air Force (RCAF) on patrol over the Atlantic came across a large surface ship. The pilot, Flight Lieutenant Jim Nutt, had not been briefed that any friendly naval vessels were expected in the area, and, quite reasonably, he believed that he had seen a German pocket battleship. With no capacity to attack the ship, short of flying into it, he returned to his Nova Scotia base to give warning and to call out the bombers. The word quickly came back: "Tell F/L Nutt to forget what he saw." What the RCAF aircraft had seen, of course, was the USS *Augusta*, with President Franklin Roosevelt aboard, en route to Argentia, Newfoundland, and the historic meeting with Prime Minister Winston Churchill.[1] Aside from a few Royal Canadian Navy ships that played a small part in escorting the British leader's battleships to the meeting, Flight Lieutenant Nutt had come as close as any Canadian to the makers of the Atlantic Charter. Certainly he was rather more involved than was Prime Minister Mackenzie King.

Canada had gone to war on 10 September 1939, symbolically seven days after Britain had made its declaration of war, with little enthusiasm. The dominion was divided: French Canadians were apathetic or opposed to participation, Canadians of European origin were unhappy, and even among those of British stock, though there was support from the majority, there were also strong neutralist and isolationist sentiments among the intelligentsia and widespread and painful memories of casualties in the Great War.[2] Prime Minister Mackenzie King, however, took his country into the war with almost no overt opposition, a feat accomplished by his promise to Quebec that there would be no conscription for overseas service and his assurance to the rest of the nation that this war, unlike the previous one, would be one of "limited liability."[3] The major effort would be in the air, notably through the British Commonwealth Air Training Plan, and in the provision of supplies and arms.

If only events had permitted these promises to be kept. The disastrous defeats of May and June 1940 forced an armistice on France and drove Britain from the Continent. That summer, the 1st Canadian Division was literally the only fully equipped, if still largely untrained, division in the British Isles, and Canada quickly dropped its blinkers and turned to total war. From being a small and reluctant player, the dominion had suddenly become Britain's ranking ally. Men, ships, and aircraft, all that a badly shaken Canada had, were dispatched overseas.[4] All the stops were pulled but one: Although conscription for home defense was put in place in the summer of 1940, domestic politics demanded that a legislative barrier to sending conscripts overseas be retained.

The sudden turn in the war also forced Canada seriously to consider its own security for the first (but not the last) time in the twentieth century. Britain was now virtually incapable of preventing invasion and exceedingly hard-pressed to defend its waters, let alone to fulfill its traditional role of protecting Canada from seaborne attack on both the Atlantic and Pacific coasts; and if Britain was invaded and conquered, as many expected and feared, then the fate of the Royal Navy became of critical import. If it fell into Hitler's hands, North America was in real peril, in danger of invasion.

These concerns weighed so heavily on President Franklin Roosevelt that in May 1940 he asked Mackenzie King to sound out the new British prime minister, Winston Churchill, on the fate of the British fleet. The approach roused in King mixed feelings of shame and apprehension, but it led Churchill to brave public speeches that Britain would never surrender and more realistic private communications that, while he would not surrender the navy, he could not guarantee what a successor Quisling government might do.[5]

That was true enough, but it did little to ease minds in Washington or Ottawa. The defeat on the Continent and the fear it engendered led inevitably to a closer defense relationship between the two North American capitals. There had never been much in the way of joint military planning between Canada and the United States prior to 1940, beyond some tentative air and naval cooperation after US entry in the Great War of 1917 and some rudimentary staff discussions just prior to the outbreak of war in 1939. Both general staffs, in fact, had continued to plan for the possibility of war against the other into the 1930s.[6]

The situation was vastly different now, however. In the State Department, officials had begun to consider American options in the event that only the Western Hemisphere might remain free of German or Japanese control, calculations that gave Canada an important place on both the economic and military sides. In Ottawa, with Canada facing the loss of its trained air force and army personnel overseas and the disappearance of its overseas markets, there was a precipitous rush to strengthen bonds with the United States, now the country's only and ultimate protector. Britain's military weakness had forced Canada to look to the United States for protection.[7]

The Ogdensburg Agreement of August 1940, done by Roosevelt and King over dinner in the president's railway car on a siding near Ogdensburg, New York, created the Permanent Joint Board of Defense (PJBD). The board was a mixed military and civilian body charged with making recommendations to the two governments on the defense of North America, and it set to work within two weeks and began preparing plans. The results of Ogdensburg were hailed with virtual unanimity both in Canada, where all but a few imperialist-minded Tories hailed the PJBD's formation, and in the United States, where Roosevelt, running for a third term and under isolationist attack, suffered not at all from this bolstering of military links on his country's northern flank. In London, however, Churchill grumbled bitterly about Canada's scuttling to save itself. This shattered Mackenzie King, who believed (and rightly so) that he had helped the cause by welding the neutral United States to a belligerent Canada and had pushed the Americans a step closer to entering the war. In a telegram that stopped just short of accusing King of cowardice, Churchill stated:

> I am deeply interested in the arrangements you are making for Canada and America's mutual defence. Here again there may be two opinions on some of the points mentioned. Supposing Mr. Hitler cannot invade us and his Air Force begins to blench under the strain all these transactions will be judged in a mood different to that prevailing while the issue still hangs in the balance.[8]

The British leader had missed the point. The creation of the PJBD allowed Canada to do its utmost for Britain without having to fear for the safety of its own shores.

But there had been one potentially ominous note in the discussions at Ogdensburg when King and Roosevelt talked about the "destroyers-for- bases" deal, then in process, and the prime minister had made clear that there were limits to how far he was prepared to go with the United States. The subject was the question of American bases in Newfoundland. King had explained that "as we had undertaken protection of Newfoundland and were spending money there, the British Government would probably want our Government to co-operate in that part" of the destroyers-for-bases arrangement. Canada, in the prime minister's view, had present and future rights in Newfoundland, then being governed as a virtual crown colony by a commission of government appointed in London, and had no intention of seeing the United States take control of the island.[9] Perhaps King's protection of Canadian "rights" got under Roosevelt's skin. When King explained further "that we would not wish to sell or lease any sites in Canada but would be ready to work out matters of facilities," Roosevelt first replied that "he had mostly in mind the need, if Canada were invaded, for getting troops quickly into Canada." Of course, that was "all right," as far as King was concerned; so too were annual manoeuvres on each other's soil. But then Roosevelt remarked, or so King recorded it, that he had told Lord Lothian, the British ambassador to the United States, that he could not understand why Britain had hesitated about leasing West Indian bases to the United States; "That as a matter of fact, if war developed with Germany and he felt it necessary to seize them to protect the United States, he would do that in any event. That it was much better to have a friendly agreement in advance."

An implicit threat and a warning was there, a Rooseveltian iron fist draped in the velvet of warmest good fellowship, though one presented wholly in a British-American context. If King, ordinarily a man of great shrewdness and perception, recognized the meaning of FDR's words, however, he never gave any indication in his diary or papers then or later. The president had raised the question of bases and King had rejected any such idea quite firmly. Roosevelt's response was to put the prime minister on notice: To ensure the safety of the United States in the Western Hemisphere, to be certain that Canada's lamentably weak defenses on the Atlantic and Pacific did not put his country in jeopardy, he would do whatever he judged necessary. To put it in its most extreme form, for example, if necessity required the seizure of facilities in Halifax or Saint John or St. John's, so be it. A "friendly agreement in advance" was the president's aim, and with the PJBD he had achieved it, just as he had with the destroyers-for-bases deal.[10]

That potential unpleasantness aside, the creation of the PJBD and the close defense ties it fostered demonstrated the importance of Canada and the United States to each other. There was a threat to North America, and so long as it existed the two nations perforce had to cooperate closely. Canadians soon had the freest of access to the bureaucracy in

Washington, Mackenzie King had the president's ear, and the chiefs of staff in both countries began to consider the defense of the continent as a shared responsibility.

The next spring, the cooperative spirit that had animated Ogdensburg was repeated when King and Roosevelt met at the president's home at Hyde Park, New York, this time to consider the economic side of the North American relationship. The Lend-Lease Act had offered enormous assistance to a hard-pressed Britain, and while that was gratefully acknowledged in Canada, the government, if few Canadians, was all too aware of the problem this "most unsordid act" posed for Canada. If Britain could get goods free of cost from the United States, why should it pay for food and munitions from Canada? The British, always ruthless in defending their own interests, bargained toughly with Canada, trying to squeeze financial concessions out of the government. But the Chancellor of the Exchequer's negotiators failed to understand that Canada was in a bind: Domestic industry was developing apace to meet wartime needs, but Canada could not produce all the components necessary for modern munitions. Engines and specialty steels, detonators and machine tools all had to be brought in from the United States, and the burgeoning flow of imports had drained Ottawa's holding of U.S. dollars. Nor was there any desire to take Lend-Lease – that was fine for Britain, separated by an ocean from the Yankees, but official Ottawa feared that sharing a continent with the superpower that was helping you today might be too great a risk tomorrow. The Hyde Park agreement staunched the flow of US dollars and obviated the necessity of accepting direct aid by charging the British Lend-Lease account for the components Canada imported for incorporation in goods to be re-exported to Britain. At the same time, Roosevelt agreed to increase American purchases, most notably of raw materials, in Canada. "Done by Mackenzie and F.D.R. at Hyde Park on a grand Sunday, April 20, 1942," Roosevelt had written on the copy of the economic agreement.[11] It was a grand Sunday for Canada, rescued from financial ruination. Even so, no one failed to notice that Canada had been bound ever more tightly into the American continental economy and that Britain's economic weakness, its complete inability to pay for its purchases from Canada, had forced Ottawa to turn to the south for help.[12]

So long as the Roosevelt administration thought primarily in hemispheric terms, a period that lasted for perhaps a year after the fall of France, Canada was a most favoured nation, perhaps even *the* most favoured nation, in Washington. Obviously, that was important for Canada's physical and financial survival; it was also one of the strongest cards Mackenzie King had to play at home, for the relationship he had built with Roosevelt and the impression he had fostered that he personally was a critical link between Britain and the United States were of incalculable political weight in domestic politics. But once the 1940 American presidential election was over, once the Lend-Lease bill was passed into law, and when, early in 1941, the United States secretly began to negotiate and plan with Britain for its participation in the war against Hitler, then Canada's importance in and to Washington inevitably began to decline.[13]

The first signs of this became apparent in the spring and summer of 1941 when, because of its concerns about those secret negotiations and about its exclusion from them, Canada asked Washington to allow it to create a military mission there "to ensure that strategic discussion in areas of Canadian responsibility were adequately coordinated" with British and American planning. Advised of this request, London was not amused, and it offered instead to add Canadian representation on the British Joint Staff Mission in the United States. That, Mackenzie King said bluntly, "would not be satisfactory," for Canada was insistent on separate representation in the United States. Soundings at the State Department had indicated no objection from that quarter, one ordinarily sympathetic to Canadian concerns, but when the Navy and War departments objected to the proposal and indicated that the PJBD seemed able to do all that was necessary, the Cabinet War Committee in Ottawa was disconcerted. Even more startling was the American response that there would be no objection if Canada was represented at U.S.-U.K. staff conversations when Canadian interests were involved; suddenly even Washington had come to prefer to deal with Canada as part of a British delegation rather than as a separate nation.[14] What had changed, of course, was that the British and Americans were dealing directly now, and suddenly Canada, hitherto the most valued ally of both powers, had been reduced to the status of a pest with its perpetual clamour to be present. On the other hand, there was some doubt that Canada really required a military mission. As Pierrepont Moffat, the able American minister to Canada, noted, "I had been forced to conclude that Canada's interest in the Mission was largely psychological and that for domestic reasons she attached importance to the title 'Mission' and to having constant interchanges between [sic, with] our respective Services rather than occasional meetings plus intermediate telephone conversations."[15] Undoubtedly that was so, but psychological pain can be as sharp as physical pain, and the hurt in Ottawa was deep.

Canada had become accustomed to good treatment in Washington, in substantial part because this compensated for the lack of interest and weight accorded it in Britain and because this created a tension in

London that sometimes was useful to Canada.[16] Like Neville Chamberlain before him, Churchill was not a leader disposed to consult the colonies on foreign policy questions or on grand strategy; what he wanted from Canada was its willing compliance in British decisions, and in truth, he almost always received it. All through the interwar years, Mackenzie King had brilliantly resisted being entrapped by the schemes of Whitehall, and he was chary of commitments. He had taken Canada to war in 1939 but that scarcely changed his approach and attitude, which were marked by a deep reluctance to be consulted about and a complete refusal to accept any responsibility for Britain's actions, mixed with a strong desire to be seen to be important. Much of that was King's insecure personality at work; but some of it too was a shrewd awareness of the play of opinion in Canada, not least in Quebec, where a paranoiac suspicion of Downing Street's wiles was a mainstay of the public discourse. For this reason King had resisted efforts in London and Canberra to call a wartime Imperial Conference of prime ministers, arguing with only limited sincerity that his continued presence was necessary in Canada to keep the war effort moving ahead. He had similarly refused even to pay a visit to Britain for consultation with British leaders and to see Canadian servicemen there.[17]

By late July 1941, however, Canada's position as the ranking ally of Britain and as the closest friend of the United States suddenly seemed on the verge of becoming untenable. The special relationship with Washington was still there, but the American refusal to countenance the establishment of a military mission and the beginnings of direct military planning with the British suggested that Canada's place in the Washington constellation was no longer as important as it had been a few months before. There was probably little chance of securing due recognition for Canada's role in Churchill's London, even if Canadian domestic conditions suddenly altered to make that desirable. The meeting of Roosevelt and Churchill at Argentia would bring these considerations to the fore.

In April 1941, when Mackenzie King visited Roosevelt at his home in Hyde Park, the president had talked about his desire to meet with Winston Churchill. As King recorded it in his diary, Roosevelt "thought it very important that the two of them should meet and be able to talk over things together." For his part, King was little surprised at this: "My real feeling was that it was taking too great a risk for anything that could come out of it.... Also that Churchill would be pretty certain to view the matter with great caution and might not find it possible to get away." But King added, if Churchill felt the same way as the president, "which he may, there might be an advantage in their having a word together which would ensure certain definite combined lines of action."[18]

Churchill did feel the *same* way about the need to meet Roosevelt, and the Argentia meeting was the result. The Canadian government had not been advised that the meeting was to take place, and it was not until Churchill sent a telegram on 6 August emphasizing the importance of the coming event and expressing the hope that his decision to accept Roosevelt's decision would be approved.[19] In fact, King did approve though he had some serious concerns. As he told the British high commissioner, Malcolm MacDonald, that day, he feared that "it is taking a gambler's risk" to bring the leaders and their chiefs of staff together, "with large stakes, appalling losses, even to that of an Empire, should some disaster overtake the gamble." It was all about publicity and show, King wrote privately, for there was no need for such a meeting. It could all have been handled by cable and conference of officials, and "it makes me more satisfied than ever that I have held out against going to England to an Imperial Conference simply for the show that this might create."

More important, King said to the high commissioner, was that "the public in Canada and certainly some of my colleagues will think it extraordinary that Churchill should have brought his own staff to negotiate with the United States staff, and ignored Canada altogether." To leave Canada out, "simply saying that we would be told what had been done," was not acceptable. "I said I did not propose to make any difficulties about the matter but that it was on all fours with what has thus far been done between Britain and the States since they have been brought together." In his diary, King added bluntly that the snub to Canada bore "out my view that the only real position for Canada to take is that of a nation wholly on her own vis-à-vis Britain and the United States. That we can never expect to have any recognition ... in any other way."[20] That comment would have substantial importance.

A week later, when MacDonald called to give King word of the charter agreed at Argentia by the two leaders, King reiterated both his praise and some of his concerns:

> The more he thought about the meeting between the President and the Prime Minister the more warmly he approved of it, and the greater the benefit he expected to flow from it. Moreover, he realized all the difficulty of including Canada. Probably it would be invidious to treat one

Dominion differently from the rest. Because of his understanding of the difficulties of any other course than that which had been followed, he had no criticisms to offer on either public or personal grounds. But he was a little apprehensive of some reactions in Canada.[21]

Unhappy or not, King did not hesitate to send Roosevelt a long letter, handwritten in his near-illegible scrawl, that offered his "sincerest congratulations on *the Conference*" and on Roosevelt's "vision and courage in bringing it about."[22]

The public criticism of Canada's absence from Argentia was generally muted. The fact that Roosevelt and Churchill had met was hailed, though there was no overwhelming enthusiasm for the charter's text.[23] Most embarrassing, perhaps, was that *Le Devoir*, the Montreal *nationaliste* newspaper that was unfailingly antiwar, asked, "Pourquoi M. King n'en était-il pas?" adding that it was all a lesson in humility for hundreds of thousands of Canadians.[24] In private, moreover, there was a good deal of gossip about King's absence, most especially in Ottawa where politicians and officials were exquisitely sensitive to what many saw as a decline in King's popularity and public confidence in the government.[25] The *Winnipeg Free Press* reporter in Ottawa, Grant Dexter, a man to whom Cabinet leaks ordinarily flowed in a torrent, wrote in a confidential memo for his editor that he had heard that King was outraged at being left out. Norman Lambert, a Liberal senator and the campaign organizer for King in 1935 and 1940, had told him that "one of the main buttresses of Mr. King's position as prime minister is the linch pin function – the interpreter between the U.S. and Britain. When Churchill and Roosevelt got together, without the interpreter, the function at once ceased to be of great importance."[26] In fact, while King was scarcely outraged, he did put great stock in his role between London and Washington, and, as we have seen, his nationalism was stirred by his being left out. Still, his prestige, his amour propre, shaken, King quickly announced to his Cabinet that he was flying to England to meet with Churchill. While King was booed by troops left standing too long in the rain, that visit (and another one to Roosevelt in November 1941) was enthusiastically covered in the press and restored everything that might have been lost by his absence from Argentia.[27]

As for the content of the charter itself, it did not overly concern Mackenzie King. Predictably, what did upset him was that Canada again was informed of its contents after the fact. As he told the Cabinet War Committee, a telegram had said that a policy statement was to be issued, and it added that the British Cabinet, considering the matter to be one of high urgency, had given its concurrence to its release. "In this connection," King said, "it was strange that the Canadian Cabinet had not also been given an opportunity to consider the joint declaration, in which Canada would be closely concerned."²⁸ Canada was soon asked formally to associate itself with the charter. Good wartime citizen that it was, it duly did.²⁹

The only serious concern in the bureaucracy about the Atlantic Charter related to its fourth point. As Norman Robertson, the undersecretary of state for external affairs and hitherto Canada's chief trade negotiator, noted,

> its most serious defect is the reservation in Point 4, under cover of the phrase "with due respect for existing obligations," of the whole system of Imperial Preference. This must weaken the force and scope of the promise of free access for all countries to markets and materials and makes it difficult to say much about the free trade implications of the Declaration.³⁰

On his return from England, King told his colleagues that the reservation "had been inserted by Churchill as the leader of a protectionist Conservative party; his [Churchill's] private view, however, inclined towards freedom of trade."³¹ Churchill's inclination might be doubted; Norman Robertson's could not. By temperament a free trader, Robertson feared that the British reservation was another indication that London was heading toward a policy of "straight bilateralism," after the war, a trend that he knew both Canada and the United States would find hard to swallow. His testy comment was an early indication of the direction of Robertson's thinking, and as he was to be the man who would shape Canadian trade policy – and bring it into line with American policy – in the next six or seven years, that had its significance.³²

Of immediate importance in the aftermath of the Argentia meeting was what Canada would or could do now. The forging of a close link between Roosevelt and Churchill, the increasing cooperation of their two governments and militaries had pushed Canada and Canadian concerns to the backburner in Washington and London. Mackenzie King had said that Canada's only course was to be an independent nation wholly on its own vis-à-vis Britain and the United States, and the bureaucrats in the departments of External Affairs and Finance and the Privy Council Office were fast reaching similar conclusions. Once Pearl Harbor brought the Americans into the war, once Washington's turn away from hemispheric concerns and toward globalism had been irrefutably confirmed, then the urgency of developing a new Canadian approach became clearer still.

Norman Robertson, for one, sent Mackenzie King a long memorandum on relations with the United States on 22 December 1941. Canadians, he said, had tended to "take it for granted that the United States will continue to follow a friendly, cooperative and unassuming policy towards Canada." But over the last year, he went on, "There have been a number of warning developments ... which suggest that we should not be too cavalier in our confidence that the United States will always regard Canadian interests as a close second to their own and appreciably ahead of any third country." Worse still, Robertson said, "now that the world war is joined on both oceans, the United States is, not unnaturally, inclined to take Canadian concurrence and support entirely for granted." Then followed a long list of complaints about structural developments and perceived slights, including American reluctance to receive a Canadian military mission and "the negotiations of the Atlantic Charter direct between the United Kingdom and United States Governments."[33]

At much the same time, Hume Wrong, the most brilliant member of the Canadian foreign service and the member of the legation staff in Washington who did all the work, was complaining that Lord Halifax, the British ambassador there, "thinks of the war now as a U.S.-U.K. affair ... He leaves Canada out as a principal."[34] On principle too. The two senior allies soon proceeded to create the Combined Chiefs of Staff and a variety of combined boards to plan and run the war. Canada, now condemned to be a spear carrier in the back row of the Grand Alliance's chorus, was nowhere to be found in this structure.

The result of this Canadian resentment was an agonized reappraisal that culminated in a new approach and a new principle. As Wrong put it in January 1942 when he was groping for an effective approach, "The principle, I think, is that each member of the grand alliance should have a voice in the conduct of the war proportionate to its contribution to the general war effort. A subsidiary principle is that the influence of the various countries should be greatest in connection with those matters with which they are most directly concerned."[35] Such an approach would not permit Canada to claim a place on the Combined Chiefs of Staff, for instance; on the other hand, as one of world's major grain producers, Canada ought to be entitled by right to sit on the Combined Food Board.

This sensible approach, this functional principle, though not formally enunciated as such until the middle of 1943,[36] henceforth governed Canadian policy toward the allied war effort. In effect, Canada was claiming that it was now a middle power, a nation entitled to be treated as a great power in certain defined areas. Almost certainly such a position would have evolved if Mackenzie King had been invited to the Argentia meeting. But he had not been, and his concern then, his feeling that Canada had to act more as an independent nation, led in a straight line to the functional principle and to Canada's assertion of responsible independence. For the first time in its history, Canada now fought for its right to share as a nation in the power exercised by its allies and in the responsibilities that came with power. If the Atlantic Charter achieved nothing else for Canada, that was gain enough.

NOTES

1 Conversation with Jim Nutt at Canton, New York, 16 August 1990. Nutt later served in the Department of External Affairs.
2 David Lenaric, "Where Angels fear to Tread: Neutralist and Non-Interventionist Sentiment in Inter-War English Canada," Ph.D. diss., York University, 1991
3 See J.L. Granatstein, *Canada's War: The Politics of the Mackenzie King Government, 1939–1945* (Toronto: Oxford University Press, 1975, 1990), chap. 1.
4 See C.P. Stacey, *Arms, Men and Governments: The War Policies of Canada 1939–1945* (Ottawa: Department of National Defence, 1970), 31ff.
5 Granatstein, *Canada's War*, 119ff. A month earlier Roosevelt had described Churchill as "tight most of the time." King thought this was "shameful ... that arrogance and the assumed superiority that some Englishmen have that have made so many nations their enemy today." National Archives of Canada (NAC), W.L.M. King Papers, Diary, 29 April 1940, f.439.
6 See J.L. Granatstein, "The American Influence on the Canadian Military, 1939- 1963," paper presented at the Canada-United States-Mexico Conference, University of Calgary, 1991, 1–3.
7 See J.L Granatstein, *How Britain's Weakness Forced Canada into the Arms of the United States* (Toronto: University of Toronto Press, 1990), chap. 2. For a contemporary comment, see Frank Underhill, "North American Front," *Canadian Forum* 20 (September 1941), 165–166.
8 NAC, King Papers, Black Binders, 20, Churchill message att. to Sir Gerald Campbell to King, 22 August 1940; see also J.L. Granatstein, "Mackenzie King and Canada at Ogdensburg, August 1940," Paper presented at "The Road from Ogdensburg: Fifty Years of Canada-United States Defence Cooperation," St Lawrence University, August 1990.
9 On this, see Peter Neary, "Great Britain and the Future of Newfoundland, 1939–45," *Newfoundland Studies* 1 (1985), 30ff. Lord Beaverbrook claimed later that he had heard Roosevelt stake a claim to Newfoundland: "I was present at a meeting at the White House when Roosevelt, forgetting my Canadian origin said to the assembled company "Don't let Canada get Newfoundland. We want it." NAC, Gerald Graham Papers, Beaverbrook to Graham, 21 October 1958.

10 Granatstein, "King and Canada at Ogdensburg," 19ff.
11 J.W. Pickersgill, *The Mackenzie King Record*, I, *1939–1944* (Toronto: University of Toronto Press, 1960), 200.
12 Granatstein, *Canada's War*, 132ff; Granatstein, *Britain's Weakness*, chap. 2;"Pax Americana," *Canadian Forum* 21 (June 1941), 69.
13 See Stacey, *Arms, Men and Governments*, 159–160.
14 Based on *Foreign Relations with the United States (FRUS) 1941*, III (Washington, DC: GPO, 1959), 129ff.; NAC, Privy Council Office Records, Cabinet War Committee Minutes, 23 April 1941 and subsequent dates; and documents on Public Record Office (PRO), Dominions Office (DO) Records, D035/1010, pt. III/WG476/4/6, and DO 114/114, 127ff. Agreement to the establishment of what came to be called the Canadian Joint Staff was not given until March 1942. Stacey, *Arms, Men and Government*, 165, 357.
15 *FRUS 1941*, III, 134.
16 For example, see Public Record Office, Prime Minister's Office Records, Prem 4/43/2, memo from Cranborne, Secretary of State for Dominion Affairs (SSDA), to the Prime Minister, 5 March 1941.
17 The British were not pleased by King's reluctance. Cranborne, the SSDA, said that he was "very wobbly" and even if faced with a definite invitation "he would still attempt to run out," PREM 4/43A/12, Cranborne to Churchill, 30 May 1941.
18 Pickersgill, *Mackenzie King Record*, 201. Churchill told King in London on 22 August that he and Roosevelt "had been writing each other love letters for some time. I wanted to talk with him. It was of the utmost importance that we should talk together." Ibid., 242.
19 Cabinet War Committee Minutes, 13 August 1941. The Canadian media were full of speculation about a Roosevelt-Churchill meeting from 6 August onwards. See, for example, Toronto *Globe and Mail*, 6, 7, 8 August 1941.
20 Pickersgill, *Mackenzie King Record*, 234. Of real importance for Canada was that Churchill and Roosevelt agreed at Argentia that strategic direction in the western Atlantic, including convoy protection, would henceforth be a U.S. responsibility. That put the Royal Canadian Navy, operating out of Newfoundland, under the control of an American admiral who would command from Argentia. Canada was, of course, not consulted about this, and there were hard feelings. See W.G.D. Lund, "The Royal Canadian Navy's Quest for Autonomy in the North West Atlantic: 1941–1943" in J.A. Boutilier, ed., *RCN in Retrospect 1910–1968* (Vancouver: University of British Columbia Press, 1982), 138ff., and Marc Milner, *North Atlantic Run* (Toronto: University of Toronto Press, 1985), 58.59.
21 PREM 4/44/7, Tel., High Commissioner to SSDA, 12 August 1941; Pickersgill, *Mackenzie King Records*, 233–234.

22 Roosevelt Papers, PSF Canada 1941–45, King to Roosevelt, 15 August 1941, Franklin D. Roosevelt Library, Hyde Park, NY.
23 "After reading all the gushing efforts of the editors and columnists ... we have decided that for once we don't differ much from the pundits. For they also obviously think that the eight points don't mean much of anything in particular"; *Canadian Forum* 21 (September 1941), 164. But see the article by FR. Scott, "Canadian Nationalism and the War," in the same magazine, XXI (March 1942), 360, where the charter was hailed as "the most important event since the war started to indicate that the Allies, too, are fighting for a new world order."
24 Toronto *Daily Star,* 15 August 1941, editorial; *Globe and Mail,* 18 August 1941, editorial; *Le Devoir,* 16 août 1941.
25 U.S. National Archives, Department of State Records, 842.00/509, Moffat to Secretary of State, 16 August 1941.
26 Queen's University Archives, Grant Dexter Papers, Memorandum, 16 September 1941.
27 See, for example, *Globe and Mail,* 20, 21, 22, and 23 August 1941.
28 Cabinet War Committee Minutes, 13 August 1941. See *Documents on Canadian External Relations (DCER), VII, 1939–1941, Part I* (Ottawa: Department of External Affairs, 1974), 237.
29 *DCER,* VIII ff. Those Canadians who supported the establishment of a social welfare state were greatly heartened by the charter. Leonard Marsh, the author of Ottawa's 1943 blueprint for social security, noted later that the clause calling for "the preservation of human rights and justice" was interpreted "not only [as] an avowed national aim, but [as] as international idea." Leonard Marsh, *Report on Social Security for Canada 1943* (Toronto: University of Toronto Press, 1975) xvi-xvii.
30 *DCER,* VII, 239.
31 Cabinet War Committee Minutes, 10 September 1941.
32 See J.L. Granatstein, *A Man of Influence: Norman A. Robertson and Canadian Statecraft, 1929–1968* (Ottawa: Deneau Publishers, 1981), 116ff. There was an early foreshadowing of postwar commercial disputes in the negotiations over Article VII of the agreement governing the terms and conditions of U.S. aid. See *DCER,* VII, 506ff.
33 *DCER,* IX, 1125ff.
34 National Archives of Canada, Hume Wrong Papers, 9, file 43, Memo, 14 December 1941.
35 Department of External Affairs, Ottawa, file 3265-A-40C, Wrong to Robertson, 20 January 1942.
36 On this, see J.L. Granatstein, *The Ottawa Men: The Civil Service Mandarins, 1935–57* (Toronto: Oxford University Press, 1982), 124ff.

Chapter Eleven

Happily on the Margins: Mackenzie King and Canada at the Quebec Conferences

The late Charles P. Stacey was Canada's most distinguished military historian, the official historian of the Canadian Army in the Second World War and, moreover, the author of the best book on Canadian policy in that war.[1] He was also no admirer of wartime Prime Minister William Lyon Mackenzie King[2] and, in the context of this commemoration of the Quebec Conference of 1944, a stern critic of his failure to press for a role in the negotiations over strategy between the United States and Britain. "At the two Quebec conferences," Stacey wrote, "Canada played merely the part of host, providing the whisky and soda, and was not admitted to the strategic discussions. But King was amply photographed with Churchill and Roosevelt, and few Canadians realized the true facts."[3]

Stacey's damning words suggest that the Canadian prime minister was interested only in the appearances, desirous merely that the Canadian public see him with his betters. They imply as well that King was little more than a fearful colonial, afraid to press Canada's case for equality of status or for a proper voice on the leaders of the Anglo-American alliance. No one can deny that there is more than a little truth in these charges, which have formed a part of the historical interpretation of Canada's war.

What Canadian historians, including Stacey, have not asked, however, is whether Canada had a legitimate claim to direct representation in the discussions at Quebec. Did the national contribution to the war merit such a place? Would representation at Quebec square with the Canadian arguments for application of the "functional principle" to representation in international organizations? And what consequences might have arisen with other allies had Canada participated? I will argue that the provision of whisky and soda in the historic city of Quebec was all to which Canada was entitled. Even so, by his presence, as well as his Cabinet colleagues and military staff, Mackenzie King, in fact, both acquired information and influenced events out of all proportion to Canada's role in the war.

The issue of Canadian representation at the Quebec discussions first arose when Quadrant, the 1943 meeting of Prime Minister Winston Churchill and President Franklin D. Roosevelt, was being arranged. In mid-July 1943, just after the Allies had landed in Sicily and just after the Canadian government had to fight very hard to ensure that its division-size representation in the assault received recognition in the official communiqués, Churchill indicated by telegram that he wanted to meet the president in the near future in Quebec. Mackenzie King discussed the suggestion with his Under-Secretary of State for External Affairs Norman Robertson and the British High Commissioner to Canada Malcolm MacDonald. King indicated that he had prepared a reply "cordially approving the idea," but Robertson "said immediately he thought my own position would have to be very carefully considered." MacDonald agreed and, feeling it would be embarrassing for King to raise this with Churchill, volunteered to do so to "make it quite clear that it would be a mistake to have the meeting at Quebec unless [King] were more than in the position merely of host to Churchill and Roosevelt in the eyes of the people." Very friendly with Robertson, a highly intelligent official,[4] and close to Mackenzie King (who had dandled this son of Ramsay MacDonald on his knee when he was a child), MacDonald was as full of warm feelings toward Canada as his suggestion indicated. Clearly, the high commissioner had succumbed to "localitis," the disease that often afflicts ambassadors who become advocates for the country to which they are accredited rather than for their own nation.

The prime minister, however, was dubious about the idea – "to try to get Churchill and Roosevelt to agree to this would be more than could be expected of them. They would wish to take the position that jointly they have supreme direction of the war. I have conceded them that position." In Mackenzie King's view, it would be enough if he was the host and was with them all the time they were in Quebec. Then the conference "would be regarded as between the three, as in fact it would be, in large part, without having the question raised too acutely or defended too sharply." But under the urgings of MacDonald and Robertson, King ultimately agreed to let MacDonald send a telegram to London on July 20 that set out his undersecretary's proposal.[5] "I know that Mr. Mackenzie King is assuming that in any meeting on Canadian soil he would be present throughout as host and that he would also be a party in discussions," the high commissioner said. Of course, there would be full opportunity for private Anglo-American talks, and King did not want to cause difficulties over the position of the other and absent Commonwealth premiers. Still, MacDonald added, "it would be extremely embarrassing politically" if King seemed to be "less than a fairly full partner in a meeting in Canada."[6]

Churchill grasped the matter and, in his reply on July 23, he suggested that King and the Canadian Chiefs of Staff participate in plenary sessions of the political and military discussions, a situation that would not prevent he and Roosevelt and their Combined Chiefs of Staff from having such private discussions as they wished.[7] As King noted in his diary, it was "quite clear Churchill saw the need of Conference appearing to be an Anglo-American- Canadian conference."[8]

But when the British leader put this plan to President Roosevelt, the American leader saw "insuperable difficulties in the Canadian Chiefs of Staff attending meetings of the Combined Chiefs of Staff," That would be sure to lead to demands from Brazil and China and other Allied and Commonwealth countries for representation on the Combined Chiefs.[9] This, as we shall see, was a line of argument Canadians had heard frequently before. Moreover, if the Canadians persisted, Roosevelt suggested to his friend Leighton McCarthy, the Canadian minister to the United States, he might not come to Quebec at all and would, if necessary, move the conference to Bermuda.[10] Rightly alarmed, King drew back from any suggestion that he or the Canadian chiefs ought to be directly involved, and he told Cabinet ministers, officials, and (through the Canadian minister in Washington) the president, that this did not upset him. The important thing "was to have the meeting held at Quebec. That, of itself, would cause all else to work out satisfactorily."[11] As Stacey put it, "King's anxiety nor to give Roosevelt one moment's uneasiness is almost comic." He goes on to add that the Canadian "was not interested in a share in discussing strategy, about which he knew nothing."[12] This greatly overstates matters in my view, but if it was Stacey's position that King knew nothing about strategic questions, why then should the Canadian leader have pressed for a seat at the table? Why not *be* satisfied with the role of host?

In fact, again contrary to Stacey who suggested that Canadians had no more to do with the actual Quebec Conference "than if it had been held in Timbuctoo,"[13] King did achieve much more than the provision of Scotch and soda. To start, Churchill proposed that the British and Canadian Chiefs of Staff meet and added that he and King "can confer formally on various important Imperial questions which are outstanding." King informed his Cabinet War Committee of this, took them to Quebec with him, and important discussions duly occurred.[14] There would also prove to be ample opportunity for Mackenzie King to have private discussions at Quadrant with both the prime minister and the president.[15]

The simple truth is that King had understood what was involved in the meeting at Quebec City in August 1943 better than Robertson or MacDonald. The leaders of the Anglo-American alliance had delicate issues to discuss – including further action against Italy and the timing of the invasion of France – and could not afford to let Canada, a spear-carrier in the middle rank of the Allied chorus – inside the room when they were being considered. The Combined Chiefs of Staff similarly could not allow the Canadian Chiefs to attend meetings and successfully maintain their barrier to representation of the lesser allies. Of course, King knew that his role as host and the widespread circulation of photographs in the press would be helpful to him and his government, but he and his ministers, officials, and officers also received full value from their attendance at Quebec. They were kept up-to-dare on much of the Anglo-American military and political discussions, including subjects ranging from postwar world organization, the sharing of information on the development of the atomic bomb in which Canada was a junior, but heavily involved, partner,[16] and policy to international civil aviation, aside entirely from bilateral discussions they held with their British and (less frequently) with their American counterparts. It is almost certainly true that Canadians knew more of Allied strategic plans after Quadrant than any other of the lesser Allies. Admittedly, there was much they could not find out.[17]

Above all, as Mackenzie King had grasped at once, the Quadrant Conference served Canadian domestic purposes. In the summer of 1943, the country was weary of the war it had been involved in for four years, tired of restrictions and rationing, and awaiting with increasing trepidation the heavy casualty tolls yet to come. The Liberal government was at its lowest point in popular esteem (in September, Canadian Institute of Public Opinion polls showed it with only 28 per cent support), and the fragile unity between French and English Canadians was wearing thin as complaints from Quebec about French Canadians being denied their share of field commands and contracts dashed head on with English Canada's boiling resentment that francophone enlistments were well below the average elsewhere.[18] The Quebec Conference distracted and inspired the country, and the prominent place accorded Mackenzie King, even if only in photographs, conveyed the sense that Canada was a valued partner in the Allied effort. That had to help.

One of the most important discussions Mackenzie King had during the Quebec Conference of 1943 was with Churchill on August 10. "I got a good chance both at dinner and after to speak of my problem which is Canada's problem – namely having a voice in all matters pertaining to the war."[19] There is, to be sure, a certain irony in King, having carried self-abnegation to the point he had in making the arrangements for Quadrant, raising this matter in private discussion with Churchill. In fact, however, his was a recurrent Canadian theme.

For purely domestic reasons, King had hung back from pressing Britain for much of a share in the direction of the war after September 1939.[20] In the prime minister's view, the memory of the divisions of the Great War, and the abhorrence of conscription for overseas service in what many in 1940s Quebec still persisted in viewing as an Imperial war, demanded that French Canada receive delicate handling. One aspect of this was that he not visit Britain, so that none could suggest that the Imperial War Cabinet of the earlier conflict had been re-created. Moreover, the fact that King was not invited to the Churchill-Roosevelt Atlantic Charter meeting of August 1941 and did not visit London for the first two years of the war called into question another of the public perceptions he had fostered, namely that Canada was the indispensable linchpin between Britain and the United States.[21]

The pressures on Canada soon increased even further. The United States' entry into the war in December 1941, an undoubted blessing for the hard-pressed British Commonwealth, pushed Canada into the background even further, and there was an almost schizophrenic response in Ottawa as events developed. On the one hand, there was great satisfaction that Britain and the United States were now working hand in glove; on the other, Ottawa felt left out as a result of the new Anglo-American unity that confirmed Canadian diplomats' secondary status. After Churchill visited the United States in December, the two Great Powers set out to coordinate their war effort. The Combined Chiefs of Staff Committee was set up to run the military war effort, while a series of combined boards coordinated the economic struggle. No Canadian seriously sought a place with the Combined Chiefs of Staff – the country's military contribution, large though it was in Canadian terms, was merely a small part of a vast array.[22] But Canada's economic war effort was a different matter, and Ottawa was shocked that its material contribution to the war was simply assumed. Canada was producing vast quantities of food and raw materials and, by the beginning of 1942, its factories had hit their stride, and war production moved out of the shops and across the Atlantic in a torrent.[23]

And Canada had received very little for all its efforts. It had been completely shut out of the direction of the war by an ungrateful London and Washington. Was Canada's war production now to be allocated by the new Boards without so much as a by-your-leave to Ottawa?

It fell to Hume Wrong to draft the response to the Anglo-American affront to Canadian prestige. The minister-counselor at the Washington Legation was the most clearheaded member of the Department of External Affairs, and he understood that Canada had been omitted in substantial part because "the Government has hitherto adopted in these matters what may unkindly be called a semi-colonial position.... We have tended ... to be satisfied with the form rather than the substance."[24] From the sidelines to which Canada had relegated itself, Wrong found the way out when he suggested the governing principle that should apply for Canada and other lesser allies in relations with the Great Powers: "each member of the grand alliance should have a voice in the conduct of the war proportionate to its contribution to the general war effort. A subsidiary principle is that the influence of the various countries should be greatest in connection with those matters with which they are most directly concerned."[25]

As yet there was no name for this idea (which drew on studies of functionalism then circulating through academe), though its formulation clearly marked the beginning of the middle power concept that Canada would later champion during the rest of the war and into the postwar era. Canadians nonetheless began using this argument regularly. The first charge came in July 1942 when Ottawa, the most important Allied producer of foodstuffs after the United States, tried to secure a seat on the Combined Food Board, the Anglo-American agency designed to allocate food supplies. Consulted first, London replied with the infuriating argument that membership "would not make for technical efficiency" and offered support only for Canadian membership on the much less important Combined Production and Resources Board. Prime Minister Mackenzie King, showing what one disgruntled diplomat called "the strong glove over the velvet hand,"[26] overrode his advisers and accepted the offer; Canada became a member of the Combined Production and Resources Board, one of the combined boards without much of a role.

But in March 1943, the Canadian government renewed its claim for a seat on the Combined Food Board. Again the British were reluctant, now countering Ottawa with the argument char if Canada won a seat, Australia and Argentina would demand one too. The infuriated Canadians responded that when those countries produced as much food as Canada, the second-largest food-producing Allied nation, they too would be entitled to a place on the Combined Food Board. Not until October, after much hard bargaining and threats that Canadian financial aid to Britain would cease unless Canada received its due, London and Washington finally conceded. Canada accepted membership on the board, the only smaller nation to win such status.

Victory here was hard to repeat, however. Created in 1942, the United Nations Relief and Rehabilitation Administration was the Allies' organization designed to distribute aid to liberated territories. Canada was expected to be one of the major contributors, but the Great Powers had also decided that Canada was to have no seat on the senior directing committee of UNRRA. The "Americans might not like the British side overweighed by Canadian representation,"[27] Whitehall officials said. Such a response was guaranteed to get Ottawa riled, its officials convinced that Canada was a nation in its own right and no mere British satellite. The manoeuvring went on for months, and British, American, and Soviet stalling led Ottawa to put Hume Wrong's doctrine into principled phrases. In a diplomatic note in January 1943, the Canadians pressed their argument "that no workable international system can be based on the concentration of influence and authority wholly in bodies composed of a few great powers to the exclusion of all the rest. It is not always the largest powers that have the greatest contribution to make to the work of these bodies. In international economic organizations such as the Relief Administration representation ... can often be determined on a functional basis and in our view this principle should be applied whenever it is feasible."[28]

The position had been spelled out, and Canada continued to argue its case with vigour for another three months. Unfortunately, when the British pressed King to yield, offering a place on UNRRA's supplies committee and representation on the key policy committee whenever supply questions were discussed, the prime minister yet again conceded, fearing the ill-will of the Great Powers. King was likely correct, for he had no stomach to try to bring UNRRA crashing down, almost the only alternative. As it was, Canada gave 1 per cent of its GNP to UNRRA in 1943. Similar sums followed in future years.

UNRRA was a test case for Canada. It had argued its case with great vigour and lost. But the functional principle on which the government had stood its ground was worth reiteration. On July 9, 1943, just a month before the first Quebec Conference, King explained the Canadian conception of functionalism to Parliament and the Canadian people: "A number of new international organizations are likely to be set up as a result of the war... In the view of the government, effective representations on these bodies should neither be restricted to the largest stares nor necessarily extended to all states. Representation should be determined on a functional basis which will admit to full membership those countries, large or small, which have the greatest contribution to make to the particular object in question."[29] Simply put, this meant that if, for example, Canada produced a significant share of the world's food or if it held a crucial place in civil aviation, the Great Powers could not deny it a voice in decisions on those subjects because Canada itself was not a Great Power.

Did the functional principle as enunciated by King in Parliament in July entitle Canada to a place at the table at Quebec in August? Norman Robertson and Malcolm MacDonald presumably thought it did, but Mackenzie King did not. The prime minister was right, not the undersecretary and the high commissioner. Functionalism should have qualified Canada for a key role in UNRRA and on the various economic combined boards. It did not, despite the country's very substantial military contribution, entitle Canada to a place on the Combined Chiefs of Staff. By what right, therefore, was Canada entitled to have its Chiefs of Staff sit with the Combined Chiefs at Quebec? By what right did the functional principle entitle Mackenzie King, the leader of a nation of just over 11 million people, to sit as an equal with Churchill and Roosevelt for strategic discussions on the course of the war? What Canada was entitled to, what all the lesser Allies were entitled to, was control over the disposition of their military and economic resources and full consultation on all broad questions of policy. That Canada did not always achieve these does not take away from the fact that the Dominion had no valid claim to representation at Quebec. Mackenzie King, in other words, was truer to the government's functional principle than his advisers, and if he recognized that the most that he, his government, and Canada could get from the Quadrant Conference was publicity and bilateral meetings, that was enough for him. The provision of whisky and soda was cheap at twice the price for those rewards which helped encourage the Canadian war effort – and the Liberal government.

When Mackenzie King learned on August 12, 1944, that Churchill and Roosevelt again wished to meet in Quebec the next month, he was instantly agreeable. "I supposed they would expect me to act as host as I did before," he said to Britain's deputy high commissioner. "If so, I shall be very happy to so act." The idea of another conference in Canada delighted the prime minister, in part because, as he noted, it "gives a further reason why there should be no immediate haste with an election." The main reason, however, was that "I shall really enjoy I think being at Quebec with the President and Churchill. Besides nothing could be more interesting than the questions which will be discussed and to be so completely on the inside in relation to all of them would mean a great deal. Moreover, the close relationship of Churchill, the President and myself cannot fail to be of help to me politically. Altogether I greatly welcome the prospect."[30]

Important questions were to be discussed at Octagon, as the second Quebec Conference was code-named, relating to the end of the war in Europe – which in August 1944 looked to be approaching with some speed – the prosecution of the war against Japan, the continuing development of the atomic bomb, and the establishment of a postwar world organization. From Canada's point of view, the most important of these issues requiring immediate decision was the Pacific War and the question of if and how Canada would participate.

That question had been under consideration in Ottawa for some months, with the military services and the politicians preparing their arguments and counter arguments.[31] For Canada, the Pacific theatre was largely terra incognita, and Canadian eyes, except to some extent in British Columbia, remained firmly fixed on Europe.[32] Moreover, the hasty decision in the fall of 1941 to accede to a British request to send an understrength brigade to garrison Hong Kong – a force lost to a man when the Crown colony fell to the Japanese on Christmas Day, 1941 – had left Canadians unhappy about the Far Eastern war and some less than pleased with British stewardship of it. There was almost no public desire, in other words, for a major role in the Pacific. Against this, however, was the sense of duty that impelled the government, a feeling that Canada's fine record in the war could not be allowed to be jeopardized by too scant a contribution.

Whether the United States wanted a Canadian contribution to the final phase of the war against Japan – or even a British one – was also uncertain until the Quebec Conference. The U.S. Navy, in particular, was markedly unenthusiastic about any British participation in the coming assault on Japan. London, on the other hand, had its own reasons for wanting to be in at the kill, and it most definitely wanted substantial Canadian air, ground, and sea participation to help bolster its position. The three Canadian defense ministers and their Chiefs of Staff generally agreed, making plans for a very large contribution, though there were serious concerns in the Cabinet War Committee about where and how to participate. The prime minister, for one, was dead set against participation in the Southwest Pacific, convinced that jungle warfare was unlikely to prove Canada's metier. Nor did he want Canadian forces to work with Britain in reimposing colonialism on the Imperial possessions that had been incorporated into Japan's Greater East Asia Co-Prosperity Sphere. "I held very strongly to the view that no government in Canada once the war in Europe was over," King told his ministers, "would send its men to India, Burma and Singapore to fight ... and hope to get through a general election successfully. That to permit this would be to raise at a general election, a nation-wide cry of Imperial wars versus Canada as a nation."[33] With the last national elections having been held in March 1940, King had to go to the polls in the near future, and Quebec, the heart of his party's strength, remained restive, and all the more so since Maurice Duplessis' autonomist and *nationaliste* Union Nationale had just been returned to power in provincial elections in August 1944. At the second Quebec Conference, Mackenzie King would make sure that Duplessis "was given as much recognition as possible," his aide J.W. Pickersgill later recalled, for he realized "that if a crisis arose there would be an unfriendly government in Quebec ready to fish in troubled waters."[34]

On September 6, 1944, a few days before the second Quebec Conference began, the Cabinet made the basic decisions about future participation in the war against Japan, although King took the view that Canada had to know the Anglo-American plans before Canada's role was definitively determined.[35] He noted in his diary that "all were agreed Canada should participate. Seemed to be a consensus of view of having one division prepared to go to Japan; one to remain as army of occupation in Europe. Navy to be cut down 50 per cent. The contribution of the Air Force to be made smaller than [the 58 squadrons originally] contemplated."

The formal decision was that Canadian forces would "participate in the war against Japan in operational theatres of direct interest to Canada as a North American nation, for example in the North or Central Pacific, rather than in more remote areas such as Southeast Asia." Reflecting the prime minister's view, the scale and form of the contribution were to be definitively decided after the Quebec meeting,[36] subject to the Americans allowing Canada and Britain in at the kill.

The Canadian ideas went to the meeting the Cabinet War Committee had with Churchill and the two countries' Chiefs of Staff in Quebec on September 14. The prime minister's position had stiffened even further on confining Canadian participation to the North Pacific; indeed, the day before he had told one of his ministers "that I would have to consider whether I could allow my name to be associated with a Canadian Ministry that would go that far ... If it was decided our forces had to fight in southern Asia, I would have to say as Prime Minister, I could not agree to such a policy and would have to leave it to other Members of the Government to carry it out."[37]

King explained his position to Churchill – carefully noting as one politician to another that he faced a general election and everything had to be considered in the light of that event – and Churchill accepted it. As King recorded the discussion, the British prime minister "made quite clear that he did not expect the Canadians to fight in any tropical region ... our men should not be expected to go into the South Pacific."[38] Thus, when the British leader offered a Royal Navy fleet to share in the assault on Japan and President Roosevelt accepted it, Churchill then added that Canada wanted to participate in the north Pacific. This was also agreed in principle. King confirmed all this in a private talk with the president that same evening. "I feel immensely relieved in my mind as a result," King wrote. "I can now see the road pretty clear ahead, first of all as to our contribution in the Pacific; there is no reason why it should be made one that would be costly in life."[39] Conscription, the shibboleth against which King had struggled for five years, in other words, could not become essential because of the commitment of a single division to the war in Asia.[40] Moreover, the decision to participate in this way meant that the Canadian infantry division allocated for the invasion of Japan, if not the naval and air contributions that were to be under overall British command, was destined to serve under American command and with a U.S. Army table of organisation and U.S. weapons.[41] This was a major departure for the country and yet another sign of the way global power had shifted during the war. Those decisions over the Pacific War were the major ones that directly concerned Canada at Quebec.

Mackenzie King also had ample opportunity to talk with Churchill and Roosevelt during the meetings on a host of topics. For example, the Canadian prime minister had persuaded Roosevelt and Churchill to agree to accept honorary degrees from McGill University at a special convocation on September 16. At a lunch just before the ceremony, King made a major interjection with the president, speaking out very strongly against Roosevelt's plan to have an international conference on world organization a week before the American presidential elections in early November. The Canadian leader knew the details of the Dumbarton Oaks Great Power proposals on international organization (made public only on October 10), and he feared that their being put before smaller countries might hurt the president's re-election campaign, or so King argued. "That once it was learned that the four great powers ... were to have the main authority of the Council to tell other nations what other contributions they might have to make in carrying out the decisions of the Council, there would almost certainly be strong objection on the part certainly of the small nations.... I pointed out that in Canada the nationalist feeling would be aroused in opposition to the proposals.... That what I feared was that with so many persons in the States of foreign descent, they would all likely side with anyone who became champions of the smaller nations."

It was not, of course, only Canadian "nationalist feeling" that resisted the Big Four's attempt to seize all power for themselves with their proposals – King's own government had led and continued to lead the attack against this position. Nonetheless, Churchill and Anthony Eden, present for this well-meaning Canadian advice on how to fight the American election, agreed with Mackenzie King, adding that they believed this conference "might really injure" the president's chances of re-election.[42] Roosevelt then departed, no doubt puzzled and gratified in equal part by the tactical advice he had received, and the second Quebec Conference was over.

Before Churchill left for home, he and King spoke at length on the role and manner in which Canada had played its part in the war. Churchill waxed eloquent, as the Canadian noted in his diary, about how "you have been so fine about letting England lead, not making it difficult for us by insisting always on several having direction. I said it had been difficult to maintain my position at times but that as long as I knew we were being consulted and getting informed on new policies and were able to speak about them before they were settled, I thought it was much better before the world to leave the matter of leadership in the hands of the President and himself. He said that had meant everything in the effecting of needed co-operation."[43] Whether Canada was always consulted and informed and whether it always had the opportunity to speak out before decisions were implemented might well be questioned, but of King's sincerity here there can be no question. The functional principle, in his view, entitled Canada to be treated seriously when it had the capacity to make a major contribution, as was certainly the case on economic and relief matters. But on grand strategy, it was different. On such questions, the Canadian prime minister was happily on the margins, most interested in contributing what little he could to facilitating the progress of the war.

Hanging back was not the stuff of nationalist myth, not the bold course. But it was the practical, sensible, and correct position – and doubly so as King (who knew this better than anyone) could not have crashed the table at Quebec City in 1943 or 1944 in any case. That Mackenzie King also received the opportunity to influence events and undoubted political benefits from his limited role at Quadrant and Octagon was a very large bonus, well worth the contribution of even the largest quantities of whisky. When his government won re-election in June 1945, thanks in substantial part to surprisingly heavy support from Quebec voters, he knew that his policy had been the right one.

NOTES

1 C.P. Stacey, *Arms, Men and Governments: The War Policies of Canada 1939–1945* (Ottawa, 1970).
2 For the fullest expression of Stacey's view of King, see his *A Very Double Life: The Private World of Mackenzie King* (Toronto, 1976).
3 C.P. Stacey, *Canada and the Age of Conflict: 1921–1948. The Mackenzie King Era*, vol. II (Toronto, 1981), p. 334. Much the same phrasing, happily omitting the dreadful use of "true facts" (which was most uncharacteristic of Stacey's ordinarily splendid prose), was used in his *Mackenzie King and the Atlantic Triangle* (Toronto, 1976), p. 58.
4 See on Robertson, J.L. Granatstein, *A Man of Influence: Norman Robertson and Canadian Statecraft 1929–1968* (Ottawa, 1981). There is as yet no satisfactory study of MacDonald's important tenure in Canada.
5 National Archives of Canada, W.L.M. King Papers, King Diary, July 19, 1943; J.W. Pickersgill, ed., *The Mackenzie King Record: 1939–44*, vol. I (Toronto, 1960), pp, 527–28
6 J.F. Hilliker, ed., *Documents on Canadian External Relations: 1942–1943*, vol. IX [hereafter DCER plus volume number] (Ottawa, 1980), p. 253.
7 Ibid, pp, 253–54.
8 King Diary, July 23, 1943.
9 *DCER*, vol. IX, p, 255.
10 King Diary, July 24, 1943; U.S. Dept. of State, *Foreign Relations of the United States Conferences at Washington and Quebec 1943* [hereafter FRUS plus volume title], (Washington, 1970), p. 397.
11 King Diary, July 24, 1943
12 Stacey, *Mackenzie King and the Atlantic Triangle*, p. 58.
13 Stacey, *Arms, Men and Governments*, p. 182.
14 *DCER*, vol. IX, p. 254; NAC, Privy Council Office Records, Cabinet War Committee Meetings, Aug. 10, 1943
15 Pickersgill, *Mackenzie King*, vol. I, pp. 534ff.; *DCER*, vol. IX, pp. 256–58.

16 On this subject, see Robert Bothwell's books, *Eldorado: Canada's National Uranium Company* (Toronto, 1984) and *Nucleus: The History of Atomic Energy of Canada Limited* (Toronto, 1988).
17 See, for example, *DCER*, vol. IX, pp. 256–58, and the account of Lt. Gen. Maurice Pope, *Soldiers and Politicians: The Memoirs of Lt.-Gen. Maurice A. Pope* (Toronto, 1962), pp. 221 ff. Pope's report on the 1943 conference (pp. 228–31), however, demonstrates how much he did uncover.
18 Norman Hillmer put it well in his description of the 1944 Quebec meeting: "the Prime Minister's eye was on another Quebec ... more interested in the defence of Canada than the salvation of Europe." "Canada as an Ally" (address delivered at the Society of Military History, Kingston, Ont., May 22, 1993). The usual assessment is that French Canada contributed less than 20 percent of military manpower though its population represented more than 30 percent of the Canadian total.
19 King Diary, Aug. 15, 1943. Stacey acknowledges those discussions in *Arms, Men and Governments* p. 183.
20 Before the war (at the Imperial Conference of 1937, for example), King had successfully resisted every effort by London, Canberra, and Wellington to achieve defense coordination prior to the outbreak of hostilities. His argument was based on the need to preserve Canadian unity and on the principle that each part of the Empire was primarily responsible only for its own defense.
21 See J.L Granatstein, "The Man Who Wasn't There: Mackenzie King, Canada, and the Atlantic Charter," in *The Atlantic Charter*, eds. D. Brinkley and D.R. Facey-Crowther, (New York, 1994), pp. 115ff
22 The Canadian armed forces enlisted 1.1 million men and women out of a population of less than 12 million. This produced the First Canadian Army of five divisions and two armoured brigades, plus additional units in North America; the Royal Canadian Navy, the fourth largest Allied navy, which escorted half of all convoys across the North Atlantic; and the Royal Canadian Air Force that, in addition to running the British Commonwealth Air Training Plan that trained 131,000 aircrew, operated 85 squadrons while also providing tens of thousands of aircrew for the Royal Air Force.
23 So great was the flow that in 1942 the Canadian government gave Britain a gift of a billion dollars' worth of war supplies, a testimony to Canada's support for the war effort and to its recognition that England could not pay for all it needed. Similar gifts, called Mutual Aid in an effort to allay widespread French-Canadian concerns that Britain was getting something for nothing, were repeated until the end of the war, amounting in all to $3.5 billion – or approximately one-fifth of Canada's total war costs. To put these numbers in context, the GNP in 1945 was $11 billion.

24 Department of External Affairs, Ottawa, (hereafter DEA], External Affairs Records [hereafter EAR], File 3265-A-40C, Wrong to L.B. Pearson, Feb. 3, 1942. See also J.L. Granatstein, "Hume Wrong's Road to the Functional Principle," in *Coalition Warfare,* eds. K. Neilson and R. Prete (Waterloo, Ont.,1983), pp. 53ff
25 EAR, File 3265-A-40C, Wrong to N. A. Robertson, Jan. 20, 1942.
26 King Papers, L.B. Pearson Memorandum, Mar. 18, 1943, ff. C241878.
27 King Diary, July 30, 1942.
28 DEA, File 2295-G-40, Memorandum, Robertson to King, Jan. 18, 1943.
29 House of Commons, *Debates,* July 9, 1943, p. 4558.
30 King Diary, Aug. 12, 1944.
31 A useful collection of documents on this subject are collected in *DCER,* vol. X, pp. 368ff.
32 Canada, King said later, "had not an acre of land or property in the Orient," and B. Greenhous et al., *The Crucible of War: The Official History of the Royal Canadian Air Force,* vol. III (Toronto, 1994), notes, "Canadians thought not one whit about the Pacific and the war against Japan" (p. 106).
33 King Diary, Sept. 13, 1944.
34 J.W. Pickersgill, *Seeing Canada Whole: A Memoir* (Toronto, 1994), p. 239.
35 King Diary, Aug. 31, 1944.
36 C. P. Stacey, *Arms, Men and Governments,* p. 58.
37 King Diary, Sept. 13, 1944.
38 Ibid., Sept. 14, 1944; Cabinet War Committee Minutes, Sept. 14, I 944.
39 King Diary, 14 Sept. 1944.
40 During his stay in Quebec City, King made a speech at the city's Reform Club in which he spoke indiscreetly about how he had prevented conscription and how, with the war all but won, it would never be imposed. This provoked a sharp reaction from his Defence Minister J.L Ralston. In fact, by late October the First Canadian Army in northwest Europe was desperately short of infantry reinforcements and King saved his government only through desperate manoeuvrings. See J.L. Granatstein, *Canada's War: The Politics of the Mackenzie King Government, 1939–1945* (Toronto, 1990), pp. 333ff.
41 *DCER,* vol. X, pp. 419–20, details meetings between the Canadian Chief of the General Staff and Gen. G.C. Marshall on Sept. 16, 1944, to discuss details of Canadian army participation with the U.S. forces. See on this and the conference generally, Pope, *Soldiers and Politicians,* pp. 24lff. The Canadian air contribution to the Pacific war is exhaustively detailed in Greenhous, et al., *The Crucible of War,* pp. 106ff. and more concisely in Hillmer, "Canada as an Ally," 10ff.
42 King Diary, Sept. 16, 1944.
43 Ibid., Sept. 17, 1944.

SECTION THREE

POLITICS

Chapter Twelve

Financing the Liberal Party, 1935–1945[1]

The importance of money in politics is obvious. Elections require massive amounts of advertising, organization demands money for salaries, travel expenses and long distance telephone calls, and candidates must receive some support from the headquarters of their party.[2] That much is clear, and there has never been as much secrecy about party expenditure as there has been about receipts. Anyone with patience and a calculating mind could probably come fairly close to assessing the national expenditures of a political party in a general election simply by totalling up the costs of advertising in the media, the costs of various kinds of literature, and by estimating that each constituency receives support to an average of some $3,000 to $5,000. Today the costs of a national general election are usually estimated to be between $2 and $5 million for a major party. In the period under examination, costs were normally closer to $1 million. Still, there is room for further study of expenditures and they will be dealt with below.

Much more interesting, however, is the question of receipts. Where does the money come from? The answer is known in general terms, of course, as is the usual rationale for corporate contributions. Large industrial and financial concerns contribute to political parties because they believe in the two-party system and because the two parties they support espouse the gospel of free-enterprise capitalism. Less often stated, but equally true, is that many corporate concerns contribute to both parties as a form of insurance in case the government is turned out and the opposition installed in power.

The generalities of party finance are known, but the specific details are still unclear. Who contributes? How is the money raised and spent, and by whom? What rewards do the collectors and contributors expect and receive? These are the central questions to which this paper is directed.

There is some difficulty in sorting out the financial machinery of the Liberal Party. The shock of the Beauharnois scandals of 1931 was such that the old order – which is to say Senator Andrew Haydon – was swept away. But once Mackenzie King had walked through the Valley of Humiliation, what was to be put in its place? Some form of organization, financial organization in particular, was necessary. Essentially, the new party machinery was to be based on the National Liberal Federation, a body conceived by Mackenzie King in late 1931 and established effectively in the following year.[3] "I can see it all so clearly," King wrote to Vincent Massey, his choice as the first president of the N.L.F., "a National Association from coast to coast. Dignified headquarters at the Capital. Study groups, speakers' committee, Liberal Clubs.... Above all a great body of public opinion slowly mobilizing itself – enlightened and increasingly powerful, restive until it has overthrown the powers that be."[4] "Restive until it has overthrown the powers that be": that was a splendid goal, a forerunner of the catch phrases of the "participatory democracy" of our day. Far more important for the National Liberal Federation, however, was its task of dealing with the powers that be, particularly in connection with election financing.

This is not to say that the post-Beauharnois Liberal Party did not try to cut itself loose from the traditional sources of party finance. It did. In March, 1933, a campaign was launched to encourage popular subscriptions to the N.L.F., partially at least with the hope of tapping a new source of financing so that the party's organization could be maintained on a day-to-day basis. Unfortunately, the innate suspicion of the Canadian public and the hardships of the Depression doomed this appeal, and from it the N.L.F. received only a paltry $1,942.83 to the end of February, 1934.[5] This disheartening experience forced the Liberals back to the traditional methods, and in December, 1933, a financial committee was appointed at the N.L.F. annual meeting. Chaired by Albert Matthews, head of a Toronto investment house, the financial committee was recognized as the working executive of the federation and directed to appoint collectors in each of the provinces.[6] But even this system did not produce as expected, and instead of its projected $50,000 annual budget, the N.L.F. had to get by on $24,000 in fiscal 1934.[7]

Most of this work of organization and fund raising was slightly distasteful to Vincent Massey, the federation president, and consequently those tasks fell to the organization's secretary, Norman Lambert. Born in 1885, Lambert had been a journalist with the Toronto *Globe,* secretary to the Canadian Council of Agriculture in Winnipeg, and a businessman. He brought to his new task a wide acquaintance across the country, a familiarity with the levers of power, and the fortunate habit of faithfully keeping a diary. And in the election of 1935, the only election he participated in that saw the Liberals begin in opposition, he was to exercise his greatest influence.

The Liberals began organizing for the election of 1935 the day after the third of Prime Minister Bennett's "New Deal" speeches.[8] Plans were prepared for radio addresses by Mackenzie King, a contribution of $4,000 from Senator A.C. Hardy of Brockville already being promised to cover the cost of two such speeches, and arrangements were made to get Prof. Norman Rogers of Queen's University to assist the Liberal leader in his campaign. By the end of January, when Vincent Massey passed through Ottawa en route home from a Bermuda vacation, the basic organization for the campaign was in hand. "Sketched situation," Lambert wrote in his diary on January 28, "and impressed necessity [on Massey] of getting busy on finances in Toronto. He said he would do so."

The importance of Toronto was evident. With Montreal, Toronto was basically responsible for financing the campaign throughout the whole country. Essentially, Montreal's responsibility extended to the provinces to the east while Toronto assisted those to the west. But owing to the confused chain of command in the party organization, it was by no means clear just how firm the responsibility to the outlying areas was. And to whom was Montreal responsible for its actions? The chief collector there was Senator Donat Raymond, and it is evident that he ran what was virtually an autonomous operation, far more so certainly than that of Frank O'Connor, the president of Laura Secord Candy Shops, who appears to have headed the Toronto collection apparatus. With O'Connor, Lambert seems to have had a close relationship, co-operating well, drawing on him for funds for the national office when needed, and allocating funds to the western provinces as they arrived. But with Raymond the story seems to have varied. Not until three weeks after the election did Lambert get an effective accounting from the senator of his receipts and expenditures. A total of $626,000 had been raised, of which $53,000 went to Nova Scotia, $45,000 to New Brunswick, and $15,000 to Prince Edward Island, leaving a total of $513,000 for Quebec uses, a sum that Raymond said left his organization $46,000 in debt.[9] Just how accurate Raymond's accounting was is unclear, simply because Quebec finances and the French-language advertising campaign were run independently of the national headquarters, and few records seem to have survived. Literature was different and was fed to constituencies from Montreal or Quebec City; advertising was handled by different agencies; and the tactical direction of the campaign was handled by the local party nabobs. In 1935, at any rate, the National Liberal Party campaign was really two separate campaigns, and the Quebec Liberals had a special status of their own.[10]

If Quebec was autonomous within the Liberal campaign machine, no other province was. From January until the election in October, 1935, Lambert, who held the purse strings, was continuously being importuned for funds from the prairies, British Columbia, and Ontario. As early as January 29, British Columbia's bagman had asked for $10,000 for six constituencies and a Young Liberal rally. In March, after a meeting with his key bagmen, Lambert had worked out a tentative election budget that allocated $75,000 for Saskatchewan, $40,000 for Manitoba, $30,000 for Alberta, and $50,000 for British Columbia. The total to be sent to the western provinces was $195,000, and Lambert estimated his remaining needs as $100,000 for the central office and $225,000 for Ontario. The grand total, exclusive of Quebec and the eastern provinces, was $520,000.[11] The estimates were just that, an assessment of the amount needed to win doubtful constituencies, a guess at how much outside money the provinces would need to supplement the sums that could be raised locally. To spend the money was a simple matter, of course, but to raise it was a horrendous task.

The problems were immense. How, for example, did one deal with firms that operated large offices in both Montreal and Toronto? Who collected from them? Co-ordination was necessary, and in February, Senator Raymond met with Frank O'Connor to arrange an equitable division of the spoils.[12] Similarly, there were some companies with headquarters in Montreal that conducted extensive operations in the west, for example, and understandably the prairie politicians felt a certain right to approach these companies for contributions. Senator Raymond helped Charles A. Dunning, soon to be Liberal Finance Minister, to get $5,000 for the west in Montreal in a not untypical arrangement.[13] Presumably that small sum did not count when the provincial allocations were calculated, and about all Lambert could bank on was that he would be kept informed of such transactions.

Lambert had other difficulties, too. His relations with Frank O'Connor in Toronto were excellent, but he had some trouble in bringing Mackenzie King to share his point of view. "K. called at my house in evening," Lambert wrote in his diary on May 10: "I asked him to speak to F. O'Connor about finances, on account of the needs of the West etc.; but he said he did not want to put himself under any obligation to O'C; that he had had a lesson from the Beauharnois affair and from MacDougall [sic: the senator and friend who had got King into difficulty with Beauharnois] and never again would he put himself in the power of any man. He did not trust an Irish Catholic drinking man any too far anyhow ... "

Still, O'Connor was a wealthy man, a key figure in the party machinery and a useful link to Premier Hepburn's organization. And when in September party fund-raising was proceeding very slowly, and when Massey and Lambert were talking seriously of writing to King and absolving themselves of responsibility for the results "on account of poor financial response,"[14] some desperate measures were necessary. Sen. Raymond came to Toronto on September 20 to discuss the crisis with Lambert, Massey and O'Connor, and in separate conversations with the latter two men he suggested that O'Connor put up $100,000 for the campaign in return for the support of Massey's "influence for Senatorship". Raymond also indicated that he was providing $50,000 himself. A few days later, Lambert learned that O'Connor had said "'no' re R.'s proposition of last Fri.; that he had put up 25 [000] and that was all."[15] In any case Prime Minister King made O'Connor a Senator in December, 1935, his party services evidently being great enough to be so rewarded even without the extra $75,000.

The nature of this aborted arrangement is striking enough, but equally interesting is the information that the Liberals were having financial difficulties. The usual assessment of this election is that the Bennett "New Deal" had frightened off Tory contributors and that the Liberal coffers were overflowing.[16] Vincent Massey had noted shortly after the New Deal speeches, to cite one example, that Bennett's proposed unemployment insurance scheme would cost Eaton's in Toronto over $300,000 a year and he clearly anticipated that such statistics would be useful in collections.[17] Evidently this was not so, for Liberal collections from Toronto were very slow, amounting only to $121,164.94 on August 15, two months before the election, rising to $154,599.94 on September 1 and only to $184,231.10 on September 15.[18] The results were so disappointing that Mackenzie King himself had to be pressed into service to jog contributors' memories and pocketbooks.[19] Whatever the effect of King's intervention, collections picked up as the election drew nearer, some $160,000 being raised in the last two weeks of September, and $186,000 in the first two weeks of October.[20] Clearly the contributors had waited until the trend was clear before committing scarce Depression dollars to the Liberals.

These difficulties with money destroyed the relations between Lambert and Massey. The frugal businessman Massey insisted on paying the bills for advertising and publicity before meeting the demands of the constituencies, particularly on the prairies. On September 2, Lambert was short by $110,000 in his budget for the prairies and British

Columbia. Two weeks later the situation had eased a little, but Lambert noted that "V.M. said he wouldn't have anything paid out until his bills for publicity were paid. I said if the West didn't get its due first, I would write him a letter and quit."[21] The next Wednesday, September 25, Lambert and several western bagmen met with Massey and squeezed promises of support from him, only to have him renege a few days later. "Had heated argument with V.M. over failure to turn funds to West as agreed," Lambert wrote on September 27, "& compared situation to heavy artillery in rear under camouflage while the front line trenches being deprived of ammunition." As a result of Lambert's concern, J.S. McLean of Canada Packers and Sir Joseph Flavelle, the chairman of the National Trust and the Bank of Commerce and a nominal Conservative, approached the banks in Toronto personally for donations, and although the results were not completely successful, $35,000 more was found somewhere for the west.[22] By October 12, two days before the election, however, Massey was able to report that Toronto had collected $517, 000[23] just $3,000 short of the estimates Lambert had prepared months earlier.

The final returns, as prepared by Lambert, indicated that $558,487.10 was raised in Ontario. The Liberals' total English-language publicity costs amounted to $116,329.13, including $46,696.53 for radio time.[24] In all, this publicity effort included the distribution of almost nine million pieces of literature.[25] About half of the money raised in Ontario was spent there, some $265,763.75 being allocated to this purpose, of which $258,510 went directly to the constituencies. Just how the decision was made to allocate specific sums to the various constituencies is unclear. The average for each riding was $3,150, but some constituencies got almost nothing (the two Hamilton seats received only $100 *in toto,* for example) while others received a relatively large amount. Nor was there any apparent effort to favour the already Liberal-held constituencies, for the same number received financial aid above as below the average. And curiously, among the 31 ridings that switched from Conservative to Liberal, fully 21 received less than the average grant from party headquarters.[26]

Contributors in Ontario numbered some 240, with amounts ranging from $50 to $25,000. Among the major individual contributors were Joe Atkinson of the *Toronto Star* ($5,000), C.L. Burton of the Robert Simpson Co. ($2,500), J.P. Bickell, mining entrepreneur ($8,000), and Frank O'Connor of Laura Secord Candy ($25,500). Corporate contributors included Canadian General Electric, Atlantic Sugar, Algoma Steel, Imperial Oil, Labatt's, the T. Eaton Co., and a large number of additional firms.[27] This money had been raised for the most part as a result of a canvass by E.G. Long, a Toronto lawyer and director of the National Trust, who called on almost 50 firms himself.[28]

Of the total amount raised in Ontario, only $115,900 was sent to the west, a figure substantially below Lambert's original intentions. Manitoba, for example, received only $8,500 according to Lambert's records, but the total expenditure in the province was $67,347. Presumably some $59,000 was raised in the province and spent there.[29]

To Lambert, the lessons of the 1935 election were plain. Somehow or other the collection of funds had to be regularized. Somehow or other one man had to be in charge throughout the country. And, somehow, he had to be assured of his position. The last of these three requirements was effectively met at an extraordinary meeting Lambert had with the Prime Minister on December 20, 1935. By this date Vincent Massey had gone off to his reward at the Court of St James, and there was no obstacle to Lambert's becoming President of the National Liberal Federation. Lambert, however, also asked King for a Senate seat, telling the Prime Minister that he would agree to carry on the work of organization if he could have this. Mackenzie King indicated that this was an acceptable bargain, and he observed that the third year of the administration would be the best time for this appointment.[30] The bargain was struck, and Lambert for the next six years would head the N.L.F. As promised, in 1938 he was made a Senator.

To regularize the party's collections, Lambert resorted to an instalment system based on a 1.5 to 2 percentage-point cut of federal contracts. Lump-sum payments in election years were inconvenient, businessmen complained, causing difficulties at income-tax time, and as Lambert was fully aware after the 1935 difficulties, an instalment scheme would allow cash to be stockpiled.[31] The system worked well, and in the period from November 30, 1935 to November 30, 1938, Lambert raised and spent at least $150,000 and banked even more.[32] Results got even better after this period and in the absolutely ordinary period from March 24 to June 5, 1939, for example, the instalment system brought in some $15,000, including $2,500 from C.L. Burton, $5,000 from the National Steel Car Co., and $2,500 from one George Raynar of Toronto who had government contracts in Moncton, N.B. Raynar's contribution was evidently insufficient, and as Lambert noted in his diary on June 5: "Spoke to Raynar over phone in Toronto: and told him that his Moncton job was 159,000 vs. 140,000 last year therefore another payment in addition to Saturday's 2500 would be expected later." The instalment system was obviously also useful to the bagman because it permitted him to apply pressure continuously to contributors.

The instalment system helped build up the party bank balance, but unless and until Lambert could secure control over the party organization throughout Canada, his N.L.F. would be little more than a facade. The sticking points were Quebec and Ontario, and a completely satisfactory *modus vivendi* was never really found in either province. Raymond had been difficult enough to deal with in the election of 1935, but the problems were compounded when Lambert was told by Mackenzie King "to leave the Province of Quebec alone"[33] and when as a result P.J.A. Cardin, King's Minister of Public Works, seized control of the Montreal machine and became involved in a struggle with Senator Raymond. A pragmatist, Lambert was on the side of power, and after conversations with the Prime Minister and with Cardin, he made his position clear in March, 1939: "I said I was willing to work with Cardin, but strictly on the same basis as with other provinces and C must be responsible for the man who would collect in Montreal."[34] The final arrangements were soon agreed upon: Raymond was to be thanked for his past services and firmly told that new arrangements were in force: the new collectors in Montreal were to be Élie Beauregard, Montreal lawyer and industrialist (Senator, 1940), and Hon. Gordon Scott, formerly the Provincial Treasurer in the Taschereau government; and, as Lambert insisted firmly, "I made it clear that Montreal must raise own funds; but I would help from here."[35] Within a few days, the list of past contributors was turned over to Beauregard. The symbols of authority had changed hands.

In Ontario, the difficulties sprang from the growing antagonism between Premier Hepburn and the federal government. The causes were complex, compounded of equal parts of personal pique and federal-provincial difficulties, but for Lambert the effect was, first, the fear that Hepburn was financing potential anti-King movements in Saskatchewan[36] and, second, repeated attempts by Hepburn to interfere with collections in Ontario.[37] Contractors there were warned to have nothing to do with Ottawa if they hoped to keep their provincial contracts,[38] and there were suggestions that the Premier was extending his operations eastward across the provincial border and trying to interfere with fund-raising in Quebec. Once Hepburn had directed the Ontario Liberal Association to secede from the national organization,[39] Lambert's only solution was the creation of a separate federal headquarters in Ontario, and by the spring of 1939 a National Liberal Committee for Ontario, little more than an office for publicity purposes, was in operation. But at last the Liberal organization in the two main provinces seemed to be sorted out and functioning.

The outbreak of war and the subsequent snap election in Quebec were soon to test the N.L.F. The war led quickly to a demand for non-partisanship and for the closing of all party headquarters in this time of national emergency. The Conservative Party closed up shop completely, and while the Liberals ostensibly followed suit, the N.L.F. carefully maintained "a small office to preserve contact with Liberal organizations throughout the country – having in mind a general election next year."[40] King and his Cabinet were agreed that this was the wise course, and they instructed Lambert to ensure that material was ready for the election which, as King wrote to his organizer, "may come at any time once Parliament has assembled."[41]

Quebec posed different problems after Maurice Duplessis suddenly dissolved the legislature and caught the Quebec Liberals with their organization and finances down. One principle of the N.L.F. while it was under Lambert's control was that the provinces were responsible for financing their own local elections: the reserve of money built up for federal campaigns was untouchable for provincial purposes. The N.L.F. would not be brought into the election, Lambert said: "Now was the time for Beauregarde [sic] and Cardin's organization."[42]

A request for a loan of $5,000 to the Quebec organization was dealt with on similar grounds: "I said no on ground that we couldn't support provl campaigns."[43] Lambert's stubbornness soon brought new men into the field, and J.G. Gardiner, the Minister of Agriculture and one of the few federal Liberals still on speaking terms with Mitch Hepburn, became directly involved in raising money in Toronto. J.S. McLean, C.L. Burton, and George McCullagh of the *Globe and Mail* were all recipients of Gardiner's importunings – and to judge by the thank-you notes Gardiner sent them, all donors as well.[44] In addition and on his own authority, Gardiner lent $25,000 of the Saskatchewan Liberal Party's funds to tide over the Quebec organization.[45] Still the financial pressures mounted, and one week before the election Mackenzie King himself asked Lambert to help the Quebec party. Under this pressure Lambert conceded and agreed to assist Chubby Power, King's Postmaster-General, who was running the fight against Premier Duplessis.[46] Just how much aid was provided is unclear, but Power noted in his memoirs that there were "no great difficulties" with money by the end of the campaign.[47] Similarly the cost of the election is not certain, but there are indications in Lambert's diary that at least $50,000 in contributions passed through his reluctant hands, including $10,000 from J.W. McConnell of the Montreal *Star* and $5,000 from J.S. McLean of Canada Packers. Another feature of the election was the re-emergence of Senator Donat Raymond as a key collector in Montreal. Beauregard, who was later to become a very important bagman, was apparently unable to produce the goods in 1939, and Raymond, the man with the contacts and the entrée to the board rooms of St James Street, had to be brought back.

The victorious Quebec election was a rehearsal for the general election of 1940. The collection apparatus was well established, and Lambert had written to King as early as July, 1939, that "I can guarantee sufficient funds to meet the national expenses of a campaign ... "[48] The instalment system had worked well. Still, the work of fund raising was started again, much of it undertaken by Lambert himself,[49] assisted by two new recruits in Toronto. Peter Campbell, a lawyer and corporation director, was the key figure, aided by C.P. Fell, a partner in the Matthews investment house and a son-in-law of the former chairman of the N.L.F. finance committee. In addition, a committee of members of Parliament representing the regions of the province was created to assist and advise on the Ontario constituency allocations.[50] In Montreal, Senator Raymond was in charge, assisted from Quebec City by J. Gordon Ross, and collectors had been chosen in all provinces except Prince Edward Island to raise money and advise on the distribution of funds from Lambert's office. Some provincial collectors were:

B.C. – S.S. McKeen, shipping company operator (Senator, 1947)
    J.W. de B. Farris, lawyer (Senator, 1937)
Alta. – George O'Connor, lawyer (Justice, Alberta Supreme Court, 1941)
    Hon. J. McKinnon, Minister without Portfolio (Senator, 1949)
Man. – John C. Davis, engineer and company president (Senator, 1949)
Sask. – Frank Ross, shipbuilding
    Neil McLean, businessman (Senator, 1945)
N.S. – W. McL. Robertson, company president (Senator, 1943)

The appointment of recognized collectors for each province greatly simplified Lambert's task, but there were still problems of co-ordination and control. Hon. T.A. Crerar, for example, told Lambert on January 27 that he had asked J.B. Coyne, who played a large part in financing the Manitoba campaign in 1935, to call on the Hudson Bay Mining Co., a lumber company in Minnesota, and the Terminal Association in Winnipeg. The mining company, Crerar said, should be worth $50,000. Aside entirely from the propriety of the Minister of Mines and Resources steering collectors to companies with which he dealt in his official duties, this posed difficulties for Lambert. His collector in Manitoba was J.C. Davis of Winnipeg, and he insisted that Coyne keep his man completely informed.[51] Another difficulty was caused by T.H. Wood, the Saskatchewan collector, who came to Toronto at the beginning of

February to call on contributors. This was defeating the system Lambert had created and at a meeting with Wood on February 2, he insisted that the Saskatchewan bagman cease his independentist activities and cooperate with Peter Campbell, the chief Toronto collector. Wood's response was that he needed $50,000, and if he could be assured of this he would go home. The next day Wood was told to complete the transaction he had started with British-American Oil Co., promised that he would get his $50,000, and sent back to Regina.[52]

Another detail with which Lambert had to deal was the insistence of some contributors in directing where their contribution should go. The wise Chubby Power later noted that this was done so that both the party bagman and the candidate "will in case of necessity demonstrate an appropriate sense of gratitude"[53] J.S. McLean, for example, gave $25,000 to the party, but earmarked $5,000 for the use of the Minister of Agriculture.[54] As Canada Packers had extensive dealing with Mr Gardiner's department, that part of the contribution, presumably, could be written off as a business expense. In Ottawa West, the retiring member, Thomas Ahearn, a man of substantial personal wealth, similarly directed that his contribution should be used for his chosen successor, George McIlraith.[55] Special arrangements and special understandings were frequent enough that they could scarcely be treated as exceptions.

Whether or not *quid pro quo* arrangements were in effect in such cases is not clear, but a suspicion that this may have been the case is understandable. Cabinet members such as Finance Minister J.L. Ralston and Transport Minister C.D. Howe were prevailed on to attend private dinners for potential contributors.[56] Reluctant corporate donors were chivvied along with reminders of just how much business they had received from the government. The three steel car companies in Montreal, Lambert reminded Senator Raymond, had done $7, $6, and $3 millions of business with the government and had not yet been canvassed: all three were soon approached and all three apparently donated.[57] On occasions, however, some contributors were "difficult". One Brophy of Northern Electric was told by Lambert that the party expected a contribution of $25,000 on the $1 million of business the company had received from the government. This hint apparently had no effect, and Lambert again saw Brophy and reminded him that Northern Electric had contributed $25,000 to the Liberals in 1935. For all the arm-twisting, however, only a mere $5,000 was received.[58] In addition, some offices apparently were available to large contributors. W.G. Clark, the Liberal M.P. for York-Sunbury, N.B., since 1935, had designs on the lieutenant-governorship of his province. Anything could be arranged and was – for a $30,000 contribution to the provincial collector.[59] This promise too was honoured, and on March 20, 1940, a few days before the election, Mr Clark became the King's representative. On the other hand, Lambert recorded in his diary that he was incensed when Walter Turnbull, the Prime Minister's secretary, insinuated that Peter Campbell was receiving special consideration from the War Supply Board in some private dealings because of his role as party bagman.[60] Some rewards were apparently "proper" and others were not.

The money raised in the few months before the election totalled only $458,000 in Toronto, a sum below the total raised in 1935,[61] but as the process of collection had been under way almost continuously since 1936, and as the Liberal coffers were full there were no problems whatsoever with money. Certainly the Conservatives were in far worse shape. Dr R.J. Manion's unacceptability as a leader to business, his difficulties with the Canadian Pacific Railway, and the disorganization caused to his election preparations by the snap dissolution of Parliament, ensured that the Liberals would have a clear run.[62] The party's publicity cost $68,222.30 for all provinces except Quebec, and involved 14 national advertisements, posters, 2.4 million booklets, 2.7 million handbills, and 725 billboards. Only 78,000 pieces of literature went into Quebec from the N.L.F. office, an indication that Quebec again remained independent in the campaign of 1940.[63] The rest of the money raised would seem to have been allocated to candidates and to the provincial organizations, but there was at least $50,000 left over on March 16 after this had been done, and some collections after that date were simply banked.[64] It is worth noting, too, that the provinces raised substantial sums on their own. In British Columbia, the campaign cost $170,000, Ian Mackenzie, the Minister of Pensions, told Lambert, and most of the money had been found in the province.[65] Local constituency organizations also raised and spent money in varying amounts depending on their candidate and location. Mackenzie's Vancouver-Centre seat absorbed $30,000, while Liberal candidate Brooke Claxton's St Lawrence-St George seat in Montreal cost only some $8,000, and according to Chubby Power, the costs in Quebec City constituencies were relatively low.[66] The total figure of Liberal expenditures in this election, including the provincial totals and the amounts raised in the constituencies, was probably on the order of $2 million.

The election of 1940 marked the last major campaign Norman Lambert directed. Both immediately before and immediately after the election he had told the Prime Minister of his intention to resign as president of the N.L.F., and his decision was accepted.[67] Thereafter he would advise his successors, but his role was never again so vital, and without his leadership the organization floundered. In fact, the N.L.F. virtually ceased to exist. Patronage, that flourishing weed of government, virtually disappeared after the election as the government genuinely sought to run an efficient and nonpartisan war effort. By 1941 complaints from ministers, backbenchers and organization officials about this policy were loud, and there were frequently expressed fears that with neither patronage nor organization the party would die.[68]

To prevent this unhappy fate, various schemes were presented to reorganize the federation. The cabinet considered the question in January, 1941, and a cabinet committee recommended that Senator A.N.K. Hugessen, a Montreal lawyer, become Lambert's successor as N.L.F. president.[69] The senator took over in May, only to discover that the questions of party finance and organization were to be left to the control of a sub-committee of Cabinet. The N.L.F. was to be "identified exclusively as an educational and promotional office,"[70] a state of affairs that might have been satisfactory if the ministers concerned had had the time or the energy to keep the federation financed. Hampered by his guidelines, Hugessen was not a success, and in September, 1942, Norman McLarty, the Secretary of State, was writing to King, bemoaning the "dry bones of the Liberal Federation" and claiming that there "has been no leadership from the Federation ...."[71] This view was increasingly shared, and as Liberal fortunes began to decline in the opinion polls at the end of 1942, others took up the cry.[72]

Early in 1943, McLarty himself was put in charge of the N.L.F. by a new cabinet committee on organization.[73] The same committee recommended that Peter Campbell should be made both the unofficial party treasurer and a Senator. He had all the "necessary qualifications" for the Senate, McLarty wrote to the Prime Minister, and Campbell went to his reward in February, 1943.[74] At the end of July, 1943, McLarty opened the new N.L.F. offices in Ottawa and began organizing mailing lists and collecting material.[75] The party organization in each province was examined – and found to be completely inactive in three and disorganized in another. In addition, McLarty was warned off Quebec by Chubby Power, speaking for the Quebec ministers, who "felt that they were in a better position to judge as to the suitable publicity and methods of organization to be used in that province".[76] From that kind of response there could be no recovery, and McLarty's efforts – which were probably not too great – accomplished little.

The first genuine signs of rejuvenation came after the political disasters of August, 1943. The loss of Ontario to George Drew's Tories and the defeat of Liberal candidates in four federal by-elections were sufficient to frighten even the most complacent Liberals. At a meeting of the N.L.F. in Ottawa in September the party organization was finally put into operation again. Sen. Wishart Robertson, selected as the new president, began meeting regularly with other organization officials. Money-raising began once more, distribution of leaflets commenced, and plans were prepared – but never used – for a large pre-election party advertising campaign.[77] At the same time, Jimmy Gardiner, the Agriculture Minister and reputedly one of the more efficient machine politicians in Canada, was named party organizer by the Prime Minister. He was to be assisted by a sub-committee of Cabinet on Liberal organization and another sub-committee on party finance,[78] the latter consisting of Howe, Power and Gardiner himself. Peter Campbell would take care of collections in Toronto and Armand Daigle (Senator, 1944) would canvass in Montreal. Lambert's advice to his friend Campbell was "to get Howe and JG [Gardiner] to do their jobs in Toronto & clear the ground before proceeding to actual collections."[79] As it turned out, however, it was Lambert who ended up doing much of the spadework. C.D. Howe, he recorded in his diary, spoke to him on March 15, 1944, about "taking hold of finances of organization. I told him that ... I would help him organize the thing after certain lists were supplied from M[unitions] and S[upply], but I was not going to Toronto ... to collect funds." The next day, Lambert noted in his diary that he "prepared list of 37 names of people who served Govt during the last four years mainly through M&S who should be asked by CDH to help now." Results were quickly apparent, and by the end of October, 1944, Campbell and Daigle bad raised at least $88,000 for the N.L.F.[80]

The N.L.F., nonetheless, was soon to be phased out of the picture. At the beginning of May, 1944, Cabinet decided on C.D. Howe's recommendation and without consulting either Robertson, the N.L.F. president, or Campbell, the chief bagman, that J. Gordon Fogo, a Nova Scotia lawyer who had been serving in the Department of Munitions and Supply since 1942, should become party chairman. As such, Fogo soon won effective control of the party's election machinery and by January, 1945, the N.L.F. formally withdrew, leaving the field to Fogo's campaign committee.[81] Fogo's task was essentially that of organizing the party for the election, and he soon prepared plans for an advertising campaign to cost an estimated $200,000. The skimpiness of this "third-class publicity" proposal aroused the ire of Postmaster-General W.J. Mulock, who wrote to Mackenzie King on September 21, 1944 that "it is inadequate and will almost certainly result in the failure of the party to reach the people with the consequent result that we will be defeated."[82] The budget was not only not increased, however, but cut further, and by April 1945, the Liberals were committed to an advertising campaign that called for only $110,000 worth of space in newspapers

Financing the Liberal Party   225

and magazines and for $33,000 to be spent on posters and other literature in the English-speaking provinces.[83]

Even this rather modest expenditure was soon in jeopardy. Liberal advertising was handled completely for the first time by Cockfield, Brown, a Montreal-based agency that had had Liberal connections since 1926, on an arrangement that, according to Gordon Fogo, was "not intended to show them any ultimate profit."[84] Perhaps this was the reason for Cockfield, Brown's rage in May when the Liberals were so short of money that they were unable to pay their bills. Fogo needed a breathing space, Bob Kidd, the agency's man at party headquarters, wrote to Montreal, especially as his "maximum outgo hit at a time when funds were just coming in". It was, he added, unfortunate and bad faith to broadcast the impression that the Liberals were hard up. That was simply untrue.[85] In fact, the Liberals were hard up. Fogo was "at the end of his tether," Lambert recorded on May 12, "& was advising the P.M. about the situation re publicity which demanded 35M by noon Monday." Fortunately for Fogo, Sen. Daigle in Montreal agreed to advance the necessary amount. By the end of the campaign the agency was somewhat mollified, having billed the Liberals for $186,000 in commissionable expenses and having earned, according to their party contact, $34,000 since May, 1944, out of their arrangement with the Liberal Party.[86] How this fact squared with Fogo's belief that Cockfield, Brown was working without profit is unclear.

Why the Liberals were so strapped financially is also unclear. In 1940 the money had rolled in, almost without urging the contributors to produce. Presumably after five more years of cost-plus war contracts, companies might have been expected to demonstrate anew their gratitude to the King government. Certainly the Conservatives had few difficulties with money in this election, probably raising and spending at least $1.5 million,[87] and it may be that business believed the Tories had the best chance of stopping the C.C.F., unquestionably the major goal for business all across Canada in the election of 1945. Or it may be that some businessmen simply resented the calls that cabinet ministers such as C.D. Howe made on them, the calls that were immediately followed by a visit from the area bagman.[88] Perhaps, too, the simple fact that so many firms were controlled from the United States had its effect. "Met Deakins of R.C.A. Victor," Lambert noted on May 3, "who couldn't see any way of his Co'y doing anything.... Because so subject to headquarters in N.Y." Whatever the reason, the Liberals were in trouble. Of course, this trouble was a relative matter. Peter Campbell told Lambert at the end of May, 1945, that over $700,000 had passed through his hands since October, 1944, and while he had $63,000 on hand then, he needed another $100,000 to get by on until the end of the campaign.[89] There is sufficient evidence, in any case, to indicate that those Conservatives who claimed that the Liberals had a "slush" fund of $5 million were far off base. In all likelihood, the Conservatives spent more than the Liberals in the election of 1945.[90]

What does this study tell us about Liberal Party finances? In the first place it is evident that the party financial organization was loose and informal. There was usually one man in charge at the top, there were always chief collectors in Toronto and Montreal, and there appear to have been recognized bagmen for each of the provinces. But what is striking is the extent to which "free-lance" collections were carried out. Virtually any individual with ready access to the banks or to industrial companies could be pressed into service, as were J.S. McLean and J.W. Flavelle in 1935. Moreover there seemed to be no effective way of stopping out-of-province collectors from coming to Toronto to try their hand there. Also complicating matters were the efforts of individual cabinet ministers to raise money, the continuing inability of the national party organizer to control satisfactorily the situation in Quebec, and the difficulties in apportioning money collected in Montreal and Toronto for use elsewhere.

Because of this anarchic organization it is difficult to trace accurately the flow of money from donor to party to constituency. It seems clear that money given to provincial collectors was used only in that province and presumably was allocated by the bagman in consultation with party notables to the places where it was most needed. Clearly, money collected in Toronto and Montreal was sent to the provinces. Quite often, however, the national organizer could allocate money to specific constituencies. Sometimes this was done at the contributor's request, sometimes in response to the demands of the candidate, and sometimes simply because the national organizer believed that money was needed there. The system operated on an *ad hoc* basis: that it operated at all is a minor miracle.

For there to have been no abuses in this system would have required a major miracle. Clearly there were offices available for sale. Clearly companies were virtually forced to contribute to party coffers out of fear of losing their government contracts. Clearly cabinet ministers were involved in collecting from firms with which their departments did business. And clearly abuses of a serious kind did exist. Whether such a system still exists is unknown, but at the very least the easy assertion of the Committee on Election Expenses' volume, *Studies in Canadian Party Finance,* that "most corporations give donations in the interest of 'good government relations' rather than in the hopes of

Financing the Liberal Party 227

special favours," deserves serious examination.[91] So too does the whole system of party finance, for so long as abuses of the kind detailed here can exist, the entire political process is justly suspect.

There is another side to this coin. The party fund raiser is essential but even such a professional politician as Mackenzie King could look on him as being in something less than the most honourable of professions. This became evident at a long and unpleasant interview Senator Lambert had with King on March 8, 1945. The Prime Minister wanted Lambert to take charge of the organization once again, but Lambert was adamant in his refusal:

> ... I felt that the Presidency or Chief Organizership of the party was an important post in the eyes of the people in the country & in the Party; and carried with it a responsibility on the part of an occupant of those posts to the membership of the Party; because of this recognition & full cooperation should be given to it by the P.M. & the Govt. I had felt and still felt that one's identity with Pol. organizn was regarded as a stigma & barrier by the P.M. & his colleagues to any form of public service outside, as for example during the war years I bad wanted to do certain things as he knew, and was denied them because of too close an association with pol. organizn.... [I had] a strong objection and antipathy to being subject to invidious treatment as President of the N.L.F & because of that bringing the post into an unfavourable light ...[92]

There is a certain poignancy about that. Bagmen were clearly necessary, but not necessary enough that they could be trusted with roles in the public service more onerous than posts in the Senate. Whether this is *prima facie* evidence of the need for Senate reform is unfortunately outside the scope of this paper.

NOTES

1 *The Report of the Committee on Election Expenses* (1966), its companion volume, *Studies in Canadian Party Finance* (1966), and K. Paltiel's book based on them, have told Canadian historians and political scientists a great deal about party finances. There is ample information on public attitudes to party fund raising, on the responses of candidates to the need for controls in this area, and on the C.C.F./N.D.P. and Social Credit methods of fund raising. There is much less detailed information on the old parties, however, except for a study of a brief period in the history of the Conservative Party. The Liberals, pre-eminently the successful party of the twentieth

century, go virtually unanalyzed for most of their history, although the *Report* and the *Studies* volumes do present long but undetailed essays on the party, and there is some good material in Neil McKenty's *Mitch Hepburn*. Unfortunately, those studies were largely prepared before access to some valuable archival collections became available, and there is substantial new information ready for analysis. The best of the new collections are the Norman Lambert Papers and Diaries (Queen's University, Kingston); the National Liberal Federation Papers (Public Archives of Canada), the W.L.M. King Papers (P.A.C.), the C.G. Power Papers (Queen's}; the T.A. Crerar Papers (Queen's); the J.G. Gardiner Papers (Sask. Archives); the J.L. Ralston Papers (P.A.C.); and the Brooke Claxton Papers (P.A.C.). This paper is based on these sources.
2 For some interesting comments on other uses of money in elections, see P.A.C., Escott Reid Papers, "Canadian Politics," Notes on Interviews, 54, 78, 114.
3 J. Lederle, "The National Organization of the Liberal and Conservative Parties in Canada," unpub. Ph.D. thesis, Univ. of Michigan, 1942, 149; H. B. Neatby, *William Lyon Mackenzie*, II: *The Lonely Heights:* Toronto, 1963, 386 ff.
4 Vincent Massey, *What's Past is Prologue:* Toronto, 1963, 210
5 P.A.C., W.L.M. King Papers, ff. Cl35086–96
6 *Ibid.*, "Summary of Proceedings 1 N.LF. Annual Meeting, 1933." f. Cl35148
7 *Ibid.*, N.L.F. statement, f. C135095
8 Queen's Univ., Norman Lambert Papers, Diary, Jan. 8, 1935.
9 *Ibid.*, Nov. 5, 1935. Part of the problem may have been pique, caused by Raymond's feeling in July that another collector was operating in Montreal and undercutting his authority. *Ibid.*, Box 2, Lambert to Raymond, July 29, 1935.
10 See K. Paltiel and J. Van Loon, "Financing the Liberal Party, 1867–1945", in Committee on Election Expenses, *Studies in Canadian Party Finance:* Ottawa, 1966, 186.
11 Queen's Univ., Lambert Diary, Mar. 9, 1935.
12 Lambert Diary, Feb. 20, 1935.
13 *Ibid.*, Feb. 6, 1935. The money was said to be for Alberta.
14 *Ibid.*, Sept. 9, 1935. King toyed with the idea of launching another public appeal for funds in August, feeling that the party "has everything to gain and nothing to lose politically" by such a move. If the Liberals remained silent, he said, "it will be assumed ... that we are depending on the big interests." But on the advice of Massey, King in the end did nothing. King Papers, King to Massey, Aug. 19, 1935 and reply, Aug. 24, 1935, ff. 179796–802
15 Lambert Diary, Sept. 20, 26, 1935.
16 See, for e.g., J. Granatstein, *The Politics of Survival:* Toronto, 1967, 7.

Financing the Liberal Party   229

17 Lambert Diary, Feb. 5, 1935.
18 Lambert Papers, Box 13, Statement.
19 P.A.C., King Papers, Massey to King, Sept. 15, 1935, f. 173813.
20 Lambert Papers, Box 13. Statement.
21 Lambert Diary, Sept. 20, 1935.
22 *Ibid.*, Sept. 28, 1935. One bank apparently did contribute.
23 *Ibid.*, Oct. 12, 1935. Neil McKenty, *Mitch Hepburn:* Toronto, 1967, 73 n. indicates that final collections were $558,478.10.
24 Lambert Papers, Box 8, Statement.
25 *Ibid.;* King Papers Memo re N.L.F. Meeting, 1936, ff. C135190 ff.
26 Lambert Papers, Box 13, Statement.
27 *Ibid.*
28 *Ibid.*, card file (E.G. Long).
29 *Ibid.*, Box 8, Manitoba receipts and expenditures and Box 13, letter J.B. Coyne to Lambert, Apr. 24, 1936.
30 Lambert Diary, Dec. 20, 1935; Lambert Papers, King to Lambert, Jan. 11, 1936 and reply, Jan. 13, 1936. King also created a committee of Cabinet (Dunning, Mackenzie, Power, Howe and Gardiner) to work with Lambert.
31 P. Hippe, "The Liberal Party of Canada," unpub. Ph.D. thesis, Univ. of Wisconsin, 1956, 143 ff; McKenty, *op. cit.*, 168.
32 King Papers, Lambert to King, Nov. 27, 1937, ff. 69015–6 and Lambert to King, Dec. 30, 1938, f. 215198.
33 *Ibid.*, Memo re Exec. Committee N.L.F., 1937, f.CI35210
34 Lambert Diary, March 16, 1939.
35 *Ibid.* March 22, 1939
36 King Papers, Memo for Prime Minister, July 14, 1918, f. C134984
37 Lambert Diary, Apr. 18, 1936.
38 McKenty, *op. cit.*, 168
39 Lambert Papers, Memo re N.L.F., n.d. Box 8
40 King Papers, Meeting of Exec Ctee N.L.F., Sept. 19, 1939, ff. 228035–6
41 *Ibid.*, King to Lambert, Nov. 18, 1939, ff. 229011–2; Memo by Lambert, Nov. 20, 1939, ff. 229023–4.
42 Lambert Diary, Sept. 25, 1939
43 *Ibid.*, Sept. 26, 1939.
44 Saskatchewan Archives, J.G. Gardiner Papers: Gardiner to Burton, McCullagh and McLean, Oct. 27, 1939.
45 N. Ward (ed.), *A Party Politician: The Memoirs of Chubby Power:* Toronto, 1966, 128. In the 1935 election Lambert noted that Gardiner took $30,000 out of the provincial treasury (Lambert Diary, Nov. 4, 1935).
46 Lambert Diary, Oct. 18, 1939.
47 Power *Memoirs*, 348. He also noted (p. 349) that no federal cash came into Quebec. This seems incorrect.

230 Section Three: Politics

48 King Papers, King to Lambert. July 24, 1939, f. 228966.
49 Queen's Univ., Grant Dexter Papers, Memo, Apr. 15, 1940.
50 The M.P.s were Chevrier, Fraser, Golding, Taylor and McLean.
51 Lambert Diary, Jan. 27, 1940.
52 *Ibid.*, Feb. 2–3, 1940.
53 Queen's Univ., C.G. Power Papers, Memo, n.d., "Political Expenditures".
54 Lambert Diary, Feb. 24, 1940.
55 *Ibid.*, Feb. 7–8, 1940.
56 *Ibid.*, Feb. 13, 1940.
57 *Ibid.*, Feb. 6, 21, 28–9, Mar. 12, 19, 1940.
58 *Ibid.*, Feb. 6, 29, Mar. 6, 1940.
59 *Ibid.*, Jan. 30, 1940.
60 *Ibid.*, Mar. 12, 1940.
61 McKenty, *op. cit.*, 217n.
62 See Granatstein, *Politics of Survival*, Chapter 3
63 Lederle, *op. cit.*, 180; Lambert Diary, Jan. 25, 29, Feb. 5–6, 1940; P.A.C., National Liberal Federation Papers, v. 602, Fin. Statements file, Memo, n.d.; *ibid.*, v. 801, 1940 el. file, "Advertising and Publicity for General Election", n.d
64 Lambert Diary, Mar. 16, 18, 1940.
65 *Ibid.*, Apr. 2, 1940.
66 *Ibid.*, Apr. 3, 1940; P.A.C., Brooke Claxton Paper v. 137, Claxton to L.B. Pearson, Apr. 27, 1940; *ibid.*, v. 150, budget, shows expenditures of $13,691.46, however; Power *Memoirs*, 355
67 Lambert Papers, Memo, "The National Liberal Federation", n.d.
68 P.A.C., W.L.M. King Papers, "Memo re National Liberal Federation", n.d. [Jan., '41?], f. 5264 ff.; Lambert Diary, Jan. 5, 1941.
69 Public Archives of Nova Scotia, A.L. Macdonald Papers, file 4–2 Personal, H. Henry to Macdonald, Jan 10, 1941; King Papers, Ian Mackenzie to King, Jan. 14, 1941, ff. 52961–3; *ibid.*, Jan. 18, 1941, ff. 52967–9.
70 Lambert Papers, Box 8, Lambert to Ian Mackenzie, May 10, 1941 and atts.
71 King Papers, McLarty to King, Sept. 1, 1942, f. 741370.
72 *Ibid.*, J4, v. 240, Memo, Turnbull to King, Dec. 28, 1942.
73 *Ibid.*, v. 46, McLarty to King, Sept. 1, 1942. The committee consisted of Power, Mackenzie. McLarty and Mulock.
74 *Ibid.*, v. 62, McLarty to King, Jan. 9, 1943 and Mackenzie to King, Jan. 6, 1943. See Lambert Papers, Memo to Campbell, n.d., which half-urges Campbell not to take the post.
75 King Papers, McLarty to King, July 28, 1943, f. 87790
76 *Ibid.* Sept. 1, 1943, ff. 81802–3.
77 J.W. Pickersgill (ed.), *The Mackenzie King Record*, I: 1939–44: Toronto, 1960, 575; Lambert Diary, Sept. 29, 1943; N.F.L. Papers, v. 603, "Memo for Sen.

Robertson on Liberal Organization" (Claxton) n.d.; *ibid.*, v. 597, Memo regarding Election Campaign Literature, Sept. 15, 1944; *ibid.*, v. 802, H.E. Kidd to A.G. McLean, Sept. 1, 1944.
78 Gardiner Papers, Gardiner to T.H. Wood, Jan. 7, 1944; Lambert Diary, Dec. 28, 1943 and March 8, 1944; King Papers, v. 62, McLarty to Sen. Robertson, Oct. 14, 1943.
79 Lambert Diary, Mar. 8–9, 1944.
80 *Ibid.*, Apr. 26, 28, 1944; Macdonald Papers, file 6–30 personal, Robertson to Macdonald, Jan. 5, 1945; N.L.F. Papers, v. 596, A. G. McLean to J.G. Fogo, July 3, 1944; Gardiner Papers, W.W. Dawson to Gardiner, Nov. 29, 1944. By contrast, Tory expenditures were far higher: 1943 – $173,000; 1944 – $478,000. J. Granatstein, "Conservative Party Finances, 1939–45", in *Studies in Canadian Party Finance*, 301
81 Lambert Diary, May 3–7, 1944; Jan. 17, 1945; P.A.C., J.L. Ralston Papers, Box 53, 1945 campaign file, Robertson to Ralston, May 11, 1945; N.LF. Papers, v. 596, Robertson to Fogo, Jan. 24, 1945.
82 King Papers, v. 84, Mulock to King, Sept. 21, 1944; Pickersgill and Forster, *King Record*, II: *1944–45:* Toronto, 1968, 95; N.L.F. Papers, v. 603, Memo, H.E. Kidd to T.L. Anderson, Jan. 26, 1945.
83 *Ibid.*, v. 602, "Estimates for advertising", Apr. 24, 1945
84 *Ibid.*, v. 596, Fogo to A.G. McLean, Feb. 7, 1945
85 *Ibid.*, v. 602, Kidd to Hammond, May 11, 1945.
86 *Ibid.*, Kidd to Archibald, June 8, 1945.
87 Granatstein, "Conservative Party Finances", 303 ff.
88 Lambert Diary, May 16, 1945.
89 *Ibid.*, May 25, 1945.
90 Granatstein, *Politics of Survival*, 189, 191.
91 Paltiel and Van Loon, *op. cit.*, 170. Cf. Hon. R.A. Bell's comments in "The Political Party – Its Organization, Candidates and Finances", in G. Hawkins (ed.), *Order and Good Government:* Toronto, 1965, 105–6; Power Papers, Memo on "Political Expenditures", p.7.
92 Lambert Diary, March 8, 1945; Pickersgill, *op. cit.*, II, 323.

Chapter Thirteen

King and His Cabinet: The War Years

Still the standard textbook, R. Macgregor Dawson's *The Government of Canada* remains a delight to read, its tart observations and hard common sense fresh despite the passage of years. Nowhere arc these qualities more evident than in the discussion about the role and relations of a prime minister and his cabinet.

A prime minister, Dawson says, is not just *primus inter pares*. "He cannot be first among his equals for the very excellent reason that he has no equals." But, the author went on, the prime minister is not a despot and the "other Ministers are the colleagues of their chief and not his obedient and unquestioning subordinates." If the leader interferes too often with ministers in the running of their departments, for example, he would soon be out of office, a victim of their combined influence in the House of Commons and the party. On the other hand, as Dawson cheerfully admits, "A fair proportion of the Cabinet are barely capable of performing their own departmental duties efficiently, and these are probably useless also as consultants in the wider field of general Government policy."

Thus while a main task of the prime minister is to make his cabinet function as a team, in trust and confidence, for practical reasons a prime minister will usually have to rely on a few ministers of exceptional ability and judgment for advice on all matters of great import.

The task is a difficult one at the best of times. Dawson concludes that the successful prime minister will be one "who can be both unchallenged master of his administration and yet at the same time avoid the faults and dangers of absolutism ... he must always strive to have it both ways...." He continues:

> The Prime Minister may have enormous powers, but the basic conditions under which he governs compel him to wield his authority strictly

on sufferance: he moves in an atmosphere of friendliness, tolerance, and suspended judgement in his own party, in one of constant criticism, suspicion, and outspoken condemnation elsewhere, His retention of office is thus continually under attack; he can never ignore incipient dissatisfaction and revolt among his own supporters, and he must soothe the ruffled feelings and anticipate the indignant outbreaks before they reach the acute stage. He can never lose sight of the paramount necessity of retaining the confidence of the House and, behind the House, of the electorate. No matter how lofty his position, he can always be defeated and displaced. The war for political supremacy is unending, and a victorious engagement today may be speedily followed by disastrous defeat tomorrow. The most any Prime Minister can hope for is a temporary success, which will give him time and opportunity to consolidate his position and prepare his defences for the next encounter.[1]

A hard job for any man, and one that those not covetous of power before everything else could scarcely contemplate. Fortunately, or perhaps unfortunately, there is no shortage of aspirants and never has been.

Dawson's description of the criteria required to lead a government in Canada can readily be applied to Macdonald, to Laurier, and to Mackenzie King. All governed successfully, well, and long; all managed to keep colleagues generally contented and dependent on them. Macdonald set the mould, Laurier refined it, and Mackenzie King perhaps brought prime-ministership to its tactical perfection. This paper will focus on the last of this trinity of successful first ministers. How did King operate in Cabinet during the Second World War? How did he select his ministers? manage them? control their enthusiasms and still their doubts? How did he deal with the dissidents and crush the disloyal?

Certainly Mackenzie King had few qualms about his ability as prime minister. It was his job to lead the government and the House of Commons, the party and the country in the proper direction. It was his task to direct and control policy, to form a consensus out of the disparate views of race, religion, region, and economic interest that existed in the party, the caucus, and the cabinet. To King, the cabinet was the focal point, the place where all the pressures came to bear, and not least among Mackenzie King's many political skills was his ability to manage his ministers. All the problems of which MacGregor Dawson wrote existed in plenty in King's cabinets, and occasionally King could muster barely a corporal's guard of competent departmental heads. In the 1920s, that tiny band might have been sufficient to administer a small government with small resources; in the 1930s it was completely inadequate to its task; in the war years, it would have been disastrous.

Fortunately, with the coming of war in September 1939 Mackenzie King put together an efficient cabinet: J.L. Ralston, Norman Rogers, J.L. Ilsley, C.D. Howe, Ernest Lapointe – that is a roster that demands respect. In addition, the war produced some new and able ministers while others blossomed. Louis St. Laurent came to the government after Lapointe's death and brought new strength to the Department of Justice and to the government as a whole, while Chubby Power, the Minister of National Defence for Air, was in some ways one of the most effective ministers King had despite his notorious drinking problem. Still, the cabinet table was surrounded by more than a few genuine mediocrities, political hacks, and patronage seekers. As Dawson noted, there were no more than four or five ministers at any time on whom King could rely. The prime minister needed advice and sought it constantly, but he had been in power for a long time and Mackenzie King was convinced that his judgment, while not infallible, was usually correct.

This self-confidence was the central factor in Canadian politics in the period of the war. King had led Liberalism with success for twenty years; he had been prime minister for thirteen years by 1939; and he had restored the Liberal party as a major force in the nation after the trauma of the Great War. This was a record in which King took justifiable pride, a record he continually pointed out to his colleagues (sometimes to the brink of boredom and even nausea). King's long experience and his extraordinary record of success tended to shape the way the government responded during the war years to crises and challenges.

Not least among the prime minister's abilities was the knack of judging men. King knew his Members of Parliament, their strengths and interests, their weaknesses and foibles. Even though the war years taxed his strength severely and filled his hours with the greatly increased responsibilities the expansion of government put on him, King still found a substantial amount of time to meet with ordinary backbenchers in his office in the Parliament Buildings, to learn something of his people, to sound opinion. In addition, the prime minister spent many hours in the House listening to the debates. His was the generation that could be greatly impressed by a good speech, and King remained party man enough to admire orators who vigorously attacked the Conservative or CCF enemy and defended the Liberal government – and particularly its leader.

But a prime minister had to consider carefully before a man was brought into the government. For example, in July 1940, in the midst of general discussions on the need to strengthen the cabinet and give it a more appealing and less partisan cast, King pondered the possibility of bringing in Sam Factor, a Toronto Jewish MP. "I was ready to appoint Sam Factor," King wrote in his diary:

> French colleagues seemed afraid of the prejudice against Jews still being shown. I said the persecuted would be becoming the most numerous elements in countries today. I thought they should be represented in the Cabinet. I could see, however, that there would be difficulties with Quebec colleagues if he were taken in.[2]

Factor was left out. However much he might have wished to make a gesture to the persecuted, King was not willing to upset his Quebec colleagues over a matter as unimportant as this.

Again in May 1941 King worried about his colleagues' weaknesses and about the need for new blood. The two best backbenchers in his view were English-speaking Montrealers, Brooke Claxton and Douglas Abbott, both able men indeed with long government careers ahead of them. Abbott was more popular, King observed in his diary, but he had been impressed with the flood of memoranda with which Claxton deluged him. There was also J.T. Thorson from Manitoba. He was a possibility for the cabinet, but King thought he was doing well as chairman of the House's Expenditures Committee, and in any case Thorson had already indicated that he wanted a place on the Exchequer Court rather than in government. With these thoughts in mind King then talked with Lapointe and P.J.A. Cardin, the senior Quebec ministers, about the need to bring in a new English-speaking representative from their province. Both men were vehemently opposed to Claxton, King learned, and their feelings were so strong that they were prepared to see the portfolio go to another province rather than to Claxton. They would support Abbott, they said, but King worried that if he was brought in, Claxton would feel left out. The solution was clear – Thorson – and the Manitoba member took his place in the Privy Council as Minister of National War Services.[3] As it turned out, Thorson was not a great success and by October 1942 he had gone to the bench.

As difficult for King as for any other prime minister was disposing of unwanted ministers. In May 1940, for example, shortly after the sweeping election victory that put the Liberals firmly in command for the war, the problem of W.D. Euler, the Minister of Trade and Commerce from North Waterloo had to be resolved. Mackenzie King had never looked on Euler as a tower of strength; in fact, before the election King had had to exert himself to keep the minister in the cabinet so he could present a united and undivided team to the electorate. But now, after the people had spoken, Euler suddenly preferred to remain rather than go to the Senate. "His whole point of view was purely Euler and what would suit his convenience," King wrote furiously on May 7 after his interview with the departing minister. "I told him I needed a portfolio for [James A.] MacKinnon [from Alberta and Minister without portfolio since January 1939] and intended to make him Minister of Trade and Commerce." On May 9, still angry, King told the assembled cabinet with Euler in attendance that if the minister had not pressed so hard for a Senate seat before the election he would probably have stayed in the cabinet.[4] But the prime minister was not so annoyed that he cut off Euler completely – the former minister did become a Senator.

Later the prime minister had problems with Pierre Casgrain, Secretary of State since May 1940. Casgrain had been the Speaker of the House since 1935, and King, who had no high opinion of his abilities, had been exceedingly reluctant to bring him into the government. In the end he agreed to make him Secretary of State on the understanding that he would stay in the government only for a short period after which he would be elevated to the bench. As King noted in his diary, Casgrain was getting consideration for one reason only – the loyalty and party service he and his wife, Thérèse, had shown. In fact, King noted, "the ability lies with her."[5] By December 1941 the time had come for Casgrain to become a judge, and the prime minister offered him a place on the Superior Court of Quebec. The Quebec minister was unhappy with this proposal and he came to see Mackenzie King on December 15, 1941, to seek a place on the province's Court of Appeals. The prime minister patiently reviewed the understanding that had been made in May 1940 and told Casgrain that "Lapointe, Dandurand and Cardin all felt that the Superior Court was the best he could do." The ex-minister pressed his case, and this time King let go: "That as he knew, he had written letters himself as Secretary of State asking that firms in his constituency should be considered for the award of contracts...." The Tories had these letters, King added, and if they had raised the question in Parliament, Casgrain would not even have got the Superior Court which he was lucky to have. "I also told him he owed everything to Therese [sic] in his appointment as Speaker as well as to the Cabinet," the prime minister went on, turning the knife just a bit. Later in the day Mme. Casgrain came to see him, but King remained adamant and Pierre Casgrain went to the Superior Court.[6]

As any prime minister must, King could wield his axe ruthlessly when necessary. If the balky ministers went quietly they would get their rewards on the bench or in the Senate, thus being assured of continuing income and status. And in fact virtually everyone got his reward. In the war years, with the exception of Ralston, Cardin, and Power, all of whom resigned on grounds of principle, every retiring minister who wanted an appointment elsewhere got something if not always the precise position he sought.

Firing ministers was sometimes easier than shuffling them. To be fired meant leaving politics and ascending to the bench or to the Senate, a process that could be masked as retirement. A cabinet shuffle, however, leaving a minister in a less important post, could be camouflaged only with difficulty, and this hurt status-conscious politicians. The task for the prime minister, in such instances, was to minimize the pain. That King could do this well can be seen in the way he handled Ian Mackenzie's transfer from National Defence to Pensions and Health in September 1939.

Mackenzie was a Vancouver Member, one of the boys, a bibulous, amusing, loyal party stalwart, a good House of Commons man, but regrettably no great administrator. As Minister of National Defence for the four years prior to the war, he had had indifferent success, seeing himself and his department enmeshed in the Bren Gun affair of 1938, watching the *Financial Post* attack contract procedures with gusto – and too many facts. There was an evident lack of direction and organization that could not be tolerated once war had come, and Mackenzie had to go. How could it be done?

King's tactics were very clever. His own mind was virtually made up when he met on September 13 with Ralston, the Minister of Finance who, despite his entry into the cabinet only one week before, already ranked with Lapointe as King's closest advisor. Ralston agreed that Mackenzie would have to go, "that now was the time to have him placed elsewhere...." Ralston believed Norman Rogers, the Minister of Labour and one of King's special favourites, could do the job in Defence, and King agreed: "I have all along been thinking of this myself.... Would have given Power Defence," King added, "but fear he might break out.... I am debating between finding an outside post for Mackenzie or keeping him in the government. Might possibly arrange an immediate exchange between him and Power [the Minister of Pensions and National Health].... Have, of course, to watch Quebec portfolios.... Best at present to keep Cabinet intact and avoid by-elections."[7]

The next day King talked the matter over with Lapointe. The two agreed that Mackenzie "would have to leave Defence ... that he could not stay in Defence without the whole Government being injured. It was not a question of not having faith in his integrity, but a matter of how the public was feeling. We had to consider the wishes of the public at this time rather than the personal side of the question."[8] King now had the backing of his two key ministers for a shift in Defence. A few days later he brought Lapointe back along with C.D. Howe, the Minister of Transport. He was thinking of Power for National Defence, he said, but there was the problem caused by his drinking. Howe agreed: "We would never be forgiven if anything happened when the country was actually at war." King, having the response he had wanted, agreed, and both ministers concurred in believing Rogers was the best choice. Lapointe added that Power should be consulted.[9]

A realistic man, well aware of the difficulties his friend Ian Mackenzie was in, Power did not seem surprised when Mackenzie King told him that it was the unanimous view of his cabinet colleagues that he should go to National Defence. If he was not surprised, however, Power was not about to be swayed by any desire to take on the job. His own third-person memorandum of this conversation indicated the reasons he offered:

1 Personal.
2 In view of the policy cutting down and also of restricting recruiting thinks his appointment would be bad as general public would attack him as Catholic, anti-Conscriptionist from Quebec desiring to thwart Canada's efforts to assist G[reat] B[ritain].
3 If, in time, conscription became necessary, [Power] pledged against it and would have to get out just when organization brought up to efficient standard.
4 With the responsibilities incident to the portfolio [Power] would have no time for the various other important [political organizing] jobs which the PM desires he should undertake.

Then, as Power recorded, King called in Lapointe "who strongly urges C.G. to accept but is finally convinced by his argument that it would be unwise." Ralston was summoned and he "terms C.G.'s refusal as ingenuous – but is also more or less convinced of soundness of argument."[10]

So King had achieved his end. Lapointe and Ralston, already having told King that Power would not be safe in National Defence, found themselves in the happy position of having Power himself argue against his going to that department. In addition, as Mackenzie's closest friend in the cabinet, Power had implicitly accepted that Mackenzie would have to be moved from Defence; and Power had also volunteered that he needed a light portfolio so that he could undertake political chores for Mackenzie King. The way was now open for the prime minister to move Mackenzie to Pensions and National Health, and to put Rogers into National Defence, and Power into the Postmaster-Generalship. The government would be greatly strengthened by this shuffle, its greatest embarrassment eliminated.

All that remained was to let Mackenzie down gently. On September 19, the cabinet agreed to let Mackenzie issue the press release announcing the despatch of an expeditionary force to Britain. "I at once said that was what I would prefer to anything," King wrote, adding that when the cabinet photograph had been taken the day before he had put Mackenzie directly behind him. The prime minister also noted "That now we were announcing Canada's war effort, our final policies, and that if those were made by him as Minister of Defence, it would then seem the natural moment at which to turn over the task of carrying on along the lines indicated."[11] So Mackenzie had been eased out of Defence by King in a way that kept his goodwill and that of the key ministers while greatly strengthening the administration. A day or two later after Rogers' first presentation to the cabinet in his new portfolio, the prime minister wrote that "We got the first intelligent and clear-cut statement from a Minister of the Department we have had in a year past."[12]

Intelligence was an important attribute of a cabinet minister in King's eyes. And to get it he was willing to override some of the more traditional factors in constructing a cabinet. He realized, of course, that any cabinet had to include strong Quebec representation; he knew that Catholics could not be slighted; that English-speaking Quebeckers had to be included; that each province needed its own man; and that class interests had to be considered. King was as aware of these factors as any prime minister. But sometimes such considerations could be sacrificed.

In the spring of 1945, for example, with an election only a few months away, King had to reconstruct his cabinet. Angus L. Macdonald and T.A. Crerar, both very unhappy with King's course in the conscription crisis of November 1944, were leaving; J.A. Michaud, a New Brunswick Acadian, hoped for the bench; General L.R. LaFlèche would be happy with a suitable diplomatic post; Norman McLarty and W.P. Mulock had to be replaced on grounds of incompetence and illness. Six ministers were departing, leaving plenty of room for new blood.

From New Brunswick, King brought in D.L. MacLaren of Saint John, a man he had apparently never met and one he accepted entirely on the recommendation of Michaud. In Manitoba his choice was J.A. Glen, the Speaker of the Commons since 1940. These were relatively simple choices (although MacLaren's appointment was unusual), but the Ontario and Quebec posts were harder to fill.

Ontario clearly would be the key to the election, and the portfolios vacated by Mulock, McLarty, and Macdonald (who, although a Nova Scotian, had been elected in Kingston) had to be filled with men able to bring support to a government that still seemed in political trouble. In these circumstances, King acted somewhat atypically. His new ministers were J.J. McCann, a doctor from Renfrew South; Lionel Chevrier from Cornwall; and Paul Martin from Windsor. All were able men, but all were Catholics and two were French Canadians, and King took them into the government in spite of this.[13] This sounds only slightly unusual today, but to have even an English-speaking Catholic from Ontario was very rare, Charles Murphy and Robert Manion being the solitary examples in living memory. To have French-speaking Catholics was unheard of. In King's mind presumably the quality of the men counted substantially, but so must his awareness that Liberal support tended traditionally to come from Catholics. Perhaps what he was trying to do was to bolster his Ontario electorate at its strongest point, counting on the Tories to win most of that province's seats in any case.

In Quebec (where the presence of Chevrier and Martin would do no harm) King again defied tradition. Brooke Claxton had been brought into the cabinet as Minister of National Health and Welfare in October 1944, and the Montreal Member seemed to fill the traditional English-Quebec seat. But King wanted Abbott, the Westmount MP, in his government too, again in the face of upsetting the traditional cabinet balance, and he brought him in. One additional Quebec minister was added, Joseph Jean. Jean had opposed conscription in the fall of 1944, but he had done so in a way that had minimized harm. This had impressed King, and he was swayed by St. Laurent's argument that Jean's elevation would give hope to other less than brilliant backbenchers that they too could aspire to the cabinet.[14]

King's selections in Ontario and Quebec, then, however unusual they may have been in traditional terms, were undoubted successes. Abbott strengthened the cabinet, and he won Westmount narrowly in the 1945 election, probably the only Liberal who could have carried that riding in the face of the conscription crisis. McCann, Chevrier, and Martin also held their seats and were exceptionally strong ministers. King had chosen ability over tradition, and he had chosen well.

Naturally enough, King was not always happy with the men around him, however able they might be. Strong ministers are strong men, arguing tenaciously about important questions, and a government that did not squabble would be unique. As a result King's diary and the diaries and correspondence of his colleagues are full of tart observations on people. J.L. Ilsley, for one, was probably the hardest-working, most able, and most intelligent of King's ministers His role during the war in administering the Department of Finance was outstanding in every regard, particularly in the way the war was financed and price controls were administered. But to King, Ilsley was too often a dour Maritimer. "Ilsley has a very narrow mind," King noted in September 1940 after a testy Cabinet War Committee meeting, "has no vision with respect to international problems. Is of the old colonial mind. Might better be a resident of Newfoundland than of N.S."[15] More than two years later King again complained about the Finance minister, grumping that he was "absolutely irrational when it comes to a possible conflict between the human values of industry and the material considerations of his price ceiling policy."[16]

Another who troubled the prime minister was Humphrey Mitchell, his Minister of Labour since December 1941. Mitchell had come to the government after long years in the Trades and Labour Congress and in the Labour Department, but despite this, or perhaps because of it, he never had labour's confidence in any measure. This worried King who considered Mitchell "more a source of uncertainty than of strength...."[17] Indeed at one extraordinary Cabinet War Committee meeting on September 15, 1 943, the officials were sent out of the room so the ministers could discuss what to do about the Minister of Labour. There was "a long and earnest talk," King wrote later. "They were all agreed that a change would have to be made." All were agreed but no one was willing to clean up the mess. King, characteristically, pointed out the difficulty in opening a seat to a by-election, and he objected to having a minister for the Department of Labour in the Senate. Would Macdonald take the post? he asked. "No reply." How about Abbott? "Ilsley did not think he was capable of sustained effort." Ralston suggested Claxton, an idea King liked, but in the end nothing was done.[18] The circumstances did not allow for a shift to be made in a fashion King could accept, and as a result Mitchell hung on until 1950 in the same portfolio. His only achievement was to create difficult government-labour relations, and King would have been better off to have followed his instincts and his judgment rather than to worry over by-elections.

Equally difficult to deal with were the personal foibles of ministers. In this period King did not have to deal with the problems of promiscuous ministers, possibly a reflection less of morality than of simple overwork. But the drinking minister was no rarity. Power continued to worry him, going off on periodic drinking sprees from which he would eventually emerge bleary-eyed but ready for more work. In October 1941 the Governor General actually raised his case with the prime minister, even volunteering to take the pledge himself if Power would do the same. "I told him he should not be called upon to do that," King replied.[19] What could be excused in Power because of his great ability was less acceptable in other ministers. Norman McLarty, for example, was demoted from Minister of Labour to Secretary of State in December 1941 in part because his behaviour at a labour conference in New York had "more or less humiliated and disgraced" the Canadian delegation.[20]

This dismal state of affairs reduced King near to despair. He looked around the Council chamber, noting "Cardin really unfit to ever take hold again.... Power liable to get on a spree at any moment...." Dandurand was old; Casgrain was "really useless and worse than useless"; while Crerar was aging fast. Ralston and Howe were carrying heavy loads and could not take any more, which made King's own burdens all the heavier. Ernest Lapointe's death, then a few weeks off, would weaken the government further, particularly in its Quebec representation.[21] There would be other occasions during the war when King would similarly conclude that he and one or two others were carrying the weight of the war without much assistance. But in fact the government went on relatively smoothly. In part this was a consequence of the concentration of real authority in the Cabinet War Committee, where all the able ministers gathered. In part it was the related consequence of a decline in the spending and hence the power of peacetime departments. The Cabinet War Committee had the power, the money, and the access to the secret information; the ordinary ministers, members of a cabinet that met with increasing irregularity, had only the shadow of prestige. So long as able men filled the key posts, the worst errors could be – and were – avoided.

But on some issues the entire cabinet was brought together. At the beginning of 1944, for example, there were long discussions about the government's social-welfare platform that revealed King's method of operating. For one thing, unanimity did not seem a requirement for action. The family-allowances question was settled with Howe dead against the decision; T.A. Crerar, known to oppose it as one that would weaken the moral fibre, was away; and Ilsley, although his department officials strongly supported the proposal, was lukewarm, and eventually would turn sharply against the measure. So too would Angus Macdonald.[22] But none of these men felt so strongly about the measure that they would resign over it, and the disagreements, although not forgotten, tended to fade.

But if Mackenzie King opposed something and was willing to make a stand, then action would be in doubt. The key was evidently his willingness to fight. In October 1941, for example, the cabinet was grappling with the proposals for a freeze, for complete wage and price controls, that had emerged from Ilsley's department. To King this was foolish and dangerous, like taking off in an aircraft with no place to land. He resisted, but when on October 10 King found himself the solitary member of the cabinet to oppose Ilsley's plan, he gave in quickly, even indicating

> ... how I thought approach should be made as to announcement of policy, making clear it was not intended as a cure-all; that the problem was a most difficult one to deal with. Later appealing to the public to co-operate with the government to save an appalling situation that might develop, stressing influence of foreign conditions, making very difficult any real solution, and leaving the way open for making clear the methods that would have to be adopted to effect adjustments which time and experience would occasion. Making clear it was only a trial of what seemed the best thing to do.[23]

King had not been prepared to veto price controls, given the unanimity of his colleagues and the civil servants, but instinctively he tried to provide an escape-hatch should one be necessary. Fortunately for the government and country, price controls were a smashing success.

On foreign policy questions, his area of expertise, King was more likely to insist on his views being followed. One example involved the question of Canadian representation in the directing body of the United Nations Relief and Rehabilitation Administration, a matter that seriously concerned the Cabinet War Committee in the first months of 1943 and one that led to the formal articulation of the functional principle of representation as the keystone of Canada's policy.[24] The great powers insisted that the direction of UNRRA should stay in their hands alone; Canadians argued that as one of the great producing nations, as one that would be expected to donate huge sums to help rebuild Europe, Canada was entitled to a place. Compromises were proposed and negotiations ensured, but the essential positions remained. The great powers would not budge, and King and his War Committee were adamant, even going so far as to sanction a message to London, Washington, and Moscow that Canada would not participate in UNRRA if it did not receive due consideration.[25]

Finally at the end of March 1943, the British Foreign Secretary, Anthony Eden, came to Ottawa to talk over the matter with King. If Canada refused the latest compromise offer, Eden said, "the whole business would have to fall through."[26] This frightened King, and he went to the Cabinet War Committee to propose acceptance of the last offer:

> I said to my colleagues that in considering the matter, we would have to consider how the Canadian people would view the rejection of a proposal of the kind with its possible consequences and repercussions as against refusing to participate at all because not given full recognition....

> Before going into the Cabinet, I had felt the only thing for us to do was to accept. We would have gained nothing by refusing ... [except] the illwill of the four great powers.... The whole business is very involved and is one of the cases where it is clearly impossible for a lesser power to do other than be largely governed by the views of the greater powers....
> This was one of the cases where, as Prime Minister, I would have had to decide regardless of what the others might have said in discussion.[27]

So King caved in. He had been put in a difficult position, faced with a choice between seeing Canada get what it deserved in the way of representation or seeing the dominion possibly blamed for destroying UNRRA. In the circumstances he had no option, and what is significant is that on an issue like this he was prepared to force his views on the rest of his colleagues, even if they had been in the majority. Fortunately, Howe and Ralston went along with King's reasoning and the matter did not come to the brink. No prime minister could take such a position very often, and King did not. The test was necessity, and King was as good a judge of the necessary as any prime minister we have had.

Occasionally, necessity required quick decisions without the full consultation with colleagues that Mackenzie King might have believed desirable in ordinary circumstances. One example was King's visit to Ogdensburg, New York, in August 1940 to meet with President Roosevelt. The president had called him up one day and the next King was in the United States striking an arrangement for a Permanent Joint Board on Defence. There was no consultation with the cabinet on this far-reaching event, nor was there any criticism of King's assumption of virtual presidential powers in making such an arrangement without so much as a "by-your-leave". On the contrary, ministers and others realized clearly that Canadian safety had now been achieved regardless of Britain's fate, and King was hailed for his success at Ogdensburg.[28]

His colleagues, however, did not always look so kindly on their leader, and in some instances their opinions changed dramatically over the course of the war. Ralston, the Minister of Finance until Rogers' death and the Minister of National Defence from July 1940 through to the 1944 conscription crisis, was one whose views underwent dramatic changes. In June 1940, for example, as the *Winnipeg Free Press* reporter, Grant Dexter, tells it, Ralston passed by King's office late at night to find the prime minister still hard at work, drafting telegrams and desperately filling the middleman's role between Roosevelt and Churchill. "King had said that he was played out, finished and couldn't carry the load," Dexter reported the equally harassed Ralston as saying. "Ralston told me he said: 'Chief you've got to go through. The despatch you are working on may mean

King and His Cabinet 245

victory, the saving of civilization.' King agreed." Dexter was normally an amused and cynical observer of the politicians and he added his own comment: "Which indicates Ralston's position fairly well. Willie may be doing all he says but, in any event, he sure has J.L. buffaloed."[29]

If Ralston had been buffaloed in June 1940, over the course of the next four years of strain his views altered dramatically. The long and fierce cabinet debates about manpower and conscription that began in earnest in the spring of 1941 and continued through to Ralston's near resignation in the summer of 1942 were the cause of the growing gulf between the minister and the prime minister. And by the time the Canadian army was fully committed to action in mid-1944 there was little trust left. In September of that year, with victory seemingly within the Allies' grasp, King spoke at a Reform Club meeting in Quebec City and said, according to some of those present, that he had prevented conscription, that it would never come. Ralston, elsewhere that day, learned of King's remarks and went to see the prime minister:

> I have something I want to speak of which unfortunately is disagreeable [King noted that Ralston had begun] ... he understood that I had said yesterday ... that I would not stand for conscription or be at the head of a government that would. He said he had been one of the team and had wondered whether I was changing our policy. That it made a pretty hard time with him in dealing with his staff and others in trying to squeeze out the numbers that they need for reserves. That there might be a holocaust when they try to get into Germany.... I told him I had made no statement of the kind. That what I had said was that I had mentioned that conscription would not be resorted to unless it was necessary. That now it was apparent the war was going to end soon and that it would be to the glory of the men overseas to be able to say they had enlisted voluntarily.... What I had said about there being no conscription to be feared was that we would certainly not have conscription for any participation with Japan.... I would not certainly be head of any government that sought conscription against Japan. He said he had not thought of that difference.[30]

Ostensibly the matter was smoothed over, but Ralston, almost certainly told by his friends that King had indeed pledged there would never be conscription anywhere, remained deeply suspicious. Grant Dexter, close to Angus Macdonald, Ralston, and T.A. Crerar, noted that "the Col. hates [King's] guts more than ever,"[31] an indelicate but accurate enough description of the relationship between King and his most powerful colleague. In such circumstances, the events of October 1944, the hard line taken by Ralston in his attempts to force the sending of home defence soldiers overseas, seem understandable. And King's ruthless chopping of Ralston on November 1 similarly becomes comprehensible. Events had taken their toll on both men.

Significantly, despite his hate for King and his policies, Ralston did not set out to topple the government. He had been shabbily treated, dismissed with scarcely a word of gratitude for five years of unremitting toil, but his sense of duty, his loyalty to the troops and to his colleagues was such that even in this moment of truth he held back from any attempts to destroy King. This is a tribute to Ralston's decency, but it might also be considered as a measure of the way Mackenzie King judged men. He had assessed his man well, and although it was a gamble he was probably convinced that Ralston would act much as he did.

King also played the rest of the cabinet skilfully in this period. When he fired Ralston, again he gambled that the shock would keep Ralston's friends pinned to their seats around the council table. He had guessed right, and once the ministers had swallowed that, they were virtually bound together for good – or at least until General McNaughton, Ralston's hapless successor, had the opportunity to demonstrate that he had no answers to the manpower questions. In the end, only Chubby Power left the ministry, objecting to any implementation of compulsion for overseas service. King would have preferred that Power stay with him, of course, but even here his luck held. With Ralston out because he wanted compulsion, and with Power out because he opposed it, King remained where he usually chose to be, firmly in the middle.

There is a story, again told by Grant Dexter, of the way Senator Norman Lambert, King's chief bagman in the elections of 1935 and 1940, viewed his leader. He was a worm, Lambert would say, surrounded by a fetid unhealthy atmosphere, like living close to some filthy object. But, Lambert would grudgingly admit, "stand off a ways and King looked better and better."[32] This comment has truth in it. Like those of other prime ministers, King's separate acts do not always appear honourable, fair, or just. Too often expediency, power considerations, or patronage appear to shape policy, and the individual parts of the whole often look pretty shabby. But the entire picture should not be distorted by too much emphasis on the bits and pieces.

Dawson's dicta on prime ministers tell us that the war for political supremacy never ends and every prime minister knows this. King knew it well, and he always acted to ensure his own ascendancy. He was a traditional prime minister, a professional, hard when he had to be, ruthless in disposing of other men when necessary. He was the giver of place, of rewards, of honours. He was simply the prime minister, running the country and the party. And if we can stand off a ways and look at his career without rancour, we may find that Mackenzie King does look better and better.

NOTES

1 R. MacGregor Dawson, *The Government of Canada*, 3rd ed. (Toronto, 1959), pp. 221ff.
2 PAC, King Diaries (July 2. 1940).
3 King Diaries (June 4, 1941).
4 King Diaries (May 7, 1940: May 9, 1940).
5 King Diaries (May 8, 1940: May 9, 1940).
6 King Diaries (December 15, 1941).
7 King Diaries, (September 13, 1939) Mackenzie's ouster from Defence had been in the wind at least as far back as September 2, 1939. See Floyd Chalmers Papers (Toronto), "Memo on Conversation with Norman Robertson" (September 2, 1939). For a comment on Mackenzie's relations with the service personnel under him, sec PAC, Adm. L.W. Murray Papers, extract of interview with Capt. E.S. Brand (February 22, 1967).
8 King Diaries (September 14, 1939).
9 King Diaries (September 19, 1939).
10 Queen's University, C.G. Power Papers, "Alarums and Excursions Incident to Re-Organization of Cabinet, September 19th, 1939".
11 King Diaries (September 19, 1939).
12 J.W. Pickersgill and D.F. Forster (eds.), *The Mackenzie King Record*, Vol. 1, *1939–1944* (Toronto, 1960), p. 26.
13 King Diaries (April 17, 1945; April 18, 1945). Sec also Paul Martin, "King: The View from the Backbench and the Cabinet Table", in this volume.
14 King Diaries (April 17, 1945).
15 King Diaries (September 5, 1940).
16 King Diaries (January 31, 1943).
17 ibid.
18 King Diaries (September 15, 1943).
19 King Diaries (October 30, 1941).
20 King Diaries (November 4, 1941). On January 13, 1942 King tried to persuade McLarty to go to the Senate, but was told that he enjoyed being Secretary of State and did not want to leave Windsor up for grabs in a by-election. King Diaries (January 13, 1942).
21 King Diaries (November 4, 1941). For a good rundown of potential Quebec ministers, see King Diaries (December 4, 1941).
22 Pickersgill and Forster, *The Mackenzie King Record*, Vol. I, p. 634; Public Archives of Nova Scotia, A.L. Macdonald Papers, Diary (January 13, 1944;

January 20, 1944; June 15, 1944); King Diaries (June 15, 1944); J.W. Pickersgill and D.F. Forster, (eds.), *The Mackenzie King Record*, Vol. II, *1944–45* (Toronto, 1968), pp. 27–28.
23 King Diaries (October 10, 1941).
24 J.L. Granatstein, *Canada's War: The Politics of the Mackenzie King Government, 1939–1945* (Toronto, 1975), pp. 295–307.
25 Department of External Affairs, Records, Robertson memo (February 26, 1943); PAC, Privy Council Records, Cabinet War Committee Records, Minutes (February 24, 1943).
26 King Diaries (March 31, 1943); Cabinet War Committee Minutes (March 31, 1943); L.B. Pearson, *Mike. The Memoirs of the Rt. Hon. Lester 8. Pearson*, Vol. I, *1897–1948* (Toronto, 1972), p. 253.
27 King Diaries (April 7, 1943); Cabinet War Committee Minutes (April 7, 1943).
28 The Cabinet War Committee heard King's report on August 20, 1940. Pickersgill and Forster, *The Mackenzie King Record*, Vol. I, p. 137 indicates the cabinet approved a minute approving the PJBD "later."
29 Queen's University, Grant Dexter Papers, memo (June 7, 1940).
30 King Diaries (September 15, 1944).
31 Dexter Papers, memo (September 25, 1944).
32 Dexter Papers (April 19, 1941).

Chapter Fourteen

The Evacuation of the Japanese Canadians, 1942: A Realist Critique of the Received Version

J.L. GRANATSTEIN AND GREGORY A. JOHNSON

The popular accepted version of the evacuation of the Japanese Canadians from the Pacific Coast in 1941–1942 and the background to it runs roughly like this. The white population of British Columbia had long cherished resentments against the Asians who lived among them and most particularly against the Japanese Canadians. Much of this sprang from envy of the Japanese Canadians' hard-work and industry, much at the substantial share held by Japanese Canadians of the fishing, market gardening, and lumbering industry. Moreover, white British Columbians (and Canadians generally) had long had fears that the Japanese Canadians were unassimilable into Canadian society and, beginning early in this century and intensifying as the interwar period wore on, that many might secretly be acting as agents of their original homeland, now an aggressive and expansionist Japan. Liberal and Conservative politicians at the federal, provincial and municipal levels played upon the racist fears of the majority for their own political purposes. Thus, when the Second World War began in September 1939, and when its early course ran disastrously against the Allies, there was already substantial fear about "aliens" in British Columbia (and elsewhere) and a desire to ensure that Japanese Canadians would be exempted from military training and service. The federal government concurred in this, despite the desire of many young Japanese Canadians to show their loyalty to Canada by enlisting.

After 7 December 1941 and the beginning of the Pacific War, public and political pressures upon the Japanese Canadians increased exponentially. Suspected subversives were rounded up by the RCMP in the first hours of the war, and over the next ten weeks a variety of actions took place that resulted in the seizure of fishing vessels, arms, cars. cameras, radio transmitters and short wave receivers owned by Japanese Canadians, and then escalated through the evacuation from the coast of male Japanese nationals between the ages of 18 and 45 to the removal of all Japanese, whether Canadian citizens by birth or naturalization and regardless of age or sex, into the interior. The legalized theft of the property of these Japanese Canadians then followed, and even before the war ended the government moved to deport large numbers to Japan. These events occurred despite the facts that the RCMP and Canada's senior military officers considered the removal of the Japanese from the coast unnecessary, there being no credible military or security threat; that the responsible politicians in Ottawa, and particularly Ian Mackenzie, BC's representative in the Cabinet, knew that the Japanese Canadians posed no threat to national security and acted out of a desire to pander to the bigotry of some whites or for political motives relating to the conduct of the war at home.

This bald summary is based on such books as Ken Adachi's *The Enemy that Never Was* (Toronto, 1976), the second volume of Hugh Keenleyside's *Memoirs* (Toronto, 1982), and Ann Gomer Sunahara's *The Politics of Racism* (Toronto, 1981), as well as on the National Association of Japanese Canadians' brief to the federal government, *Democracy Betrayed: The Case for Redress* (1985). There are variations of emphasis in these accounts, naturally enough, but the received version is a composite that does not pay much attention to these differences.

That Canadians should be interested in the events of 1942 is understandable. That they should attempt to fix blame for the events of those days is no less so, and historians, whose trade obliges them to rummage with more or less science through the past, have not been immune from this tendency. It is the responsibility of historians, however, to try to put themselves back into the circumstances of the past and, while never becoming apologists for the horrors of those times, to seek to understand why people acted as they did. This paper is an attempt to do precisely that, and to look afresh at some points which are encompassed in the received version of the 1942 evacuation and open for examination and some which are not.

The Intelligence Services

The first question that must be raised and one that has not been asked before is this: what resources did Ottawa's civil, military and police authorities have on the West Coast before the outbreak of war to secure information about the 22,000 Japanese Canadians living in British Columbia? The answer is readily available.

The responsibility for internal security rested with the RCMP, assisted as necessary by the armed forces.[1] In July 1941, five months before the outbreak of war with Japan, the RCMP's "E" Division responsible for the Pacific Coast had on its staff three persons concerned with gathering intelligence on the Japanese Canadians in British Columbia: a sergeant who did not speak Japanese, a constable who did, and a civilian translator. These three were in charge of the "active personnel intelligence work on enemy and potential enemy aliens and agents." There was in addition a lieutenant-commander at Naval Headquarters in Esquimalt charged with intelligence duties who was "greatly interested in the Japanese problem generally," but who had many other tasks. The Royal Canadian Air Force's intelligence section in the province, which like the Royal Canadian Navy's had a wide range of duties over and above collecting information on Japanese Canadians, consisted of two officers, both of whom had lived in Japan and spoke Japanese. The senior officer, a Squadron Leader Wynd, however, could read Japanese only with difficulty: whether his colleague was any more fluent is uncertain. The army's intelligence on the coast was in the hands of two very busy officers, neither of whom spoke Japanese. In addition, the British Columbia Provincial Police had four officers working in the Japanese-Canadian community. Cooperation between the various services was hampered by RCMP regulations that forbade the Mounties to share information with their colleagues without first securing permission from Ottawa headquarters. Even so, the West Coast Joint Intelligence Committee had been created to coordinate the information collected by the military and police.[2] There is one additional point worth mentioning: the British intelligence services had some representation on the West Coast, and there exists in RCMP files one very long (and very inflammatory) report on "Japanese Activities in British Columbia," prepared by someone unnamed for William Stephenson's British Security Coordination.[3]

This intelligence presence did not amount to very much. As Hugh Keenleyside of the Department of External Affairs, a British Columbian who had served in the Legation in Japan and who was genuinely sympathetic to the Japanese Canadians, wrote in June 1940, there was a danger of subversive activities on the part of some elements in the Japanese community. "The police," he went on, "are not in a position to ferret out the dangerous Japanese as they have done with the Germans and Italians; they have lines on a few Japanese who might be expected to take part in attempts at sabotage.... But that would not really solve the problem."[4] Even, therefore, in the view of someone in a position to know (and understand), the intelligence information gathered on the Japanese Canadians was strictly limited, the officers involved pathetically few in number and largely baffled by the impenetrability of the

Japanese language and the tendency of the Japanese Canadians to stay together, separate, and (with good historical reasons) not to trust whites.

The discussion thus far has said nothing about the quality of the information gathered. The available intelligence evidence on the Japanese Canadians is very slim (and the Privacy Act prevents us from seeing whatever else there might be), but we can state with confidence that when the RCMP looked at Communist questions, towards which it had a definite *idée fixe,* or the activities of suspected Nazis in this period, its work was far from competent.[5] In November 1939, J.W. Pickersgill of the prime minister's office complained that the force could not distinguish between facts and hearsay, or discriminate between legitimate social and political criticism and subversive doctrine. There was, moreover, "no suggestion that there is any co-ordination with Military Intelligence, or with the Immigration authorities, or with the Department of External Affairs, or even with the Censorship." More disturbing still to Pickersgill was "the evidence of a total lack of the capacity, education and training required for real intelligence work...."[6] Whether the RCMP's efforts on the Japanese Canadians were any better remains speculative, at least until all the files are open to research; the existing documents offer no grounds for optimism.

There is little more information available on the quality of military intelligence gathered. But as the regular forces before the war were tiny and as military intelligence, a skill requiring years of preparation. was not among the best developed areas of the permanent forces, there is no reason to believe that the army, navy or air force by 1941 were any less clumsy or more sophisticated in their ability to gather and assess information on the Japanese Canadians than the RCMP. Evidence for this conclusion is suggested by the efforts of the Examination Unit, a secret operation of External Affairs and National Defence set up under the shelter of the National Research Council, among other things to attempt to decipher Japanese diplomatic and military wireless messages in response to a British request before Pearl Harbor. As the just declassified manuscript history of the Examination Unit notes, two people were engaged for this purpose in August 1941, a Mr. and Mrs. T.L. Colton. "It was hoped that Mrs. Colton, who was very well educated in Japanese but could not handle translation into English, might be able to explain the contents of messages to her husband who could then write them out in English. This system," the history notes dryly, "did not prove very satisfactory" and the Coltons were replaced in April 1942.[7]

In this atmosphere of improvisation and amateurism, many of the available reports by the RCMP and the military on the Japanese Canadians tended to focus on investigations of alleged "unlawful drilling [with weapons]" by male Japanese Canadians, reports of caches of Japanese rifles and ammunition, and accounts of suspicious fishing parties of well-dressed Japanese who did not appear to be fishermen. Rumours, plain and fanciful.[8] On the other hand, there were just as many assertions offered with great confidence that 95 per cent of Japanese Canadians were law abiding and satisfied with their lot in Canada and that "No fear of sabotage need be expected from the Japanese in Canada." That last statement by Assistant Commissioner Frederick J. Mead of the RCMP, one of the Mounties' specialists in security matters and Communist subversion, was, he added, "broad [but] at the same time I know it to be true."[9]

Mead was soon a member of the British Columbia Security Commission where activist *Nisei* (or second generation Canadian Japanese) correctly believed he depended on intelligence from Etsuji Morii, a man suspected of blackmailing other Japanese Canadians and a notorious underworld figure. Morii was in turn the Commission's appointed chairman of the "Japanese Liaison Committee," whose mandate was to convey news and information in 1942 to the community.[10] As Mead was the senior RCMP official on the coast early in 1942, he was almost certainly the main source for RCMP Commissioner S.T. Wood's defence of Morii and his assertion to William Stephenson (in response to the British Security Coordination report mentioned earlier) in August 1942 that "we have searched without let-up for evidence detrimental to the interests of the state and we feel that our coverage has been good, but to date no such evidence has been uncovered."[11] The RCMP's firmly-stated position may have been correct, but again the small size of its resources and the lack of sophistication of all its operations in this period tend to raise doubts. From 45 years' distance, the fairest thing that can be said is that the RCMP had uncovered relatively little hard information about possible subversion among the Japanese Canadians before 7 December 1941, if there were indeed subversive intentions within the community, because it lacked the competence and skills to do so. Moreover, much of the information that the RCMP had before and after that date came from sources that even many Japanese Canadians considered self-interested and tainted.

The Role of the Japanese Consulate

Such intelligence information as there was tended to agree that the Japanese Consulate in Vancouver was the focus of Japanese nationalism, propaganda and possible subversive activities in BC. One RCMP report surveying the general activities of the Japanese Canadians noted that the Consul and his staff regularly visited areas where Japanese Canadians lived to deliver speeches and to talk privately with individuals about the Tokyo government's views of world events. One RCAF intelligence officer was sufficiently alarmed by these activities to tell his superior that he considered British Columbia's Japanese Canadians to be "directly under the control of the Japanese Government through their consul at Vancouver."[12] The Consul was also thought to exercise considerable influence on the local Japanese language schools and press. Roles of these sorts, of course, were well within the bounds of diplomatic niceties. And since, under Japanese law, *Nisei* born abroad before 1924 were considered as Imperial subjects, while those born abroad after that date could register at Japanese consulates and secure Japanese citizenship in addition to their status as British subjects, the Consul in Vancouver had substantial work to do in dealing with the approximately 7,200 Japanese nationals, 2,400 naturalized British subjects, and the unknown (but very large) number of Japanese Canadians holding dual citizenship in the BC community.[13] A military intelligence paper surveying the situation on the coast added that the Consul "through his agents, and through the Japanese schoolmasters, and the Japanese patriotic societies cultivates a strong Japanese spirit and a consciousness among the BC Japanese of being 'sons of Japan abroad' rather than Canadian citizens."[14] That was no different than the role of the Italian and German consuls in this pre-war period.

There were, however, grounds for believing that in this instance the Japanese. Consulate's officials had duties of a more dangerous kind. On 18 February 1941. Vincent Massey, the high commissioner in London. reported to Prime Minister Mackenzie King that "reliable information of a most secret character" had revealed that "official Japanese circles" were taking great interest in the British Columbia Coast. "Reference is also made to large numbers of Japanese settled in British Columbia and in Western Coast of United States, who are all said to have their duties,"[15] an ominous phrase.

The source of that information was possibly Britain's Government Code & Cypher School which had been reading some Japanese military and diplomatic messages since the 1920s,[16] or more probably "Magic," the name given by the Americans to their armed forces' decryption operation that in January 1941 had cracked the "Purple" code used for the most secret Japanese diplomatic traffic. Britain and the United States soon started to cooperate in reading Japanese codes, and by the spring of 1941 the two countries had pooled their intelligence.[17] The Americans also began reading their hitherto unbroken files of Japanese messages back to 1938.

The Evacuation of the Japanese Canadians   255

The decryption team had intercepted important telegrams from the Foreign Office in Tokyo to the Japanese Embassy in Washington dated 30 January 1941, which gave the *Gaimushuo*'s orders to its officials in North America to de-emphasize propaganda and to strengthen intelligence gathering. Special reference was made to "Utilization of our 'Second Generations' [Nisei] and our resident nationals" and to the necessity for great caution so as not to bring persecution down on their beads. Those messages were copied to Ottawa and Vancouver as "Minister's orders" – instructions, in other words, that were to be carried out in Canada just as in the United States. The Consulate's success in carrying out these orders remains unknown.

A further message from Tokyo to Washington, dated 15 February 1941, was also sent to Ottawa and Vancouver as a "Minister's instruction." In this telegram, the Foreign Ministry specified the "information we particularly desire with regard to intelligence involving US and Canada," especially the strengthening of Pacific Coast defences, ship and aircraft movements. In a telegram the day before, the Consulate in Vancouver was instructed to pay special attention to paragraph 10 of the order to Washington: "General outlooks on Alaska and the Aleutian Islands, with particular stress on items involving plane movements and shipment of military supplies to those localities." The next month, the Consulate was asked to report on RCN ship movements. Whether these particular telegrams were the basis for Massey's despatch to Ottawa is unclear.[18]

A thorough search of the "Magic" intercepts in the United States National Archives makes clear that at least as early as 1939 intelligence and counter-intelligence work was carried on from the Vancouver Consulate, exactly as was taking place in the Japanese Consulates all over the United States and throughout the Western Hemisphere. As we have seen, the 1941 telegrams also stress efforts to involve the resident nationals and the second generation *Nisei*, at whom radio broadcasts from Tokyo had been deliberately aimed for some years. How much, if anything, Ottawa knew of all this, beyond the RCMP's suspicions and the information conveyed in the Massey telegram, is still indeterminate. But surely there was ample justification in the light of the Massey telegram for the government to have increased surveillance on the Consulate and the Japanese-Canadian community. There is no sign that it did so.[19]

One contemporary assessment of the Canadian situation by an RCAF intelligence officer noted that "espionage and subversive activity is largely carried on by a few key Japanese working under the Consul and *seriously* involves only a few – say 60 at most – Japanese individuals."

256   Section Three: Politics

This same officer then tried to assess the response of Japanese Canadians in the event of war, particularly if the Japanese authorities instructed them to engage in sabotage, and if such orders were reinforced by "disorderly demonstrations of white antipathy." His answer was that "No one knows; but no one in his senses would take a chance on Japanese loyalty under those circumstances."[20]

The Pre-War Pro-Japan Actions of Japanese Canadians

If that sounds harsh, there were reasons why it should not. Throughout the 1930s and especially after 1937, Japan had aggressively expanded its influences in northern China, and the Imperial Japanese Army had campaigned with great brutality in that country. The Japanese government, naturally enough, tried to put the best face possible on its actions, and it encouraged the creation and spread of propaganda on its behalf abroad, something in which Japanese Canadians directly assisted by writing and distributing leaflets. The most widely distributed pamphlet, dated 1 October 1937 and published by the Canadian Japanese Association. the largest Japanese-Canadian association with over 3,000 members, was "Sino-Japanese Conflict Elucidated," a far from unbiased examination of the struggle in China, despite its claim to be circulated "in the interests of truth, to meet unfair and untrue propaganda:" Moreover, money, comforts for the troops, medical supplies and tin foil were collected for Japan by first generation *Nisei* and second generation *Nisei* groups."[21] There was, of course, nothing remotely improper about this, and other ethnic groups in Canada at that time (Italians, say. during the Italo-Ethiopian war) and more recently (Jews during the Arab-Israeli wars, for example) have acted similarly in comparable circumstances.

But the wholly justifiable outrage in Canada over such incidents as the brutal rape of Nanking, with its estimated 200,000 or more dead (and the Japanese army assaults on Canadian missionaries stationed there) led many Canadians to boycott Japanese products and to call upon the federal government to take steps to cease strategic metal exports to Japan. Such measures were eventually taken.[22] And the *New Canadian*, the newspaper of British Columbia's *Nisei*, began publication in late 1938, noted its founder, Edward Ouchi, the General Secretary of the main *Nisei* organization, the Japanese Canadian Citizens' League, to counter the "vicious" anti-Japanese propaganda of North American Chinese that was hurting Japanese-Canadian businesses. Although the newspaper did not offer frequent support for Japan's war in China in its pages, it did give close and favourable coverage to the activities of

The Evacuation of the Japanese Canadians 257

the Consul in Vancouver and even ran an occasional rotogravure section of propagandistic photographs on life in Japan.[23]

Inevitably Japanese-Canadian support for Japan's war on China focussed much attention upon the *Issei* and *Nisei*. As Professor Henry Angus of the University of British Columbia wrote in October 1940:

> The young Japanese understand the position well enough. At first they (in all good faith I think) distributed a good deal of pro-Japanese, anti-Chinese propaganda., Now they say, "we are not responsible for what Japan may do." l tell them that they have unfortunately made people feel that they are identified with Japan by their action in distributing propaganda, and that it is very difficult to find a way of removing this impression.[24]

Angus was always very sympathetic to the Japanese Canadians (and after he had joined External Affairs, he and Hugh Keenleyside would find themselves under attack in Parliament because of the vigour of their resistance to the evacuation in January and February 1942),[25] but he was surely correct in his assessment. Even such supportive British Columbia politicians as CCF Member of Parliament Angus MacInnis agreed.[26] The Japanese Canadians by their support for Japan "impaired [their] standing with those circles most disposed to press [their] cause," Professor Angus lamented.[27]

We can say today that Canadians should have understood the difficulties that a small minority would have faced in not supporting its belligerent mother country in those days in the late 1930s and early 1940s. But after the Pearl Harbor attack and the fall of Hong Kong, British Columbians, already predisposed to expect the worst of the Japanese Canadians and motivated by deep rooted racism against them, and Canadians generally could not reasonably have been expected to make such judgments. Many Japanese Canadians had supported Japan against China before 7 December and few, if any, had opposed her; after Pearl Harbor, China was an ally and Japan an enemy. Therefore, the supporters of Japan before 7 December were now supporters of Canada's enemy and possibly (or probably) disloyal, particularly as there seemed no way of distinguishing the active few from the passive majority. The syllogism was flawed (and certainly the vast majority of German and Italian Canadians had been treated far differently in the comparable circumstances of September 1939 and June 1940), but few were prepared to challenge its logic.

Norman Robertson, the undersecretary of state for external affairs, a British Columbian and no bigot, expressed something of the same reasoning when he told Pierrepont Moffat, the American minister to Canada, on 8 December 1941 that the Government had hoped not to have to intern all Japanese. However, this might be very difficult in view of the treacherous nature of the Japanese attack, [and] the evidences of premeditation...."[28] Robertson's description of the attack mirrored the public's response: "In the wake of Pearl Harbor, the single word favoured by Americans as best characterizing the Japanese people," John Dower has noted, "was 'treacherous' ...."[29]

The Attitudes of Japanese Canadians after 7 December

In August 1944, Prime Minister King told the House of Commons that "no person of Japanese race born in Canada has been charged with any act of sabotage or disloyalty during the year of war." In his account Ken Adachi added that "no alien Japanese or naturalized citizen had ever been found guilty of the same crime."[30] Those statements are undoubtedly true, but they do not tell the whole story.

Thirty-seven or thirty-eight Japanese nationals were arrested and interned by the RCMP at the outbreak of the war presumably because they were thought to be engaged in espionage or subversive activities. None of the standard accounts offers any detailed information on the allegations against or the fate of these people.[31]

More important, it seems certain that support for Japan remained strong among some Japanese Canadians after the war began. The *Issei* Takeo Nakano, in his book *Within the Barbed Wire Fence*, notes that "We Japanese, largely working class immigrants, were, generally speaking, not given to sophisticated political thinking. Rather we had in common a blind faith in Japan's eventual victory." John J. Stephan's study, *Hawaii under the Rising Sun*, cites the conclusions of Japanese historians Nobuhiro Adachi and Hidehiko Ushijima that most first generation Japanese in Hawaii remained loyal to Japan: "even among those who considered the Pearl Harbor attack a betrayal were many who believed in and hoped for an ultimate Japanese victory.... Radio reports of Japanese advances ... confirmed for many their motherland's invincibility." Nakano's book demonstrates that the "same response existed in British Columbia, and even Sunahara notes that the Japanese vice-consul encouraged some Japanese Canadians to seek internment as a gesture of support for Japan.[32] Those of Japanese origin, of course, formed a greater proportion of the Hawaiian population (about 35 per cent) than did the Japanese Canadians in British Columbia (about three per cent). Moreover, at this point it is impossible to determine if the links between the Japanese Canadians and Japan were stronger or weaker than those between Hawaiian Japanese and the mother country. These two factors could certainly have affected the situation.

The Evacuation of the Japanese Canadians 259

Nakano also underlines the presence in the Japanese Canadian community of a substantial number of hardliners or *gambariya*, "best described as rebels against the treatment they were receiving in time of war. The *Nisei gambariya* were protesting such unjust treatment of Canadian citizens," he continues, an understandable response. He goes on, however, to note that "the *Nisei gambariya* firmly believed in Japan's eventual victory and looked forward to the Canadian government's enforced compensation to them."[33] That attitude is less understandable if the revised version is to be accepted. More than 750 *gambariya*, a fairly substantial number of the approximately 9,000 adult males over the age of sixteen in a BC community of 22,000, were interned at Angler in Northern Ontario, and Nakano, in part as a result of misunderstanding, he says, ended up there as well. Nakano's story is stylistically elliptical, but it rings true. None of the historical accounts make much mention of the *gambariya*, other than to skirt the evidence by saying that there were some who refused to have anything to do with the evacuation or to cooperate with the Canadian authorities.

Perhaps a last word here should belong to Stephan, whose study of Hawaii is an exemplary and sensitive one. "It has been common to write about Hawaii's Japanese before and during the Second World War as if their 'loyalty' were a self-evident, quantifiable phenomenon," he said. "In the justifiable impulse to indict the relocation of West Coast Japanese and Japanese Americans ... writers have in many cases dealt simplistically with what is full of complex nuances and ambiguities."[34] Those comments apply with equal force to the Canadian accounts, almost all of which have been remarkably one-dimensional.

The Role of the Military in the Evacuation

There is no doubt that senior officers of the armed forces and the RCMP in Ottawa were remarkably unperturbed by the presence of large numbers of Japanese Canadians in British Columbia.[35] General Maurice Pope, the vice chief of the General Staff, attended the Conference on the Japanese Problem in British Columbia in Ottawa on 8–9 January 1942, which brought together representatives from British Columbia, the federal bureaucracy, and political figures, and his memoir provides the standard account. The navy, he wrote, had no fears, now that the Japanese Canadian fishing fleet was in secure hands; the RCMP expressed no concern, and Pope himself, offering the army position, said that if the RCMP was not perturbed, "neither was the Army." Pope adds that several days after the meeting adjourned, the angry and frightened British Columbians who had attended "must have got busy on the telephone" for "we received an urgent message from the [Army's] Pacific Command recommending positive action against the Japanese in the interests of national security. With the receipt of this message, completely reversing the Command's previous stand," the minister of national defence, Colonel J.L. Ralston, "was anything but pleased."[36]

The evidence simply does not support Pope's account. While it is clear that the Department of National Defences representatives on the Special Committee on Measures to be Taken in the Event of War with Japan agreed in mid-1941 with the Committee's recommendation to Cabinet that "the bulk of the Japanese population in Canada can continue its normal activities,"[37] and while it is equally certain in mid-December the Chiefs of Staff Committee told the Cabinet War Committee that fears of a Japanese assault on BC were unwarranted,[38] there is absolutely no doubt that the military commanders *in* British Columbia and the military members of the Permanent Joint Board on Defence were seriously concerned about the possible threat posed by the Japanese Canadian population both before and after 7 December 1941. The real question that remains unanswered is why in this instance the generals, admirals and air marshals in Ottawa were so ready to ignore the advice of their commanders in the field.

Certainly the military advice from BC was completely unambiguous, The Joint Service Committee, Pacific Coast, the key coordinating military body that brought together the three service commanders in British Columbia, had prepared plans in July 1940 for preventive actions directed at the Japanese Canadian in the event of war with Japan."[39] The Committee also recommended on 17 June 1941 that "the Japanese population of approximately 230 residing in the vicinity of the Royal Canadian Air Force Advanced Base at Ucluelet [on the West Coast of Vancouver Island] should, in the event of an emergency, be evacuated for reasons of security. It was felt that similar steps should be taken in connection with Japanese resident near other important defence areas, and particularly those established near air bases." There were about two hundred Japanese Canadians living at Port Alice near the Coal Harbour RCAF base and the same number in Prince Rupert near another air station. The Committee's recommendation, had been forwarded to the Chiefs of Staff Committee in Ottawa no later than 20 September 1941.[40]

In addition, the RCN on the coast had long been concerned with the fleet of up to 1,200 fishing vessels operated by Japanese Canadians. In 1937, for example, the Navy's staff officer (intelligence) at Esquimalt had said that "The fact that there are a large number of Japanese fishermen operating in British Columbia waters ... and having a thorough and practical knowledge of the coast, is in itself a matter of some concern to the Naval authorities."[41] In August 1941, the naval officer commanding on the coast asked Ottawa for authority to round up the fishing boats in the event of war. The Department of External Affairs refused to agree to this *in toto*, however, and in October orders were issued for seizure only of boats "owned and operated by Japanese *nationals*." "Vessels owned and operated by British subjects of Japanese origin," the RCN was told, "will only be interfered with where there are positive grounds for suspicion, comparable to those which would justify the internment of a British subject of Japanese origin."[42] When war came five weeks later, those orders would be overridden in the urgency of the moment.

Furthermore, before the outbreak of war in the Pacific, both the Canadians and the Americans worried about the concentration of Japanese Americans and Canadians living along the common coastline. The Joint Service Committee, Pacific Coast, had urged Ottawa on 20 September 1941 to coordinate any actions with Washington. In its opinion, "inequality in the treatment of persons of Japanese race in the territories of the Dominion of Canada and the United States would be liable to prove a source of danger to the effective prosecution of such measures of control as may be ordered by either government and to furnish grounds for grievance by the persons immediately concerned."[43] The Permanent Joint Board on Defence at its meeting on 10-11 November at Montreal had also considered the question of the "population of Japanese racial origin." Just as the Joint Service Committee on the West Coast had urged, the Canadian and American members agreed that there should be consultation to produce "policies of a similar character in relation to these racial groups" if war with Japan broke out. The aim was "a practicable coincidence of policy."[44] That did not imply evacuation from the Pacific Coast, but it did suggest that there was a shared realization of a "problem." And as John Hickerson, the senior State Department official regularly concerned with Canadian affairs, noted after that PJBD meeting, it would "cause the Canadians considerable political difficulty in British Columbia if we adopted more rigid treatment of Japanese in California than that prescribed in British Columbia." That, he added, is why the Canadians suggest "that at the proper time there be consultation" between the two governments "with the view to adopting similar policies in Canada and in continental United States."[45]

After Pearl Harbor, but before the Conference in Ottawa, the three senior officers on the coast wrote to Ottawa with their views. Major General R.O. Alexander, the GOC of Pacific Command, told the chief of the General Staff on 30 December that he believed "internment of Japanese males between the ages of 18 and 45, their removal from the coast and their organization into paid units on public works would be advisable." Such action, Alexander added, "might prevent interracial riots and bloodshed, and will undoubtedly do a great deal to calm the local population." There is no doubt that General Pope saw this letter, because he sent a copy of it to Hugh Keenleyside of the Department of External Affairs and Keenleyside wrote back to him with suggestions on 3 January – before the "Japanese Problem" conference in Ottawa took place."[46]

The senior RCAF officer in BC shared the view of his army colleague. Air Commodore L.F. Stevenson informed RCAF headquarters in Ottawa in January that security "cannot rest on precarious discernment between those who would actively support Japan and those who might at present be apathetic." If the government had doubts about the wisdom of moving the Japanese out, Stevenson said, "'I suggest a strong commission be appointed immediately to ... obtain the opinion of a good cross section of the BC public and the officers charged with the defence of the Pacific Coast." The senior naval officer agreed, Commodore W.J.R. Beech telling his headquarters on 27 December that "Public opinion is very much against the Japanese all over the Queen Charlotte Islands and in view of the strategic position of these Islands I would strongly recommend that all the Japanese be removed."[47]

All three officers stressed public opinion at least as much as military needs, and it is reasonable to assume that their positions often put them in close contact with politicians and journalists likely to be pressing for stern action. But this does not alter the fact that the responsible military commanders in British Columbia, after 7 December and before the Ottawa conference, called for removal of the Japanese Canadians from all or part of the coastal region; so too had their staff urged removal before 7 December from the vicinity of military bases and after Pearl Harbor from coastal areas of the province.[48] Moreover, on 13 February 1942, the Joint Services Committee, Pacific Coast, decided that in view of "the deterioration of the situation in the Pacific theatre of war ... the continued presence of enemy aliens and persons of Japanese racial origin [in the coastal areas] constitutes a serious danger and prejudices the effective defence of the Pacific Coast of Canada."[49] And as late as 26 February, the RCN commanding officer on the coast was advised by his security intelligence officer that "The removal of all Japanese from this coastal area would undoubtedly relieve what is becoming more and more a very dangerous situation from the point of view of sabotage and aid to the enemy as well as the great danger of development of inter-racial strife."[50] Again, public opinion was given equal weight with the fear of sabotage, but it is significant that this advice was proffered after adult male Japanese citizens living on the coast had been ordered inland.

Even after the great majority of Japanese Canadians had been cleared from the government's designated defence zone, moreover, substantial concern was expressed repeatedly by the American military and by the US members of the Permanent Joint Board on Defence on 26–27 May and 1 September 1942 at the relocation of Japanese Canadians inland to road camp sites near railway lines or other strategic points. Under pressure, the Canadian government then acted to resolve matters to reassure its ally. Similar concerns had been expressed in June 1942 in the British Security Coordination report.[51]

An additional factor that played an unquantifiable but important part in events in BC were the reports that Japanese living in Hawaii, Hong Kong and Malaya had helped the attacking Japanese forces.[52] Undoubtedly the lurid tales of fifth column activities from Europe in 1940 also fed popular fears. The Hawaii stories eventually proved to be mere rumours, but their impact was great in the first months of 1942. In Hong Kong and particularly in Malaya, however, there was substantial truth to the reports in January and February that local Japanese had hidden arms and ammunition, planted explosive charges at military installations, docks and ships, and sniped at troops, as well as providing information to the invaders.[53] It is virtually immaterial if the stories were true; what is important is that they circulated widely among a generally anti-Japanese public and a fearful military that were prepared to believe them. As the *Vancouver Sun* put it on 2 January 1942, "we may expect Japanese civilians to do all in their power to assist the attacker."[54]

Finally, the stories, all too true, of the brutality of the Japanese victors towards captured Allied servicemen and civilians had substantial impact on both the public and political leaders. As early as 12 February, telegrams from London to Ottawa spoke of atrocities against captured Hong Kong prisoners and of deplorable conditions in the POW camps. Within the week, Cabinet ministers in Ottawa were talking about the fate of the Hong Kong force with their intimates, and on 10 March, the widespread rumours were given official sanction by statements in Parliament in London and Ottawa. The "devilish" Japanese, or so M.J. Coldwell of the CCF said in the House of Commons, would be punished after the war for their atrocities. The Canadian Japanese wholly innocent of the crimes of the Imperial Japanese Army, nonetheless were denied sympathy as a result.[55]

Was There a Military Threat to the Coast?

Whether there was a direct military threat to the coast from the Imperial Japanese forces is also worth some consideration if only because the received version denies any. In September 1941, RCAF headquarters in Ottawa had been confident that the United States Navy was the ultimate guarantor of the safety of the Pacific Coast: "Unless the United States Navy is seriously defeated or loses its northern bases," Air Vice Marshal G.M. Croil told his minister, C.G. Power all Canada had to do was remain in "watchful readiness" on the West Coast.[56] With that attitude in the ascendant, the coast of British Columbia was left "poorly defended," the words employed to describe matters by Robert Rossow, Jr., the American Vice-Consul in Vancouver, in August 1941.[57] After Pearl Harbor, however, the worst possible case seemed to have occurred, and Canada was largely unprepared. Certainly there were few modern aircraft, few ships and relatively few trained soldiers in the area until the outbreak of war[58] and it took some time before more could be rushed to the coast.[59] That caused concern.

So too did the course of the war. The Japanese hit Pearl Harbor on 7 December and simultaneously attacked Malaya, Hong Kong, the Philippines and Wake and Midway Islands. On 8 December, Japan occupied Thailand, captured Guam on 13 December, Wake on 24 December, and Hong Kong on 25 December. Manila fell on 2 January, Singapore followed on 15 February, a staggering blow to the British position in Asia (and something that frightened British Columbia[60]) and the Imperial Japanese Navy crushed an allied fleet in the Java Sea on 27 February, the date that the Canadian government's decision to move all Japanese Canadians inland was in the newspapers. Closer to home, a Japanese submarine had shelled Santa Barbara, California, on 23 February, two days later the "Battle of Los Angeles" took place with much ammunition expended against (apparently) imaginary targets, and there were submarine attacks on points in Oregon. (On 20 June a Japanese submarine shelled Estevan point on Vancouver Island.) The Dutch East Indies and most of Burma were then captured in March, capping an extraordinary four months of conquest.

At the beginning of June, the Japanese launched what H.P. Willmott, the leading historian of Pacific war strategy, called "their main endeavour, a twin offensive against the Aleutians," designed to draw the American fleet to battle to protect their territory, "and against the western Hawaiian Islands," intended to lead to an invasion once the Americans' Pacific Fleet had been destroyed. At least two plans for such an invasion existed before and after the attack on Pearl Harbor, and one plan saw the capture of Hawaii "as preparatory to strikes against the United States mainland."[61] (Whether attacks against the Canadian Coast were intended remains unclear until such Japanese military records that survived the war are searched.) Dutch Harbor, Alaska was attacked by carrier-based aircraft on 3 June as part of this plan. Four days later Kiska and Attu in the Aleutian Islands were taken.

Although in retrospect the American naval victory at Midway in June, aided beyond measure by "Magic" intercepts, put an end to the Hawaiian adventure and truly marked the beginning of the end for Japanese imperial ambitions as a whole, its significance was not quite so apparent in mid-1942 as it has since become. Certainly the Canadian government did not slacken its defence efforts on the coast after the American victory. In mid-February 1942, a military appreciation prepared by the chiefs of staff for the minister of national defence's use at a secret session of Parliament noted that "probable" Japanese strategy included containing "North American forces in America" by raids on the North American Pacific seaboard. "Possible" enemy aims included an "invasion of the West Coast of North America," although the chiefs noted that "Under present conditions" such invasion was "not considered to be a practicable operation of war."[62]

The next month, with the Japanese forces seemingly roaming at will throughout the Pacific and with the politicians anxious to satisfy the public clamour for stronger local defences in British Columbia, the chief of the General Staff in Ottawa was estimating the possible scale of a Japanese attack on the Pacific Coast to be two brigades strong (i.e., two Japanese regiments of three battalions each or approximately 5,200 to 6,000 men), and he was recommending the raising of new forces.[63] At the beginning of April, President Roosevelt used the occasion of the first meeting of the Pacific Council, made up of representatives of all the belligerent allies to say that he had invited Canada because "he thought that Canada might do more than she was now doing."[64] That disturbed Ottawa, perhaps because it mirrored British Columbia public opinion so clearly, and Mackenzie King hastened to discuss the matter with the president.[65]

Later that month, after Lieutenant Colonel James Doolittle's B-25 bombers, launched from the carrier *Hornet*, had hit Tokyo. Canadian intelligence reports predicted that eleven enemy aircraft carriers would launch retaliatory attacks against the West Coast in May.[66] By June, there were nineteen battalions on the west coast, a response to Japan's invasion of the Aleutians and continued and growing public concern. Even so, the military commanders were far from satisfied. The Joint Canadian United States Services Committee at Prince Rupert believed that military strength in the area was "entirely inadequate against many types attack that are possible and probable from the West."[67] The air officer commanding on the coast asked for sixteen squadrons to deal with the maximum scale of attack by battleships, cruisers and carrier-borne aircraft. There were also blackouts, and dimouts, and active plans underway in July and August 1942 for the evacuating of Vancouver Island and the lower mainland in the event of a Japanese attack.[68]

The Cabinet War Committee was assured by the chief of the General Staff in late September that he saw "no reason to fear any invasion from the Pacific Coast at present time,"[69] but two months later the Combined Chiefs of Staff, the highest Allied military authority, determined that while "carrier-borne air attacks and sporadic naval bombardment" were the most probable form of attack, the possibility of "a small scale destructive raid cannot be ignored." By that, the British and American planners meant "a force comprising 10/15 fast merchant ships carrying up to two brigades."[70] And as late as March 1943, there was a flurry of reports of Japanese activity in North American waters that stirred fears about a possible attack of the precise sort the planners had anticipated.[71] In other words, and contrary to the arguments of those who have argued that there was never any threat from Japan to the coast and hence no justification on grounds of national security for the evacuation of the Japanese Canadians, there *was* a credible – if limited – military threat into 1943.

The intent of this paper was to present some new and re-state some old evidence on several aspects of the Japanese-Canadian question. What has our account done to the received version? It has pointed to the gross weaknesses of and wishful thinking in RCMP and military intelligence about the Japanese Canadians. It has demonstrated irrefutably that the Japanese Consulate in Vancouver had orders from the Foreign Ministry to employ British Columbia *Nisei* in information collection or spying. It has called into question the advice of the military planners in Ottawa, brought forward once more the widespread concerns of the senior officers and staff planners of all three armed forces in British Columbia, and argued that there was a limited but credible military threat to North America from early 1942 into 1943 from the Imperial Japanese forces. It has noted that the attitudes of some Japanese Canadians by their support for Japan's war with China before 7 December 1941 raised understandable concerns on the part of British Columbians and Canadians generally. And although the attitudes of Japanese Canadians before and during the war have yet to be thoroughly studied despite all the work on the subject, Nakano's memoir is important for its account of the wartime attitudes and divisions in the community and especially so because of its resonance with Stephan's account of Hawaii. Finally, although little has been made of this here, it is certainly germane to recall that there was a war on and that Canada and its Allies were losing it at the beginning of 1942. As the civil libertarian and historian Arthur Lower wrote in October 1941, "The temper of the Canadian people seems to be becoming more and more arbitrary and we are fast losing whatever tolerance and magnanimity we once possessed."[72] That explains much that happened.

None of this alters the conclusion that the Japanese Canadians were victims of the racism of the society in which they lived and an uncaring government that failed to defend the ideals for which its leaders claimed to have taken Canada and Canadians to war. Even so, this paper does maintain that there were military and intelligence concerns that, in the face of the sudden attack at Pearl Harbor, could have provided Ottawa with a justification for the evacuation of the Japanese Canadians from the coast. The government in December 1941 was unaware of much of the data that has since emerged, and even if it had had it all, it simply lacked the assessment capability to put it together. If it had had the information and the intelligence capacity to appraise it properly, the arguments for evacuation would certainly have appeared far stronger than they already did.

However arguable this case, there is, of course, no necessary connection between the later confiscation of property and the still later effort to deport the Japanese Canadians and the reasons for the evacuation that seemed compelling to some in January and February 1942. The anger that persists at the evacuation might be misplaced; that at the confiscation of property and the attempt at deportation still seems wholly justifiable. In any case, this paper should demonstrate that there remains ample room for further work, broader interpretations and, perhaps, a changed emphasis in this area of research.

NOTES

1 National Archives of Canada (NA), Department of National Defence Records, mf reel 5257, f. 8704, "Instructions for the Guidance of General Officers Commanding-in-Chief Atlantic and Pacific Commands," 26 February 1941
2 NA. Department of External Affairs Records, vol. 2007, f. 1939-212. pt. 2, "Report on the State of Intelligence on the Pacific Coast with Particular Reference to the Problem of the Japanese Minority," 27 July 1941: Department of National Defence Records, vol. 11913, "Japanese" file, Cmdr Hart to R.B.C. Mundy, 21 August 1940.
3 PAC, RCMP Records, declassified report, "Japanese Activities in British Columbia" and attached correspondence. See also External Affairs Records, vol. 2007, f. 1939-212, pt. 2 "Report on the State..."

4 External Affairs Records, vol. 2007, f. 1939-212. pt. 1, Keenleyside to H.F. Angus, 28 June 1940. After the order to remove the Japanese from the coast, Keenleyside noted that American "control of enemy aliens seems to be rather more severe than ours while their action with regard to their own citizens is somewhat less severe than ours." *Ibid.* Acc. 83–84/259, box 171, f. 2915-40, pt. 1. Keenleyside to Wrong, 14 March 1942.
5 See, e.g., Robert H. Keyserlingk, "'Agents within the Gates': The Search for Nazi Subversives in Canada during World War II," 216–17; J.L. Granatstein, *A Man of Influence* (Ottawa, 1981), pp. 81ff; Reg Whitaker, "Official Repression of Communism during World War II," *Labour/Le Travail*, XVII (Spring 1986), 137 and *passim*.
6 NA. W.L.M. King Papers, "Note on a War-Time Intelligence Service," 27 November 1939, f. C257903ff. We are indebted to Professor W.R. Young for this reference.
7 Department of National Defence Records, Declassified Examination Unit Files, memorandum for chairman, Supervisory Committee, 15 August 1941, Lt. C.H. Little memorandum, 18 April 1942, Draft History, chapter VI "Japanese Diplomatic Section," 1
8 The spy scares in British Columbia sound much the same as those in Britain before the Great War. See Christopher Andrew, *Secret Service* (London, 1985), 34ff.
9 Department of National Defence Records, vol. 11917, f. 5-1-128, 1938–9, RCMP report. 3 June 1938: *ibid.*, vol. 11913, "Japanese" file, "Vancouver" [an agent] to Cmdr Hart. 30 June and 13 July 1940; External Affairs Records, vol. 2007, f. 1939-212, pt. 2. RCMP report, 29 July 1941; Ann Sunahara, *The Politics of Racism* (Toronto, 1981), 23
10 See Roy Miki, ed., *This Is My Own: Letters to Wes & Other Writings on Japanese Canadians. 1941–48 by Muriel Kitagawa* (Vancouver. 1985), 98–9.
11 RCMP Records, declassified material, Commissioner S.T. Wood to Stephenson, 5 August 1942
12 Department of National Defence Records, vol. 3864, f. N.S.S. 1023-18-2, vol. I, memorandum, F/L Wynd to senior air staff officer, 24 June 1940
13 External Affairs Records, vol. 2007, RCMP report, 29 July 1941. Under a Japanese law of 1899, Japanese men liable for military service did not lose Japanese nationality upon naturalization abroad unless they had performed their military service. After 1934, Canada would not accept Japanese for naturalization without certification that they had completed military service. See *ibid.*, Acc. 83-84/259, box 171, f. 2915-40, pt. 3, memorandum, "Postwar Treatment of Japanese in Canada." n.d.; John J. Stephan, *Hawaii under the Rising Sun* (Honolulu, 1984), 24; and Ken Adachi. *The Enemy That Never Was* (Toronto, 1976). Adachi, 175, says that in 1934, 86 percent of *Nisei* were dual citizens. The population numbers used here

The Evacuation of the Japanese Canadians   269

are those in the *Report and Recommendations of the Special Committee on Orientals in British Columbia, December 1940* (copy in NA, Privy Council Office Records, vol. 1, f. C-10-3), not those of the 1941 Census which were, of course, not available at the time.

14 External Affairs Records, vol. 2007, f. 1939-212, pt. 2, "Report on the State...." See also the pamphlet by the Vancouver unit of the Fellowship for a Christian Social Order, "Canada's Japanese" (Vancouver [1942?]), 7–8, with its explanation of the role of the Consulate.

15 External Affairs Records, f. 28-C(s), Massey to prime minister, 28 February 1941. This telegram was discussed by the Cabinet War Committee, the key comment being that by Angus L. Macdonald, the minister of national defence (naval services), that there was "little danger of serious attack by Japan" on the Pacific Coast. Privy Council Office Records, Cabinet War Committee Minutes, 5 March 1941. This type of attitude presumably was responsible for the fact that, as late as July 1941, as we have seen above, the RCMP still had only three people responsible for Japanese-Canadian questions. For a plausible hypothesis on how the information might have reached Massey – from US undersecretary of state, S. Welles, to the British ambassador, Halifax, to London and thence to Massey – see Ruth Harris, "The 'Magic' Leak of 1941 and Japanese-American Relations," *Pacific Historical Review*, L (1981), 83.

16 Andrew, 261, 353. Ronald Lewin, *The American Magic* (New York, 1982) 44ff

17 *Ibid.* 45–6

18 United States National Archives (USNA), General Records of the Department of the Navy, RG 80, "Magic" Documents, box 56, Tokyo to Washington, 30 January 1941 (2 parts), *ibid.* Tokyo to Washington, 15 February 1941, *ibid.* Los Angeles to Tokyo, 9 May 1941; *ibid,* Tokyo to Vancouver, March 1941, USNA, Records of the National Security Agency, RG 457. "Magic" Documents, SRH 018. SRDJ nos. 1233-4, 1246-9, 1370, 1525, Vancouver to Tokyo, 14 July to 19 August 1939. Some of this information is contained in *The "Magic" Background to Pearl Harbor* (Washington 1977), 1, no. 131 and especially no. 135 which is the Tokyo to Vancouver, 14 February 1941, telegram referred to. See also *New York Times* 22 May 1983, and Gregory A. Johnson's research paper "Mackenzie King and the Cancer in the Pacific" (York University, 1984).

19 Indeed, as late as 21 October 1941, and despite the Massey telegram referred to above, Keenleyside, the assistant under secretary of state for external affairs told the undersecretary that "While it might be possible to find Japanese nationals in British Columbia against whom some meagre suspicion exists, there is certainly no Japanese national at large in that Province or elsewhere in Canada against whom any really convincing case can be made out." That comment likely reflected both RCMP advice,

which is suspect, and Keenleyside's own extensive knowledge. Whether his certainty was justified – in light of the Consulate's activities – is another question. D.R. Murray, ed., *Documents on Canadian External Relations*, vol. XIII *1939–41*, 2 (Ottawa, 1976) 5169

20 Foreign Affairs Records, vol. 2007, f. 1939-212 pt 2 "Report on the State..." c.f. H.F. Angus critique of this report in Department of National Defence Record, f. 292–392, 15 August 1941 and his memorandum of an interview with the officer F.O. Neil 15 August 1941. We are indebted to Professor Patricia Roy for the Angus critique. It is worth noting that even missionaries shared alarmist views. A United Church China missionary, in Vancouver in January 1941, wrote that "I have had too much experience with the Japanese to trust them ... there is a war in progress and we in Vancouver are in the front line. And the front line is no place for thousands of enemy citizens." United Church Archives, Board of Foreign Missions, Honan box 11 f. 174 Stewart to Reverend Armstrong 20 January 1942.

21 Adachi, 184–5, Membership figures for the Canadian Japanese Association are in University of British Columbia Archives, Japanese Canadian Collection, Miyasaki Collection b4. A copy of the pamphlet is in *ibid*, P.H. Meadows, Japanese Association Papers.

22 Granatstein, 98ff; King Papers, f. C144716ff contains petitions and other material on Canadian policy to Japan after 1937. See also Murray, 1203ff for extensive documentation on metals exports policy.

23 Ed Ouchi, ed., *'Till We See the Light of Hope* (Vernon BC, 1982), 70. *The New Canadian* is available in the UBC Archives. For support for the war, see the 20 October 1939 issues; on the consul, see e.g., 8 September 1939. The rotogravure sections began in late 1939 and ran well into 1940. On the economic boycott launched by Chinese groups, see UBC Archives, *Chinese Times* translations for 1937.

24 NA, J.W. Dafoe Papers, Angus to Dafoe, 15 October 1940. Mackenzie King told the Japanese minister to Canada in January 1941 that Japanese Canadians would not be called up for NRMA service: "he must remember that Japan and China were at war and we might be encouraging a little civil war if we supply both Chinese and Japanese with rifles etc., in BC at this time. He laughed very heartily at that." King Papers, Diary, 8 January 1941

25 University of British Columbia, Special Collections, H.F. Angus Papers. vol. I, folder 2, draft memoir, 320–1: H.L Keenleyside. *Memoirs of Hugh L Keenleyside*, vol. II: *On the Bridge of Time* (Toronto, 1982), 171.

26 University of British Columbia Archives, Special Collections, MacInnis Papers, Box 54A, f. 8, MacInnis to the Canadian Japanese Association, 11 December 1937; *ibid.*, f. 12, MacInnis to T. Umezuki, 18 April 1939. The CCF did not live up to its ideals once the Pacific War started and the BC party

supported removal of Japanese Canadians. See Werner Cohn. "The Persecution of Japanese Canadians and the Political Left in British Columbia. December 1941 – March 1942." *BC Studies*. LXVIII (Winter 1985–6), 3ff.
27 H.F. Angus, "The Effect of the War on Oriental Minorities in Canada." *Canadian Journal of Economics and Political Science*. VII (November 1941). 508
28 Harvard University. J. Pierrepont Moffat Papers, "Memorandum of Conversations with Mr. Norman Robertson ...." 8 December 1941
29 John W. Dower. *War without Mercy: Race and Power in the Pacific War* (New York, 1986), 36. See also Christopher Thorne, *Racial Aspects of the Far Eastern War of 1941–1945* (London, 1982) and chapter 11 of his *The Issue of War* (London, 1985).
30 Canada. House of Commons *Debates*, 4 August 1944, 5948; Adachi. 276
31 RCMP Records, "Japanese Activities in British Columbia," Appendix 6, lists the names. Adachi, 199, says 38 were arrested. Sunahara, 28, agrees.
32 Takeo Nakano, *Within the Barbed Wire Fence* (Toronto. 1980), 8; Sunahara, 70; Stephan, 171
33 Nakano, 44–45. Sunahara, 69, says that many *Nisei gambariya* had been educated in Japan.
34 Stephan, 177
35 To what extent the post-7 December military response was a reflection of prewar contempt for Japanese military capabilities remains unknown. Dower, 98ff, discusses the responses of the American and British military and civilians both before and after the outbreak of war.
36 Maurice Pope, *Soldiers and Politicians* (Toronto, 1962), 176–8. Escott Reid, who attended the Conference for the Department of External Affairs, later wrote that delegates from BC "spoke of the Japanese Canadians in a way that Nazis would have spoken about Jewish Germans. I felt in that room the physical presence of evil." "The Conscience of a Diplomat: A Personal Testament." *Queen's Quarterly*, LXXIV (Winter 1967). 6–8
37 External Affairs Records, Acc. 83–84/259, box 115, f. 1698-A-40. "Report of Special Committee ...," 28 July 1941. Ottawa had not always been so calm. The Joint Staff Committee at Defence Headquarters on 5 September 1936 had foreseen circumstances in which "the Western Coast of Canada will be within the area of hostilities and is likely to be attacked not only by Japanese naval and air forces, but, in the case of important shore objectives, by Japanese landing parties operating in some strength." An abridged version of the document is in James Eayrs, *In Defence of Canada*, vol. II: *Appeasement and Rearmament* (Toronto, 1965), 213ff. Two years later Defence Headquarters had concluded that "there was a problem of possible sabotage in wartime and recommended that Japanese Canadians not be allowed to purchase property adjacent to areas of military importance." Cited in

272 Section Three: Politics

John Saywell, "Canadian Political Dynamics and Canada-Japan Relations: Retrospect and Prospect," 26, a paper published in Japanese only ("Nikkakankei No Kaiko To Tembo," *Kokusai Seiji* (May 1985), 121–36)
38 W.A.B. Douglas, *The Creation of a National Air Force*, vol. II: *The Official History of the Royal Canadian Air Force* (Toronto, 1986), 405. The British and American planners meeting at the Arcadia conference later in December agreed. *Ibid.*, 410. On 29 December !941, the chief of the General Staff told the Cabinet War Committee that he had just returned from the Pacific Coast where he found the military and police more concerned with the possibility of attacks on Japanese Canadians than with subversion. Cabinet War Committee Minutes, 29 December 1941. The enormous difficulties that the military would have faced in dealing with racist attacks on Japanese Canadians should not be underestimated: the limited number of trained troops in the area and the very real problem of using white troops against white British Columbians in defence of Japanese Canadians would have frightened any realistic commander.
39 Department of National Defence Records, vol. 2730, f. HQS-5l99X, "Memorandum of the Joint Service Committee, Pacific Coast, on the matter of the Defences of the Pacific Coast of Canada," 12 July 1940
40 *Ibid.*, vol. 3864, f. N.S.S. 1023-18-2, vol. I, N.A. Robertson to LCol K.S. Maclachlan, 14 August 1941; *ibid.*, vol. 2730, f. HQS 5199X, "Memorandum of the Joint Service Committee, Pacific Coast, on the Subject of Dealing With Persons of Japanese Origin in the Event of an Emergency," 20 September 1941. See Peter Ward, *White Canada Forever* (Montreal, 1978), 145, which notes that as early as June 1938, the military were thinking of widespread wartime internment of Japanese Canadians. The numbers near RCAF stations are from NA, Ian Mackenzie Papers, vol. 32, f. X-8 l, Commander Parsons to Attorney General Maitland, 17 February 1942
41 Department of National Defence Records, vol. 3864, f. N.S.S. 1023–18–2, vol. I, "Extract from Report on Japanese Activities on the West Coast of Canada," 10 March 1937. See also Privy Council Office Records, vol. 3, f. D-19–1 Pacific Area, for AVM Croil's "Appreciation of the Situation Likely to Arise on the West Coast...," 11 September 1941.
42 External Affairs Records, Acc. 83–84/259, box 115, f. 1698-A-40, memorandum for Robertson, 21 October 1941. London soon urged that as many Japanese fishing vessels as possible be seized in the event of war. External Affairs Records, f. 28-C(s). secretary of state for dominion affairs to prime minister, 23 October 1941
43 National Defence Records, vol 2688, f. HQS-5199-1. vol. I, "Memorandum of the Joint Service Committee. Pacific Coast. on the Subject of Dealing with Persons of Japanese Origin in the Event of an Emergency," 20 September 1941

The Evacuation of the Japanese Canadians 273

44 USNA, Department of State Records, RG 59, PJBD Records, box 14, meeting 12
45 *Ibid.*, 842.20 Defense/140 1/2, Hickerson to Hackworth, 2 December 1941. We are indebted to Professor Robert Bothwell for this reference.
46 RCMP Records, vol. 3564, f. C11-19-2-24, General Alexander to CGS, 30 December 1941; *ibid.*, Keenleyside to Pope, 3 January 1942
47 Mackenzie Papers, vol. 32, f. X-81, "Extracts from Secret Letters," 30, 27 December 1941. See also C.P. Stacey. *Six Years of War* (Ottawa, 1955), 169, and W.A.B. Douglas, "The RCAF and the Defence of the Pacific Coast, 1939–1945," an unpublished paper presented to the Western Studies Conference, Banff, Alberta, January 1981. 8.
48 Department of National Defence. Directorate of History, f. 193.009 (D3), Pacific Command, Joint Service Committee, minutes, 9 January 1942
49 Department of National Defence Records, Acc. 83–84/216, f. S-801-100-P5-1, minutes of Joint Service Committee, Pacific Coast, 13 February 1942
50 *Ibid.*, vol. 11767, f. PC019-2-7, P.A. Hoare to commanding officer, 26 February 1942. The Joint Service Committee recommended on 20 February that all aliens and all Japanese regardless of age and sex should be removed from certain areas on the coast, particularly those near defence installations and in isolated areas. Cited in Patricia Roy, "Why Did Canada Evacuate the Japanese?" unpublished paper, 6–7
51 USNA, Records of US Army Commands, RG 338, box 4, f. 291.2, contains ample evidence of US concern from April 1942; RCMP Records, declassified material, "Japanese Activities in British Columbia." See also Department of National Defence Records, mf. reel 5258, f. 8704–11 for indications of National Defence's concern about sabotage in August 1942 and especially the vice chief of the General Staff's fear that the RCMP lacked "a realistic appreciation of the present danger of sabotage." *Ibid.*, General Murchie to Ralston, 19 August 1942.
52 Mackenzie papers, vol 32, f. X-81, BC Police Commissioner T.W.S. Parsons to Attorney General Maitland, 17 February 1941: "With these people neither Canadian birth nor naturalization guarantees good faith. Something to remember in the case of invasion or planned sabotage."
53 On Pearl Harbor, see Roger Daniels, *Concentration Camps U.S.A: Japanese Americans in World War II* (New York, 1972), 36–8 and Gordon W. Prange, *Pearl Harbor: The Verdict of History* (New York, 1986), 348ff; on Hong Kong, see Stacey. 467, Oliver Lindsay, *The Lasting Honour* (London, 1978), 28. Carl Vincent, *No Reason Why* (Stittsville, 1981), 137, 139 and 146, and Ted Ferguson *Desperate Siege: The Battle of Hong Kong* (Toronto, 1980), 57, 127–8, I 37–9; on Malaya, see Ian Morrison, *Malayan Postscript* (London, 1942), 32–3. and the book by the British official historian of the war in Asia,

General S. Woodburn Kirby, *Singapore: The Chain of Disaster* (New York, 1971), 30, 37, 152, 251, as well as the British Security Coordination report cited above from declassified RCMP records.
54 *Vancouver Sun*, 2 January 1942
55 External Affairs Records, Acc. 83–84/259. box 160, f. 2670 D-40, high commissioner in Great Britain to secretary of state for external affairs, 12 February 1942; Queen's University Archives, T.A. Crerar Papers, Crerar to J.W. Dafoe, 20 February 1942; Montreal *Gazette* 11 March 1942. See also *Times* (London), 13 March 1942.
56 Privy Council Office Records, vol. 3, f. D-19- J, Pacific Area, memorandum A.V.M. Croil to minister for air, 11 September 1941
57 Department of State Records, 842.20 Defence/100, "Observations on the General Defense Status of the Province of British Columbia," 1 August 1941
58 See Stacey, 165ff, and Department of National Defence Records, vol. 2730. f. HQS-5199X, "Memorandum of the Joint Service Committee, Pacific Coast. on the Matter of the Defences of the Pacific Coast of Canada," 12 July 1940, Privy Council Office Records, vol. 3, f. D-19-1, Pacific Area, appreciations of 18 November 1941 and 10 December 1941.
59 See, e.g. Dafoe Papers, Bruce Hutchison to Dafoe. January 1942; Mackenzie Papers, vol. 30, chief of air staff to minister for air, to March 1942 and various memoranda.
60 Dower, 112, notes that, as the Japanese victories continued through early 1942, "Suddenly, instead of being treacherous and cunning, the Japanese had become of monstrous and inhuman ... invested in the eyes of both civilians and soldiers with superhuman qualities."
61 The best accounts of Pacific war strategy are H.P. Willmott, *Empires in the Balance* {Annapolis, 1982) and *The Barrier and the Javelin* (Annapolis 1983). On the Aleutian and Midway plans, see Willmott, *Barrier*, chapter 3; Stephan, chapters 6–7. Note, however, Willmott's cool assessment of the difficulties Japan would face in trying to take Hawaii. *Empires*, 437. The importance of the Aleutian thrust was seen by the Americans' Special Branch, Military Intelligence Service, based on an analysis of "Magic" traffic. See USNA, RG 457, box 2. SRS-668, supplement to Magic summary, 30 July 1942, and on the Special Branch, Lewin, 141ff. One interesting assessment of the Japanese attack in the Aleutians was offered to Japanese Ambassador Oshima in Berlin by General von Boettichcr, a former military attaché in Washington: "the Aleutian attack has closed the only practicable route for an attack on Japan and is a serious threat to Canada and the West Coast." *Ibid.*, box 1, SRS-640, Magic summary, 26 June 1942
62 NA, J.L. Ralston Papers, vol. 72, Secret Session file, chiefs of staff appreciation, 19 February 1942

The Evacuation of the Japanese Canadians 275

63 Stacey, 171. Sec also Cabinet War Committee Minutes. 18 February 1942, and National Defence Records. vol. 2688. f. HQS-5159-1, vol. 2, "Report of Meeting Held at Headquarters. 13th Naval District Seattle, 6 March 1942," where Canadian and American commanders agreed with the Canadian estimates of scales of attack and suggested that "nuisance raids" were most likely. Additional information on defence preparations is in John F. Hilliker, ed., *Documents on Canadian External Relations, vol. IX: 1942–1943* (Ottawa, 1980), 1162ff. For a good example of hindsight 20/20 vision on the impossibilities of a Japanese attack on the coast, see Adachi. 201–8.
64 Privy Council Office Records, vol. 14, f. W-29-1. "First Meeting of the Pacific Council in Washington," n.d. [1 April 1942] and attached documents
65 *Ibid.*, "Memorandum re Prime Minister's Visit to Washington. April 14th to 17th, 1942"
66 Department of National Defence Records. vol. 11764, f. PC05-11-5, naval message to NOI/C, Vancouver and Prince Rupert 29 April 1942
67 *Ibid.*, vol. 11764, f. PC0I0-9-18, memorandum. "Defence of the West Coast." 7 July 1942
68 See *Vancouver Sun*, 10 August 1942; *Vancouver Province*. 13 August 1942; documents on External Affairs Records, Acc. 83–84/259, box 216, f. 3942–40; Douglas, *Creation*, 354. We are indebted to Professor John Saywell for his recollections of this period on Vancouver Island and to his father's book, John F.T. Saywell, *Kaatza: The Chronicles of Cowichan Lake* (Sidney. BC, 1967), 197–8, which briefly details the role of the Pacific Coast Militia Rangers, a force largely of skilled woodsmen and hunters.
69 King Papers, f. C249469, memorandum for file, 25 September 1942. See also Cabinet War Committee Minutes, 25 September 1942, where the chief of the General Staff said he would be "surprised" if the Japanese attacked the coast.
70 USNA, RG 218, Records of the US Joint Chiefs of Staff, mr. reel 10, r. 39322ff. Combined Chiefs of Staff. "Probable Maximum Scale of Attack on West Coast of North America," CCS 127, 29 November 1942. See also *ibid.*, f. A4024ff, CCS 127/1, "Probable Scale of Attack on the West Coast of North America." 16 January 1943. Not until August 1943 (in CCS 127/3) did the Combined Chiefs declare the possibility of any serious attack on the coast "very unlikely." Douglas, *Creation*, 368–9. C.P. Stacey's comment in *Arms, Men and Governments* (Ottawa, 1970), 46, that "No informed and competent officer ever suggested that the Japanese were in a position to undertake anything more than nuisance raids" seems exaggerated in the light of the CCS papers. It is worth recalling that the Canadian raid on Dieppe involved about 5,000 men and was intended, among other purposes, to lead the Nazis to strengthen the French Coast at the expense of the Eastern front. The Japanese planners could (and should?) have been thinking

similarly. Certainly a raid in force would have resulted in a massive public demand for the stationing of more troops on the coast; indeed, the simple prospect of such a raid did lead to the strengthening of defences.
71 Department of National Defence Records, vol. 11764, f. PC05-11-7, naval messages, 30–31 March 1943. This may have been based on false information. A secret US Federal Communications Commission project had reported on landing barges in the area; Washington discounted these reports but turned the information over to Canada, which sent them to the West Coast and then back into the American intelligence net where "they were believed to be authentic. Hence military action was ordered." See USNA, RG 457, SRMN-007, memorandum, 19 April 1943
72 Lower to Frank Underhill, 15 October 1941, quoted in Doug Owram, *The Government Generation* (Toronto, 1986), 263

Chapter Fifteen

Arming the Nation: Canada's Industrial War Effort 1939–1945

In the course of the Second World War, Canada's factories, mines, and fields produced billions and billions of dollars' worth of goods and foods to support the war effort. The nation created and produced more than Canada's million men and women in uniform needed to fight and win, so arms, equipment, food, minerals and metals were sold or, if our Allies did not have the money to pay, given away for the cause of victory. This was an astonishing feat of production and organization, a massive effort by every sector of the Canadian economy and by Canadian workers and business leaders. Canadians won the economic war, and their efforts from 1939 to 1945 also ensured that the postwar years would be very different than the bleak decade that had preceded the war.

Canada was a small and weak country in 1939. The Gross National Product, the sum total of all the goods and services created by the population of 11.2 million Canadians, was only $5.6 billion. The federal government's expenditures in 1939 were only $680 million, and Canadian corporations paid only $115 million in taxes while income taxes generated only an additional $112 million.

Unemployment remained very high, though down from the worst years of the Great Depression.* There were still hundreds of thousands on relief and men who continued to "ride the rods" across the country, seeking work at a time when jobs were few. The nation's mines

---

* There are no wholly reliable unemployment data for the 1930s, but in 1933, generally judged to be the worst year of the Depression, there were 2.2 million Canadians with nonfarm jobs; in 1938, the last full year of peace, there were 2.7 million men and women so employed. By contrast in 1943, with hundreds of thousands serving in the military, there were 3.37 million civilians employed in Canada in non-agricultural work. In 1943, the Unemployment Insurance Commission, created two years before and collecting hard data, reported that only 62,000 Canadians were listed as unemployed.

produced metals and minerals – gold, copper, zinc – and the factories produced automobiles, trucks, steel, durable goods and clothing; most heavy industrial goods were imported, and even the auto sector relied heavily on American motors. Moreover, there were almost no munitions plants in that last year of peace. There was only a small federally owned arsenal in Quebec City (that primarily made limited quantities of small arms ammunition), and a subsidiary plant in Lindsay, Ontario, re-opened in 1937. The British government just before the war started had placed a small contract with Marine Industries Limited of Sorel, Quebec, to make one hundred 25-pounder artillery field guns. There were a few tiny aircraft manufacturers that produced airplanes on an almost piecework basis (in 1933, no aircraft were produced in Canada; in 1938, 282 worth $4 million). In Toronto, the John Inglis Company in March 1938 had won a contract to build seven thousand Bren light machine guns for the Canadian military and five thousand for Britain – through a contracting process that produced cries of scandal and resulted in a Royal Commission to investigate. Perhaps the Bren gun fiasco had something to do with the cancellation of the order placed by the United Kingdom in Canada for one hundred Bren gun tracked carriers, an order extraordinarily ended by London just *after* the outbreak of war.

Nor was there much of a legacy from the industrial war effort of the Great War of 1914–1918. The British government then had arranged its own procurement in Canada through the Imperial Munitions Board, and the Dominion had produced mainly artillery shells, an effort that had proved difficult enough and one which had generated a succession of scandals and many production failures, eventually resolved. In all, the industrial effort had generated a billion dollars' worth of munitions, a figure then seen as huge. The country's shipyards had built some small ships and a few aircraft factories produced tiny numbers of "flying machines." But the main effort had come in the form of shells, automobiles, and the produce of the fields and mines.

Few in the dark years of the Depression believed, should there be another war, that Canada could do much more. There had been a "Survey of Industry" in 1936, the first full-scale attempt to catalogue what resources Canada might have for war production. But the difficulty was that few Canadians in government or industry could foresee the creation of war industries in Canada if only the Canadian forces were to be equipped. British orders were needed to make the creation or re-tooling of factories economical and, the British order for Bren guns aside, orders for Britain's armed forces almost always went only to British firms. Nor were there prospects of orders from the United

States – America was neutral in word and deed and its small armed forces used different patterns of military equipment.

Partly as a result of the Bren gun affair, the Liberal government of Mackenzie King in June 1939 had passed the "Defence Purchasing, Profits Control and Financial Act" which aimed to control profits and the costs of defence contracts. Profits could not exceed 5 per cent, a stipulation that meant that soon after the war began, C.D. Howe, the Minister of Transport, told the House of Commons that Canada had not managed to place a single contract. The Act had also created the Defence Purchasing Board to coordinate purchases, and in its short life (July 14 to October 31, 1939) the Board managed to buy only $43.7 million worth of goods, with three-quarters of the orders placed after Nazi Germany had invaded Poland in September 1939 and Britain and France had declared war against the Hitler regime on September 3; Canada had followed with its own declaration of war one week later.

One of the first casualties of the Second World War was this system of profit controls, quickly repealed so that war orders could be placed. A second casualty was the Defence Purchasing Board itself, replaced on November 1, 1939 by the War Supply Board, led by Wallace Campbell, the president of the Ford Motor Company of Canada. Initially, the new Board fell under the control of the Finance Minister, but in mid-November, in a fateful and fortunate move, the Board came under the ambit of the Minister of Transport, the just-named Minister of Munitions and Supply, Clarence Decatur Howe. Howe had no department as yet, only a title. But when the War Supply Board was swallowed by the new department on April 9, 1940, just days after the King Liberals' election victory, Canadian war production had found its czar.

Howe was American-born, a graduate of the Massachusetts Institute of Technology, a former engineering professor at Dalhousie University, and a man who had made himself rich by constructing grain elevators throughout the west. In 1935, he had won election to Parliament from Port Arthur, Ontario, as a Liberal, and he instantly went into Mackenzie King's Cabinet. Tough, blunt, familiar with business and the men who ran it, Howe proved to be the right minister to lead the nation's wartime industrial mobilization.

But even Howe could do little until the urgency of war began to drive matters. The Nazi invasion of Denmark and Norway was quickly followed by the stunning victory of the Wehrmacht in the Low Countries and France. The Dunkirk evacuation at the end of May 1940 was the only grace note in the requiem for the European democracies. But now, at least, the financial concerns that had crimped British armaments orders in Canada and restrained Ottawa's own purchases were gone. In

April 1940, $11.6 million in contracts were placed; in May $31 million; in June $45 million; in July $82 million; in October 1940 $148 million. Both London and Ottawa wanted everything now, right now. The dollar no longer reigned; the idea that Canada would fight a "limited liability" war had disappeared, a casualty of the Hitlerian blitzkrieg.

Howe set out to seize the initiative. He began to look to Canadian business for executives who could step in to organize and galvanize war production and allocate scarce commodities. He expected their employers to pay their salaries, and he offered nothing beyond a dollar a year, only expenses; many of those he brought to Ottawa declined to take their expenses at all. The "dollar a year men," as they quickly became known, were the cream of Canadian business, men like H.J. Carmichael of General Motors, R.C. Berkinshaw from Goodyear Tire and Rubber, Henry Borden, a powerful corporate lawyer from Toronto, E.P. Taylor, a Toronto businessman and brewery owner, H.R. MacMillan, the British Columbia lumber giant, and W.C. Woodward, the West Coast department store owner. There were many more – a parliamentary return in late February 1941 noted that 107 dollar a year men were employed across the government; Howe's department with its array of executives, accountants, and lawyers had by far the most. There would be many more as the war went on.

The Department of Munitions and Supply had control over all orders placed by Britain in Canada, soon had similar sway over a re-arming United States' orders, and, of course, controlled all Canadian orders. The Act that had created the department was amended by Parliament in August 1940, giving Howe the power to "mobilize, control, restrict or regulate to such extent as the Minister may, in his absolute discretion, deem necessary, any branch or trade or industry in Canada or any munitions of war or supplies." Moreover, the amended Act gave Howe exclusive power to buy, manufacture or produce munitions and supplies required by the Department of National Defence. Howe was in charge, the one man directing the Canadian industrial war effort. And Canada was the only Allied nation that had one agency handling all war procurement. There was no competition for scarce supplies between the armed forces. The Cabinet and Howe decided, and Howe's voice was the clearest in the decisions.

Howe and his men did everything in a hurry. As his biographer, historian Robert Bothwell, noted, "There was no time to consider production programs in detail. No one could hope to know when production would actually come on stream – merely that a commitment to production must be made, often orally, and ratified with government dollars." Munitions and Supply offered loans and grants, it purchased licenses to permit

Canadian production of foreign-owned weapons and equipment, and it helped secure the British and American experts to let Canadian firms get up and running. This was usually sufficient to get detailed planning underway; getting the actual armaments produced was more difficult.

Canadian industry was small and slow, plant was often obsolete, machine tools were scarce, and skilled workers in short supply. Howe's production chief, Harry Carmichael who had come to Ottawa from his post as Vice-President of General Motors, had the answer – sub-contracting. The lead firm could likely produce a few artillery pieces a month, for example, if it worked on its own. But if it could get carefully machined parts from other smaller plants across the country that could be screwed into place at the main shops, production could be stepped up. That was how the big automobile plants worked, Carmichael said, so why couldn't the same methods be employed in building artillery or ships or aircraft? It required planning and control, a careful allocation of scarce materials, and a high level of inspection to ensure that the requisite quality was maintained, but it could be done. Yes, it was a "bits and pieces" program, just as Howe called it. But it worked and, moreover, it spread wartime jobs across the country and not just in central Canada. That was a political necessity if complaints from the Maritimes and the West that Ontario and Quebec received all the jobs were to be dealt with. "Will Saskatoon get its share [of jobs]?" election campaigners asked in a 1939 by-election. In fact, Saskatoon and virtually every city and province did.

There were inevitable bottlenecks and failures, of course, but one way around them was to create Crown corporations. There was a shortage of rubber? Set up a Crown company to produce synthetic rubber. Wood veneers for aircraft were in scarce supply? A Crown corporation could do the job. Machine tools? Howe's Citadel Merchandising could get them and make sure they went where they were most needed. In all, 28 Crown corporations came into being during the war, some manufacturing, some purchasing and distributing, others supervising and controlling. The establishment of Crown companies, operating with great flexibility outside the usual bureaucratic restraints, allowed for efficiencies. Even so, Howe and his advisers believed that private enterprise was inherently more efficient than government-run operations. The Second World War made the government – or at least C.D. Howe's part of it – operate much like a corporation. The state helped with plant expansion and re-tooling, and corporate Canada itself put its money into wartime growth. It had to – more than half of Canadian war production came from plants that had not existed in 1939. In 1939, some $3.65 billion had been invested in the country's factories. Four years later, capital invested was $6.3 billion, a huge jump. Much of that was government money, but because Howe and his controllers ran what the press called "a graftless war," one almost wholly without patronage and preferment, there were relatively few complaints.

But there were some, and not everyone was happy. H.R. MacMillan was Howe's Timber Controller, and by the end of 1940, he had become displeased with the minister's management style and with what he saw as the bloated, confused bureaucracy of Ottawa. Munitions and Supply needed to be run in a business-like fashion – by him? – if war production was to get moving properly. But to the B.C. tycoon's surprise, few listened to MacMillan, and he found himself effectively isolated within Munitions and Supply where all of the other dollar a year men understood that the sleeping giant that was Canadian production required time to get moving. MacMillan left Ottawa later in 1941, just as production in Canada began to get untracked, and went to Montreal where a charitable Howe put his undoubted talents to work as president of Wartime Merchant Shipping, charged with the task of building cargo ships. He proved hugely successful in that role.

MacMillan's were not the only complaints. The social-democratic left in Canada, just beginning to sprout during the hothouse atmosphere of war, worried about the ways in which Howe's men were doing business. T.C. Douglas, the Cooperative Commonwealth Federation Member of Parliament from Weyburn, Saskatchewan, said in July 1942 that "Instead of government taking over industry, industry has taken over government." Canada needed, Douglas said, to be able to get its government back again. There was some truth in Tommy Douglas' complaints, but only some.

Certainly, Canadian business was paying its full share of the war's costs, for one thing. Business contributed billions of dollars to Victory Loans, helping the government finance the war – for interest rates that ranged from 1.5 to 3 per cent. Corporation taxes had increased from a rate of 18 to 40 per cent, generating $636 million – or nearly half of all corporate profits – in 1943 and $850 million the next year. Excess profits taxes produced even more revenue. Profit on government contracts was limited to 10 per cent, and all profits in excess of 116 2/3 per cent of standard profits (the average of an individual corporation's profits for the lean years from 1936 to 1939) were taxed at 100 per cent by 1942. In 1945, this generated $466 million. Corporations, however, could claim double depreciation against taxes for plant renovations, machinery acquisition, and other expenses, and they were to receive a 20 per cent rebate on their excess profits taxes after the war, a conscious attempt to help in the eventual reconversion to peacetime production. "No great fortunes," Finance minister J.L. Ilsley said in 1941, "can be accumulated out of wartime profits." H.R. MacMillan said the same thing in a speech to British Columbia lumbermen: "We must kill off that hangover from the last war – great profits. There can be no profits in this war to capitalists, labour or anyone else. Instead, there will be a sharing of losses."

For most Canadians working in war industry, in fact, there were gains. Average wages increased dramatically, rising from $956 in 1938 to $1525 in 1943. There was as much overtime as people wanted, and many worked fifty or even sixty hours a week. Families that had struggled to keep one breadwinner employed in the Depression years now had a son in the army and two, three, or more family members bringing home good pay cheques each week from factory work. The government's National Selective Service system controlled where people could work in an economy struggling to find enough workers for factories and men for the army, navy, and air force, and the flood from small town and rural Canada into the urban factories was enormous, not least the huge numbers of women who went to work for the first time. By 1943, 261,000 women were employed in war factories and making almost equivalent wages to male workers. The growth in wages across the country, moreover, outstripped inflation, thanks to the federal government's wage and price control system. And wartime Canadians ate better and spent more, despite rationing and controls, than they had in the 1930s.

No one begrudged the improvements in wages and living standards. What mattered most during the war years was victory and victory could only be won through the efforts of fighting men. Their triumph demanded production and more production. Canada delivered the goods, producing 40 per cent of Allied aluminum and 95 per cent of the nickel. It mined 75 per cent of the asbestos, 20 per cent of the zinc, 12 per cent of the copper, and 15 per cent of the lead. Very simply, without the aluminum provided by the Dominion, the Royal Air Force could not have fought the war. At the same time, in great secrecy, Howe secured majority control for the government of Eldorado Gold Mines Limited, the sole producer of uranium under Allied control (other than the more inaccessible Belgian Congo) from a mine at Great Bear Lake in the North West Territories and a refinery at Port Hope, Ontario. Whether or not Canadian uranium was used in the atomic bombs that brought the war with Japan to an end and the world into a new era is uncertain; what is beyond doubt is that Canadian uranium played a key role in the research and development of the bomb. Canada's raw materials, $5.8 billion in all produced from 1939 to 1945, made an extraordinary contribution to victory.

At the same time, Canada produced an array of military equipment, its war production overall ranking fourth among the Allies, behind only the United States, the United Kingdom, and the Soviet Union. For a nation of just 11 million people, this was little short of amazing. The orders, for example, went out for Anson aircraft so that training under the British Commonwealth Air Training Plan could speed up, with $58.4 million provided for this in December 1940. Canadian firms could build the airframes but none could manufacture the engines which had to be imported. In 1941 only 88 Ansons came off the lines; in 1942, total production had risen to 1432; and by the end of 1943 to 2269. The story was much the same for other aircraft types, Canadian firms producing 1451 Hurricane fighters, 894 Curtiss Helldivers, more than a thousand DeHavilland Mosquitos, 676 giant Catalina flying boats, 2000 Harvard and 2800 Cornell trainers. More than 16,400 aircraft in all were produced in Canada by 116,000 workers of whom more than 30,000 were women. It was a massive, hugely successful effort even if the engines had to be brought into the country or installed in aircraft once the airframes reached Britain or the United States, all the more so for beginning from a standing start.

But sometimes Howe and his men could overreach Canada's productive capacity. The Minister had agreed in September 1941 that Canada would build 15 Lancaster heavy bombers a month beginning in 1943 at the Malton, Ontario plant of what became Victory Aircraft, a Crown corporation. The Lanes would go to the Royal Canadian Air Force's No. 6 Bomber Group, based in Yorkshire, England. But the huge aircraft were complex, and there were a succession of management, labour, and equipment problems that slowed production (and led to Howe's turning the plant into a Crown corporation). The first Canadian-made Lancaster, the *Ruhr Express,* it was dubbed, took part in a raid in November 1943, but no others saw service until March and April 1944. By V-E Day, only three RCAF squadrons had the Canadian-made bombers. Even so, Victory Aircraft produced 450 Lanes all told, exceeding Howe's promised production rate.

The story was very similar for naval and merchant ship construction. At the beginning of the war, the Canadian shipbuilding industry was tiny with only some 2000 skilled workers employed. There were four shipyards with a total of only nine berths capable of handling a 10,000 tonne vessel. The first such cargo ship was delivered in December 1941. Two years later, there were 38 berths and 70 yards (and by the war's end 90 yards), and H.R. MacMillan's Wartime Merchant Shipping was turning out three 10,000 tonne merchant ships a week. One cargo ship, the *SS Fort Romaine* was built from scratch in just 58 days in the summer of 1943. In all, Canada produced 410 merchant ships, as well as an array of boilers, generators and other marine equipment. MacMillan's empire at its peak employed almost a hundred thousand men and women, while over 300 Canadian firms were involved in the supply of everything from steel plate to rivets to engines.

The growth was as rapid in naval construction which eventually employed some 30,000 workers. The first orders for corvettes, the Royal Canadian Navy's main anti-submarine and convoy escort vessel, were placed in February 1940 and the first ten keels were laid that month. By the end of the year, 44 corvettes had been launched and an even dozen were manned. In all, 206 corvettes were built in Canada, most on the east and west coasts but many in Great Lakes ports and on the St Lawrence. At the same time, Canadian yards built frigates and minesweepers, tugs and landing craft, motor torpedo boats, patrol boats, and Tribal class destroyers. The last class of ships, greatly desired by the Navy, was the shipbuilding equivalent of the Lancaster, a step too far.

Half as big again as the destroyers with which the RCN began the war, the Tribals were heavily armed and fast, almost as powerful as a light cruiser. The Navy secured four such destroyers from the Royal Navy (*Haida, Athabaskan, Huron,* and *Iroquois*), but it wanted more and, late in the war, it secured Munitions and Supply's permission to build four Tribals in Halifax yards. It was a quantum leap forward from constructing corvettes and frigates to building Tribals and, while they were completed, none was in the water and crewed before the war against the U-boats had ended on V-E Day, May 8, 1945.

For army equipment, the equivalent to the Lancaster and Tribals story was the Ram tank. The Nazi blitzkrieg had demonstrated the superiority of the Germans' *panzers*, and the British, Canadians, and Americans scrambled to find something better than the weak, slow, under-armed tanks with which they had begun the war. The army's two armoured divisions and two armoured brigades needed tanks, and the Montreal Locomotive Works received Howe's authorization to set up a tank factory to manufacture an American-designed tank, the M-3 Grant. But the Grant had a fixed gun, and Canadian armoured specialists recognized this as a flaw. Instead, Canada would manufacture a modified Grant with its gun on a revolving turret, thus giving it a 360-degree range of fire and a lower silhouette. The prototype of the Ram, with its engines imported from the United States, was ready in the summer of 1941. The story is long and complicated but, while almost two thousand Rams eventually came off the lines, the lengthy production time, engineering and armour plate problems, and the relatively high costs guaranteed that the Ram was superseded by the American-made Sherman, soon designated as the Allies' main tank. The Sherman was much superior to the Ram (though much inferior to German Tiger and Panther tanks), and U.S. productive capacity simply swamped the potential of the Montreal factory. The Rams nonetheless equipped Canada's armoured divisions until they acquired Shermans, and the Canadian-made tanks ended the war converted into Kangaroos, the first armoured personnel carriers.

If the Ram experience showed the limitation of Canada's heavy industry, the Canadian and Allied armies were huge beneficiaries of the production of the nation's factories. The major contribution – indeed, arguably Canada's biggest industrial contribution to victory – was in the form of trucks, most particularly Canadian Military Pattern vehicles. These CMP vehicles, produced in huge numbers by Ford and General Motors (along with some 180,000 military versions of Chrysler's 060 truck model), came in a bewildering variety. There were three types of wireless trucks, four of ambulances, thirteen of field workshop vehicles, and 90 types of army vehicles on twelve different chassis. In all, Canada's General Motors, Ford, and Chrysler auto plants produced 815,729 military vehicles that equipped the Canadian and British Commonwealth armies. Britain's Eighth Army, fighting in North Africa and Italy, used huge numbers of CMP vehicles.

Other than the Ram, the only tanks Canada produced in quantity were Valentines, a small, lightly-armed and weakly-armoured tank. Many of the 1420 Valentines, made in the Canadian Pacific's shops in Montreal, went to Britain; some went to the Soviet Union's Red Army.* Howe's department also had built 188 Grizzlies, a Sherman variant; more significantly, Montreal's factories turned out 2150 self-propelled 25-pounder guns, a major contribution to Allied firepower. Other factories made armoured cars, scout cars, fire trucks, and universal carriers, the ubiquitous Bren Gun Carrier used by British and Canadian forces. Still others produced weapons large and small – field artillery, heavy anti-aircraft guns, anti-tank weapons, mortars, machine guns, and rifles.

Does it overstate matters to suggest that the British army ran on Canadian vehicles? Yes and no. Large as it was, Canadian war production amounted in all only to ten per cent of the total of British Commonwealth production. On the other hand, only 34 per cent of Canadian war production was used by the Canadian services, while 53 per cent went to

---

* The Canadian War Museum in Ottawa has a Canadian-made Valentine tank which was recovered long after the end of the Second World War from a bog in Ukraine near the town of Telepino into which it had sunk in an offensive in January 1944. It was acquired by the Museum in 1991–92 in return for a donation of medicines and other items.

the British and Commonwealth nations, 12 per cent to the United States, and one per cent to other Allied states. In all, Canadian wartime industrial production was valued at more than $9.5 billion in 1940s dollars (the equivalent in today's dollars would be more than $100 billion). Another $1.5 billion was spent on defence construction and the expansion of war plants, all paid for by the government. For a nation that had begun the war with a Gross National Product of $5.6 billion, this was incredible. That Canada's GNP in 1945 was $11.8 billion, more than double the total six years before, is accounted for in large part by the extraordinary production of the nation's war factories and mines.

On June 12, 1943, the *Globe and Mail* printed a chart showing one week's production from Canada's factories. Each week, the newspaper noted, 900,000 Canadian workers, men and women, made at least six vessels, 80 aircraft, 4000 motor vehicles, 450 armoured fighting vehicles, 940 heavy guns, 13,000 smaller weapons, 525,000 artillery shells, 25 million cartridges, 10,000 tons of explosives, and at least $4 million worth of instruments and communications equipment. It was not until 1944 that Canada reached its peaks in production, so there was more to come. That almost none of these weapons, ammunition, and equipment had been produced in Canada in 1939 – that very few in fact were even capable of being produced – is an indication of just how effective Canada's wartime industrial mobilization had been.

Just as striking, the federal government – and not least C.D. Howe who became the Minister of Reconstruction in 1944 – actively worked to ensure that the industrial economy was able to make the conversion from war to peace. There were jobs for returning veterans, and soon there were new houses, refrigerators, baby carriages, and clothing for those men and women who had won the war overseas and in the factories of Montreal, Toronto, and Saskatoon and fifty more cities and towns.

The workers of Canada, the Canadian people, and C.D. Howe and his dollar a year men had won the industrial war, they had changed Canada, and they had ensured that the postwar nation would be stronger and more prosperous than it had ever been before the war.

SECTION FOUR

Reflections

Chapter Sixteen

A Half-Century On: The Veterans' Experience

Thanks to the Canadian Broadcasting Corporation, I had the good fortune to be able to attend the 50th anniversary celebrations of D-Day in Normandy and in London in June 1994 and the 50th anniversary commemoration of VE-Day in Apeldoorn and London in May 1995. These were both astonishing events, at once of supreme interest to a historian of Canada's part in World War II and also deeply, wrenchingly emotional. As I think back on them, it seems to me that I spent both trips in tears most of the time. To watch the old men once young march through the streets of Courseulles and St. Aubin and Apeldoorn, Amsterdam, Groningen and fifty small Dutch towns was at once to realize how quickly time passes, how soon we all become old. The two trips, the two commemorative events, also made me aware again how little, in contrast to many Western Europeans, Canadians know of what their soldiers did a half century ago.

To be sure, London paid very little attention to the Canadians or to other Commonwealth and Allied troops who had helped Britain survive and triumph in World War II. The focus in the huge celebrations and superbly staged ceremonies in 1994 and 1995 was on the Battle of Britain, on surviving the Blitz, on the long, hard road back from defeat in 1940, on the role of British troops, and on the songs and travails of wartime daily life. Perhaps the monochromatic focus was justified, but I could not help thinking that, just as Britain no longer means very much to Canadians, so too do Canada and the Commonwealth matter not a whit to the United Kingdom.

Then there was France. The French, in truth, did not seem particularly grateful for their 1944 liberation, although fifty years later they clearly appreciated the surge in business brought by the thousands of celebrants who poured into Normandy in June 1994. World War II was a time of shame and glory for France, a time of collaboration as much as it was a time of resistance, and the memories of the collapse of May and June 1940 seem to be alive still (and to lead to such vainglory as President Chirac's nuclear tests which aim to prove that France remains a great power with its own independent nuclear deterrent and global policy).

It was utterly different in May 1995 in the Netherlands, the one country in the world where Canadians are universally hailed as liberators. Every house was decorated in the colours of the House of Orange and with Canadian flags, and home-made banners, most obviously erected by ordinary citizens or neighbourhood associations and not by the state or municipalities, seemed to stretch across every street. The theme of gratitude, written in English on one banner I saw in Apeldoorn, was everywhere clear: "Bless You, Boys."

The Dutch remember the war. They remember the brutality of the Nazi occupation, the starvation winter of 1944–45, the executions of resistance fighters that went on into May 1945, and the collaboration of many of their men and women with the oppressors. They remember, but no longer hate the Germans, with whom, for example, they willingly cooperate in a combined German-Dutch corps in the North Atlantic Treaty Organization. They remember, above all, those who fought and died to liberate them, those men of the First Canadian Army who came from afar to drive the Germans out of Holland, those Royal Canadian Air Force (RCAF) pilots who supported the armies and who dropped food to them in the hungry days just before liberation, and the Royal Canadian Navy (RCN) sailors who cleared mines and ferried supplies.

You could see their acts of remembrance in the Canadian war cemeteries at Groesbeek and Holten, both of which are supremely beautiful places – if one can say such a thing of graveyards where thousands of your countrymen are buried so far from home. When I went to Holten, several days before VE-Day, there were perhaps a hundred ordinary Dutch families wandering among the endless rows of headstones that, beneath a carved maple leaf, list the rank, name, dates of birth and death, regiment or corps, and sometimes a message from parents, wives, or children. Small children looked solemn as their parents talked to them – I could not understand what they were saying, but I had no doubt of the message that was being conveyed. These men, these boys – and so many of them were boys who had the demographic bad luck to be born in the 1920s and to grow up knowing little else but depression and war – had died to free their nation from oppression a half century before. Do not forget what they did for your country. Remember that you are free because of them.

A Half-Century On 293

Those Canadians who assume that the liberation of Holland was a cakewalk against a beaten Wehrmacht would be disabused of that notion by the thousands buried in these war cemeteries. I was especially struck at Holten by the twenty men of the Cape Breton Highlanders whose headstones reveal that they were killed in action on 1 May 1945 in liberating the little port of Delfzijl, a battle that the history of their regiment calls its hardest fight of the war. On 1 May – with Hitler already a suicide and the war inexorably drawing to its close! The Dutch families at Holten that day understood what their liberation had cost.

The same public display of memory was evident for all to see in the single most extraordinary event I have ever been privileged to attend, the amazing Victory parade of Canadians through Apeldoorn, a few days before the VE-Day anniversary. Apeldoorn is a pleasant town of about 100,000 people in central Holland, quiet, staid in the reserved Dutch way. But that day, just as fifty years before when the Canadian Shermans rolled into their towns, the Dutch were far from staid. In May 1995, Apeldoorn's streets were lined by at least a half million men and women, children and babes in arms. The 15,000 or so Canadian vets who marched through the streets were mobbed, showered with kisses, handed drinks, smokes, and flags in the most sincere and astonishing outpouring of love, affection, and gratitude I have ever seen. The parade, scheduled to run for about two hours, lasted for eight, so slow was the triumphal progress through the happy crowds. That the vets lasted that long was a tribute to the power of exhilaration to overcome the aches and pains inherent to seventy-five-year-old bodies.

I will never forget the sight of young mothers in their twenties, weeping and cheering simultaneously while holding their babies up to get a sobbing veteran's kiss. Nor will I forget the Dutch mothers telling astonished and typically blasé Canadian reporters that they were doing this because they wanted their children to be able to say that they had been touched by one of the men who liberated the Netherlands a half century before.

Obviously, the Dutch remember. They teach their children about the war in their schools; they teach that freedom is everything and that, if not defended, freedom can be lost. They take whole schools to the Canadian cemeteries each year to lay flowers on the graves and to make the point that the preservation of freedom has a price. And all of this attention to the past showed during that moving, wonderful, amazing day in Apeldoorn.

How different it is here in Canada today. World War II was a time of supreme national effort for Canadians who produced a military, industrial, and agricultural contribution to victory that was frankly astonishing. Ten per cent of the population was in uniform; our war production, starting from effectively nothing, became large enough that we could give away billions of dollars' worth of weapons and foodstuffs to our Allies on a proportionate scale greater than that of the United States. There was scarcely a family in the land that did not have someone in the service, either as a volunteer, as were the vast majority, or as a conscript.

We all know that every ethnic group has the data, carefully massaged, to demonstrate that its sons enlisted in disproportionate numbers. The Toronto Globe and Mail noted on 5 October 1995, for example, that French Canadians had enlisted in "huge" numbers. A letter in the same newspaper a few weeks before argued that Ukrainian- Canadians had enlisted in numbers above their proportionate share, and Jewish groups make the same claim, as do other ethnic organizations. I do not believe these filiopietistic interpretations, I am afraid, and I continue to suspect that World War II was largely fought by Canadians of British extraction. The gravestones at Holten and Groesbeek certainly suggest this.

Let me personalize this sweeping generalization. My own immediate family's contribution to the war was lamentably small – one cousin in the RCAF who did not leave Canada and one uncle who saw action in North-West Europe with the United States Army. No one from my father's side was in the Canadian Forces. This was a source of enormous and continuing shame for me as I grew up in postwar Canada. I believed then, and continue to do so, that the sons of Eastern European Jewish immigrants should have had a special urgency to help defeat Hitler, but neither my father nor his two brothers who were of appropriate age volunteered or were called up for service. I am sure the Granatsteins would *have* been dreadful soldiers, but they ought to *have* enlisted nonetheless in what was unquestionably a just and necessary war, and especially so for Jews. The result of my embarrassment at their lack of the voluntary spirit was a succession of family arguments, followed by my going into the army when I was seventeen years old – to expiate my family shame and, as teenagers are wont to do, to act in the way most certain to infuriate my parents. I suspect that I was a lousy soldier too – but that is a question for another day.

If I am correct that Canada's war was largely fought by those of British origins, then this may partly explain the curious way we study the war in our schools. In this new multicultural Canada, the history of the world wars is seen as a *divisive* force, something that is almost too dangerous to teach in primary and secondary schools. What might a child of German or Slovakian or Croatian origin think, how might

A Half-Century On 295

he or she feel, if World War II were discussed? Better to say nothing – which is the case in most public and high schools – or to look at the war only in its economic impact on women munitions plant workers or to stress the cruel and unjust way Canada treated its Japanese Canadians or barred Jewish refugees from Hitler – which is the case in most university courses and the newest textbooks on Canadian history. The pride that Canadians should feel over their very substantial role in the war, the lessons that its events should hold for us, are brushed aside by the efforts to create a history that suits the misguided ideas of contemporary Canada held by successive federal and provincial ministers of Canadian Heritage and Multiculturalism and Education and by far too many academics who, unlike the cabinet ministers, might at least be expected to know better.

"Freedom's just another word for nothing left to lose," as a once popular song put it, and certainly that is how Canadian schools and universities treat it in their scanting of our war history. But the song is dead wrong; freedom is the word for that which is most precious, for that which cannot be lost, a word and a concept for which so many Canadians fought and died. The children and grandchildren of the Dutch who lived through the war and brutal occupation understand this and remember what can happen if freedom is lost; pathetically, terribly, the children and grandchildren of those who liberated them do not.

Our veterans still remember, however. They have become inured to public indifference, to sincere, well-meaning, but largely unattended ceremonies on Remembrance Day (a public service holiday, of course), and to the small crowds that, the valiant and underfunded efforts of "Canada Remembers" notwithstanding, celebrated the events of a half-century ago. Still, the celebrations of the milestones of the war – the 50th anniversary commemorations of the Battle of Britain, the Battle of the Atlantic, the D-Day invasion and VE-Day (the Italian campaign was largely neglected, just as it was during the war!) that have now come to their end – were critically important to the vets. All now old men and women with their memories becoming ever more important, the 50th anniversaries were their swansong. How fortunate that the Dutch knew how to sing their praises, even if most Canadians did not.

Why are we so ignorant, so diffident? The lamentable failure of our schools, as I have suggested, is a large part of it, but it may also have something to do with the subject of this book. It is almost as if the national effort to provide the Veterans Charter during the war excused Canadians from having to do anything for veterans after it.

Certainly the Veterans Charter was a great accomplishment, the best package of veterans legislation put together by any of the belligerents, and a model of wartime generosity, gratitude, and compassion that stands in marked contrast to the mean-spirited approach that seemed to dominate the legislative mind in the years after 1918.

Perhaps that is why the veterans after World War II played a lesser part in politics than their fathers after the Great War. We all know of the government's panic in 1919 that the returned men might side with the strikers at Winnipeg and elsewhere if the general strike spread. We remember the political efforts of the Great War Veterans' Association for better benefits and bigger pensions. We recall the efforts of the Canadian Legion and the Canadian Corps Association to demand conscription in World War II. And we know that two World War I veterans – John Diefenbaker and Lester Pearson – became prime minister.

It was much different after 1945. The demobilization of the armies went smoothly, and the reconstruction period was handled with great skill. There was scarcely anything for which the veterans could ask that was not given to them. There was a large packet of crisp notes, a suit of clothes, money for a farm or schooling or a house, cash to start a business and to learn a trade, care for the wounded in body and mind, and a system of pensions that, while inevitably bureaucratic, was generous and tax-free.

Of course, there were veterans in politics. Some, like Davie Fulton, George Hees, Cecil Merritt, Ernest Sansom, George Pearkes, Walter Harris and Ernest Halpenny came home from the war in uniform to run for Parliament in 1945. Some got elected; some did not. But no World War II veteran became prime minister. King and St Laurent, neither a veteran, passed power to Diefenbaker and Pearson, Great War vets, and the torch then was handed on to Trudeau who, while of an age to be a participant in World War II, was not. Clark, Turner, Mulroney, Campbell, and Chrétien all were either too young for war service or born after the war.

The absence of veterans from the highest office is in itself striking. (Compare the United States, where Presidents Eisenhower, Kennedy, Johnson (after a fashion), Nixon, Ford, Carter, Reagan (in his own mind if not in reality) and Bush served.) Even more striking is that veterans as a class played almost no part in politics in this country after the war. The only great issue on which the Canadian Legion spoke out with force, the only issue that I can remember and the only time that I believed the vets should remember why they fought the war, was not the "Valour and the Horror" controversy, but the struggle over the new Canadian flag that occupied the early years of Mike Pearson's Liberal administration. When an early three-leaf design was shown to the Canadian Legion convention by Pearson in 1964, the vets booed and then campaigned as hard as they could to retain the Union Jack and the Red Ensign as Canada's flags. It was as if they hadn't worn maple leaves in their cap badges, as many did, or served under First Canadian Army's flag or the RCAF's, both of which had maple leaves on them, or sailed in RCN ships with a maple leaf on the funnel; it was as if none had wandered through the cemeteries where every headstone had the maple leaf front and centre. The veterans were wrong in 1964–65, and they discredited themselves – not least because they seemed to have interpreted a distinctive Canadian flag as pandering to Quebec, and Quebec, in veterans' eyes, had not carried its share of the war's burdens.

Still, that sole example of political intervention is a relatively minor one, the exception that proves the rule. The political influence of veterans as a class was markedly less after 1945 than after 1919, and I suspect this was because Mackenzie King, so much wiser than Robert Borden, gave the nation's soldiers, sailors, airmen – and, as Peter Neary and Shaun Brown have pointed out, the members of its women's units – a Veterans Charter that generously fulfilled the promises that were made when the armies went overseas.

There is now no chance that veterans have the capacity to affect the great public issues of our time. The rollback of social services our politicians and bankers are forcing on us might be one such area where the elderly veterans could exercise some influence, but no government has dared to tamper very much with veterans benefits, and the Royal Canadian Legion has largely remained silent.

All the veterans now care about is the rectification of past injustices. They have campaigned successfully for a Dieppe and Hong Kong bar to wear on their medals; the Merchant Navy veterans still try, less successfully, to secure the full veterans benefits they certainly merit; and the Hong Kong survivors continue to seek in vain for government support for their efforts to secure their due compensation from Japan for their endless years of suffering in PoW cages during the war.

There is very little bitterness left towards the Germans against whom our armies fought. The German government has accepted responsibility for the monstrous actions of the Nazis, and today's Germans overwhelmingly understand and do not condone the sins of their grandfathers. But the Japanese, as I have suggested, have neither offered totally sincere apologies nor appropriate compensation; nor have they educated their citizens about Japan's expansionist war. When the Queen spoke at the V-J Day commemoration in London in mid-August 1995, she mentioned the reconciliation that had been achieved with Germany and pointedly did not refer to any such reconciliation with Japan. Her remarks were, for all practical purposes, a statement of British government policy – and certainly they reflect the bitterness that still lives in the minds of the few Canadian survivors of Hong Kong.

Well, what now do we owe the veterans who won World War II? We owe them, most importantly, our freedom, our right to live as we wish in a nation, however troubled, however divided at times, that was and still remains God's country. Beyond some fine-tuning, we do not owe them new programs, so complete were the Veterans Charter and the other programs that came into operation after the war. We do owe the half million surviving veterans continuing care and compassion. Above all, for putting their lives on the line to protect their country, we owe them gratitude and remembrance, and regrettably, these are the two things their countrymen have not given them in the last generation.

I think back to that banner that hung over the street in Apeldoorn in May 1995, and I wish that even one such a banner had flown over just one street in one city or town in this country. In Apeldoorn, "Bless You, Boys" seemed to me to be a particularly appropriate phrase. It seems to me still to be precisely what all Canadians should say. So, "Bless You, Boys." Some of us have not forgotten what you did; some of us will always remember.

Chapter Seventeen

"What Is to Be Done?" The Future of Canadian Second World War History

"What Is to Be Done?" was the title of Lenin's book/pamphlet published in 1902, well before he seized power in Russia. The Bolshevik leader was calling for the formation of a cadre of professional revolutionaries, a vanguard to direct the efforts of the working class. Only a revolutionary party, only an educated elite, Lenin maintained, could lead a scientific socialist revolution.

I am no Leninist – in fact, I'm a committed Groucho Marxist – but I do believe that only a group of dedicated professional historians can take back Canadian history. Increasing numbers of "Canadianists" are beginning to bemoan the state of Canadian history in the universities, and to suggest that it is being all but driven out of history departments by declining faculty numbers and dropping enrolments. Canadian history, one friend says, is becoming the subject that dare not speak its name. Certainly, there are some signs that the concerns are correct across the country. Why? There will be many answers, but I point the finger at tiny particularist courses and narrow, boring, ideologically dense, and badly-written books and articles. Francophone plumbers in North Winnipeg. The first female dentist in Moose Jaw. A Marxist history of Canadian identity in the 1960s. I am only making some of this up. Women's history, labour history, cultural history ought to be intrinsically interesting to a wide reading public. It certainly has not become so.

But what is striking is that wherever Canadian *military* history is taught, the situation, certainly in terms of enrolments, appears to be very good. There are lineups at the University of New Brunswick where Marc Milner teaches, at Wilfrid Laurier University with Terry Copp and Roger Sarty, at the University of Western Ontario with Jonathan Vance, and at the University of Calgary with David Bercuson and a dozen others of his colleagues, to cite by name only a few. Moreover, while astonishingly little of note is being published in most areas of Canadian history, there are more books being published than ever before in Canadian military history, more, I believe, than in any other field of Canadian history. The University of British Columbia Press's terrific series with the Canadian War Museum (and the Museum's support for publications by the Gregg Centre for the Study of War and Society at the University of New Brunswick, and for *Canadian Military History* at Wilfrid Laurier University) deserves special mention, but so do McGill-Queen's University Press, University of Toronto Press, Robin Brass Studio, Douglas & McIntyre, Vanwell Publishing, the Dundurn Group, and the extraordinary volume of hooks produced by the Canadian Defence Academy, based at the Royal Military College of Canada in Kingston, Ontario. Very simply, there is a flood of good scholarly and popular military history coming from trade and university presses. And all this is happening when relatively few universities even teach military history at all. The largest numbers of academic military historians in one city, the extraordinary gathering at the University of Calgary excepted, are located, not in academic institutions, but at the Directorate of History and Heritage at National Defence Headquarters, and at the War Museum in Ottawa, both of which have long been the spawning ground for the best practitioners of present Canadian military history.

What is clear is that students, the reading public, and publishers want Canadian military history, even if most of the university history departments think it "old hat" and boring. They are wrong – the theory-laden social/cultural/gender historians, slowly killing Canadian history in the universities and writing textbooks on Canada that completely omit the nation's military history, are now the ones well behind the curve. At some point, a few bold department chairs may even decide to hire a military historian or two to get their enrolments back up. Canadian military historians have become the revolutionary vanguard, using the tools of the new military history with great effect.

But enough preening. Lenin's title "What Is to Be Done?" can also mean: what *remains* to be done? What does this present large generation of Canadian military historians need to turn to in the next decade when it looks at Canada's part in the Second World War? Let me talk in broad strokes about books and research, and let me put my remarks in the way historians ought to think of Second World War history – the entire political, industrial, economic, social, cultural, and military story of Canada in the war.

I will begin with the political sphere first, which is where I began my own research more than 45 years ago. There are only two scholarly books that try to deal with the whole of the Canadian government during the war – Charles Stacey's *Arms Men and Governments: The War*

Policies of Canada, 1939–1945, and my *Canada's War: The Politics of the Mackenzie King Government, 1939–1945.* Stacey's official history came out in 1970, and my book, five years later. In other words, it is 35 years since anyone tried to look at the overarching subject of how Canada fought the war. Given the availability of new sources and the different perspectives now available, that is far too long. We badly need a new look at Canada's war.

Similarly, there is no biography of Mackenzie King when he was the wartime prime minister. There must be five hundred books on each of Winston Churchill and Franklin Roosevelt as war leaders, but there is nothing on King, who ran the massive Canadian war effort. It is no longer sufficient to talk about King as if his dog and his table-rapping sessions with mediums were all there was to him. Why did he act as such a "colonial choir boy" on so many issues? How did he manage his Cabinet? How did he lead on such issues as the political management of French Canada and the introduction of social welfare, to cite only a few? Why did King hang back in getting a voice in strategy for Canada? Did no one else in the government think of national strategy in Canada during the Second World War? The war effort was vastly greater and better organized in all aspects than that in the Great War, but do Canadians know this, or know why it was so? Has their image of Mackenzie King affected how they think of the two wars? And is it not time to change this to the reality? How could such a biography remain unwritten? This is one subject that, if done well, will make its writer a great scholarly reputation.

Nor is there a study of the Cabinet War Committee, or biographies of King's Minister of National Defence, Colonel J. Layton Ralston, or of Charles "Chubby" Power, the Air Minister. There is one good study of the Navy Minister, Stephen Henderson's *Angus L. Macdonald: A Provincial Liberal,* published in 2007, and Robert Bothwell and William Kilbourn's very good examination of the "Minister of Everything," *C.D. Howe: A Biography,* published 30 years ago. But these are all subjects crying out for examination or re-examination. There should also be a good, solid examination of wartime public opinion and new studies of the Liberal, Conservative, and CCF parties during the war.

We also need a military history of Newfoundland from 1939 to 1945, where Canada, the United States, and Britain all had interests and bases. How did they get on? Not very well, is the answer, but no-one has explored this fully. Peter Neary's fine book, *Newfoundland in the North Atlantic World 1929–1949* (1996), and David Mackenzie's *Inside the North Atlantic Triangle: Canada and the Entrance of Newfoundland into Confederation, 1939–1949* (1986), do the political-economic side very well, but neither asks why military enlistment in the other North American Dominion was so low in percentage terms. This needs full examination. Did everyone on the island decide to stay home and take a job at an American or Canadian base?

Nor are there serious studies of Canada's industrial, agricultural, and timber, mineral, and mining effort. There are works in train on the aviation industry and shipbuilding, but if, as I believe, Canada's vehicle production was the country's key contribution to victory, why is there no study of the wartime automobile industry? We should have a full appraisal of what Canadian industry did overall, how it did it, and who directed the task. Did everything run smoothly in the Department of Munitions and Supply? We don't know – there is no serious scholarly study of the Department. Or were the *Ram* tank, the inadequate Royal Canadian Navy radar sets, and the expensive, drawn-out saga of building *Lancaster* bombers at Malton, Ontario, more the norm than the exceptions? Was Howe the organizational genius we are always assured he was? What was the impact of the war on modernizing Canadian industry and agriculture? What did the nation's economic elite believe they wanted – and got – out of the war? What impact, if any, did they have on shaping wartime policy in their own interests? We need a full historical study of Canada's economic war, its Wartime Prices and Trade Board (there is one unpublished dissertation done by Christopher Waddell at York University almost 30 years ago), its treatment of labour, unionized and not, and how Canada raised the funds needed to fight the war and give away billions in gifts and Mutual Aid. We need a full study of women in the war – why so few, not so many – went into the factories and why they returned in such large numbers to domesticity in 1945. Ruth Pierson ably covered women in uniform in her *"They're Still Women after All": The Second World War and Canadian Womanhood,* published in 1986, but more remains unwritten.

There is also much more to be said on re-establishing veterans, more than Peter Neary and I could get into the essays we edited in *The Veterans Charter and Post World War II Canada* (1998), although Neary is now writing on this topic. Why, for example, did no Second World War veteran become prime minister? What does that say of us? What influence did the vets have on Canadian life, good or bad? What role did veterans organizations play, contrasted with that after 1918?

We desperately need a good examination of the entire area of wartime mobilization. Why was it so light in its effects? What was the contribution of ethnic groups – of German- Canadians, Italian-Canadians, Ukrainian-Canadians and others? Did – as I believe – British-Canadians disproportionately fight the war on their own as they had done in

1914–1918? I ask this because I continue to wonder why my father – and his four brothers – neither volunteered nor got called up. Why did my mother stay at home during the war? Why did Pierre Trudeau not get called up? Why was he permitted to leave Canada to go to Harvard in 1944? Jeffrey Keshen's fine study, *Saints, Sinners and Soldiers: Canada's Second World War* (2004), looks at the grimy underbelly of some domestic areas, including black marketeering, the first major examination of the whole Canadian home front, including – for the first time in a researched way – the lives of children growing up with fathers overseas and with their mothers working.

Unfortunately, there are no book-length wartime regional economic studies. We need studies of Ontario, the Maritimes, the West, British Columbia, and Quebec. And as Roger Sarty and B.D. Tennyson's *Guardian of the Gulf: Sydney, Cape Breton and the Atlantic Wars* (2000) and Serge Durflinger's *Fighting from Home: The Second World War in Verdun, Quebec* (2006) confirm, we could use more first-class city histories.

Above all, one of the great gaps in all Canadian history is the absence of a study of Quebec and the war, a big, important book that would examine how and why francophones acted and reacted as they did during the war. (We need this for the First World War as well.) The young Pierre Trudeau thought the war another imperialist conflict driven only by the British and their Anglo-Canadian supporters. How could someone so intelligent think that, and so misread the Nazis? What does that say of francophone attitudes? How many French Canadians actually volunteered, and why? The estimates of those who served, volunteers and conscripts, range from 90,000 Québécois to 200.000 French-speaking Canadians. Who did and did not volunteer, and why? John Macfarlane's *Triquet's Cross: Some Societal and Political Dimensions of Military Heroism*, a study of Captain Paul Triquet, VC, is one attempt to examine Quebec in the war through a unique lens, but it does not succeed. Durflinger's very fine study of Verdun *does* succeed, and it provides some answers for one Montreal suburb. We need a study of the whole province, and, indeed, of all French- speaking Canada that is hard-eyed, hard-edged, and willing to tell the truth. It would be best if it was written by a francophone, but it still may be too contentious a topic for anyone in Quebec to tackle. Someone must. This is another book that will make a great career.

While there are specific small areas that need coverage, most war-time foreign policy history has been written. With the multi-volume works of Charles Stacey *(Canada and the Age of Conflict)* and John Holmes *(The Shaping of Peace)* and detailed studies by many others, as well as a host of biographies and memoirs *by* and *on* men such as Escott Reid, L.B.

Pearson, Norman Robertson, and, with a study of O.D. Skelton forthcoming from Norman Hillmer, there is likely enough fine recent work on most subjects. But that said, there is still a requirement for full-scale histories that bring together the whole story of Canada–United Kingdom and Canada–United States military, economic and diplomatic relations, or better yet, a Canada-U.S.-U.K. study. R.B. Bryce's *Canada and the Cost of World War II* (2005), his post-mortem account of Canadian international finance during the Second World War, is a good starting point.

On the military aspects of Canada's war, history is still not well served. There is *The Official History of the Royal Canadian Air Force*, which is first rate in research, if sometimes strangely skewed in argument. Even so, it deliberately did not look at the 55 per cent of RCAF aircrew overseas who served in Royal Air Force squadrons, or as ground crew or as women in the RCAF. Those are very large gaps. We have the superb Official *Operational History of the Royal Canadian Navy in the Second World War* well underway. There are the three volumes of the *Official History of the Canadian Army*, which are first class, but now 50 years old or more. These should be re-done or, at least, the subjects should be tackled by non-official historians. We do have much good work on the RCN and the RCAF by academic and popular historians, but there are still no major books on how the RCN was raised from nothing to 100,000 men and 400 ships in a few years (Richard Mayne's *Betrayed: Scandal, Politics and Canadian Naval Leadership* (2006)) suggests there is much more to this than we yet know) and how a half-million soldiers and airmen were transported to Britain. Where is the thoroughly researched and readable book on how the British Commonwealth Air Training Plan was set up and run, and its massive impact upon the country? What did it mean to have Brits, Aussies, and Kiwis in Yorkton, Saskatchewan and Springbank, Alberta? And were there really street brawls in Quebec City between airmen and civilians? We have some fine operational histories by able scholars, not least Terry Copp, Brian Reid, and Jack English, but readers and researchers still need to know more about how the army was recruited and trained. What were the motivations of home defence conscripts, or of volunteers for overseas service? What were public attitudes to home defence "Zombies" during and after the war? That the Canadian Legion refused to admit even conscripts who fought overseas until 1950 suggests that feelings against those who refused to volunteer remained strong after the peace.

I also believe that the overall Canadian experience in the Second World War may be similar to that of the other Dominions. Is there not room for a comparative history (or perhaps first a large international conference) on the efforts of the Dominions, all of which experienced major problems in the field? On recent trips to Australia and New Zealand, I was struck by the need for comparative research.

To change tack, it does not serve much purpose any more to blame London for the disasters at Hong Kong and Dieppe. Instead, we need to do as Beatrice Richard did in *La mémoire de Dieppe: Radioscopie d'un mythe* (2002), and examine what the debacle *at* Dieppe *meant* and *means* still to Canadians' memory of the war, their relations with Britain, and their sense of themselves. But that does not mean that we should not look even more closely at the state of Canadian training and the lack of our own military and diplomatic intelligence capabilities. Historians also need to ask generally if high casualty rates are a measure of *effectiveness* – or of *ineffectiveness*. And the real question scholars must ask is why the Canadian services were so colonial during the war. Canadians brag about how much better and more innovative the Canadian Corps was than the British in the Great War, but during the Second World War the Canadian Army slavishly followed the British lead in operations, training, and doctrine. Why? Jack English's fine 1991 book *(The Canadian Army and the Normandy Campaign)* on the failings of the army in Normandy gave some answers, but much more work is needed here.

And it is not only the army. How can a flat-out colonial issue like Canadianization in the RCAF arise more than a decade after the Statute of Westminster? How did Canada allow the Royal Navy to fob off the Royal Canadian Navy (RCN) with lousy equipment for so long? Why did Ottawa not demand that the Canadian services fight together? Why did the government allow the RCAF's tactical fighters to support British, not Canadian, troops in Northwest Europe? (Or I Canadian Armoured Brigade to not support I Canadian Division in Italy?) Why does Canada produce a superb fighting soldier like Sir Arthur Currie in the Great War, and a political-military bureaucrat like Harry Crerar during the Second World War? To raise questions like these is, among other things, to ask what the Great War did to shape Canada's Second World War.

I do not believe in the "great man" theory of history, but there is no doubt that biography offers a way into the past. Happily, we do have a good study of Crerar, Paul Dickson's *A Thoroughly Canadian General* (2007), and a new study by John Rickard on General A.G.L. McNaughton entitled *The Politics of Command*. There are good memoirs by Maurice Pope and E.L.M. Burns, for example, and a few horrors, such as that of Christopher Vokes. But other than Douglas Delaney's *The Soldier's General* (2005) on Bert Hoffmeister of the 5th Canadian Armoured Division, there are no first-rate new published studies of other

Canadian commanders. We could do with books on brigade, battalion, company, and platoon commanders as well. There are no studies at all on senior air officers, and none on the Royal Canadian Navy's leaders. Even with a population of just 11 million, Canada was, in some ways, the fourth greatest power in the greatest European war in history and, 65 years after the war ended that is all we have? This is an amazing state of affairs. We need biographies of the country's key military, air, and naval leaders – a fully researched book on Guy Simonds, biographies of Charles Foulkes, Ken Stuart. Percy Nelles, Gus Edwards (or, at least, one not by his daughter), and "Black Mike" McEwen of No. 6 (RCAF) Group in Bomber Command. The edited volumes organized by Richard Gimblett, Michael Whitby, and Jim Bouthilier and others on the RCN and its leaders are a very good start – we desperately need something like that for RCAF commanders – but scholars of the war need researched book-length biographies much more than edited collections.

I believe we need to stop the soft commemorations of anniversaries (in which Parks Canada, Veterans Affairs Canada, and others wallow) and cease "playing cheerleader" for every aspect of Canada's military efforts. I admit that I have done as much of this as anyone – and perhaps more. Why can more historians not deal with the failures of First Canadian Army openly and honestly as Jack English did, and now Yves Tremblay's *Instruire une armée: les officiers canadiens et la guerre moderne, 1919–1944* (2007) does? Why can we not begin to treat Canadian failings as honestly as British and American scholars do theirs? Max Hastings, in the *New York Review of Books* on 13 August 2009 ("A Very Chilly Victory") wrote that the British Army "... disgraced itself for the first three years of the war, and seldom thereafter surpassed adequacy." Hastings was right and was also correct when he pointed to the US Army's weaknesses. It and the British did only enough "... to make a respectable subordinate contribution to the destruction of Nazism," he wrote, while the Red Army "did the heavy lifting." At the very least, Hastings is being brutally honest in expressing his views of the British and American forces. Can Canadians not do the same?

Why can scholars – and museums – not talk about the RCAF part in the bombing campaign openly, and without fear of denunciation? *The Valour and the Horror* TV series of fifteen years ago was dreadful – but at least the McKenna brothers raised hard critical questions, if in an appalling, ignorant, "presentist" way. But their questions, if only they had been stripped of bias and spin, were good ones. Historians need to bring a critical perspective to every aspect of the war. Essentially, the spectrum of comment must widen from its present focus on the "good war" to a more realistic approach that encompasses good and bad, success and failure. Jeff Keshen's book, mentioned earlier, consciously set out to examine unsparingly "the good war" thesis – although in the "unkindest cut of all" from one of my own PhD students, he used me as his target. Let us look at why Canada went to war, how Ottawa ran and fought it, and what the nation did right and wrong, without worrying about "exposing all the warts." There are relatively few warts – we have flogged Canadian sins about the forcible evacuation (not internment) of Japanese Canadians enough to make up for all the others – but it would do us good to be open and honest – and modest. It would also be very helpful if someone emulated Jonathan Vance's fine *Death So Noble: Memory, Meaning and the First World War* (1997) by looking at the memory and remembrance of the Second World War in Canada more than 70 years after its outbreak. We might also ask what impact – I think it was significant – the massive TV and print coverage of the 50th and 60th anniversaries of D-Day and V-E Day had upon the rejuvenation of military history, and upon the public memory of the war.

So, what does the history of Canada's Second World War now demand? More. More of everything. But above all, we need gifted story-tellers writing big histories that are based upon hard research and rigorous "number-crunching." We need to re-envisage the present narrative of Canada and the war in a way similar to the fashions in which American historians regularly re-examine – and broaden the discussion upon – their Civil War. We do not want to abandon guns and trumpets, but we do need to go beyond them to take into account everything that the social and cultural approaches can offer.

Above all, military historians need to ensure that big syntheses get written. After 40 years of dominance by social and cultural historians in Canada, there is not a single major book that synthesizes those approaches and offers a full assessment of their impact upon Canada's history.

Students of the Second World War cannot make the same mistake of focusing upon the particular or the trivial, or of producing endless edited books of essays that too often add very little except padding for Curriculum Vitae, when what we need are serious books by first-rate historians who will write hard-researched examinations of the truly important issues.

Chapter Eighteen

Thirty Years in the Trenches: A Military Historian's Report on the War between Teaching and Research

Ezio Cappadocia was my teacher from 1959 to 1961 at the Royal Military College of Canada in Kingston, Ontario. RMC had begun to give degrees only in 1959 (my sometime co-author Desmond Morton received the first one), but it had strength in engineering, history, political science, economics and English. It was a college with a specialized purpose, namely producing officers for the army, navy, and air force, but there was a recognition that the quality of the new degree, and hence of the regard in which it would be held, depended on the reputation of the teaching staff in the broader scholarly community. That meant their research had to be known.

I had arrived at RMC from three years at Le Collège Militaire Royal de St. Jean, which then fed all its students to Kingston, intending to take a degree in Political Science and Economics, but I quickly discovered that economics was beyond me. I gravitated instead to history, a wise choice. The History Department at RMC was tiny, but very fine indeed. George F.G. Stanley was the chair, but he was on sabbatical leave when I arrived. The key figure was Richard Preston, and under him were Donald Schurman, Fred Thompson, and Ezio. They were all different but all very capable, and I did most of my work, including a hugely long undergraduate thesis on the early history of Canadian peacekeeping operations, for Preston. Preston taught me to love research, and I turned out to be a good scrounger, able to get access to hitherto closed records. I have lived off that knack ever since.

Ezio taught American and European history, and I have not a single recollection of a specific lecture that I heard him deliver. What I do remember was his enthusiastic lecturing style, his short, stocky body flying around the classroom as he gesticulated at us or scribbled on the board. I had never had a lecturer like him before. At CMR, I had literally slept through most of the history lectures I took. It was impossible to sleep in Ezio's classes – there was so much noise from the lectern, so many ideas being tossed out, so much going on. It was simply wonderful, the first time that history was fun.

The barriers of discipline and rank at RMC were so great at the beginning of the 1960s that it was impossible for a cadet to be a friend of a professor. But I was closer to Cappodocia than to Dick Preston, my supervisor, and I loved that he was so overtly unmilitary and discreetly anti-military. An RMC professor then would not have criticized the Canadian military in class or even privately in discussion with a cadet, but I was sure that Cappodocia thought that I was in the wrong place, heading in the wrong direction if I intended a career in the Canadian Army. Of course, he was right. And when the army let me go to the University of Toronto in the autumn of 1961 to do my Master's degree in history, I realized how right he was.

A few years later, still in the army and working off my obligatory three-year period of service, l was applying to do PhD work at a number of American graduate schools. I had come out of RMC infatuated with American history, likely because Ezio had taught the subject, and I wanted to do my dissertation on some aspect of Franklin Roosevelt's career. Cappodocia and Preston were my main RMC referees and I talked with the two of them. Ezio was still in Kingston and I still remember going to see him over lunch and his dissuading me from doing U.S. history and especially Roosevelt. There was already too much on FDR, he said, something surely incorrect in 1963. Where he was right, however, was in saying that there was much too little work yet done on Canadian history and that this was where I should do my dissertation. Being an obedient fellow, that conversation pushed me toward Duke University which had a Commonwealth Studies Centre and where a number of historians and political scientists knew something of Canada. I have been grateful to Ezio ever since.

By 1966, I was out of the army and on the faculty of York University. My dissertation, finished in the fall of 1966 was on the Conservative Party in the Second World War, a good Canadian political history topic. I had written a paper on this subject in Jack Saywell's political history seminar at the University of Toronto, and Saywell was now the Dean of Arts and Science at the new York University. The university then had a campus at Glendon College in the north of Toronto and was constructing a campus in the far northwestern reaches of the city. There was already much history behind the new institution, many divisions over the direction it should go, and much bad blood between faculty and administration. I knew nothing of this in my first year as a professor as I scrambled to prepare courses in Canadian, American, and Commonwealth history.

I modelled myself on the good teachers I had had. Because I had had full scholarships as an MA and PhD student, I had never given a lecture or taught a tutorial, so I looked for exemplars to those whose teaching I had enjoyed. Jack Saywell at Toronto had run the best seminar I had ever had, offering new and challenging interpretations of post-Confederation Canada, and William Hamilton at Duke had devastatingly effective methods of making the graduate students appraise the work of their peers. I emulated both. There was no doubt to whom I looked as a model for my lectures. Cappodocia had been the finest lecturer I had heard, and while I couldn't muster the same degree of total enthusiasm for my subjects as he did, I tried. I shouted, waved my arms, and threw chalk at the students who dozed. I looked for anecdotes and stories, and I deliberately and consciously sought parallels to the past in current events. It was pretty rough at the start, but I learned and improved. I like to think that I became a better than average teacher and lecturer in a few years.

At the same time, I was trying to publish. No one told me I had to do so; no one said I should not – at the outset. I simply assumed that professors published, and l had done so much research for my dissertation that it would have been a crime to waste it. The book, *The Politics of Survival: The Conservative Party of Canada, 1939–1945*, came out with the University of Toronto Press in 1967.

By then I had gone to York's main campus. Saywell had told me I could stay at Glendon, which was to remain a geographically separate and small college, or go to the muddy wastes of Keele and Finch where there would eventually be masses of students, both undergraduates and graduates. He was going north, so I did too, making a fateful choice without thinking much about it. Glendon eventually solidified into a "teaching" institution, a bilingual college that to my mind, at least, would never amount to very much. The University's main campus had the chance of doing great things as a major research institution.

And at the beginning it seemed to be full of promise as a teaching institution as well. The students were superb, those I had in the next five years simply the best I have ever taught. I used the Duke seminar techniques Bill Hamilton had taught me, and the kids travelled to Ottawa to do research in the National Archives and wrote fifty-page primary source papers that they defended and attacked brilliantly. It was simply amazing, and when students went on to graduate school and published their papers, I felt exactly as Cappodocia did when I moved forward. If this was what teaching could be like, I understood why Ezio had loved it. But I also wanted to do research and to write.

I hope I have suggested that I am – or was – a bit of a naïf. I went off to Duke because Ezio told me so, and I left Glendon because Jack Saywell suggested the main campus might be fun. And, as I have said, I simply assumed that all professors published. I think I knew that Cappodocia wasn't a major publisher, but I never had the slightest doubt that he was a scholar and that he understood and respected research and scholarship.

But at York in the late 1960s, I came to realize for the first time that there were academics who thought research and scholarship were a waste of time that diverted a faculty member's attention from the important work of teaching, administration, and serving on committees. I can still remember when this realization hit me. I was talking to Sydney Eisen, a British historian who had come to York and back to his native Toronto from a teaching career in the United States. It must have been early 1968 because my book had been out for only a few months, and he was not yet the chair of the department. Eisen said to me, "Well, you've proved you can do it. So now you don't have to publish anymore." I was stunned at this, not least because I had spent the last summer doing archival research in Ottawa, was publishing academic articles and starting to get opinion pieces into the media, and was already well underway on my next book Eisen was a senior figure in the new and growing department and in the university, and we were friendly. So, still being a good soldier, I didn't bite his head off. But neither did I salute and march away. I told him that I was doing research and intended to keep on publishing. He looked at me as if I'd thrown up on his shoes. The long process of losing my academic innocence had begun.

My next shock came in 1970 when I went up for tenure and promotion to associate professor. York at that time had few rules or regulations in this area, a university-wide committee simply deciding who to recommend to the President. The former chair of the History Department, Lewis Hertzman, was on the committee, and I was turned down for tenure because, I learned several years later from the secretary of the committee, I "had published too much." The reason in truth was that Hertzman and I had had a long-running dispute over the role of students in the department's business. My fourth-year seminar students had been leading the revolution, and I had supported them. It was the late 1960s, after all. But what was interesting was Hertzman's rationale: I had published too much. I started looking elsewhere for employment but, on appeal, received tenure a few months after the blockade was cracked.

As I later discovered, there was a *de facto* double jeopardy system in effect at York. If you did not publish, the assumption was that you were a good teacher or good administrator and, therefore, deserving of tenure and promotion. If you published, by definition you were less likely to be a good teacher or committee member and, moreover, the quality of your scholarship had to be closely appraised. Not that anyone on the tenure and promotion committee in those casual days had either read my work or had it appraised by outside referees.

I had my future at stake here, and I was no unbiased observer. But I thought this raising of teachers over scholars was nonsense. There was no separation of the two roles in my mind. The History Department at York had attracted some absolutely first-rate scholars such as Ramsay Cook, John Bosher, Gabriel Kolko, and Jerome Chen, most of whom, as far as I could tell, had a good reputation in the classroom and certainly seemed to do their share of the burdensome work of committees. What hurt the department in my view was that its efforts to build its reputation – all the new universities in Canada were seen as upstart institutions and York, located in the same city as the "national university," the University of Toronto, was especially so – had been hampered by the number of "anti-publishing" faculty who had been brought aboard. It was, of course, hard to recruit first-class faculty in a period of rapid national expansion, and Jack Saywell's York had, by and large, done exceptionally well. But there were aberrations, a deliberate effort, or so I thought, by some in the History Department to replicate themselves and their approach to the proper role of faculty. (I have not forgotten a History hiring committee some years later where unpublished faculty members grilled a well-published candidate and turned him down for a job over my objections. His several books and many articles were "too traditional," they decided.)

The tenure rules soon were codified at York, and a rigid three-track system devised. Scholarship, teaching and service were the routes upward, and the gradings were labelled as excellence, high competence, and competence. Three ratings of high competence were enough for promotion and/or tenure. Excellence in research could get one tenure and promotion but only if there was at least competence in the other two areas. This was fair. But excellence in teaching required only competence in scholarship and service and, as I discovered when I sat on the Faculty of Arts tenure and promotion committee (with Sydney Eisen as Dean running the committee), the definition of competence in scholarship was rather more flexible than it was in teaching. Faculty members' creativity in drafting their curriculum vitae was unbounded, and a non-publishing scholar could get his satisfactory grade with a book review, a talk to a service club, or a great and unfunded research project on which he had been working for years and might, someday, publish. At the same time, he still was assumed to be a great teacher and/or a great committee person for if he did not publish, he must be. A great scholar, on the other hand, had her published works dissected line by line, often by those who had not published much or at all, her teaching record scrutinized very closely, and her membership on and attendance at committees pored over. Double jeopardy still ruled. It took many years to have defensible standards prevail in the History Department, if not at York as a whole. Those eventual departmental standards took both teaching and scholarship very seriously, as they should, as they must.

Soon the unionization of faculty entered the York picture, a process in which I played a major role. In 1974, the small pool of merit pay money for History had been unilaterally awarded by the department chairman to those who were the lowest paid. I believed that I was entitled to merit pay that year (every year, in fact!) and thought that one's salary should have nothing to do with how merit was awarded. I appealed my exclusion to the chair and was turned down; I went to the Dean and the President with a similar result. I then used the existing grievance procedures which followed precisely the same route up the food chain and was turned down once more. By this time I was furious and ran for president of the York University Faculty Association. In a matter of months, and not because of History's merit pay allocation procedures, we were involved in a long process of seeking certification, collective bargaining, and strife. The university had more than its share of troubles, the administration was less than competent, and the wellsprings of faculty resentment at weak administrative procedures flowed very freely.

What was striking in the present context was the attitudinal split in the university. While there were many exceptions, the good scholars tended to shy away from unionization and the junior and the weaker supported it. I counted myself a strong scholar, and I brought along some of my well-published colleagues to support unionization, but it was an uphill struggle. I discovered yet again that publishing scholars were simply despised by those whose interests lay elsewhere – I cannot forget one member of the YUFA bargaining committee, a Glendon College assistant professor of English, saying precisely that. My purpose in supporting unionization was to see a rules-based employment relationship and to end sweetheart deals. I could not conceive of strikes and said this repeatedly in meeting after meeting. The resulting contract achieved what l had hoped for, but the union, as l discovered to my regret within a few years, could only run well if the best faculty took an interest in it. They did not. The most productive people at the university wanted to do research and write books, not bargain over the amendment of clause 96(2)(b), and the tenured assistant professors, the lifetime associates, and the Marxists who thought the university was only another shop floor assumed control of the faculty union. The strikes duly followed, poisoning the work relationship at York

And merit pay, the reason I had plunged into the mess? The union turned out, not surprisingly, to support the view that the university's professorial workers should get the same raises. Some departments actually passed resolutions giving everyone the same merit pay allocation. The administration presumably decided not to stir the pot and either went along with the union or reduced the money going to merit pay to trifling sums in contract after contract. My unhappy experiment with labour relations led me to concentrate on my research and to focus on my department. A naïf at the beginning, I remained one to the end.

In the History Department itself, the struggle for control of the future hinged on a second year course in historiography. First-year courses at York were "Gen Ed," a hopelessly inadequate mishmash of general education courses that all students took. Not until the second year did undergraduates go to their major departments, and the department in its wisdom had decided that a course in historiography should be compulsory for all History majors. This course had become the property of the anti-publishing wing, and it aroused the ire of the rest in ways that now seem hard to credit. I don't think any of the publishing historians objected to historiography as such, only to the compulsion involved and to the fact that symbolically this course suggested that the anti-scholarship wing's hold on the department remained unassailable. Certainly, this issue upset me, not least because this was the only compulsory course in the department when I, as a good Canadian nationalist in a period of very strong Canadianism in the universities, thought that every undergraduate should be obliged to take a course in Canadian history. This was sharply and successfully opposed by the historiography faction (and some others) which was, like many York faculty at the time, heavily American-born.

It took years to end the compulsory historiography course, but when it did the power in the department shifted for the better. Hiring now was more often conducted to seek out good scholars, and promotions became heavily biased toward publishing scholars. There would no longer be full professors with blank curriculum vitae holding key administrative posts in the department or teaching graduate students. It was, I think, no coincidence that the History Department came to be recognized as a "power" department in the university and, by the early 1980s, as the best in the country. Certainly York's Canadianists were unchallenged. The best group of Canadian historians ever, or so Jack Saywell later described a cadre that included Ramsay Cook, Fernand Ouellet, Viv Nelles, Chris Armstrong, Peter Oliver, Irving Abella, Michiel Horn, and Saywell himself.

But what was "good" history? When I had started teaching in 1966, there had been no divisions here. Good history was soundly researched and well written, plain and simple. But by the 1970s, ideology had begun to creep into Canadian history on its hobnailed and steel-toed boots, initially in labour history. Were you a Marxist (almost the norm)? Were you writing about the workers (which was good)? Or the union institutions (which was evil)? Soon, stories of conferences that had turned into denunciatory bloodbaths began to circulate, journals denied space to those on the wrong side of the ideological divide, and historians began to switch fields, leaving Canadian labour history to the ideologues and seeking friendlier terrain in foreign policy or military history. I was a political historian working on the Great and Second World Wars and largely oblivious to all this, but I ought to have paid more attention.

Before long, I came to realize that no matter how much I published or how good it might have been, I was doing the wrong kind of history. I remember a social historian friend saying that mine was the only political history he read. I remember others pronouncing what I did as old-fashioned, irrelevant, out-of-date. Social history was in, and I was out. "It's a war," labour historian-turned-military historian Terry Copp of Wilfrid Laurier University said to me, "and we're losing."

He was right, but I nonetheless found this puzzling. Students still seemed more interested by and large in the "old" history than in the "new," as enrolments all across the nation testified. Copp's classes, for example, had waiting lists, and he had more graduate students than everyone else in his department added together. The young wanted to hear about military history, or Canadian-American relations, or the rise and fall of Canadian political leaders. Those were the areas I taught, those were the areas I wrote about as my interests changed and re-focussed, and it was startling to hear historians at York and elsewhere dismiss those subjects as boring, old hat, and unimportant. How could any Canadian pronounce the nation's role in the Second World War of no interest or suggest that Canada's relations with its superpower neighbour didn't matter? How could it be that a strike in 1943 was of interest but Prime Minister Mackenzie King's efforts to control the pressures for conscription in World War II were not? How was it that work on the maltreatment of women was path-breaking, while studies of Canada's dollar crisis in 1947–48 or of the abortive free trade negotiations of 1948 with the United States were boring? I didn't object to those who worked on social history topics, so why should they trash me? My focus in the university had been on the differences between those who published and those who did not, but suddenly that had been overridden by the division between the old and the new in Canadian history.

So powerful was this trend that I suddenly realized that political history, broadly defined as politics, military history, foreign policy, and public policy, or what I called national history, was on the verge of disappearing in the university, as older faculty retired and were replaced by the trendy young. Similar things were happening in the high schools. The new Canadian reality of multiculturalism changed the way high school history was taught, where it was still taught at all, and the Charter of Rights and Freedoms seemed to require little case studies to demonstrate how beastly Canadians had been in the dark ages before 1982. History by snippet, history by object lesson, was the new rule, and the memory of a past to which Canadians, native-born or immigrants, could relate was fast disappearing. This made me uncomfortable and not simply because my own relevance to my subject of Canadian history was in question. I believed then, and believe still, that Canadians need to understand their national and their local history, their political and their social history. The ideas and concerns that were to become *Who Killed Canadian History?* (1998) had started to percolate.

By the 1980s, curiously, I found that the "old hat" and "conservative" work I did was increasingly of interest to the media, and I spent substantial time doing newspaper interviews and radio and television work. This, I quickly discovered, upset some of my colleagues, and soon I heard accusations to my face that I was both publishing so much and doing so much media that I had to be ignoring my students. I wasn't, and not one single student ever complained that I was, but the unfounded complaints were still hurled at me. I took my teaching seriously until the day I left York in 1995, but I will admit that I found that the quality of both undergraduate and graduate students had deteriorated in the years since 1966 – and that the decline had accelerated over time. My guesstimate was that academic standards fell by at least a third between the late 60s and the mid-90s. My own research continued.

I had continued my focus on the world wars, looking at politics, foreign policy, economic policy, the bureaucracy, and the web of interrelationships between Canada, the United States and Britain. But increasingly I found myself drawn to military history. In 1984, the fortieth anniversary of D-Day, I did a popular treatment of the Canadian role in the great invasion with another of Cappodocia's former students,

Desmond Morton. This was a great success, and we followed it with books on Canada's role in the Great War and in World War II. I soon turned my interest to a collective biography of Canadian Second World War senior officers, published as *The Generals* in 1993. Then I did some work for the Department of National Defence as a commissioner on the Special Commission on the Restructuring of the Canadian Forces Reserves. I was soon a consultant to the Minister of National Defence on the future of the Canadian Forces, and I began to consider writing a one-volume history of Canada's Army, eventually published in 2002.

By the beginning of the 1990s, by then in my early fifties, I had begun to look for a way out of the university. The chance came in 1995 when York University offered a modest buyout for faculty over 55 years of age, and I seized the opportunity. At 56, I was free, out of the university life for good and out of York completely. I also took my pension out of the university after discovering an error of approximately 5 per cent in the university's calculation of my entitlement. No explanation or apology was ever offered. I quickly discovered that retirement meant that my income rose, my stress level declined, and my time became my own. Thirty wearying years was long enough, and the task of participating in the doomed counterattacks against the entrenched opponents of scholarship, sound history, and standards now belonged to others.

For me, the fighting was over and, as far as I was concerned, I had won. What did you do in the French Revolution? Talleyrand was supposed to have been asked. "I survived," he replied. Me, too.

www.ingramcontent.com/pod-product-compliance
Lightning Source LLC
Chambersburg PA
CBHW030304080526
44584CB00012B/436